THE PRINCIPLES OF ETHICS

HERBERT SPENCER

THE PRINCIPLES OF ETHICS

HERBERT SPENCER

Introduction by Tibor R. Machan

In Two Volumes
Vol. II

Liberty Fund
INDIANAPOLIS
1978

This book is published by Liberty Fund, Inc., a foundation established to encourage study of the ideal of a society of free and responsible individuals.

The cuneiform inscription that serves as the design motif for our endpapers is the earliest-known written appearance of the word "freedom" (*amagi*), or liberty. It is taken from a clay document written about 2300 B.C. in the Sumerian city-state of Lagash.

This edition of *The Principles of Ethics* follows the text of the edition published in New York in 1897 by D. Appleton and Company.

Frontispiece photograph: Bettmann Archive, Inc.

Library of Congress Cataloging in Publication Data

Spencer, Herbert, 1820–1903.
    The principles of ethics.

    Includes bibliographical references and index.
    1. Ethics. 2. Ethics, Evolutionary. I. Title.
BJ1311.S75 1977   170   77-1274

0-913966-33-9   Set (HC)
0-913966-76-2   Volume I (HC)
0-913966-74-6   Volume II (HC)
0-913966-34-7   Set (SC)
0-913966-77-0   Volume I (SC)
0-913966-75-4   Volume II (SC)

01 00 99 98 97 C 7 6 5 4 3
01 00 99 98 97 P 7 6 5 4 3a

CONTENTS OF VOLUME II

Preface to Volume II 11
Preface to Part IV 15

PART IV
THE ETHICS OF SOCIAL LIFE: JUSTICE

1. Animal Ethics 19
2. Subhuman Justice 25
3. Human Justice....................................... 33
4. The Sentiment of Justice............................. 41
5. The Idea of Justice 51
6. The Formula of Justice 61
7. The Authority of This Formula 65
8. Its Corollaries 79
9. The Right to Physical Integrity 81
10. The Rights to Free Motion and Locomotion 89
11. The Rights to the Uses of Natural Media 97
12. The Right of Property 111
13. The Right of Incorporeal Property 121
14. The Rights of Gift and Bequest....................... 135
15. The Rights of Free Exchange and Free Contract 143
16. The Right to Free Industry........................... 149
17. The Rights of Free Belief and Worship 153
18. The Rights of Free Speech and Publication 157
19. A Retrospect with an Addition 165
20. The Rights of Women 175
21. The Rights of Children 185
22. Political Rights—So-Called........................... 193

23. The Nature of the State 201
24. The Constitution of the State 209
25. The Duties of the State 221
26. The Limits of State Duties 235
27. The Limits of State Duties—Continued 247
28. The Limits of State Duties—Continued 257
29. The Limits of State Duties—Concluded 271

PART V
THE ETHICS OF SOCIAL LIFE: NEGATIVE BENEFICENCE

1. Kinds of Altruism.................................... 283
2. Restraints on Free Competition 297
3. Restraints on Free Contract 307
4. Restraints on Undeserved Payments 317
5. Restraints on Displays of Ability 325
6. Restraints on Blame.................................. 331
7. Restraints on Praise.................................. 339
8. The Ultimate Sanctions............................... 347

PART VI
THE ETHICS OF SOCIAL LIFE: POSITIVE BENEFICENCE

1. Marital Beneficence 353
2. Parental Beneficence 361
3. Filial Beneficence 369
4. Aiding the Sick and the Injured 373
5. Succor to the Ill-Used and the Endangered 379
6. Pecuniary Aid to Relatives and Friends 387
7. Relief of the Poor 393
8. Social Beneficence 411
9. Political Beneficence................................. 425
10. Beneficence at Large 437

APPENDICES

Appendix A. The Kantian Idea of Rights 451
Appendix B. The Land Question 455
Appendix C. The Moral Motive 461
Appendix D. Conscience in Animals 469
Appendix E. Replies to Criticisms 483
References 505
Index to Volume II..................................... 511

THE PRINCIPLES OF ETHICS

PREFACE TO VOLUME II

Now that, by this issue of Parts V and VI, along with Part IV previously published, I have succeeded in completing the second volume of *The Principles of Ethics,* which some years since I despaired of doing, my satisfaction is dashed by the thought that these new parts are less definite in their conclusions than I had hoped to make them. Complete definiteness was of course not to be expected. Right regulation of the actions of so complex a being as man, living under conditions so complex as those presented by a society, evidently forms a subject matter unlikely to admit of specific statements throughout its entire range.

The primary division of it—private conduct—necessarily dependent in part on the nature of the individual and his circumstances, can be prescribed but approximately; and guidance must, in most cases, be partly determined by a judicial balancing of requirements and avoidance of extremes. Entrance on the first great division of public conduct—Justice—does, indeed, introduce us to conclusions which are in large degree definite. Happily, into this most important portion of ethics, treating of certain right relations between individuals, irrespective of their natures or circumstances, there enters the ruling conception of equity or equalness—

there is introduced the idea of *measure;* and the inferences reached acquire a certain quantitative character, which partially assimilates them to those of exact science. But when, leaving this all-important division, the injunctions of which are peremptory, and take no cognizance of personal elements, we pass into the remaining divisions—Negative and Positive Beneficence—we enter a region in which the complexities of private conduct are involved with the complexities of relations to the no less complex conduct of those around: presenting problems for the solution of which we have nothing in the nature of measure to guide us, and must commonly be led by empirical judgments.

In view of these admissions some will contend that no aid is here furnished by the general doctrine of evolution. The first reply is that in that chief division of ethics treating of justice, it furnishes aid both as verifying conclusions empirically drawn and as leading to certain unaccepted conclusions of importance. If it be said that throughout the final divisions of ethics, dealing with beneficence, negative and positive, the conclusions must, as above implied, be chiefly empirical; and that therefore here, at any rate, the doctrine of evolution does not help us; the reply is that it helps us in general ways though not in special ways. In the first place, for certain modes of conduct which at present are supposed to have no sanction if they have not a supernatural sanction, it yields us a natural sanction—shows us that such modes of conduct fall within the lines of an evolving humanity—are conducive to a higher life, and are for this reason obligatory. In the second place, where it leaves us to form empirical judgments, it brings into view those general truths by which our empirical judgments should be guided—indicates the limits within which they are to be found.

Beyond serving to reinforce the injunctions of beneficence, by adding to the empirical sanction a rational sanction, the contents of Parts V and VI have these claims to attention: First, that under each head there are definitely set down the various requirements and restraints which should be taken into account: so aiding the formation of balanced judgments. Second, that by this methodic treatment there is given a certain coherence to the confused and often inconsistent ideas on the subject of beneficence, which are at present lying all abroad. And third, that the coherent body of doctrine which results, is made to include regulation of sundry kinds of conduct which are not taken cognizance of by ethics as ordinarily conceived.

H. S.

London
April 1893

PREFACE TO PART IV
When First Issued Separately

In the Preface to *The Data of Ethics,* published in June 1879, there occurred the sentence: "Hints, repeated of late years with increasing frequency and distinctness, have shown me that health may permanently fail, even if life does not end, before I reached the last part of the task I have marked out for myself." There followed the statement that since "this last part of the task"—the affiliation of ethics on the doctrine of evolution—was that "to which I regard all the preceding parts as subsidiary," I did not like to contemplate the probability of failure in executing it. Hence the decision to write *The Data of Ethics* in advance.

Something like the catastrophe foreseen gradually came. Years of declining health and decreasing power of work, brought, in 1886, a complete collapse; and further elaboration of the Synthetic Philosophy was suspended until the beginning of 1890, when it became again possible to get through a small amount of serious work daily. Of course there arose the question—What work to undertake first? Completion of *The Principles of Ethics* was, without hesitation, decided upon: the leading divisions of *The Principles of Sociology* having been executed. A further question presented itself—What part of *The Principles of Ethics* should have precedence? Led by the belief that my remaining energies would probably not carry me through the whole, I concluded that it would be best to begin with the part of most importance. Hence, passing over Part II, "The Inductions of Ethics," and Part III, "The Ethics of Individual Life," I devoted myself to Part IV, "The Ethics of Social Life: Justice," and have now, to my great satisfaction, succeeded in finishing it.

Should improved health be maintained, I hope that, before the close of next year, I may issue parts II and III, completing the first volume; and should I be able to continue, I shall then turn my attention to Part V, "The Ethics of Social Life: Negative Beneficence," and Part VI, "The Ethics of Social Life: Positive Beneficence."

Between this Part IV of *The Principles of Ethics*, and my first work, *Social Statics*, with the constructive portion of which it coincides in area, there are considerable differences. One difference is that what there was in my first book of supernaturalistic interpretation has disappeared, and the interpretation has become exclusively naturalistic—that is, evolutionary. With this difference may be joined the concomitant difference, that whereas a biological origin for ethics was, in *Social Statics*, only indicated, such origin has now been definitely set forth; and the elaboration of its consequences has become the cardinal trait. And a further distinction is that induction has been more habitually brought in support of deduction. It has in every case been shown that the corollaries from the first principle laid down, have severally been in course of verification during the progress of mankind.

It seems proper to add that the first five chapters have already been published in *The Nineteenth Century* for March and April 1890.

H. S.

London
June 1891

PART IV
THE ETHICS OF SOCIAL LIFE:
JUSTICE

CHAPTER 1

Animal Ethics

246.   Those who have not read the first division of this work will be surprised by the above title. But the chapters "Conduct in General" and "The Evolution of Conduct" will have made clear to those who have read them that something which may be regarded as animal ethics is implied.

It was there shown that the conduct which ethics treats of is not separable from conduct at large; that the highest conduct is that which conduces to the greatest length, breadth, and completeness of life; and that, by implication, there is a conduct proper to each species of animal, which is the relatively good conduct—a conduct which stands toward that species as the conduct we morally approve stands toward the human species.

Most people regard the subject matter of ethics as being conduct considered as calling forth approbation or reprobation. But the primary subject matter of ethics is conduct considered objectively as producing good or bad results to self or others or both.

Even those who think of ethics as concerned only with conduct which deserves praise or blame, tacitly recognize an animal ethics; for certain acts of animals excite in them antipathy or sympathy. A bird which feeds its mate while she is sitting is regarded with a sentiment of approval. For a hen which refuses to sit upon her eggs there is a feeling of aversion; while one which fights in defense of her chickens is admired.

Egoistic acts, as well as altruistic acts, in animals are classed as good or bad. A squirrel which lays up a store of food for the winter is thought of as doing that which a squirrel ought to do; and, contrariwise, one which idly makes no provision and dies of starvation, is thought of as properly paying the penalty of improvidence. A dog which surrenders its bone to another without a struggle, and runs away, we call a coward—a word of reprobation.

Thus, then, it is clear that acts which are conducive to preservation of offspring or of the individual we consider as good relatively to the species, and conversely.

247. The two classes of cases of altruistic acts and egoistic acts just exemplified, show us the two cardinal and opposed principles of animal ethics.

During immaturity benefits received must be inversely proportionate to capacities possessed. Within the family group most must be given where least is deserved, if desert is measured by worth. Contrariwise, after maturity is reached benefit must vary directly as worth: worth being measured by fitness to the conditions of existence. The ill fitted must suffer the evils of unfitness, and the well fitted profit by their fitness.

These are the two laws which a species must conform to if it is to be preserved. Limiting the proposition to the higher types (for in the lower types, parents give to offspring no other aid than that of laying up small amounts of nutriment with their germs: the result being that an enormous mortality has to be balanced by an enormous fertility)—thus limiting the proposition, I say, it is clear that if, among the young, benefit were proportioned to efficiency the species would disappear forthwith; and that if, among adults, benefit were proportioned to inefficiency, the species would disappear by decay in a few generations (see *Principles of Sociology*, sec. 322).

248. What is the ethical aspect of these principles? In the first place, animal life of all but the lowest kinds has been maintained by virtue of them. Excluding the protozoa, among which their operation is scarcely discernible, we see that without *gratis* benefits to offspring, and earned benefits to adults, life could not have continued.

In the second place, by virtue of them life has gradually evolved into higher forms. By care of offspring, which has become greater with advancing organization, and by survival of the fittest in the competition among adults, which has become more habitual with advancing organization, superiority has been perpetually fostered and further advances caused.

On the other hand, it is true that to this self-sacrificing care for the young and this struggle for existence among adults, has been due the carnage and the death by starvation which have characterized the evolution of life from the beginning. It is also true that the processes consequent on conformity to these principles are responsible for the production of torturing parasites, which outnumber in their kinds all other creatures.

To those who take a pessimist view of animal life in general, contemplation of these principles can of course yield only dissatisfaction. But to those who take an optimist view, or a meliorist view, of life in general, and who accept the postulate of hedonism, contemplation of these principles must yield greater or less satisfaction, and fulfillment of them must be ethically approved.

Otherwise considered, these principles are, according to the current belief, expressions of the Divine will, or else, according to the agnostic belief, indicate the mode in which works the Unknowable Power throughout the universe; and in either case they have the warrant hence derived.

249. But here, leaving aside the ultimate controversy of pessimism versus optimism, it will suffice for present purposes to set out with a hypothetical postulate, and to limit it to a single species. If the preservation and prosperity of such species is to be desired, there inevitably emerge one most general conclusion and from it three less general conclusions.

The most general conclusion is that, in order of obligation, the preservation of the species takes precedence of the preservation of the individual. It is true that the species has no existence save as an aggregate of individuals; and it is true that, therefore, the welfare of the species is an end to be subserved only as subserving the welfares of individuals. But since disappearance of the species, implying disappearance of all individuals, involves absolute failure in achieving the end, whereas disappearance of individuals, though carried to a great extent, may leave outstanding such number as can, by the continuance of the species, make subsequent fulfillment of the end possible; the preservation of the individual must, in a variable degree according to circumstances, be subordinated to the preservation of the species, where the two conflict. The resulting corollaries are these:

First, that among adults there must be conformity to the law that benefits received shall be directly proportionate to merits possessed: merits being measured by power of self-sustentation. For, otherwise, the species must suffer in two ways. It must suffer immediately by sacrifice of superior to inferior, which entails a general diminution of welfare; and it must suffer remotely by further increase of the inferior which, by implication, hinders increase of the superior, and causes a general deterioration, ending in extinction if it is continued.

Second, that during early life, before self-sustentation has become possible, and also while it can be but partial, the aid given must be the greatest where the worth shown is the smallest—benefits received must be inversely proportionate to merits possessed: merits being measured by power of self-sustentation. Unless there are *gratis* benefits to offspring, unqualified at first and afterward qualified by decrease as maturity is approached, the species must disappear by extinction of its young. There is, of course, necessitated a proportionate self-subordination of adults.

Third, to this self-subordination entailed by parenthood has, in certain cases, to be added a further self-subordination. If the constitution of the species and its conditions of existence are such that sacrifices, partial or complete, of some of its individuals, so subserve the welfare of the species that its numbers are better maintained than they would otherwise be, then there results a justification for such sacrifices.

Such are the laws by conformity to which a species is maintained; and if we assume that the preservation of a particular species is a desideratum, there arises in it an obligation to conform to these laws, which we may call, according to the case in question, quasi-ethical or ethical.

CHAPTER 2

Subhuman Justice

250.   Of the two essential but opposed principles of action
by pursuance of which each species is preserved,
we are here concerned only with the second. Passing over the
law of the family as composed of adults and young, we have
now to consider exclusively the law of the species as composed of adults only.

This law we have seen to be that individuals of most worth,
as measured by their fitness to the conditions of existence,
shall have the greatest benefits, and that inferior individuals
shall receive smaller benefits, or suffer greater evils, or
both—a law which, under its biological aspect, has for its
implication the survival of the fittest. Interpreted in ethical
terms, it is that each individual ought to be subject to the
effects of its own nature and resulting conduct. Throughout
subhuman life this law holds without qualification; for there
exists no agency by which, among adults, the relations between conduct and consequence can be interfered with.

Fully to appreciate the import of this law, we may with
advantage pause a moment to contemplate an analogous law;
or, rather, the same law as exhibited in another sphere. Besides being displayed in the relations among members of a
species, as respectively well sustained or ill sustained accord-

ing to their well-adapted activities or ill-adapted activities, it is displayed in the relations of the parts of each organism to one another.

Every muscle, every viscus, every gland, receives blood in proportion to function. If it does little it is ill fed and dwindles; if it does much it is well fed and grows. By this balancing of expenditure and nutrition, there is, at the same time, a balancing of the relative powers of the parts of the organism; so that the organism as a whole is fitted to its existence by having its parts continuously proportioned to the requirements. And clearly this principle of self-adjustment within each individual, is parallel to that principle of self-adjustment by which the species as a whole keeps itself fitted to its environment. For by the better nutrition and greater power of propagation which come to members of the species that have faculties and consequent activities best adapted to the needs, joined with the lower sustentation of self and offspring which accompany less adapted faculties and activities, there is caused such special growth of the species as most conduces to its survival in face of surrounding conditions.

This, then, is the law of subhuman justice, that each individual shall receive the benefits and the evils of its own nature and its consequent conduct.

251. But subhuman justice is extremely imperfect, alike in general and in detail.

In general, it is imperfect in the sense that there exist multitudinous species the sustentation of which depends on the wholesale destruction of other species; and this wholesale destruction implies that the species serving as prey have the relations between conduct and consequence so habitually broken that in very few individuals are they long maintained. It is true that in such cases the premature loss of life suffered from enemies by nearly all members of the species, must be considered as resulting from their natures—their inability to contend with the destructive agencies they are exposed to. But we may fitly recognize the truth that this violent ending of the immense majority of its lives, implies that the species is one in which justice, as above conceived, is displayed in but small measure.

Subhuman justice is extremely imperfect in detail, in the sense that the relation between conduct and consequence is in such an immense proportion of cases broken by accidents— accidents of kinds which fall indiscriminately upon inferior and superior individuals. There are the multitudinous deaths caused by inclemencies of weather, which, in the great majority of cases, the best members of the species are liable to like the worst. There are other multitudinous deaths caused by scarcity of food, which, if not wholly, still in large measure, carries off good and bad alike. Among low types, too, enemies are causes of death which so operate that superior as well as inferior are sacrificed. And the like holds with invasions by parasites, often widely fatal. These frequently destroy the best individuals as readily as the worst.

The high rate of multiplication among low animals, required to balance the immense mortality, at once shows us that among them long survival is not insured by superiority; and that thus the subhuman justice, consisting in continued receipt of the results of conduct, holds individually in but few cases.

252. And here we come upon a truth of great significance—the truth that subhuman justice becomes more decided as organization becomes higher.

Whether this or that fly is taken by a swallow, whether among a brood of caterpillars an ichneumon settles on this or that, whether out of a shoal of herrings this or that is swallowed by a cetacean, is an event quite independent of individual peculiarity: good and bad samples fare alike. With high types of creatures it is otherwise. Keen senses, sagacity, agility, give a particular carnivore special power to secure prey. In a herd of herbivorous creatures, the one with quickest hearing, clearest vision, most sensitive nostril, or greatest speed, is the one most likely to save itself.

Evidently, in proportion as the endowments, mental and bodily, of a species are high, and as, consequently, its ability to deal with the incidents of the environment is great, the continued life of each individual is less dependent on accidents against which it cannot guard. And, evidently, in proportion as this result of general superiority becomes marked, the results of special superiorities are felt. Individual differences of faculty play larger parts in determining individual fates. Now deficiency of a power shortens life, and now a large endowment prolongs it. That is to say, individuals experience more fully the results of their own natures—the justice is more decided.

253. As displayed among creatures which lead solitary lives, the nature of subhuman justice is thus sufficiently expressed; but on passing to gregarious creatures we discover in it an element not yet specified.

Simple association, as of deer, profits the individual and the species only by that more efficient safeguarding which results from the superiority of a multitude of eyes, ears, and noses over the eyes, ears, and nose of a single individual. Through the alarms more quickly given, all benefit by the senses of the most acute. Where this, which we may call passive cooperation, rises into active cooperation, as among rooks where one of the flock keeps watch while the rest feed, or as among the cimarrons, a much-hunted variety of mountain sheep in Central America, which similarly place sentries, or as among beavers where a number work together in making dams, or as among wolves where, by a plan of attack in which the individuals play different parts, prey is caught which would otherwise not be caught; there are still greater advantages to the individuals and to the species. And, speaking generally, we may say that gregariousness, and cooperation more or less active, establish themselves in a species only because they are profitable to it; since, otherwise, survival of the fittest must prevent establishment of them.

But now mark that this profitable association is made possible only by observance of certain conditions. The acts directed to self-sustentation which each performs, are performed more or less in presence of others performing like acts; and there tends to result more or less interference. If the interference is great, it may render the association unprofitable. For the association to be profitable the acts must be restrained to such extent as to leave a balance of advantage. Survival of the fittest will else exterminate that variety of the species in which association begins.

Here, then, we find a further factor in subhuman justice. Each individual, receiving the benefits and the injuries due to its own nature and consequent conduct, has to carry on that conduct subject to the restriction that it shall not in any large measure impede the conduct by which each other individual achieves benefits or brings on itself injuries. The average conduct must not be so aggressive as to cause evils which outbalance the good obtained by cooperation. Thus, to the positive element in subhuman justice has to be added, among gregarious creatures, a negative element.

254. The necessity for observance of the condition that each member of the group, while carrying on self-sustentation and sustentation of offspring, shall not seriously impede the like pursuits of others, makes itself so felt, where association is established, as to mould the species to it. The mischiefs from time to time experienced when the limits are transgressed, continually discipline all in such ways as to produce regard for the limits; so that such regard becomes, in course of time, a natural trait of the species. For, manifestly, regardlessness of the limits, if great and general, causes dissolution of the group. Those varieties only can survive as gregarious varieties in which there is an inherited tendency to maintain the limits.

Yet further, there arises such general consciousness of the need for maintaining the limits, that punishments are inflicted on transgressors—not only by aggrieved members of the group, but by the group as a whole. A "rogue" elephant (always distinguished as unusually malicious) is one which has been expelled from the herd: doubtless because of conduct obnoxious to the rest—probably aggressive. It is said that from a colony of beavers an idler is banished, and thus prevented from profiting by labors in which he does not join: a statement made credible by the fact that drones, when no longer needed, are killed by worker-bees. The testimonies of observers in different countries show that a flock of crows, after prolonged noise of consultation, will summarily execute an offending member. And an eyewitness affirms that among rooks, a pair which steals the sticks from neighboring nests has its own nest pulled to pieces by the rest.

Here, then, we see that the *a priori* condition to harmonious cooperation comes to be tacitly recognized as something like a law; and there is a penalty consequent on breach of it.

255. That the individual shall experience all the consequences, good and evil, of its own nature and consequent conduct, which is that primary principle of subhuman justice whence results survival of the fittest, is, in creatures that lead solitary lives, a principle complicated only by the responsibilities of parenthood. Among them the purely egoistic actions of self-sustentation have, during the reproductive period, to be qualified by that self-subordination which the rearing of offspring necessitates, but by no other self-subordination. Among gregarious creatures of considerable intelligence, however, disciplined, as we have just seen, into due regard for the limits imposed by other's presence, the welfare of the species, besides demanding self-subordination in the rearing of offspring, occasionally demands a further self-subordination.

We read of bisons that, during the calving season, the bulls form an encircling guard round the herd of cows and calves, to protect them against wolves and other predatory animals: a proceeding which entails on each bull some danger, but which conduces to the preservation of the species. Out of a herd of elephants about to emerge from a forest to reach a drinking place, one will first appear and look round in search of dangers, and, not discerning any, will then post some others of the herd to act as watchers; after which the main body comes forth and enters the water. Here a certain extra risk is run by the few that the many may be the safer. In a still greater degree we are shown this kind of action by a troop of monkeys, the members of which will combine to defend or rescue one of their number, or will fitly arrange themselves when retreating from an enemy—"the females, with their young, leading the way, the old males bringing up the rear . . . the place of danger"; for though in any particular case the species may not profit, since more mortality may result than would have resulted, yet it profits in the long run by the display of a character which makes attack on its groups dangerous.

Evidently, then, if by such conduct one variety of a gregarious species keeps up, or increases, its numbers, while other varieties, in which self-subordination thus directed does not exist, fail to do this, a certain sanction is acquired for such conduct. The preservation of the species being the higher end, it results that where an occasional mortality of individuals in defense of the species furthers this preservation in a greater degree than would pursuit of exclusive benefit by each individual, that which we recognize as subhuman justice may rightly have this second limitation.

256. It remains only to point out the order of priority, and the respective ranges, of these principles. The law of relation between conduct and consequence, which, throughout the animal kingdom at large, brings prosperity to those individuals which are structurally best adapted to their conditions of existence, and which, under its ethical aspect, is expressed in the principle that each individual ought to receive the good and the evil which arises from its own nature, is the primary law holding of all creatures; and is applicable without qualification to creatures which lead solitary lives, save by that self-subordination needed among the higher of them for the rearing of offspring.

Among gregarious creatures, and in an increasing degree as

they cooperate more, there comes into play the law, second in order of time and authority, that those actions through which, in fulfillment of its nature, the individual achieves benefits and avoids evils, shall be restrained by the need for noninterference with the like actions of associated individuals. A substantial respect for this law in the average of cases, being the condition under which alone gregariousness can continue, it becomes an imperative law for creatures to which gregariousness is a benefit. But, obviously, this secondary law is simply a specification of that form which the primary law takes under the conditions of gregarious life; since, by asserting that in each individual the interactions of conduct and consequence must be restricted in the specified way, it tacitly reasserts that these interactions must be maintained in other individuals, that is in all individuals.

Later in origin, and narrower in range, is the third law, that under conditions such that, by the occasional sacrifices of some members of a species, the species as a whole prospers, there arises a sanction for such sacrifices, and a consequent qualification of the law that each individual shall receive the benefits and evils of its own nature.

Finally, it should be observed that whereas the first law is absolute for animals in general, and whereas the second law is absolute for gregarious animals, the third law is relative to the existence of enemies of such kinds that, in contending with them, the species gains more than it loses by the sacrifice of a few members; and in the absence of such enemies this qualification imposed by the third law disappears.

CHAPTER 3

Human Justice

257.   The contents of the last chapter foreshadow the contents of this. As, from the evolution point of view,
human life must be regarded as a further development of
subhuman life, it follows that from this same point of view,
human justice must be a further development of subhuman
justice. For convenience the two are here separately treated,
but they are essentially of the same nature, and form parts of a
continuous whole.

Of man, as of all inferior creatures, the law by conformity to
which the species is preserved, is that among adults the individuals best adapted to the conditions of their existence shall
prosper most, and that individuals least adapted to the conditions of their existence shall prosper least—a law which, if
uninterfered with, entails survival of the fittest, and spread of
the most adapted varieties. And as before so here, we see that,
ethically considered, this law implies that each individual
ought to receive the benefits and the evils of his own nature
and consequent conduct: neither being prevented from having whatever good his actions normally bring to him, nor
allowed to shoulder off on to other persons whatever ill is
brought to him by his actions.

To what extent such ill, naturally following from his actions, may be voluntarily borne by other persons, it does not concern us now to inquire. The qualifying effects of pity, mercy, and generosity, will be considered hereafter in the parts dealing with "Negative Beneficence" and "Positive Beneficence." Here we are concerned only with pure justice.

The law thus originating, and thus ethically expressed, is obviously that which commends itself to the common apprehension as just. Sayings and criticisms daily heard imply a perception that conduct and consequence ought not to be dissociated. When, of some one who suffers a disaster, it is said, "He has no one to blame but himself," there is implied the belief that he has not been inequitably dealt with. The comment on one whose misjudgment or misbehavior has entailed evil upon him, that "he has made his own bed, and now he must lie in it," has behind it the conviction that this connection of cause and effect is proper. Similarly with the remark, "He got no more than he deserved." A kindred conviction is implied when, conversely, there results good instead of evil. "He has fairly earned his reward"; "He has not received due recompense"; are remarks indicating the consciousness that there should be a proportion between effort put forth and advantage achieved—that justice demands such a proportion.

258. The truth that justice becomes more pronounced as organization becomes higher, which we contemplated in the last chapter, is further exemplified on passing from subhuman justice to human justice. The degree of justice and the degree of organization simultaneously make advances. These are shown alike by the entire human race, and by its superior varieties as contrasted with its inferior.

We saw that a high species of animal is distinguished from a low species, in the respect that since its aggregate suffers less mortality from incidental destructive agencies, each of its members continues on the average for a longer time subject to the normal relation between conduct and consequence; and here we see that the human race as a whole, far lower in its rate of mortality than nearly all races of inferior kinds, usually subjects its members for much longer periods to the good and evil results of well-adapted and ill-adapted conduct. We also saw that as, among the higher animals, a greater average longevity makes it possible for individual differences to show their effects for longer periods, it results that the unlike fates of different individuals are to a greater extent determined by that normal relation between conduct and consequence which constitutes justice; and we here see that in mankind, unlikenesses of faculty in still greater degrees, and for still longer periods, work out their effects in advantaging the superior and disadvantaging the inferior in the continuous play of conduct and consequence.

Similarly is it with the civilized varieties of mankind as compared with the savage varieties. A still further diminished rate of mortality implies that there is a still larger proportion, the members of which gain good from well-adapted acts and suffer evil from ill-adapted acts. While also it is manifest that both the greater differences of longevity among individuals, and the greater differences of social position, imply that in civilized societies more than in savage societies, differences of endowment, and consequent differences of conduct, are enabled to cause their appropriate differences of results, good or evil: the justice is greater.

259. More clearly in the human race than in lower races, we are shown that gregariousness establishes itself because it profits the variety in which it arises; partly by furthering general safety and partly by facilitating sustentation. And we are shown that the degree of gregariousness is determined by the degree in which it thus subserves the interests of the variety. For where the variety is one of which the members live on wild food, they associate only in small groups: game and fruits widely distributed, can support these only. But greater gregariousness arises where agriculture makes possible the

support of a large number on a small area; and where the accompanying development of industries introduces many and various cooperations.

We come now to the truth—faintly indicated among lower beings and conspicuously displayed among human beings— that the advantages of cooperation can be had only by conformity to certain requirements which association imposes. The mutual hindrances liable to arise during the pursuit of their ends by individuals living in proximity, must be kept within such limits as to leave a surplus of advantage obtained by associated life. Some types of men, as the Abors, lead solitary lives, because their aggressiveness is such that they cannot live together. And this extreme case makes it clear that though, in many primitive groups, individual antagonisms often cause quarrels, yet the groups are maintained because their members derive a balance of benefit—chiefly in greater safety. It is also clear that in proportion as communities become developed, their division of labor complex, and their transactions multiplied, the advantages of cooperation can be gained only by a still better maintenance of those limits to each man's activities necessitated by the simultaneous activities of others. This truth is illustrated by the unprosperous or decaying state of communities in which the trespasses of individuals on one another are so numerous and great as generally to prevent them from severally receiving the normal results of their labors.

The requirement that individual activities must be mutually restrained, which we saw is so felt among certain inferior gregarious creatures that they inflict punishments on those who do not duly restrain them, is a requirement which, more imperative among men, and more distinctly felt by them to be a requirement, causes a still more marked habit of inflicting punishments on offenders. Though in primitive groups it is commonly left to any one who is injured to revenge himself on the injurer; and though even in the societies of feudal Europe, the defending and enforcing of his claims was in many cases held to be each man's personal concern; yet there has ever tended to grow up such perception of the need for internal order, and such sentiment accompanying the perception, that infliction of punishments by the community as a whole, or by its established agents, has become habitual. And that a system of laws enacting restrictions on conduct, and punishments for breaking them, is a natural product of human life carried on under social conditions, is shown by the fact that in numerous nations composed of various types of mankind, similar actions, similarly regarded as trespasses, have been similarly forbidden.

Through all which sets of facts is manifested the truth, recognized practically if not theoretically, that each individual carrying on the actions which subserve his life, and not prevented from receiving their normal results, good and bad, shall carry on these actions under such restraints as are imposed by the carrying on of kindred actions by other individuals, who have similarly to receive such normal results, good and bad. And vaguely, if not definitely, this is seen to constitute what is called justice.

260. We saw that among inferior gregarious creatures, justice in its universal simple form, besides being qualified by the self-subordination which parenthood implies, and in some measure by the self-restraint necessitated by association, is, in a few cases, further qualified in a small degree by the partial or complete sacrifice of individuals made in defense of the species. And now, in the highest gregarious creature, we see that this further qualification of primitive justice assumes large proportions.

No longer, as among inferior beings, demanded only by the need for defense against enemies of other kinds, this further self-subordination is, among human beings, also demanded by the need for defense against enemies of the same kind. Having spread wherever there is food, groups of men have come to be everywhere in one another's way; and the mutual enmities hence resulting, have made the sacrifices entailed by wars between groups, far greater than the sacrifices made in defense of groups against inferior animals. It is doubtless true with the human race, as with lower races, that destruction of the group, or the variety, does not imply destruction of the species; and it follows that such obligation as exists for self-subordination in the interests of the group, or the variety, is an obligation of lower degree than is that of care of offspring, without fulfillment of which the species will disappear, and of lower degree than the obligation to restrain actions within the limits imposed by social conditions, without fulfillment, or partial fulfillment, of which the group will dissolve. Still, it must be regarded as an obligation to the extent to which the maintenance of the species is subserved by the maintenance of each of its groups.

But the self-subordination thus justified, and in a sense rendered obligatory, is limited to that which is required for defensive war. Only because the preservation of the group as a whole conduces to preservation of its members' lives, and their ability to pursue the objects of life, is there a reason for the sacrifice of some of its members; and this reason no longer exists when war is offensive instead of defensive.

It may, indeed, be contended that since offensive wars initiate those struggles between groups which end in the destruction of the weaker, offensive wars, furthering the peopling of the earth by the stronger, subserve the interests of the race. But even supposing that the conquered groups always consisted of men having smaller mental or bodily fitness for war (which they do not; for it is in part a question of numbers, and the smaller groups may consist of the more capable warriors), there would still be an adequate answer. It is only during the earlier stages of human progress that the development of strength, courage, and cunning, are of chief importance. After societies of considerable size have been formed, and the subordination needed for organizing them produced, other and higher faculties become those of chief importance; and the struggle for existence carried on by violence, does not always further the survival of the fittest. The fact that but for a mere accident Persia would have conquered Greece, and the fact that the Tartar hordes very nearly overwhelmed European civilization, show that offensive war can be trusted to subserve the interests of the race only when the capacity for a high social life does not exist; and that in proportion as this capacity develops, offensive war tends more and more to hinder, rather than to further, human welfare. In brief we may say that the arrival at a stage in which ethical considerations come to be entertained, is the arrival at a stage in which offensive war, by no means certain to further predominance of races fitted for a high social life, and certain to cause injurious moral reactions on the conquering as well as on the conquered, ceases to be justifiable; and only defensive war retains a quasi-ethical justification.

And here it is to be remarked that the self-subordination which defensive war involves, and the need for such qualification of the abstract principle of justice as it implies, belong to that transitional state necessitated by the physical-force conflict of races; and that they must disappear when there is reached a peaceful state. That is to say, all questions concerning the extent of such qualifications pertain to what we have distinguished as relative ethics; and are not recognized by that absolute ethics which is concerned with the principles of right conduct in a society formed of men fully adapted to social life.

This distinction I emphasize here because, throughout succeeding chapters, we shall find that recognition of it helps us to disentangle the involved problems of political ethics.

CHAPTER 4

The Sentiment of Justice

261. Acceptance of the doctrine of organic evolution determines certain ethical conceptions. The doctrine implies that the numerous organs in each of the innumerable species of animals, have been either directly or indirectly moulded into fitness for the requirements of life by constant converse with those requirements. Simultaneously, through nervous modifications, there have been developments of the sensations, instincts, emotions, and intellectual aptitudes, needed for the appropriate uses of these organs; as we see in caged rodents which exercise their jaw muscles and incisors by purposeless gnawing, in gregarious creatures which are miserable if they cannot join their fellows, in beavers which, kept in confinement, show their passion for dam building by heaping up whatever sticks and stones they can find.

Has this process of mental adaptation ended with primitive man? Are human beings incapable of having their feelings and ideas progressively adjusted to the modes of life imposed on them by the social state into which they have grown? Shall we suppose that the nature which fitted them to the exigencies of savage life has remained unchanged, and will remain unchanged, by the exigencies of civilized life? Or shall we suppose that this aboriginal nature, by repression of some traits and fostering of others, is made to approach more and more to a nature which finds developed society its appropriate environment, and the required activities its normal ones? There are many believers in the doctrine of evolution who seem to have no faith in the continued adaptability of man-kind. While glancing but carelessly at the evidence furnished by comparisons of different human races with one another, and of the same races in different ages, they ignore entirely the induction from the phenomena of life at large. But if there is an abuse of the deductive method of reasoning there is also an abuse of the inductive method. One who refused to believe that a new moon would in a fortnight become full and then wane, and, disregarding observations accumulated through-out the past, insisted on watching the successive phases be-fore he was convinced, would be considered inductive in an irrational degree. But there might not unfairly be classed with him those who, slighting the inductive proof of unlimited adjustability, bodily and mental, which the animal kingdom at large presents, will not admit the adjustability of human na-ture to social life until the adjustment has taken place: nay, even ignore the evidence that it is taking place.

Here we shall assume it to be an inevitable inference from the doctrine of organic evolution, that the highest type of living being, no less than all lower types, must go on molding itself to those requirements which circumstances impose. And we shall, by implication, assume that moral changes are among the changes thus wrought out.

262. The fact that when surfeit of a favorite food has caused sickness, there is apt to follow an aversion to that food, shows how, in the region of the sensations, experiences establish associations which influence conduct. And the fact that the house in which a wife or child died, or in which a long illness was suffered, becomes so associated with painful states of mind as to be shunned, sufficiently illustrates, in the emo-tional region, the mode in which actions may be determined by mental connections formed in the course of life. When the

circumstances of a species make certain relations between conduct and consequence habitual, the appropriately linked feelings may come to characterize the species. Either inheritances of modifications produced by habit, or more numerous survivals of individuals having nervous structures which have varied in fit ways, gradually form guiding tendencies, prompting appropriate behavior and deterring from inappropriate. The contrast between fearless birds found on islands never before visited by man, and the birds around us, which show fear of man immediately they are out of the nest, exemplifies such adaptations.

By virtue of this process there have been produced to some extent among lower creatures, and there are being further produced in man, the sentiments appropriate to social life. Aggressive actions, while they are habitually injurious to the group in which they occur, are not unfrequently injurious to the individuals committing them; since, though certain pleasures may be gained by them, they often entail pains greater than the pleasures. Conversely, conduct restrained within the required limits, calling out no antagonistic passions, favors harmonious cooperation, profits the group, and, by implication, profits the average of its individuals. Consequently, there results, other things equal, a tendency for groups formed of members having this adaptation of nature, to survive and spread.

Among the social sentiments thus evolved, one of chief importance is the sentiment of justice. Let us now consider more closely its nature.

263. Stop an animal's nostrils, and it makes frantic efforts to free its head. Tie its limbs together, and its struggles to get them at liberty are violent. Chain it by the neck or leg, and it is some time before it ceases its attempts to escape. Put it in a cage, and it long continues restless. Generalizing these instances, we see that in proportion as the restraints on actions by which life is maintained are extreme, the resistances to them are great. Conversely, the eagerness with which a bird

seizes the opportunity for taking flight, and the joy of a dog when liberated, show how strong is the love of unfettered movement.

Displaying like feelings in like ways, man displays them in other and wider ways. He is irritated by invisible restraints as well as by visible ones; and as his evolution becomes higher, he is affected by circumstances and actions which in more remote ways aid or hinder the pursuit of ends. A parallel will elucidate this truth. Primitively the love of property is gratified only by possession of food and shelter, and, presently, of clothing; but afterwards it is gratified by possession of the weapons and tools which aid in obtaining these, then by possession of the raw materials that serve for making weapons and tools and for other purposes, then by possession of the coin which purchases them as well as things at large, then by possession of promises to pay exchangeable for the coin, then by a lien on a banker, registered in a passbook. That is, there comes to be pleasure in an ownership more and more abstract and more remote from material satisfactions. Similarly with the sentiment of justice. Beginning with the joy felt in ability to use the bodily powers and gain the resulting benefits, accompanied by irritation at direct interferences, this gradually responds to wider relations: being excited now by the incidents of personal bondage, now by those of political bondage, now by those of class privilege, and now by small political changes. Eventually this sentiment, sometimes so little developed in the Negro that he jeers at a liberated companion because he has no master to take care of him, becomes so much developed in the Englishman that the slightest infraction of some mode of formal procedure at a public meeting or in Parliament, which cannot intrinsically concern him, is vehemently opposed because in some distant and indirect way it may help to give possible powers to unnamed authorities who may perhaps impose unforeseen burdens or restrictions.

Clearly, then, the egoistic sentiment of justice is a subjective attribute which answers to that objective requirement constituting justice—the requirement that each adult shall receive the results of his own nature and consequent actions. For unless the faculties of all kinds have free play, these results cannot be gained or suffered, and unless there exists a sentiment which prompts maintenance of the sphere for this free play, it will be trenched upon and the free play impeded.

264. While we may thus understand how the egoistic sentiment of justice is developed, it is much less easy to understand how there is developed the altruistic sentiment of justice. On the one hand, the implication is that the altruistic sentiment of justice can come into existence only in the course of adaptation to social life. On the other hand the implication is that social life is made possible only by maintenance of those equitable relations which imply the altruistic sentiment of justice. How can these reciprocal requirements be fulfilled?

The answer is that the altruistic sentiment of justice can come into existence only by the aid of a sentiment which temporarily supplies its place, and restrains the actions prompted by pure egoism—a proaltruistic sentiment of justice, as we may call it. This has several components which we must successively glance at.

The first deterrent from aggression is one which we see among animals at large—the fear of retaliation. Among creatures of the same species the food obtained by one, or place of vantage taken possession of by it, is in some measure insured to it by the dread which most others feel of the vengeance that may follow any attempt to take it away; and among men, especially during early stages of social life, it is chiefly such dread which secures for each man free scope for his activities, and exclusive use of whatever they bring him.

A further restraint is fear of the reprobation likely to be shown by unconcerned members of the group. Though in the expulsion of a "rogue" elephant from the herd, or the slaying of a sinning member of the flock by rooks or storks, we see that even among animals individuals suffer from an adverse public opinion; yet it is scarcely probable that among animals expectation of general dislike prevents encroachment. But among mankind, "looking before and after" to a greater extent, the thought of social disgrace is usually an additional check on ill-behavior of man to man.

To these feelings, which come into play before there is any social organization, have to be added those which arise after political authority establishes itself. When a successful leader in war acquires permanent headship, and comes to have at heart the maintenance of his power, there arises in him a desire to prevent the trespasses of his people one against another; since the resulting dissensions weaken his tribe. The rights of personal vengeance and, as in feudal times, of private war, are restricted; and, simultaneously, there grow up interdicts on the acts which cause them. Dread of the penalties which follow breaches of these, is an added restraint.

Ancestor worship in general, developing, as the society develops, into special propitiation of the dead chief's ghost, and presently the dead king's ghost, gives to the injunctions he uttered during life increased sanctity; and when, with establishment of the cult, he becomes a god, his injunctions become divine commands with dreaded punishments for breaches of them.

These four kinds of fear cooperate. The dread of retaliation, the dread of social dislike, the dread of legal punishment, and the dread of divine vengeance, united in various proportions, form a body of feeling which checks the primitive tendency to pursue the objects of desire without regard to the interests of fellow men. Containing none of the altruistic sentiment of justice, properly so called, this proaltruistic sentiment of justice serves temporarily to cause respect for one another's claims, and so to make social cooperation possible.

265. Creatures which become gregarious tend to become sympathetic in degrees proportionate to their intelligences. Not, indeed, that the resulting sympathetic tendency is exclusively, or even mainly, of that kind which the words ordinarily imply; for in some there is little beyond sympathy in fear, and

in others, little beyond sympathy in ferocity. All that is meant is that in gregarious creatures a feeling displayed by one is apt to arouse kindred feelings in others, and is apt to do this in proportion as others are intelligent enough to appreciate the signs of the feeling. In two chapters of the *Principles of Psychology*—"Sociality and Sympathy" and "Altruistic Sentiments"—I have endeavored to show how sympathy in general arises, and how there is eventually produced altruistic sympathy.

The implication is, then, that the associated state having been maintained among men by the aid of the proaltruistic sentiment of justice, there have been maintained the conditions under which the altruistic sentiment of justice itself can develop. In a permanent group there occur, generation after generation, incidents simultaneously drawing from its members manifestations of like emotions—rejoicings over victories and escapes, over prey jointly captured, over supplies of wild food discovered; as well as laments over defeats, scarcities, inclemencies, &c. And to these greater pleasures and pains felt in common by all, and so expressing themselves that each sees in others the signs of feelings like those which he has and is displaying, must be added the smaller pleasures and pains daily resulting from meals taken together, amusements, games, and from the not infrequent adverse occurrences which affect several persons at once. Thus there is fostered that sympathy which makes the altruistic sentiment of justice possible.

But the altruistic sentiment of justice is slow in assuming a high form, partly because its primary component does not become highly developed until a late phase of progress, partly because it is relatively complex, and partly because it implies a stretch of imagination not possible for low intelligences. Let us glance at each of these reasons.

Every altruistic feeling presupposes experience of the corresponding egoistic feeling. As, until pain has been felt there cannot be sympathy with pain, and as one who has no ear for music cannot enter into the pleasure which music gives to others; so, the altruistic sentiment of justice can arise only after the egoistic sentiment of justice has arisen. Hence where this has not been developed in any considerable degree, or has been repressed by a social life of an adverse kind, the altruistic sentiment of justice remains rudimentary.

The complexity of the sentiment becomes manifest on observing that it is not concerned only with concrete pleasures and pains, but is concerned mainly with certain of the circumstances under which these are obtainable or preventible. As the egoistic sentiment of justice is gratified by maintenance of those conditions which render achievement of satisfactions unimpeded, and is irritated by the breaking of those conditions, it results that the altruistic sentiment of justice requires for its excitement not only the ideas of such satisfactions but also the ideas of those conditions which are in the one case maintained and in the other case broken.

Evidently, therefore, to be capable of this sentiment in a developed form, the faculty of mental representation must be relatively great. Where the feelings with which there is to be sympathy are simple pleasures and pains, the higher gregarious animals occasionally display it: pity and generosity are from time to time felt by them as well as by human beings. But to conceive simultaneously not only the feelings produced in another, but the plexus of acts and relations involved in the production of such feelings, presupposes the putting together in thought of more elements than an inferior creature can grasp at the same time. And when we come to those most abstract forms of the sentiment of justice which are concerned with public arrangements, we see that only the higher varieties of men are capable of so conceiving the ways in which good or bad institutions and laws will eventually affect their spheres of action, as to be prompted to support or oppose them; and that only among these, therefore, is there excited, under such conditions, that sympathetic sentiment of justice which makes them defend the political interests of fellow citizens.

There is, of course, a close connection between the sentiment of justice and the social type. Predominant militancy, by the coercive form of organization it implies, alike in the fighting body and in the society which supports it, affords no scope for the egoistic sentiment of justice, but, contrariwise, perpetually tramples on it; and, at the same time, the sympathies which originate the altruistic sentiment of justice are perpetually seared by militant activities. On the other hand, in proportion as the regime of status is replaced by the regime of contract, or, in other words, as fast as voluntary cooperation which characterizes the industrial type of society, becomes more general than compulsory cooperation which characterizes the militant type of society, individual activities become less restrained, and the sentiment which rejoices in the scope for them is encouraged; while, simultaneously, the occasions for repressing the sympathies become less frequent. Hence, during warlike phases of social life the sentiment of justice retrogrades, while it advances during peaceful phases, and can reach its full development only in a permanently peaceful state.*

---

* Permanent peace does in a few places exist, and where it exists the sentiment of justice is exceptionally strong and sensitive. I am glad to have again the occasion for pointing out that among men called uncivilized, there are some, distinguished by the entire absence of warlike activities, who in their characters put to shame the peoples called civilized. In *Political Institutions,* sections 437 and 574, I have given eight examples of this connection of facts, taken from races of different types.

CHAPTER 5

The Idea of Justice

266. While describing the sentiment of justice the way has been prepared for describing the idea of justice. Though the two are intimately connected they may be clearly distinguished.

One who has dropped his pocketbook and, turning round, finds that another who has picked it up will not surrender it, is indignant. If the goods sent home by a shopkeeper are not those he purchased, he protests against the fraud. Should his seat at a theater be usurped during a momentary absence, he feels himself ill used. Morning noises from a neighbor's poultry he complains of as grievances. And, meanwhile, he sympathizes with the anger of a friend who has been led by false statements to join a disastrous enterprise, or whose action at law has been rendered futile by a flaw in the procedure. But though, in these cases, his sense of justice is offended, he may fail to distinguish the essential trait which in each case causes the offense. He may have the sentiment of justice in full measure while his idea of justice remains vague.

This relation between sentiment and idea is a matter of course. The ways in which men trespass on one another become more numerous in their kinds, and more involved, as society grows more complex; and they must be experienced in their many forms, generation after generation, before analysis can make clear the essential distinction between legitimate acts and illegitimate acts. The idea emerges and becomes definite in the course of the experiences that action may be carried up to a certain limit without causing resentment from others, but if carried beyond that limit produces resentment. Such experiences accumulate; and gradually, along with repugnance to the acts which bring reactive pains, there arises a conception of a limit to each kind of activity up to which there is freedom to act. But since the kinds of activity are many and become increasingly various with the development of social life, it is a long time before the general nature of the limit common to all cases can be conceived.*

A further reason for this slowness of development should be recognized. Ideas as well as sentiments must, on the average, be adjusted to the social state. Hence, as war has been frequent or habitual in nearly all societies, such ideas of justice as have existed have been perpetually confused by the conflicting requirements of internal amity and external enmity.

267. Already it has been made clear that the idea of justice, or at least the human idea of justice, contains two elements. On the one hand, there is that positive element implied by each man's recognition of his claims to unimpeded activities and the benefits they bring. On the other hand, there is that

---

* The genesis of the idea of simple limits to simple actions is exhibited to us by intelligent animals, and serves to elucidate the process in the case of more complex actions and less obvious limits. I refer to the dogs of Constantinople, among which, if not between individuals yet between groups of individuals, there are tacit assertions of claims and penalties for invasions of claims. This well-known statement has been recently verified in a striking way in the work of Major E. C. Johnson, *On the Track of the Crescent.* He says (pp. 58–59): "One evening I was walking [in Constantinople] with an English officer of gendarmerie when a bitch came up and licked his hand. . . . She followed us a little way, and stopped short in the middle of the street. She wagged her tail, and looked wistfully after us, but never stirred when we called her. A few nights afterwards . . . the same bitch . . . recognized me . . . and followed me to the boundary of her district."

negative element implied by the consciousness of limits which the presence of other men having like claims necessitates. Two opposite traits in these two components especially arrest the attention.

Inequality is the primordial idea suggested. For if the principle is that each shall receive the benefits and evils due to his own nature and consequent conduct, then, since men differ in their powers, there must be differences in the results of their conduct. Unequal amounts of benefit are implied.

Mutual limitations to men's actions suggest a contrary idea. When it is seen that if each pursues his ends regardless of his neighbor's claims, quarrels must result, there arises the consciousness of bounds which must be set to the doings of each to avoid the quarrels. Experience shows that these bounds are on the average the same for all. And the thought of spheres of action bounded by one another, which hence results, involves the conception of equality.

Unbalanced appreciations of these two factors in human justice, lead to divergent moral and social theories, which we must now glance at.

268. In some of the rudest men the appreciations are no higher than those which we see among inferior gregarious animals. Here the stronger takes what he pleases from the weaker without exciting general reprobation—as among the Dogribs; while, elsewhere, there is practiced and tacitly approved something like communism—as among the Fuegians. But where habitual war has developed political organization, the idea of inequality becomes predominant. If not among the conquered, who are made slaves, yet among the conquerors, who naturally think of that which conduces to their interest as that which *ought* to be, there is fostered this element in the conception of justice which implies that superiority shall have the benefits of superiority.

Though the Platonic dialogues may not be taken as measures of Greek belief, yet we may gather from them what beliefs were general. Glaucon, describing a current opinion, says:

> This, as they affirm, is the origin and nature of justice: there is a mean or compromise between the best of all, which is to do and not to suffer injustice, and the worst of all, which is to suffer without the power of retaliation; and justice, being the mean between the two, is tolerated not as good, but as the lesser evil. And immediately afterwards it is said that men are only diverted into the path of justice by the force of law.

In this significant passage several things are to be noted. There is first a recognition of the fact, above indicated, that at an early stage the practice of justice is initiated by the dread of retaliation, and the conviction, suggested by experience, that on the whole it is desirable to avoid aggression and to respect the limit which compromise implies: there is no thought of intrinsic flagitiousness in aggression, but only of its impolicy. Further, the limit to each man's actions, described as "a mean or compromise," and respect for which is called "the path of justice," is said to be established only "by the force of law." Law is not considered as an expression of justice otherwise cognizable, but as itself the source of justice; and hence results the meaning of a preceding proposition, that it is just to obey the law. Thirdly, there is an implication that were it not for retaliation and legal penalties, the stronger might with propriety take advantage of the weaker. There is a half-expressed belief that superiority ought to have all the advantages which superiority can take: the idea of inequality occupies a prominent place, while the idea of equality makes no definite appearance.

What was the opinion of Plato, or rather of Socrates, on the matter is not very easy to find out. Greek ideas on many matters had not yet reached the stage of definiteness, and throughout the dialogues the thinking is hazy. Justice, which is in some places exemplified by honesty, is elsewhere the equivalent of virtue at large, and then (to quote from Jowett's summary) is regarded as "universal order or well being, first in the state, and secondly in the individual." This last, which is the finished conclusion, implies established predominance of a ruling class and subjection of the rest. Justice consists "in each of the three classes doing the work of its own class": carpenter, shoemaker, or what not, "doing each his own business, and not another's"; and all obeying the class whose business it is to rule.* Thus the idea of justice is developed from the idea of inequality. Though there is some recognition of equality of positions and of claims among members of the same class, yet the regulations respecting community of wives &c. in the guardian class, have for their avowed purpose to establish, even within that class, unequal privileges for the benefit of the superior.

That the notion of justice had this general character among the Greeks, is further shown by the fact that it recurs in Aristotle. In Chapter V of his *Politics,* he concludes that the relation of master and slave is both advantageous and just.

But now observe that though in the Greek conception of justice there predominates the idea of inequality, while the idea of equality is inconspicuous, the inequality refers, not to the natural achievement of greater rewards by greater merits, but to the artificial apportionment of greater rewards to greater merits. It is an inequality mainly established by authority. The gradations in the civil organization are of the same nature as those in the military organization. Regimentation pervades both; and the idea of justice is conformed to the traits of the social structure.

---

* On another page there is furnished a typical example of Socratic reasoning. It is held to be a just "principle that individuals are neither to take what is another's, nor to be deprived of what is their own." From this it is inferred that justice consists in "having and *doing* what is a man's own"; and then comes the further inference that it is unjust for one man to assume another's occupation, and "force his way" out of one class into another. Here, then, because a man's own property and his own occupation are both called his own, the same conclusion is drawn concerning both. Two fallacies are involved—the one that a man can "own" a trade in the same way that he owns a coat, and the other that because he may not be *deprived* of the coat he must be *restricted* to the trade. The Platonic dialogues are everywhere vitiated by fallacies of this kind, caused by confounding words with things—unity of name with unity of nature.

And this is the idea of justice proper to the militant type at large, as we are again shown throughout Europe in subsequent ages. It will suffice to point out that along with the different law-established positions and privileges of different ranks, there went gradations in the amounts paid in composition for crimes, according to the rank of the injured. And how completely the notion of justice was determined by the notion of rightly existing inequalities, is shown by the condemnation of serfs who escaped into the towns, and were said to have "unjustly" withdrawn themselves from the control of their lords.

Thus, as might be expected, we find that while the struggle for existence between societies is going on actively, recognition of the primary factor in justice which is common to life at large, human and subhuman, is very imperfectly qualified by recognition of the secondary factor. That which we may distinguish as the brute element in the conception is but little mitigated by the human element.

269. All movements are rhythmical, and, among others, social movements, with their accompanying doctrines. After that conception of justice in which the idea of inequality unduly predominates, comes a conception in which the idea of equality unduly predominates.

A recent example of such reactions is furnished by the ethical theory of Bentham. As is shown by the following extract from Mr. Mill's *Utilitarianism* (p. 91), the idea of inequality here entirely disappears:

> The Greatest-Happiness Principle is a mere form of words without rational signification, unless one person's happiness, supposed equal in degree (with the proper allowance made for kind), is counted for exactly as much as another's. Those conditions being supplied, Bentham's dictum, "everybody to count for one, nobody for more than one," might be written under the principle of utility as an explanatory commentary.

Now though Bentham ridicules the taking of justice as our guide, saying that while happiness is an end intelligible to all, justice is a relatively unintelligible end, yet he tacitly asserts that his principle, "everybody to count for one, nobody for more than one," is just; since, otherwise, he would be obliged to admit that it is unjust, and we may not suppose he would do so. Hence the implication of his doctrine is that justice means an equal apportionment of the benefits, material and immaterial, which men's activities bring. There is no recognition of the propriety of inequalities in men's shares of happiness, consequent on inequalities in their faculties or characters.

This is the theory which communism would reduce to practice. From one who knows him, I learn that Prince Krapotkin blames the English socialists because they do not propose to act out the rule popularly worded as "share and share alike." In a recent periodical, M. de Laveleye summed up the communistic principle as being "that the individual works for the profit of the state, to which he hands over the produce of his labor for equal division among all." In the communistic utopia described in Mr. Bellamy's *Looking Backward*, it is held that each "shall make the same effort," and that if by the same effort, bodily or mental, one produces twice as much as another, he is not to be advantaged by the difference. The intellectually or physically feeble are to be quite as well off as others: the assertion being that the existing regime is one of "robbing the incapable class of their plain right in leaving them unprovided for."

The principle of inequality is thus denied absolutely. It is assumed to be unjust that superiority of nature shall bring superiority of results, or, at any rate, superiority of material results; and as no distinction appears to be made in respect either of physical qualities or intellectual qualities or moral qualities, the implication is not that strong and weak shall fare alike, but that foolish and wise, worthy and unworthy, mean and noble, shall do the same. For if, according to this conception of justice, defects of nature, physical or intellectual, ought not to count, neither ought moral defects, since they are all primarily inherited.

And here, too, we have a deliberate abolition of that cardinal distinction between the ethics of the family and the ethics of the state, emphasized at the outset: an abolition which, as we saw, must eventuate in decay and disappearance of the species or variety in which it takes place.

270. After contemplating these divergent conceptions of justice, in which the ideas of inequality and equality almost or quite exclude one another, we are now prepared for framing a true conception of justice.

In other fields of thought it has fallen to my lot to show that the right view is obtained by coordinating the antagonistic wrong views. Thus, the association theory of intellect is harmonized with the transcendental theory on perceiving that when, to the effects of individual experiences, are added the inherited effects of experiences received by all ancestors, the two views become one. So, too, when the molding of feelings into harmony with requirements, generation after generation, is recognized as causing an adapted moral nature, there results a reconciliation of the expediency theory of morals with the intuitional theory. And here we see that a like mutual correction occurs with this more special component of ethics now before us.

For if each of these opposite conceptions of justice is accepted as true in part, and then supplemented by the other, there results that conception of justice which arises on contemplating the laws of life as carried on in the social state. The equality concerns the mutually limited spheres of action which must be maintained if associated men are to cooperate harmoniously. The inequality concerns the results which each may achieve by carrying on his actions within the implied limits. No incongruity exists when the ideas of equality and inequality are applied the one to the bounds and the other to the benefits. Contrariwise, the two may be, and must be, simultaneously asserted.

Other injunctions which ethics has to utter do not here concern us. There are the self-imposed requirements and limitations of private conduct, forming that large division of ethics treated of in Part III; and there are the demands and restraints included under "Negative Beneficence" and "Positive Beneficence," to be hereafter treated of, which are at once self-imposed and in a measure imposed by public opinion. But here we have to do only with those claims and those limits which have to be maintained as conditions to harmonious cooperation, and which alone are to be enforced by society in its corporate capacity.

271. Any considerable acceptance of so definite an idea of justice is not to be expected. It is an idea appropriate to an ultimate state, and can be but partially entertained during transitional states; for the prevailing ideas must, on the average, be congruous with existing institutions and activities.

The two essentially different types of social organization, militant and industrial, based respectively on status and on contract, have, as we have above seen, feelings and beliefs severally adjusted to them; and the mixed feelings and beliefs appropriate to intermediate types, have continually to change according to the ratio between the one and the other. As I have elsewhere shown,* during the thirty—or rather forty—years' peace, and consequent weakening of the militant organization, the idea of justice became clearer: coercive regulations were relaxed and each man left more free to make the best of himself. But since then, the redevelopment of militancy has caused reversal of these changes; and, along with nominal increases of freedom, actual diminutions of freedom have resulted from multiplied restrictions and exactions. The spirit of regimentation proper to the militant type, has been spreading throughout the administration of civil life. An army of workers with appointed tasks and apportioned shares of products, which socialism, knowingly or unknowingly, aims at, shows in civil life the same characters as an army of soldiers with prescribed duties and fixed rations shows in military life; and every act of Parliament which takes money from the

---

* *Principles of Sociology*, secs. 266–67; *Political Institutions*, secs. 573–74 and 559.

individual for public purposes and gives him public benefits, tends to assimilate the two. Germany best shows this kinship. There, where militancy is most pronounced, and where the regulation of citizens is most elaborate, socialism is most highly developed; and from the head of the German military system has now come the proposal of regimental regulations for the working classes throughout Europe.

Sympathy which, a generation ago, was taking the shape of justice, is relapsing into the shape of generosity; and the generosity is exercised by inflicting injustice. Daily legislation betrays little anxiety that each shall have that which belongs to him, but great anxiety that he shall have that which belongs to somebody else. For while no energy is expended in so reforming our judicial administration that everyone may obtain and enjoy all he has earned, great energy is shown in providing for him and others benefits which they have not earned. Along with that miserable *laissez-faire* which calmly looks on while men ruin themselves in trying to enforce by law their equitable claims, there goes activity in supplying them, at other men's cost, with *gratis* novel-reading!

CHAPTER 6

The Formula of Justice

272.   After tracing up the evolution of justice in its simple form, considered objectively as a condition to the maintenance of life; after seeing how justice as so considered becomes qualified by a new factor when the life is gregarious, more especially in the human race; and after observing the corresponding subjective products—the sentiment of justice and the idea of justice—arising from converse with this condition; we are now prepared for giving to the conclusion reached a definite form. We have simply to find a precise expression for the compromise described in the last chapter.

The formula has to unite a positive element with a negative element. It must be positive in so far as it asserts for each that, since he is to receive and suffer the good and evil results of his actions, he must be allowed to act. And it must be negative in so far as, by asserting this of everyone, it implies that each can be allowed to act only under the restraint imposed by the presence of others having like claims to act. Evidently the positive element is that which expresses a prerequisite to life in general, and the negative element is that which qualifies this prerequisite in the way required when, instead of one life carried on alone, there are many lives carried on together.

Hence, that which we have to express in a precise way, is the liberty of each limited only by the like liberties of all. This we do by saying: Every man is free to do that which he wills, provided he infringes not the equal freedom of any other man.

273. A possible misapprehension must be guarded against. There are acts of aggression which the formula is presumably intended to exclude, which apparently it does not exclude. It may be said that if A strikes B, then, so long as B is not debarred from striking A in return, no greater freedom is claimed by the one than by the other; or it may be said that if A has trespassed on B's property, the requirement of the formula has not been broken so long as B can trespass on A's property. Such interpretations, however, mistake the essential meaning of the formula, which we at once see if we refer back to its origin.

For the truth to be expressed is that each in carrying on the actions which constitute his life for the time being, and conduce to the subsequent maintenance of his life, shall not be impeded further than by the carrying on of those kindred actions which maintain the lives of others. It does not countenance a superfluous interference with another's life, committed on the ground that an equal interference may balance it. Such a rendering of the formula is one which implies greater deductions from the lives of each and all than the associated state necessarily entails; and this is obviously a perversion of its meaning.

If we bear in mind that though not the immediate end, the greatest sum of happiness is the remote end, we see clearly that the sphere within which each may pursue happiness has a limit, on the other side of which lie the similarly limited spheres of action of his neighbors; and that he may not intrude on his neighbor's spheres on condition that they may intrude on his. Instead of justifying aggression and counteraggression, the intention of the formula is to fix a bound which may not be exceeded on either side.

274. And here, on this misapprehension and this rectification, an instructive comment is yielded by the facts of social

progress. For they show that, in so far as justice is concerned, there has been an advance from the incorrect interpretation to the correct interpretation.

In early stages we see habitual aggression and counter-aggression: now between societies and now between individuals. Neighboring tribes fight about the limits to their territories, trespassing first on one side and then on the other; and further fights are entailed by the requirement that mortality suffered shall be followed by mortality inflicted. In such acts of revenge and re-revenge there is displayed a vague recognition of equality of claims. This tends towards recognition of definite limits, alike in respect of territory and in respect of bloodshed; so that in some cases a balance is maintained between the numbers of deaths on either side.

Along with this growing conception of intertribal justice goes a growing conception of justice among members of each tribe. At first it is the fear of retaliation which causes such respect for one another's persons and possessions as exists. The idea of justice is that of a balancing of injuries—"An eye for an eye and a tooth for a tooth." This remains the idea during early stages of civilization. After justice, as so conceived, ceases to be enforced by the aggrieved person himself, it is this which he asks to have enforced by the constituted authority. The cry to the ruler for justice is the cry for punishment—for the infliction of an injury at least as great as the injury suffered, or, otherwise, for a compensation equivalent to the loss. Thus the equality of claims is but tacitly asserted in the demand to have rectified, as far as may be, the breaches of equality.

How there tends gradually to emerge from this crude conception of justice the finished conception of justice, it seems scarcely needful to explain. The true idea is generated by experience of the evils which accompany the false idea. Naturally, the perception of the right restraints on conduct becomes clearer as respect for these restraints is forced on men, and so rendered more habitual and more general. Men's incursions into one another's spheres constitute a kind of oscillation, which, violent at the outset, becomes gradually less with the progress towards a relatively peaceful state of society. As the oscillations decrease there is an approach to equilibrium; and along with this approach to equilibrium comes approach to a definite theory of equilibrium.

Thus that primitive idea of justice in which aggression is to be balanced by counteraggression, fades from thought as fast as it disappears from practice; and there comes the idea of justice here formulated, in which are recognized such limitations of conduct as exclude aggressions altogether.

NOTE. For the views of Kant concerning the ultimate principle of right, see Appendix A.

CHAPTER 7

The Authority of This Formula

275. **B**efore going further we must contemplate this formula under all its aspects, for the purpose of seeing what may be said against it as well as what may be said in its favor.

By those who have been brought up in the reigning school of politics and morals, nothing less than scorn is shown for every doctrine which implies restraint on the doings of immediate expediency or what appears to be such. Along with avowed contempt for "abstract principles" and generalizations, there goes unlimited faith in a motley assemblage of nominees of caucuses, ruled by ignorant and fanatical wire pullers; and it is thought intolerable that its judgments should be in any way subordinated by deductions from ethical truths.

Strangely enough we find in the world of science, too, this approval of political empiricism and disbelief in any other guidance. Though it is a trait of the scientific mind to recognize causation as universal, and though this involves a tacit admission that causation holds throughout the actions of incorporated men, this admission remains a dead letter. Notwithstanding the obvious fact that if there is no causation in public affairs one course must be as good as another; and notwithstanding the obvious fact that to repudiate this implication is to say that some cause determines the goodness or badness of this or that policy; no effort is made to identify the causation. Contrariwise, there is ridicule of those who attempt to find a definite expression for the fundamental principle of harmonious social order. The differences among their views are emphasized, rather than the traits which their views have in common; just as, by adherents of the current creed, the differences among men of science are emphasized, instead of their essential agreements.

Manifestly, then, before proceeding we must deal with the more important objections urged against the formula reached in the last chapter.

276. Every kind of evolution is from the indefinite to the definite; and one of the implications is that a distinct conception of justice can have arisen but gradually. Already the advance towards a practical recognition of justice has been shown to imply a corresponding advance towards theoretical recognition of it. It will be desirable here to observe more closely this growth of the consciousness that the activities carried on for self-conservation by each, are to be restrained by the like activities of all.

And first let us note a fact which might have been fitly included at the close of the last chapter—the fact that where men are subject to the discipline of a peaceful social life only, uninterfered with by the discipline which intersocial antagonisms entail, they quickly develop this consciousness. Entirely pacific tribes, uncivilized in the common sense of the words as some of them are, show a perception of that which constitutes equity, far clearer than the perception displayed by civilized peoples, among whom the habits of industrial life are qualified more or less largely by the habits of militant life. The amiable and conscientious Lepcha, who, while he does not desire to be killed himself, refuses absolutely to assist in killing others; the Hos, full of social virtues, who may be driven almost to suicide by the suspicion that he has committed a theft; the lowly Wood-Veddah, who can scarcely conceive it possible that one man should willingly hurt another, or take that which does not belong to him; these and sundry others show that though there is not intelligence enough to frame a conception of the fundamental social law, there is yet a strong sentiment responding to this law, and an understanding of its special applications. Where the conditions are such as do not require that respect for the claims of fellow tribesmen shall go along with frequent tramplings on the claims of men outside the tribe, there grow up simultaneously in each individual a regard for his own claims and a regard for the claims of other individuals.

It is only where the ethics of amity are entangled with the ethics of enmity, that thoughts about conduct are confused by the necessities of compromise. The habit of aggression outside the society is at variance with the habit of nonaggression inside the society, and at variance with recognition of the law implied by nonaggression. A people which gives to its soldiers the euphemistic title "defenders of their country," and then exclusively uses them as invaders of other countries—a people which so far appreciates the value of life that within its bounds it forbids prizefights, but beyond its bounds frequently takes scores of lives to avenge one life—a people which at home cannot tolerate the thought that inferiority shall bear the self-inflicted evils of inferiority, but abroad has no compunction in using bullet and bayonet to whatever extent is needful for conquest of the uncivilized, arguing that the inferior should be replaced by the superior; such a people must think crookedly about the ultimate principles of right and wrong. Now enunciating the code appropriate to its internal policy and now the code appropriate to its external policy, it cannot entertain a consistent set of ethical ideas. All through the course of that conflict of races which, by peopling the earth with the strongest, has been a preliminary to high civilization, there have gone on these incongruous activities necessitating incongruous sets of beliefs, and making a congruous set of beliefs inadmissible.

Nevertheless, where the conditions have allowed, the conception of justice has slowly evolved to some extent, and found for itself approximately true expressions. In the Hebrew commandments we see interdicts which, while they do not overtly recognize the positive element in justice, affirm in detail its negative element—specify limits to actions, and, by prescribing these limits for all Hebrews, tacitly assert that life, property, good name, &c., must be respected in one as in another. In a form which makes no distinction between generosity and justice, the Christian maxim "Do unto others as ye would that others should do unto you" vaguely implies the equality of men's claims—implies it, indeed, in too sweeping a manner, since it recognizes no reason for inequality in the shares of good respectively appropriate to men: there is in it no direct recognition of any claim which each has to the results of his own activities, but only an implied recognition of such claims in the persons of others, and by implication a prescribing of limits. Taking no note of intermediate forms of the conception, we may instance among modern forms the one which it took in the mind of Kant. His rule, "Act only on that maxim whereby thou canst at the same time will that it should become a universal law," is, indeed, an allotropic form of the Christian rule. The suggestion that every other man must be imagined to act after a manner similar to the manner proposed, joined with the tacit implication that if suffering would be caused, the act should not be performed (Kant is classed as an antiutilitarian!), indirectly assumes that the welfares of other men are to be considered as severally of like values with the welfare of the actor—an assumption which, while it covers the requirements of justice, covers much more.

But now leaving these indications of the beliefs of those who have approached the question from the religious side and from the ethical side, let us consider the beliefs of those who have approached it from the legal side.

277. Of course, when jurists set forth first principles, or appeal to them, they have in mind the bases of justice, whether they use the word justice or not; since systems of

justice, considered in general or in detail, form the subject matters of their works. This premised, let us observe the doctrines from time to time enunciated.

Sir Henry Maine, speaking of certain dangers which threatened the development of Roman law, says:

> But at any rate they had adequate protection in their theory of Natural Law. For the Natural Law of the jurisconsults was distinctly conceived by them as a system which ought gradually to absorb civil laws, without superseding them so long as they remained unrepealed. . . . The value and serviceableness of the conception arose from its keeping before the mental vision a type of perfect law, and from its inspiring the hope of an indefinite approximation to it. [*Ancient Law*, pp. 76–77, 3d ed.]

In the spirit of these Roman lawyers, one of our early judges of high repute, Chief Justice Hobart, uttered the emphatic assertion—"Even an Act of Parliament made against natural equity, as to make a man Judge in his own case, is void in itself, for *jura naturæ sunt immutabilia*, and they are *leges legum*" (*Hobart's Reports*, London, 1641, p. 120). So said a great authority of later date. Dominated by a creed which taught that natural things are supernaturally ordained, Blackstone wrote:

> This law of nature being coeval with mankind, and dictated by God himself, is of course superior in obligation to any other. . . . no human laws are of any validity if contrary to this; and such of them as are valid derive all their force and all their authority, mediately or immediately, from this original. [*Chitty's Blackstone*, vol. I., pp. 37–38.]

Of like character is another verdict, given by one who treated of legislation from a philosophical point of view. Sir James Mackintosh defines a law of nature as being

> a supreme, invariable, and uncontrollable rule of conduct to all men . . . It is "the law of nature," because its general precepts are essentially adapted to promote the happiness of man . . . because it is discoverable by natural reason, and suitable to our natural constitution; and because its fitness and wisdom are founded on the general

nature of human beings, and not on any of those temporary and accidental situations in which they may be placed. [Mackintosh's *Miscellaneous Works,* vol. I., p. 346.]

Even the despotically minded Austin, idolized by the lawyers of our days as having elaborated a theory of unlimited legislative authority, is obliged to confess that the ultimate justification for the governmental absolutism he defends, is ethical. Behind the authority, monarchical, oligarchic, or parliamentary, which enacts laws represented as supreme, there is at length recognized an authority to which it is subordinate—an authority, therefore, which is not derived from human law, but is above human law—an authority which is by implication ascribed, if not to divine enactment, then to the nature of things.

Paying some respect to these *dicta* (to which I may add that of the German jurists with their *Naturrecht*) does not imply unreasoning credulity. We may reasonably suspect that, however much they may be in form open to criticism, they are true in essence.

278. "But these are *a priori* beliefs," will be the contemptuous comment of many. "They all exemplify that vicious mode of philosophizing which consists in evolving truths out of the depths of one's own consciousness," will be said by those who hold that general truths can be reached only by conscious induction. Curiously illustrating the law that all movement is rhythmical, the absolute faith of past times in *a priori* reasoning, has given place to absolute disbelief; and now nothing is to be accepted unless it is reached *a posteriori.* Any one who contemplates the average sweep of human progress, may feel tolerably certain that this violent reaction will be followed by a re-reaction; and he may infer that both of these antithetical modes of reasoning, while they have their abuses, have also their uses.

Whence come *a priori* beliefs—how happen they to arise? I

do not of course refer to beliefs peculiar to particular persons, which may be results of intellectual perversions. I refer to those which are general, if not universal—beliefs which all, or nearly all, do not profess to base on evidence, and yet which they hold to be certain. The origin of such beliefs is either natural or supernatural. If supernatural, then unless, by believers in a devil, they are regarded as diabolically insinuated into men to mislead them, they must be regarded as divinely implanted for purposes of guidance, and therefore to be trusted. If, not satisfied with an alleged supernatural derivation, we ask for a natural derivation, then our conclusion must be that these modes of thought are determined by converse with the relations of things. One who adheres to the current creed with its good and evil agents, is not without a feasible reason for denying the value of *a priori* beliefs; but one who accepts the doctrine of evolution is obliged, if he is consistent, to admit that *a priori* beliefs entertained by men at large, must have arisen, if not from the experiences of each individual, then from the experiences of the race. When, to take a geometrical illustration, it is affirmed that two straight lines cannot inclose a space; and when it is admitted, as it must be, that this truth cannot be established *a posteriori,* since not in one case, still less in many cases, can lines be pursued out into infinity for the purpose of observing what happens to the space between them; then the inevitable admission must be that men's experiences of straight lines (or rather, having regard to primitive times, let us say objects approximately straight) have been such as to make impossible the conception of space as inclosed by two straight lines—have been such as to make it imperative to think of the lines as bending before the space can be inclosed. Unquestionably, on the evolution hypothesis, this fixed intuition must have been established by that intercourse with things which, throughout an enormous past, has, directly or indirectly, determined the organization of the nervous system and certain resulting necessities of thought; and the *a priori* beliefs determined by these necessities differ from *a posteriori* beliefs simply in this, that they are products of the experiences of innumerable successive individuals instead of the experiences of a single individual.

If, then, from the evolution point of view, this is undoubtedly so with those simple cognitions which concern space, time, and number, must we not infer that it is so, in large measure, with those more complex cognitions which concern human relations? I say "in large measure"; partly because the experiences are in this case far more involved and superficially varied, and cannot have produced anything like such definite effects on the nervous organization; and partly because, instead of reaching back through an immeasurable series of ancestral beings, they reach back through a part of the human race only. For these experiences, hardly traceable during early stages, become marked and coherent only where amicable social cooperation forms a considerable factor in social life. Hence these cognitions must be comparatively indefinite.

The qualification to be therefore made is that these ethical intuitions, far more than the mathematical intuitions, have to be subjected to methodic criticism. Even the judgments of immediate perception respecting straight lines, curves, angles, and so forth, have to be tested in ways devised by conscious reason: one line is perceived to be perpendicular to another with approximate truth, but complete perpendicularity can be ascertained only by the aid of a geometrical theorem. Evidently, then, the relatively vague internal perceptions which men have of right human relations, are not to be accepted without deliberate comparisons, rigorous cross-examinations, and careful testings of all kinds: a conclusion made obvious by the numerous minor disagreements which accompany the major agreement.

Thus even had the foregoing *dicta,* and along with them the law of equal freedom as recently formulated, no other than *a priori* derivations (and this is far from being the fact) it would still be rational to regard them as adumbrations of a truth, if not literally true.

279. But now mark that those who, in this case, urge against a system of thought the reproach that it sets out with an *a priori* intuition, may have the reproach hurled back upon them with more than equal force.

Alike in philosophy, in politics, and in science, we may see that the inductive school has been carried by its violent reaction against the deductive school to the extreme of assuming that conscious induction suffices for all purposes, and that there is no need to take anything for granted. Though giving proof of an alleged truth consists in showing that it is included in some wider established truth, and though, if this wider truth be questioned, the process is repeated by demonstrating that a still wider truth includes it; yet it is tacitly assumed that this process may go on forever without reaching a widest truth, which cannot be included in any other, and therefore cannot be proved. And the result of making this unthinking assumption is the building up of theories which, if they have not *a priori* beliefs as their bases, have no bases at all. This we shall find to be the case with the utilitarian systems of ethics and politics.*

For what is the ultimate meaning of expediency? When it is proposed to guide ourselves empirically, towards what are we to guide ourselves? If our course must always be determined by the merits of the case, by what are the merits to be judged? "By conduciveness to the welfare of society, or the good of the community," will be the answer. It will not be replied that the merit to be estimated means increase of misery; it will not be replied that it means increase of a state of indifference, sensa-

---

* There are some who not only decline to admit any truths as necessary, but deny necessity itself; apparently without consciousness of the fact that since, in reasoning, every step from premises to conclusion has no other warrant than perception of the necessity of dependence, to deny necessity is to deny the validity of every argument, including that by which it is proposed to prove the absence of necessity! I recently read a comment on the strange resurrection of a doctrine said to have been long ago killed. Doubtless remarkable enough, if true. I know only one thing more remarkable, and that is the way in which a system of thought may be seen going about in high spirits after having committed suicide!

tional and emotional; and it must therefore be replied that it means increase of happiness. By implication, if not avowedly, greatest happiness is the thing to be achieved by public action, or private action, or both. But now whence comes this postulate? Is it an inductive truth? Then where and by whom has the induction been drawn? Is it a truth of experience derived from careful observations? Then what are the observations, and when was there generalized that vast mass of them on which all politics and morals should be built? Not only are there no such experiences, no such observations, no such induction, but it is impossible that any should be assigned. Even were the intuition universal, which it is not (for it has been denied by ascetics in all ages and places, and is demurred to by an existing school of moralists), it would still have no better warrant than that of being an immediate *dictum* of consciousness.

More than this is true. There is involved a further belief no less *a priori*. Already I have referred to Bentham's rule, "Everybody to count for one, nobody for more than one," joined with Mr. Mill's comment that the greatest-happiness principle is meaningless unless "one person's happiness . . . is counted for exactly as much as another's." Hence the Benthamite theory of morals and politics posits this as a fundamental, self-evident truth. And this tacit assumption that one man's claim to happiness is as good as another's has been recently put into more concrete shape by Mr. Bellamy, who says: "The world, and everything that is in it, will ere long be recognized as the common property of all, and undertaken and administered for the equal benefit of all." That is to say, whether formulated by Bentham himself, or by Mill as his expositor, or by a communistic disciple, the assumption is that all men have equal rights to happiness. For this assumption no warrant is given, or can be given, other than alleged intuitive perception. It is an *a priori* cognition.

"But it is not a cognition properly so-called," will probably be asserted by those who wish to repudiate the communistic implication, at the same time that they wish to repudiate the *a priori* reasoning. "It is merely the product of perverted fancy. Happiness itself cannot be divided out either equally or unequally, and the greatest happiness is not to be obtained by equal division of the means to happiness, or the benefits, as they are above called. It is to be obtained rather by giving a larger share of means to those who are most capable of happiness." Raising no question about the practicability of such an adjustment, let us simply ask the warrant for this assertion. Is it an inductive warrant? Has anyone made a number of comparisons between societies in which the one method of apportioning happiness has been pursued, and societies in which the other has been pursued? Hardly so, considering that neither the one method nor the other has been pursued in any society. This alternative assumption has no more facts to stand upon than the assumption repudiated. If it does not claim for itself an *a priori* warrant, then it has no warrant.

See then the predicament. While reprobating assumptions said to be warranted only by direct intuition, this empirical system makes more such assumptions than the system to which it is opposed! One of them is implied in the assertion that happiness should be the end sought, and another of them is implied in either of the two assertions that men have equal rights to happiness or that they have not equal rights to happiness. Mark, too, that no one of these intuitions is justified by so wide a consensus as the intuition rejected as untrustworthy. Sir Henry Maine remarks that

> The happiness of mankind is, no doubt, sometimes assigned, both in the popular and in the legal literature of the Romans, as the proper object of remedial legislation, but it is very remarkable how few and faint are the testimonies to this principle compared with the tributes which are constantly offered to the overshadowing claims of the Law of Nature. [*Ancient Law,* p. 79, 3d ed.]

And it is scarcely needful to say that since Roman times, there has continued to be this contrast between the narrow recognition of happiness as an end, and the wide recognition of natural equity as an end.

280. But now let it be remembered that this principle of natural equity, expressed in the last chapter as the freedom of each limited only by the like freedom of all, is not an exclusively *a priori* belief. Though, under one aspect, it is an immediate dictum of the human consciousness after it has been subject to the discipline of prolonged social life, it is, under another aspect, a belief deducible from the conditions to be fulfilled, firstly for the maintenance of life at large, and secondly for the maintenance of social life.

Examination of the facts has shown it to be a fundamental law, by conformity to which life has evolved from its lowest up to its highest forms, that each adult individual shall take the consequences of its own nature and actions: survival of the fittest being the result. And the necessary implication is an assertion of that full liberty to act which forms the positive element in the formula of justice; since, without full liberty to act, the relation between conduct and consequence cannot be maintained. Various examples have made clear the conclusion, manifest in theory, that among gregarious creatures this freedom of each to act, has to be restricted; since if it is unrestricted there must arise such clashing of actions as prevents the gregariousness. And the fact that, relatively unintelligent though they are, inferior gregarious creatures inflict penalties for breaches of the needful restrictions, shows how regard for them has come to be unconsciously established as a condition to persistent social life.

These two laws, holding, the one of all creatures and the other of social creatures, and the display of which is clearer in proportion as the evolution is higher, find their last and fullest sphere of manifestation in human societies. We have recently seen that along with the growth of peaceful cooperation there has been an increasing conformity to this compound law under both its positive and negative aspects; and we have also seen that there has gone on simultaneously an increase of emotional regard for it and intellectual apprehension of it.

So that we have not only the reasons above given for concluding that this *a priori* belief has its origin in the experiences of the race, but we are enabled to affiliate it on the experiences of living creatures at large, and to perceive that it is but a conscious response to certain necessary relations in the order of nature.

No higher warrant can be imagined; and now, accepting the law of equal freedom as an ultimate ethical principle, having an authority transcending every other, we may proceed with our inquiry.

CHAPTER 8

Its Corollaries

281. Men's activities are many in their kinds and the consequent social relations are complex. Hence, that the general formula of justice may serve for guidance, deductions must be drawn severally applicable to special classes of cases. The statement that the liberty of each is bounded only by the like liberties of all, remains a dead letter until it is shown what are the restraints which arise under the various sets of circumstances he is exposed to.

Whoever admits that each man must have a certain restricted freedom, asserts that it is *right* he should have this restricted freedom. If it be shown to follow, now in this case and now in that, that he is free to act up to a certain limit but not beyond it, then the implied admission is that it is *right* he should have the particular freedom so defined. And hence the several particular freedoms deducible may fitly be called, as they commonly are called, his *rights*.

282. Words are sometimes profoundly discredited by misuse. The true ideas they connote become so intimately associated with false ideas, that they in large measure lose their characters. This is conspicuously the case with the word "rights."

In past times rivers of blood were shed in maintaining the "right" of this or that person to a throne. In the days of the old Poor Law the claims of the pauper were habitually urged on the ground that he had a "right" to a maintenance out of the soil. Not many years since we were made familiar with the idea, then current among French workingmen, that they had a "right" to labor; that is, a right to have labor provided for them. At the present time communists use the word "rights" in ways which entirely invert the meaning given to it by past usages. And so lax is the application of the word that those who pander to the public appetite for gossip about notable personages, defend themselves by saying that "the public has a 'right' to know."

The consequence has been that, in many of the cultivated, there has been produced a confirmed, and indeed contemptuous, denial of rights. There are no such things, say they, except such as are conferred by law. Following Bentham, they affirm that the state is the originator of rights, and that apart from it there are no rights.

But if lack of discrimination is shown in such misuse of words as includes under them more than should be included, lack of discrimination is also shown in not perceiving those true meanings which are disguised by the false meanings.

283. As is implied above, rights, truly so-called, are corollaries from the law of equal freedom, and what are falsely called rights are not deducible from it.

In treating of these corollaries, as we now proceed to do, we shall find that, in the first place, they one and all coincide with ordinary ethical conceptions, and that, in the second place, they one and all correspond with legal enactments. Further, it will become apparent that so far is it from being true that the warrant for what are properly called rights is derived from law, it is, conversely, true that law derives its warrant from them.

CHAPTER 9

The Right to Physical Integrity

284. For using a title that is so apparently pedantic, my defense must be that no other adequately expresses everything to be included in the chapter. The physical integrity which has to be claimed for each, may at the one extreme be destroyed by violence, and at the other extreme interfered with by the nausea which a neighboring nuisance causes.

It is a self-evident corollary from the law of equal freedom that, leaving other restraints out of consideration, each man's actions must be so restrained as not directly to inflict bodily injury, great or small, on any other. In the first place, actions carried beyond this limit imply the exercise on one side of greater freedom than is exercised on the other, unless it be by retaliation; and we have seen that, as rightly understood, the law does not countenance aggression and counteraggression. In the second place, considered as the statement of a condition by conforming to which the greatest sum of happiness is to be obtained, the law forbids any act which inflicts physical pain or derangement.

285. Only for form's sake is it needful to specify under this general head, the right to life and the consequent interdict on murder. This, which in civilized communities is regarded as

the blackest of crimes, may be considered as unconsciously, if not consciously, thus regarded because it is the greatest possible breach of the law of equal freedom; for by murder another's power to act is not merely interfered with but destroyed. While, however, it is not needful to insist on this first deduction from the law of equal freedom, that life is sacred, it will be instructive to observe the successive steps towards recognition of its sacredness.

Noting as an extreme case that of the Fijians, among whom murder is, or was, thought honorable, we may pass to the many cases furnished by savage tribes who kill their old, diseased, and useless members. Various of the early European peoples, too, did the like. Grimm tells us that among the Wends "the children killed their aged parents, blood and other relatives, also those who no longer were fit for war or work, and then cooked and ate them, or buried them alive." "The Herulians, also, killed their aged and sick. . . . Later traces of the custom of killing the aged and sick are found in North Germany."

Apart from this deliberate destruction of incapable members of the tribe, which very generally had the excuse that it was needful for preservation of the capable, there has habitually existed, in primitive social groups, no public recognition of murder as a crime. Of the Homeric Greeks Grote writes that the murderer had to dread only "the personal vengeance of the kinsmen and friends." These might compound for the offense by a stipulated payment. All that the chiefs did in such cases was to see that the bargains were fulfilled. In later times throughout Europe, the same ideas, sentiments, and practices prevailed. It was not so much the loss of his life by the man slain which constituted the evil, as the injury done to his family or clan: this was the wrong which had to be avenged or compounded for. Hence it was a matter of comparative indifference whether the actual murderer was killed in return, or whether some guiltless member of the murderer's kindred. And this, too, was probably a part cause for the gradation in the compensations to be made for murders according to the rank of the murdered—compensations which, after being in earlier stages matters of private agreement, came presently to be established by law. And to how small an extent the conception of the sacredness of life had grown up, is seen in the fact that the slave had no *wergeld* or *bot:* his lord could slay him if he pleased, and if slain by some one else his value as a chattel only could be demanded.

An unobtrusive step towards recognition of murder as something more than a private offense, took place when part of the money paid in compensation went to the king: the idea being, in considerable measure, still the same; since destruction of a subject was destruction of a portion of the king's power over subjects, and did, in effect, diminish the strength of his society for fighting purposes. But the continuance of the different fines adjusted to different ranks, shows how little the intrinsic criminality of murder was recognized; and this is further shown by the distinction which benefit of clergy made. Up to the time of the Plantagenets a murderer "who knew how to read escaped from nearly all punishment."

Merely noting that a great step was made under the Commonwealth, when "benefit of clergy was to be abolished absolutely"; when, "by a separate Act, wager of battle was abolished"; and when "the same Act punished dueling with extraordinary severity" (legislation which recognized the intrinsic guilt of murder) we may come at once to modern times. No class distinction can now be pleaded in mitigation, and no condonation under any form is possible.

The course of this progress presents three significant facts. Maintenance of life is in the earliest stages an entirely private affair, as among brutes; and to the taking of it there is attached scarcely more idea of wrong than among brutes. With growing social aggregation and organization, the taking of life comes to be more and more regarded as a wrong done, first to the family or the clan, and then to the society; and it is punished rather as a sin against society than as a sin against the individual. But eventually, while there is retained the conception of its criminality as a breach of the law needful for social order, there becomes predominant the conception of its criminality as an immeasurable and irremediable wrong done to the murdered man. This consciousness of the intrinsic guilt of the act, implies a consciousness of the intrinsic claim of the individual to life: the right to life has acquired the leading place in thought.

286. The connection between such degree of bodily injury as causes death, and such degree of bodily injury as causes more or less incapacity for carrying on life, has all along been too obvious to escape recognition. Hence, with that tacit assertion of the right to physical integrity which is implied by the punishment of murder, there has gone such further tacit assertion of it as is implied by punishments for inflicting mutilations, wounds, &c. Naturally, too, there has been a certain parallelism between the successive stages in the two cases; beginning with that between life for life and "an eye for an eye."

When, after the early stage in which retaliation was entirely a private affair, there was reached the stage in which it came to be an affair concerning the family or clan, we see that as the clan avenged itself by taking from an offending clan a life to balance the life it had lost, so by insisting on a substituted, if not an actual, equivalent, it sought to avenge an injury which was not fatal. This is shown by the fact that after the system of money damages had grown up, the price, not only for a life but for a limb, was to be paid by the family or house of the wrongdoer to the family or house of the wronged. A further fact implies this same conception. With the Germanic tribes and the early English, along with compensations for homicide, varying according to rank, there went "as large a scheme of compensations for minor injuries," also according to rank. The implication in both cases is that the damage to the family or clan was dominant in thought, rather than the damage to the individual. The like held in ancient Russia.

As fast as the social life of smaller groups or clans, merged into the social life of larger groups or nations, the idea of injury to the nation began to replace that of injury to the clan; and at first part, and eventually the whole, of the fine or amercement payable by one who had committed an assault, went to the state; and this usage still survives. Though in cases of personal violence the current consciousness is now mainly occupied by sympathy with the injured man, and reprobation of the offender for having inflicted pain and accompanying mischief, yet the state appropriates the condonation money, and leaves the sufferer to bear the evil as best he may.

But in modern days we see growth of a higher conception, in the awarding of compensations for injuries which have resulted from negligence. The claim of the citizen against a fellow citizen, not only for bodily damage voluntarily inflicted on him but for bodily damage caused by careless actions or inactions, dates back some centuries at least. Much more extensive applications of the principle have of late years been made; such as those which render a railway company liable for injuries caused by imperfection of its appliances or inattention of its officials, and private employers for those entailed on workmen by defective apparatus, by lack of safeguards, or by operations involving risk. These developments of law imply higher appreciations of the claims of the individual to physical integrity; and the fact that the person or company responsible for the mischief done, is called upon to pay damages to the sufferer and not to the state, is one of the proofs that the claim of the individual to physical integrity, now occupies in the general consciousness a greater space than the thought of social detriment done by disregard of such claim.

Nor must we omit to note, in proof of the same thing, that what we may call the sacredness of the person, has in our days been further insisted on by laws which regard as assaults, not only such acts of violence as cause slight injuries, but such as are constituted by intentional pushes or other forcible interferences with another's body, or even by threatening uses of the hands without actual contact; and laws which also make a kiss, taken without consent, a punishable offense.

287. One more trespass against physical integrity, not in early times thought of as such, but held to be such in our times, is that which consists in the communication of disease.

This is a kind of trespass which, though grave, and though partly recognized in law, occupies neither in law nor in the general conscience so distinct a place as it should do: probably because of the indefiniteness and uncertainty of the mischievous results. Here is a father who fetches home his boy suffering from an epidemic disease, regardless of the fact that the railway carriage in which they travel may not improbably infect others; and here is a mother who asks the doctor whether her children have sufficiently recovered from scarlet fever to go to school, and proposes to send them notwithstanding the intimation that they may very possibly convey the disease to their school fellows. Such acts are indeed, punishable; but they so commonly pass without detection, and the evils likely to be inflicted are so faintly conceived, that they are scarcely thought of as offenses; though they really ought to be regarded as something like crimes—if not actual crimes, then potential crimes.

For let us remember that there is now recognized by law and by public conscience, the truth that not only actual physical mischiefs to others but also potential physical mischiefs to others, are flagitious. We have reached a stage in which the body of each person is so far regarded as a territory inviolable by any other person, that we rank as offenses all acts which are likely to bring about violation of it.

288. Thus it is undeniable that what we see to be the primary corollary from the formula of justice, has been, in the course of social evolution and the accompanying evolution of man's mental nature, gradually establishing itself. Prolonged converse with the conditions under which alone social life can

be harmoniously carried on, has slowly molded sentiments, ideas, and laws, into conformity with this primary ethical truth deducible from those conditions.*

That which it here concerns us specially to note, is that murder, manslaughter, mutilation, assault, and all trespasses against physical integrity down to the most trivial, have not become transgressions in virtue of laws forbidding them, nor in virtue of interdicts having a supposed supernatural origin; but they have become transgressions as being breaches of certain naturally originated restraints.

It remains only to say that while, in a system of absolute ethics, the corollary here drawn from the formula of justice is unqualified, in a system of relative ethics it has to be qualified by the necessities of social self-preservation. Already we have seen that the primary law that each individual shall receive and suffer the benefits and evils of his own nature, following from conduct carried on with due regard to socially imposed limits, must, where the group is endangered by external enemies, be modified by the secondary law, which requires that there shall be such sacrifice of individuals as is required to preserve, for the aggregate of individuals, the ability thus to act and to receive the results of actions. Hence, for purposes of defensive war, there is justified such contingent loss of physical integrity as effectual defense of the society requires: supposing, always, that effectual defense is possible. For it would

---

* A barrister who has devoted much attention to the evolution of law, has obliged me by checking the statements which preceding and succeeding chapters contain respecting laws, past and present. To the above paragraph he has appended the following note:

> The late Clitheroe abduction case which establishes that a man may not forcibly detain his own wife, is an interesting example of this doctrine. In this case the right of married women to physical liberty has only just been established by a Court of Appeal; and that against the opinion of two very able judges of 1st instance, who thought that the old law was otherwise.
>
> The punishment by justices of School-board teachers, for the use of the rod on the boys, is another example of this growing feeling, which molds the law while assuming only to administer it.

seem to be an implication that where the invading force is overwhelming, such sacrifice of individuals is not justified.

We see here, indeed, as we shall see throughout all subsequent chapters, that the requirements of absolute ethics can be wholly conformed to only in a state of permanent peace; and that so long as the world continues to be occupied by peoples given to political burglary, the requirements of relative ethics only, can be fulfilled.

CHAPTER 10

The Rights to Free Motion and Locomotion

289.   As direct deductions from the formula of justice, the right of each man to the use of unshackled limbs, and the right to move from place to place without hindrance, are almost too obvious to need specifying. Indeed these rights, more perhaps than any others, are immediately recognized in thought as corollaries. Clearly, one who binds another's limbs, chains him to a post, or confines him in a dungeon, has used greater liberty of action than his captive; and no less clear is it that if, by threatened punishment or otherwise, he debars him from changing his locality, he commits a kindred breach of the law of equal freedom.

Further, it is manifest that if, in either of these ways, a man's liberty of action is destroyed or diminished, not by some one other man but by a number of other men acting jointly—if each member of a lower class thus has his power of motion and locomotion partially cut off by the regulations which a higher class has established, each member of that higher class has transgressed the ultimate principle of equity in like manner if in a smaller degree.

290. We have already seen that the instinct prompting flight, as well as the desire to escape when captured, shows us

in subhuman beings, as well as in human beings, the presence of that impulse which finally emerges as a conscious claim to free motion and locomotion. But while this positive element in the sentiment corresponding to the right, deep-rooted as it is, early manifests itself, the negative element in it, corresponding to the imposed limits, has to await the discipline of sociality before it can reach any considerable development.

We have instances showing that where governmental control does not exist, or is very feeble, the tacit claim to unhindered movement is strongly pronounced; whether the nature be of a savage kind or of a gentle kind. Of the one class may be named the Abors, who are so self-asserting that they cannot live together, and the Nagas to whom the notion of restraint is so foreign that they ridicule the idea of a ruler. Of the other class I may instance the before-named Lepchas, who, mild as they are, fly to the woods and live on roots rather than submit to coercion; and the Jakuns, who are greatly valued as servants because of their virtues, but who disappear at once if authority is injudiciously exercised over them. Having in common a strong sense of personal liberty, these types of men differ in the respect that while, in the warlike type, this sense is egoistic only, it is, in the peaceful type, altruistic also—is joined with respect for the personal liberties of others.

Out of primitive unorganized groups, or groups of which the organization is very slight, the progress to large and organized groups is effected by war. While this implies little regard for life, it also implies little regard for liberty; and hence, in the course of the process by which nations are formed, recognition of the claim to liberty, as well as of that to life, is subordinated: the sentiment is continually repressed and the idea is rendered vague. Only after social consolidation has made great progress, and social organization has become in large measure industrial—only when militancy has ceased to be constant and the militant type of structure has relaxed, do the sentiment and the idea become more marked.

Here we have to glance at some of the steps through which

the claim to freedom of motion and locomotion is gradually established, ethically and legally.

291. It has been remarked with truth that the rise of slavery was practically a limitation of cannibalism, and in so far a progress. When the prisoner of war was allowed to live and work instead of being cooked and eaten, the fundamental principle of equity was no longer absolutely negatived in his person; for the continuance of his life, even under the imposed conditions, made possible some maintenance of the relation between conduct and consequence. Where the enslaved prisoners and their descendants, fed and sheltered to the extent required for making use of them as working cattle, are also liable at any time to be made into food, as until lately among the Fijians, this mitigation of cannibalism is relatively small; but where, as among many of the uncivilized, the slave is treated in large measure as a member of the family, the restraints on his freedom are practically not much greater than those to which the children are subject.

To specify the different forms and qualifications of bondage which have existed among various peoples at different times and under changing social conditions, would be needless for our purpose here, even were it practicable. Such facts only must be named as indicate how the conception of individual liberty grew up, alike in law and in ethics. We may note that among the Hebrews, while persons of foreign blood might be bought and, with their children, inherited as possessions, those of Hebrew blood who sold themselves, either to men of their own race or to strangers sojourning among them, were subject to a slavery qualified alike in respect of length and rigor: the reason given being that, as servants of God, they could not be permanently alienated. But there was neither recognition of any wrong inflicted by enslavement, nor of any correlative right to freedom. This lack of the sentiments and ideas which, in modern times, have become so pronounced, continued to the time when Christianity arose, and was not

changed by Christianity. Neither Christ nor his apostles denounced slavery; and when, in reference to freedom, there
was given the advice to "use it rather" than slavery, there was
manifestly implied no thought of any inherent claim of each
individual to unhindered exercise of free motion and locomotion. So was it among the Greeks; as, indeed, it has been
among most peoples during early stages. In Homeric times,
captives taken in war were enslaved and might be sold or
ransomed; and throughout Greek civilization, accompanying
warfare that was practically chronic, slavery was assumed to
be a normal part of the social order. Lapse into bondage by
capture, debt, or otherwise, was regarded as a misfortune;
and no reprobation attached to the slave-owner. That is to say,
the conception of freedom as an inalienable right of each man,
had little or no place in either ethics or law. Inevitably, indeed,
it was suppressed in relation to slaves, literally so-called,
when even those who were nominally free were in reality
slaves of the state—when each citizen belonged not to himself
but to his city. And it is noteworthy that in the most warlike
Greek state, Sparta, not only was the condition of the helot
more abject than elsewhere, but the Spartan master himself
was deprived in a greater degree than elsewhere of the power
to order his own movements as he pleased.

Indeed we may recognize, generally, the fact that in states
which have grown considerably in size and structure, it has
naturally happened that since they have thus grown by external aggression and conquest, implying, as it always does,
internal coercion, individuality has been so greatly repressed
as to leave little trace in law and usage.

292. To illustrate the growth in morals and legislation of
that conception of human freedom which has now become
established among the leading civilized races, it will suffice if
we glance at some of the chief steps traceable in our own
history.

Militant as were the successive swarms of invaders who,
now subjugating and now expelling the previous possessors

of the soil, peopled the country in old English days, it of course happened that slaves existed among them—a class of the unfree, originally captives, the size of which was from time to time augmented by the addition of debtors and criminals. Along with the growth of population and accompanying advance of political organization, those who, under the original Mark system, had formed a class of free men, gradually lost much of their liberty: occasionally by conflicts within groups, in the course of which some members gained predominance, but mostly in the course of external conflicts, leading to subjugations and establishments of lordships. Peasants became subject to thegns and thegns to higher nobles; so that "by Alfred's day it was assumed that no man could exist without a lord": implying deprivation of freedom not only in members of the lowest rank (the slaves who were bought and sold) but in members of all higher ranks. Amid the changes which followed the Conquest, this limitation of liberty implied by sworn fealty continued; or rather, indeed, was increased, save in the partial abolition of trade in slaves. With the growth of towns during the 11th century, the accompanying development of industrial institutions, the implied replacing of relations of status by relations of contract, and the development of a "new moral sense of man's right to equal justice," came a "transition from pure serfage to an imperfect freedom." A century later the Great Charter put restraints on arbitrary rule, and the consequent losses of freedom by citizens. The growing influence of the trading classes was shown by the concession of liberty of journeying to foreign merchants. And then when, after another hundred years, the attachment of the serf to the soil, gradually weakened, had been broken, the fully free laborer acquired the right of unhindered locomotion. Though he partially lost this right when the Black Death caused so large a decrease of population, and consequent great rise in wages, that there was prompted a statute fixing the price of labor, and tying the laborer to his parish; yet these restraints, by the violent resistance they caused, led to a violent assertion of equality, not only in respect to right of locomotion but in respect to other things. But how little the claim to freedom was then recognized by the ruling classes, was shown when, after the subjugation of the revolting peasants, the king suggested enfranchisement; and when the landowners, asserting that their serfs were their goods, said that consent to emancipation "we have never given and never will give, were we all to die in one day." As increase of industrial activity and organization had produced increase of liberty, so, conversely, the twenty years of militant activity known as the Wars of the Roses, destroyed much of the liberty which had been obtained: not, however, the detachment of the peasant from the soil, and consequent ability to wander about, which, in the disturbed social state left by the collapse of feudalism, entailed an industrial disorganization that was remedied by again putting the laboring class under partial coercion, and partially attaching them to their localities, without otherwise restraining their movements. The freedom thus obtained had, however, still to be safeguarded; and the provisions against arbitrary imprisonment, dating from the Great Charter but often broken through, were strengthened, towards the end of the 17th century, by the Habeas Corpus Act. Save slight interferences caused by temporary panics, personal liberty in England thereafter continued intact; while such minor restraints on freedom of movement as were involved in the laws forbidding artisans to travel in search of work, were formally abolished in 1824.

And now let us not omit to note that, along with the slow legal establishment of personal liberty there has gone a growth of the responsive sentiment; and that with the egoistic assertion of liberty has been eventually joined the altruistic assertion of it. Those changes which, in the course of many centuries, have advanced social arrangements from a condition of complete slavery of the lowest, and qualified slavery of those above them, to a state of absolute freedom for all, have, towards their close, produced both sentiment and law asserting this freedom, not in English citizens only but in aliens under English rule—beginning with the emancipation of slaves who set foot on English soil, and ending with the emancipation of all who inhabited English colonies: since which time abolition of slavery elsewhere has been a constant aim.

293. Unless by those who think that civilization is a backward movement, it must, then, be admitted that induction justifies this deduction from the fundamental principle of equity. Those who think that ancient societies were of higher types than our own, and human welfare better achieved by them—those who think that feudal organization with its grades of vassalage superposed on villenage, produced a greater total of happiness than we experience now—those who, with Mr. Carlyle, yearn for a time like that of Abbot Sampson, and applaud the obedience of the Russians to their Czar; may consistently deny that growth of the sentiment of liberty, and establishment of individual freedom by law, afford any support for the abstract inference drawn in this chapter. But those who think that our days are better than those in which nobles lived in castles and wore shirts of mail—those who think that *oubliettes* and torture chambers were accompaniments of a social state less desirable than that in which princes as well as paupers are subject to the administration of justice—those who think that the regime which brought about peasant revolts was inferior to that which is characterized by multitudinous societies for furthering popular welfare, must admit that the generalization drawn from human experiences at large, is at one with the corollary above drawn from the formula of justice.

But this *dictum* of absolute ethics has to be qualified by the requirements of relative ethics. From the principle laid down at the outset, that the preservation of the species, or that variety of it constituting a society, is an end which must take precedence of the preservation of the individual, it follows that the right to individual liberty, like the right to individual life, must be asserted subject to qualifications, entailed by the measures needful for national safety. Such trespass on liberty as is required to preserve liberty, has a quasi-ethical warrant. Subject only to the condition that all capable members of the community shall be equally liable to it, that restraint on the rights of free motion and locomotion necessitated by military organization and discipline, is legitimate; provided always that the end in view is defensive war and not offensive war.

CHAPTER 11

The Rights to the Uses of Natural Media

294.   A man may be entirely uninjured in body by the actions of fellow men, and he may be entirely unimpeded in his movements by them, and he may yet be
prevented from carrying on the activities needful for maintenance of life, by traversing his relations to the physical environment on which his life depends. It is, indeed, alleged that
certain of these natural agencies cannot be removed from the
state of common possession. Thus we read:

> Some things are by nature itself incapable of appropriation, so that
> they cannot be brought under the power of anyone. These got the
> name of *res communes* by the Roman law; and were defined, things
> the property of which belongs to no person, but the use to all. Thus,
> the light, the air, running water, &c. are so adapted to the common use
> of mankind, that no individual can acquire a property in them, or
> deprive others of their use. [*An Institute of the Law of Scotland* by John
> Erskine (ed. Macallan), i, 196.]

But though light and air cannot be monopolized, the distribution of them may be interfered with by one man to the partial
deprivation of another man—may be so interfered with as to
inflict serious injury upon him.

No interference of this kind is possible without a breach of
the law of equal freedom. The habitual interception of light by

one person in such way that another person is habitually deprived of an equal share, implies disregard of the principle that the liberty of each is limited by the like liberties of all; and the like is true if free access to air is prevented.

Under the same general head there must, however, by an unusual extension of meaning, be here included something which admits of appropriation—the surface of the earth. This, as forming part of the physical environment, seems necessarily to be included among the media of which the use may be claimed under the law of equal freedom. The earth's surface cannot be denied to any one absolutely, without rendering life-sustaining activities impracticable. In the absence of standing-ground he can do nothing; and hence it appears to be a corollary from the law of equal freedom, interpreted with strictness, that the earth's surface may not be appropriated absolutely by individuals, but may be occupied by them only in such manner as recognizes ultimate ownership by other men; that is—by society at large.

Concerning the ethical and legal recognitions of these claims to the uses of media, not very much has to be said: only the last demands much attention. We will look at each of them in succession.

295. In the earliest stages, while yet urban life had not commenced, no serious obstruction of one man's light by another man could well take place. In encampments of savages and in the villages of agricultural tribes, no one was led, in pursuit of his ends, to overshadow the habitation of his neighbor. Indeed, the structures and relative positions of habitations made such aggressions almost impracticable.

In later times, when towns had grown up, it was unlikely that much respect would forthwith be paid by men to the claims of their neighbors in respect of light. During stages of social evolution in which the rights to life and liberty were little regarded, such comparatively trivial trespasses as were committed by those who built houses close in front of others' houses, were not likely to attract much notice, considered either as moral transgressions or legal wrongs. The narrow, dark streets of ancient Continental cities, in common with the courts and alleys characterizing the older part of our own towns, imply that in the days when they were built the shutting out by one man of another man's share of sun and sky, was not thought an offense. And, indeed, it may reasonably be held that recognition of such an offense was in those days impracticable; since, in walled towns, the crowding of houses became a necessity.

In modern times, however, there has arisen the perception that the natural distribution of light may not be interfered with. Though the law which forbids the building of walls, houses, or other edifices of certain heights, within prescribed distances from existing houses, does not absolutely negative the intercepting of light; yet it negatives the intercepting of it to serious degrees, and seeks to compromise the claims of adjacent owners as fairly as seems practicable.

That is to say, this corollary from the law of equal freedom, if it has not come to be overtly asserted, has come to be tacitly recognized.

296. To some extent interference with the supply of light involves interference with the supply of air; and, by interdicting the one, some interdict is, by implication, placed on the other. But the claim to use of the air, though it has been recognized by English law in the case of windmills, is less definitely established: probably because only small evils have been caused by obstructions.

There has, however, risen into definite recognition the claim to unpolluted air. Though acts of one man which may diminish the supply of air to another man, have not come to be distinctly classed as wrong; yet acts which vitiate the quality of his air are in modern times regarded as offenses— offenses for which there are in some cases moral reprobations only, and in other cases legal penalties. In some measure all are severally obliged, by their own respiration, to vitiate the air respired by others, where they are in proximity. It needs but to walk a little distance behind one who is smoking, to perceive how widely diffused are the exhalations from each person's lungs; and to what an extent, therefore, those who are adjacent, especially indoors, are compelled to breathe the air that has already been taken in and sent out time after time. But since this vitiation of air is mutual, it cannot constitute aggression. Aggression occurs only when vitiation by one, or some, has to be borne by others who do not take like shares in the vitiation; as often happens in railway carriages, where men who think themselves gentlemen smoke in other places than those provided for smokers: perhaps getting from fellow passengers a nominal, though not a real, consent, and careless of the permanent nuisance entailed on those who afterward travel in compartments reeking with stale tobacco smoke. Beyond the recognition of this by right-thinking persons as morally improper, it is forbidden as improper by railway regulations; and, in virtue of bylaws, may bring punishment by fine.

Passing from instances of this kind to instances of a graver kind, we have to note the interdicts against various nuisances—stenches resulting from certain businesses carried on near at hand, injurious fumes such as those from chemical works, and smoke proceeding from large chimneys. Legislation which forbids the acts causing such nuisances, implies the right of each citizen to unpolluted air.

Under this same head we may conveniently include another kind of trespass to which the surrounding medium is instrumental. I refer to the production of sounds of a disturbing kind. There are small and large trespasses of this class. For one who, at a table d'hote, speaks so loudly as to interfere with the conversation of others, and for those who, during the performance at a theater or concert, persist in distracting the attention of auditors around by talking, there is reprobation, if nothing more: their acts are condemned as contrary to good manners, that is, good morals, for the one is a part of the other. And then when inflictions of this kind are public, or of which all live, is antagonized by ideas and arrangements descending to us from the past. These ideas and arrangements arose when considerations of equity did not affect land tenure any more than they affected the tenure of men as slaves or serfs; and they now make acceptance of the proposition difficult. If, while possessing those ethical sentiments which social discipline has now produced, men stood in possession of a territory not yet individually portioned out, they would no more hesitate to assert equality of their claims to the land than they would hesitate to assert equality of their claims to light and air. But now that long-standing appropriation, continued culture, as well as sales and purchases, have complicated matters, the *dictum* of absolute ethics, incongruous with the state of things produced, is apt to be denied altogether. Before asking how, under these circumstances, we must decide, let us glance at some past phases of land tenure.

Partly because in early stages of agriculture, land, soon exhausted, soon ceases to be worth occupying, it has been the custom with little-civilized and semicivilized peoples, for individuals to abandon after a time the tracts they have cleared, and to clear others. Causes aside, however, the fact is that in early stages private ownership of land is unknown: only the usufruct belongs to the cultivator, while the land itself is tacitly regarded as the property of the tribe. It is thus now with the Sumatrans and others, and it was thus with our own ancestors: the members of the Mark, while they severally owned the products of the areas they respectively cultivated, did not own the areas themselves. Though it may be said that at first they were members of the same family, *gens,* or clan, and that the ownership of each tract was private ownership in so far as the tract belonged to a cluster of relations; yet since the same kind of tenure continued after the population of the Mark had come to include men who were unrelated to the rest, ownership of the tract by the community and not by individuals became an established arrangement. This primitive condition will be clearly understood after contemplating the case of the Russians, among whom it has but partially passed away.

The village lands were held in common by all the members of the association [*mir*]; the individual only possessed his harvest, and the *dvor* or enclosure immediately surrounding his house. This primitive condition of property, existing in Russia up to the present day, was once common to all European peoples. [*The History of Russia*, A. Rambaud, trans. Lang, vol. i., p. 45.]

With this let me join a number of extracts from Wallace's *Russia*, telling us of the original state of things and of the subsequent states. After noting the fact that while the Don Cossacks were purely nomadic, "agriculture was prohibited on pain of death"—apparently because it interfered with hunting and cattle breeding—he says:

Each Cossack who wished to raise a crop ploughed and sowed wherever he thought fit, and retained as long as he chose the land thus appropriated; and when the soil began to show signs of exhaustion, he abandoned his plot and ploughed elsewhere. As the number of agriculturists increased, quarrels frequently arose. Still worse evils appeared when markets were created in the vicinity. In some stanitzas [Cossack villages] the richer families appropriated enormous quantities of the common land by using several teams of oxen, or by hiring peasants in the nearest villages to come and plough for them; and instead of abandoning the land after raising two or three crops they retained possession of it. Thus the whole of the arable land, or at least the best parts of it, became actually, if not legally, the private property of a few families. [*Ibid.*, ii, 86.]

Then he explains that as a consequence of something like a revolution:

In accordance with their [the landless members of the community's] demands the appropriated land was confiscated by the Commune and the system of periodical distributions . . . was introduced. By this system each adult male possesses a share of the land." [*Ibid.*, ii, 87.]

On the Steppes a plot of land is commonly cultivated for only three or four years in succession. It is then abandoned for at least double that period, and the cultivators remove to some other portion of the communal territory. . . . Under such circumstances the principle of private property in the land is not likely to strike root; each family insists on possessing a certain *quantity* rather than a certain *plot* of

land, and contents itself with a right of usufruct, whilst the right of
property remains in the hands of the Commune. [*Ibid.*, ii, 91.]

But in the central and more advanced districts this early practice has become modified, though without destroying the
essential character of the tenure.

> According to this system [the three-field system] the cultivators do
> not migrate periodically from one part of the communal territory to
> another, but till always the same fields, and are obliged to manure the
> plots which they occupy. . . . Though the three-field system has been
> in use for many generations in the central provinces, the communal
> principle, with its periodical reallotment of the land, still remains
> intact. [*Ibid.*, ii, 92.]

Such facts, and numerous other such facts, put beyond
question the conclusion that before the progress of social
organization changed the relations of individuals to the soil,
that relation was one of joint ownership and not one of individual ownership.

How was this relation changed? How only could it be
changed? Certainly not by unforced consent. It cannot be
supposed that all, or some, of the members of the community
willingly surrendered their respective claims. Crime now and
again caused loss of an individual's share in the joint
ownership; but this must have left the relations of the rest to
the soil unchanged. A kindred result might have been entailed by debt, were it not that debt implies a creditor; and
while it is scarcely supposable that the creditor could be the
community as a whole, indebtedness to any individual of it
would not empower the debtor to transfer in payment something of which he was not individually possessed, and which
could not be individually received. Probably elsewhere there
came into play the cause described as having operated in
Russia, where some, cultivating larger areas than others, accumulated wealth and consequent power, and extra possessions; but, as is implied by the fact that in Russia this led to
a revolution and reinstitution of the original state, the process
was evidently there, and probably elsewhere, regarded as

aggressive. Obviously the chief cause must have been the exercise of direct or indirect force: sometimes internal but chiefly external. Disputes and fights within the community, leading to predominance (achieved in some cases by possession of fortified houses) prepared the way for partial usurpations. When, as among the Suanetians, we have a still-extant case in which every family in a village has its tower of defense, we may well understand how the intestine feuds in early communities commonly brought about individual supremacies, and how these ended in the establishment of special claims upon the land subordinating the general claims.

But conquest from without has everywhere been chiefly instrumental in superseding communal proprietorship by individual proprietorship. It is not to be supposed that in times when captive men were made slaves and women appropriated as spoils of war, much respect was paid to preexisting ownership of the soil. The old English buccaneers who, in their descents on the coast, slew priests at the altars, set fire to churches, and massacred the people who had taken refuge in them, would have been very incomprehensible beings had they recognized the landownership of such as survived. When the pirate Danes, who in later days ascended the rivers, had burnt the homesteads they came upon, slaughtered the men, violated the women, tossed children on pikes or sold them in the marketplace, they must have undergone a miraculous transformation had they thereafter inquired to whom the Marks belonged, and admitted the titles of their victims to them. And similarly when, two centuries later, after constant internal wars had already produced military rulers maintaining quasi-feudal claims over occupiers of lands, there came the invading Normans, the right of conquest once more overrode such kinds of possession as had grown up, and still further merged communal proprietorship in that kind of individual proprietorship which characterized feudalism. Victory, which gives unqualified power over the defeated and their belongings, is followed, according to the nature of the race, by the assertion of universal ownership, more or less qualified illustrated by the fact that year by year state authority is given for appropriating land for public purposes, after making due compensation to existing holders. Though it may be replied that this claim of the state to supreme landownership is but a part of its claim to supreme ownership in general, since it assumes the right to take anything on giving compensation; yet the first is an habitually enforced claim, while the other is but a nominal claim not enforced; as we see in the purchase of pictures for the nation, to effect which the state enters into competition with private buyers, and may or may not succeed.

It remains only to point out that the political changes which have slowly replaced the supreme power of the monarch by the supreme power of the people, have, by implication, replaced the monarch's supreme ownership of the land by the people's supreme ownership of the land. If the representative body has practically inherited the governmental powers which in past times vested in the king, it has at the same time inherited that ultimate proprietorship of the soil which in past times vested in him. And since the representative body is but the agent of the community, this ultimate proprietorship now vests in the community. Nor is this denied by landowners themselves. The report issued in December 1889 by the council of "The Liberty and Property Defense League," on which sit several peers and two judges, yields proof. After saying that the essential principle of their organization, "based upon recorded experience," is a distrust of "officialism, imperial or municipal," the council go on to say that "this principle applied to the case of land clearly points to individual ownership, qualified by State-suzerainty. . . . The land can of course be 'resumed' on payment of full compensation, and managed by the 'people' if they so will it."

And the badness of the required system of administration is the only reason urged for maintaining the existing system of landholding: the supreme ownership of the community being avowedly recognized. So that whereas, in early stages, along with the freedom of each man, there went joint ownership of the soil by the body of men; and whereas, during the long periods of that militant activity by which small communities were consolidated into great ones, there simultaneously resulted loss of individual freedom and loss of participation in landownership; there has, with the decline of militancy and the growth of industrialism, been a reacquirement of individual freedom and a reacquirement of such participation in landownership as is implied by a share in appointing the body by which the land is now held. And the implication is that the members of the community, habitually exercising as they do, through their representatives, the power of alienating and using as they think well, any portion of the land, may equitably appropriate and use, if they think fit, all portions of the land. But since equity and daily custom alike imply that existing holders of particular portions of land, may not be dispossessed without giving them in return its fairly estimated value, it is also implied that the wholesale resumption of the land by the community can be justly effected only by wholesale purchase of it. Were the direct exercise of ownership to be resumed by the community without purchase, the community would take, along with something which is its own, an immensely greater amount of something which is not its own. Even if we ignore those multitudinous complications which, in the course of century after century, have inextricably entangled men's claims, theoretically considered—even if we reduce the case to its simplest theoretical form; we must admit that all which can be claimed for the community is the surface of the country in its original unsubdued state. To all that value given to it by clearing, breaking-up, prolonged culture, fencing, draining, making roads, farm buildings, &c., constituting nearly all its value, the community has no claim. This value has been given either by personal labor, or by labor paid for, or by ancestral labor; or else the value given to it in such ways has been purchased by legitimately earned money. All this value artificially given vests in existing owners, and cannot without a gigantic robbery be taken from them. If, during the many transactions which have brought about existing landownership, there have been much violence and much fraud, these have been small compared with the violence and the fraud which the community would be guilty of did it take possession, without paying for it, of that artificial value which the labor of nearly two thousand years has given to the land.

298. Reverting to the general topic of the chapter—the rights to the uses of natural media—it chiefly concerns us here to note the way in which these rights have gradually acquired legislative sanctions as societies have advanced to higher types.

At the beginning of the chapter we saw that in modern times there have arisen legal assertions of men's equal rights to the uses of light and air: no forms of social organization or class interests having appreciably hindered recognition of these corollaries from the law of equal freedom. And we have just seen that by implication, if not in any overt or conscious way, there has in our days been recognized the equal rights of all electors to supreme ownership of the inhabited area— rights which, though latent, are asserted by every act of Parliament which alienates land. Though this right to the use of the earth possessed by each citizen, is traversed by established arrangements to so great an extent as to be practically suspended; yet its existence as an equitable claim cannot be denied without affirming that expropriation by state decree is inequitable. The right of an existing holder of land can be equitably superseded, only if there exists a prior right of the community at large; and this prior right of the community at large consists of the sum of the individual rights of its members.

NOTE. Various considerations touching this vexed question of landownership, which would occupy too much space if included here, I have included in Appendix B.

voluntarily make an exchange, neither assumes greater liberty of action than the other, and fellow men are uninterfered with—remain possessed of just as much liberty of action as before. Though completion of the exchange may shut out sundry of them from advantageous transactions, yet as their abilities to enter into such transactions depended wholly on the assent of another man, they cannot be included in their normal spheres of action. These continue what they would have been had the two persons who have bargained never existed.

Obvious as is the right of exchange, recognition of it in law has arisen but slowly; and, in most parts of the world, is still far from complete. Among the Polynesian races, exchange is variously interfered with by the chiefs: here, foreign trade being monopolized by them; there, prices fixed by them; and in other places the length of a day's work. Similarly in Africa. The right of preemption in trade is possessed by chiefs among Bechuanas and Inland Negroes; and there is no business without royal assent. In Ashanti only the king and great men can trade; and in Shoa certain choice goods can be bought only by the king. The Congo people, Dahomans, and Fulahs have commercial chiefs who regulate buying and selling. Kindred limitations existed among the Hebrews and Phoenicians, as also among the Ancient Mexicans and Central Americans. At the present time the men of some South American tribes, as the Patagonians and Mundrucus, have to obtain authority from chiefs before they can trade. Like facts, presented by the European nations, down from the time when Diocletian fixed prices and wages, need not be detailed. All it concerns us to note is that interferences with exchange have diminished as civilization has advanced. They have decreased, and in some cases have disappeared from the transactions between members of the same society; and have partially disappeared later from the transactions between members of different societies. Moreover with this, as with other rights, the interferences have become smallest where the development of the industrial type with its concomitant

free institutions, has become greatest, namely, among ourselves.

It is worthy of note, however, that the changes which established almost entire freedom of trade in England, were chiefly
urged on grounds of policy and not on grounds of equity.
Throughout the anti–Corn Law agitation little was said about
the "right" of free exchange; and at the present time such
reprobation as we hear of protectionists, at home and abroad,
is vented exclusively against the folly of their policy and not
against its inequity. Nor need we feel any surprise at this if we
remember that even still the majority of men do not admit that
there should be freedom of exchange in respect of work and
wages. Blinded by what appear to be their interests, artisans
and others tacitly deny the rights of employer and employed
to decide how much money shall be given for so much labor.
In this instance the law is in advance of the average opinion: it
insists that each citizen shall be at liberty to make whatever
bargains he pleases for his services; while the great mass of
citizens insist that each shall not be at liberty to do this.

315. Of course with the right of free exchange goes the right
of free contract: a postponement, now understood, now
specified, in the completion of an exchange, serving to turn
the one into the other.

It is needless to do more than name contracts for services on
certain terms; contracts for the uses of houses and lands;
contracts for the completion of specified works; contracts for
the loan of capital. These are samples of contracts which men
voluntarily enter into without aggressing on any others—
contracts, therefore, which they have a right to make.

In earlier times interferences with the right of exchange
were of course accompanied by interferences with the right of
contract. The multitudinous regulations of wages and prices,
which century after century encumbered the statute books of
civilized peoples, were examples. Decreasing with the decrease of coercive rule, these have, in our days, mostly disappeared. One such gradual change may be instanced as

typifying all others—that which usury laws furnish. In sundry cases where but small progress towards free institutions had been made, the taking of interest for money lent was forbidden altogether; as among the Hebrews, as among ourselves in the remote past, and as among the French at the time of the greatest monarchical power. Then, as a qualification, we have the fixing of maximum rates; as in early ages by Cicero for his Roman province; as in England by Henry VIII at 10 percent, by James I at 8 percent, by Charles II at 6 percent, by Anne at 5 percent; and as in France by Louis XV at 4 percent. Finally we have removal of all restrictions, and the leaving of lenders and borrowers to make their own bargains.

While we observe that law has in this case gradually come into correspondence with equity, we may also fitly observe one exceptional case in which the two agree in forbidding a contract. I refer to the moral interdict and the legal interdict against a man's sale of himself into slavery. If we go back to the biological origin of justice, as being the maintenance of that relation between efforts and the products of efforts which is needful for the continuance of life, we see that this relation is suspended by bondage; and that, therefore, the man who agrees to enslave himself on condition of receiving some immediate benefit, traverses that ultimate principle from which social morality grows. Or if we contemplate the case from an immediately ethical point of view, it becomes manifest that since a contract, as framed in conformity with the law of equal freedom, implies that the contracting parties shall severally give what are approximately equivalents, there can be no contract, properly so-called, in which the terms are incommensurable; as they are when, for some present enhancement of his life, a man bargains away the rest of his life. So that when, instead of recognizing the sale of self as valid, law eventually interdicted it, the exception it thus made to the right of contract was an exception which equity also makes. Here, too, law harmonized itself with ethics.

316. These rights of exchange and contract have, of course, in common with other rights, to be asserted subject to the

restrictions which social self-preservation in presence of external enemies necessitates. Where there is good evidence that freedom of exchange would endanger national defense, it may rightly be hindered.

This is a limitation of the right which, in stages characterized by permanent militancy, is obviously needful. Societies in chronic antagonism with other societies must be self-sufficing in their industrial arrangements. During the early feudal period in France, "on rural estates the most diverse trades were often exercised simultaneously"; and "the castles made almost all the articles used in them." The difficulties of communication, the risk of loss of goods in transit, and the dangers arising from perpetual feuds, made it requisite that the essential commodities should be produced at home. That which held of these small social groups has held of larger social groups; and international freedom of exchange has therefore been greatly restricted. The outcry against being "dependent on foreigners," which was common during the anti–Corn Law agitation, was not without some justification; since it is only during well-assured peace that a nation may, without risk, buy a large part of its food abroad, instead of growing it.

Beyond this qualification of the rights of exchange and contract, there remains no other having an ethical warrant. Interference with the liberty to buy and sell for other reasons than that just recognized as valid, is a trespass, by whatever agency effected. Those who have been allowed to call themselves "protectionists" should be called aggressionists; since forbidding A to buy of B, and forcing him to buy of C (usually on worse terms), is clearly a trespass on that right of free exchange which we have seen to be a corollary from the law of equal freedom.

The chief fact to be here noted, however, is that among ourselves, if not among other peoples, the ethical deduction, after being justified inductively, has gained a recognition in law; if not on moral grounds, yet on grounds of policy.

CHAPTER 16

The Right to Free Industry

317. Though, under one of its aspects, industrial freedom is implied by the rights to free motion and locomotion; and though, under another of its aspects, it is implied by the rights to free exchange and free contract; yet it has a further aspect, not clearly included in these, which must be specifically stated. Though demonstration of it is scarcely called for, yet it is needful to indicate it for the purpose of showing how little it was once recognized and how fully it is recognized now.

By the right to free industry is here meant the right of each man to carry on his occupation, whatever it may be, after whatever manner he prefers or thinks best, so long as he does not trespass against his neighbors: taking the benefits or the evils of his way, as the case may be. Self-evident as this right now seems, it seemed by no means self-evident to people in past times. Naturally, indeed, it could not well be self-evident while more obvious rights were unrecognized.

Just noting that, in the far past, industry was under regulations having a religious authority, as among the Hebrews, who, in *Deuteronomy* XXII. 8 &c., were directed concerning methods of building and agriculture, it will suffice to observe how great and persistent were the restraints on industrial liberty among European peoples during the supremacy of that militant organization which in all ways subordinates individual wills. In Old English days, the lord of the manor in Court-leet inspected industrial products; and, after the establishment of kingship, there came directions for cropping of lands, times of shearing, mode of ploughing. After the Conquest regulations for dyeing were enacted. From Edward III onwards to the time of James I, official searchers had to see that various wares were properly made. Certain traders were told how many assistants they should have; the growing of particular plants was made compulsory; tanners had to keep their hides in the pits for specified periods; and there were officers for the assize of bread and ale. With the development of institutions characterizing the industrial type, these restrictions on industrial freedom diminished; and, at the time George III began to reign, five-sixths of them had disappeared. Increasing though they did during the war period brought on by the French revolution, they again diminished subsequently; until there had been abolished nearly all state interferences with modes of production. Significantly enough, however, the recent revival of militancy here, consequent on the immense redevelopment of it on the Continent (set going, for the second time, by that greatest of all modern curses, the Bonaparte family), has been accompanied by a reaction towards industrial regulations; so that during the last thirty years there have been numerous acts saying how businesses shall be carried on: ranging from the interdict on taking meals in match factories except in certain parts, to directions for the building and cleaning of artisans' dwellings—from orders for the painting of bakehouses to acts punishing farmers if they employ uneducated children.

Meanwhile it is to be observed that in France, where the militant activities entailed by surroundings have developed more highly the militant type of structure, industrial regulations have been more elaborate and more rigorous: having been carried, during the latter days of the monarchy, to a scarcely credible extent. "Swarms of public functionaries" enforced rules continually complicated by new ones to remedy the insufficiency of the old: directing, for example, "the lengths pieces of cloth are to be woven, the pattern to be chosen, the method to be followed, and the defects to be avoided." Even after the revolution, when greater industrial freedom was temporarily achieved, interferences again multiplied; so that in 1806, according to Levasseur, public administrations fixed the length of the day's labor, the hours of meals, and the beginning and end of the day at the various seasons. Indeed, it is instructive to observe how, in France, where the idea of equality has always subordinated the idea of liberty; and where, under the guise of a free form of government, citizens have all along submitted without protest to a bureaucracy which has been as despotic under the republican form of government as under the monarchical; and where reversions to the completely militant type of structure have more than once occurred, and have more than once almost occurred; the industrial freedom of the individual, in common with other freedoms, has never been established so fully as here; where *la gloire* has not been so predominant an aim and militant organization has never been so pronounced.

But details apart, a general survey of the facts proves that during the advance from those early stages in which small respect was paid to life, liberty, and property, to those later stages in which these are held sacred, there has been an advance from a regime under which modes of production were authoritatively prescribed, to a regime under which they are left to the will of the producer; and in places where legislation most recognizes individual freedom in other respects, it most recognizes individual freedom in this respect.

CHAPTER 17

The Rights of Free Belief and Worship

318. If we interpret the meanings of words literally, to assert freedom of belief as a right is absurd; since by no external power can this be taken away. Indeed an assertion of it involves a double absurdity; for while belief cannot really be destroyed or changed by coercion from without, it cannot really be destroyed or changed by coercion from within. It is determined by causes which lie beyond external control, and in large measure beyond internal control. What is meant is, of course, the right freely to *profess* belief.

That this is a corollary from the law of equal freedom scarcely needs saying. The profession of a belief by any one, does not of itself interfere with the professions of other beliefs by others; and others, if they impose on any one their professions of belief, manifestly assume more liberty of action than he assumes.

In respect of those miscellaneous beliefs which do not concern in any obvious way the maintenance of established institutions, freedom of belief is not called in question. Ignoring exceptions presented by some uncivilized societies, we may say that it is only those beliefs, the profession of which seems at variance with the existing social order, which are interdicted. To be known as one who holds that the political system, or the social organization, is not what it ought to be, entails penalties in times and places where the militant type of organization in unqualified. But, naturally, where fundamental rights are habitually disregarded, no regard for a right less conspicuously important is to be expected. The fact that the right of political dissent is denied where rights in general are denied, affords no reason for doubting that it is a direct deduction from the law of equal freedom.

The right to profess beliefs of the religious class, has for its concomitant the right to manifest such beliefs in acts of worship. For these, too, may be performed without diminishing the like rights of fellow men, and without otherwise trespassing against them in the carrying on of their lives. So long as they do not inflict nuisances on neighboring people, as does the untimely and persistent jangling of bells in some Catholic countries, or as does the uproar of Salvation Army processions in our own (permitted with contemptible weakness by our authorities) they cannot be equitably interfered with. Those who profess other religious beliefs, in common with those who profess no religious beliefs, remain as free as before to worship in their own ways or not to worship at all.

The enunciation of these rights, needful for the symmetry of the argument, is in our day and country almost superfluous. But England is not the world; and even in England there still survive certain practical denials of these rights.

319. The savage, far from possessing that freedom which sentimental speculators about society used to imagine, has his beliefs dictated by custom, in common with those usages which peremptorily regulate his life. When we read that in Guinea, a man who does not fulfill the prophecy of the fetish by getting well, is strangled because he has made the fetish lie, we may readily understand that the expression of skepticism is practically unknown. The Fijians, who, being worshippers of cannibal gods, expressed horror at the Samoans because they had no worship like their own, and whose feeling towards Jackson for disregarding one of their religious

interdicts was shown by angrily calling him "the white infidel," are not likely to have tolerated any religious skepticism among their own common people, any more than they are likely to have tolerated any political skepticism respecting the divine authority of their chiefs: a conclusion we are compelled to draw on reading, in Williams, that a Fijian who had been in America endangered his life by saying that America was larger than Fiji.

Turning to ancient civilizations, we meet with various denials of the right of free belief. There is Plato's prescription of punishments for those who dissented from the Greek religion; there is the death of Socrates for attacking the current views concerning the gods; and there is the prosecution of Anaxagoras for implying that the sun was not the chariot of Apollo. Passing to the time when the profession of the Christian belief was penal, and then to the subsequent time when the profession of any other belief was penal, the only thing we have to note in connection with the doings of inquisitors and the martyrdoms, now of Protestants by Catholics and then of Catholics by Protestants, is that the thing insisted on was external conformity. It sufficed if there was nominal acceptance of the prescribed belief, without any evidence of real acceptance. Leaving the period of these earlier religious persecutions, during which there was a tacit denial of the right of free belief, it suffices to note that since the Toleration Act of 1688, which, while insisting on acknowledgment of certain fundamental dogmas, remitted the penalties on dissent from others, there have been successive relaxations. The disqualifications of dissenters for public posts were removed; by and by those of Catholics and eventually those of Jews; and still more recently the substitution of affirmation for oath has made it no longer legally imperative to assert or imply belief in a God, before being permitted to fulfill certain civil functions. Practically, every one is now free to entertain any creed or no creed, without incurring legal penalty, and with little or no social penalty.

By a kindred series of changes there has been gradually

established freedom of political belief. Punishment or ill-usage for rejecting such a political dogma as the divine right of kings, or for calling in question the right of some particular man to reign, has ceased. The upholders of despotism and the avowed anarchists are equally at liberty to think as they please.

320. Is freedom of belief, or rather the right freely to profess belief, subject to no qualification? Or from the postulate that the needs for social self-preservation must override the claims of individuals, are we to infer that under certain conditions the right may properly be limited?

The only cases in which limitation can be urged with manifest force, are those in which the beliefs openly entertained are such as tend directly to diminish the power of the society to defend itself against hostile societies. Effectual use of the combined forces of the community, presupposes subordination to the government and to the agencies appointed for carrying on war; and it may rationally be held that the open avowal of convictions which, if general, would paralyze the executive agency, ought not to be allowed. And here, indeed, we see once more how that militant regime which in various other ways suppresses or suspends the rights of individuals, interferes even with the right of free belief.

Only, indeed, as we pass gradually from that system of status which chronic hostilities produce, to that system of contract which replaces it as fast as industrial life becomes predominant, does the assertion of rights in general become more and more practicable and appropriate; and only in the course of this change does the change from the alleged duty of accepting beliefs prescribed by authority, to the asserted right of individually choosing beliefs, naturally go on.

Subject to this interpretation, we see that the right of free belief has had a history parallel to the histories of other rights. This corollary from the law of equal freedom, at first ignored and then gradually more and more recognized, has finally come to be fully established in law.

CHAPTER 18

The Rights of Free Speech and Publication

321.   The subject matter of this chapter is scarcely separable from that of the last. As belief, considered in itself, does not admit of being controlled by external power—as it is only the profession of belief which can be taken cognizance of by authority and permitted or prevented, it follows that the assertion of the right to freedom of belief implies the right to freedom of speech. Further, it implies the right to use speech for the propagation of belief; seeing that each of the propositions constituting an argument or arguments, used to support or enforce a belief, being itself a belief, the right to express it is included with the right to express the belief to be justified.

Of course the one right like the other is an immediate corollary from the law of equal freedom. By using speech, either for the expression of a belief or for the maintenance of a belief, no one prevents any other person from doing the like: unless, indeed, by vociferation or persistence he prevents another from being heard, in which case he is habitually recognized as unfair, that is, as breaking the law of equal freedom.

Evidently with change of terms, the same things may be said concerning the right of publication—"the liberty of unlicensed printing." In respect of their ethical relations, there exists no essential difference between the act of speaking and the act of symbolizing speech by writing, or the act of multiplying copies of that which has been written.

One qualification, implied by preceding chapters, has to be named. Freedom of speech, spoken, written, or printed, does not include freedom to use speech for the utterance of calumny or the propagation of it; nor does it include freedom to use speech for prompting the commission of injuries to others. Both these employments of it are obviously excluded by those limits to individual liberty which have been set forth.

322. Though in our time and country defense of these rights seems needless, it may be well to deal with such arguments against them as were urged among ourselves in comparatively recent times and are still urged in other countries.

It is said that a government ought to guarantee its subjects "security and a sense of security"; whence it is inferred that magistrates ought to keep ears open to the declamations of popular orators, and stop such as are calculated to create alarm. This inference, however, is met by the difficulty that since every considerable change, political or religious, is, when first urged, dreaded by the majority, and thus diminishes their sense of security, the advocacy of it should be prevented. There were multitudes of people who suffered chronic alarm during the Reform Bill agitation; and had the prevention of that alarm been imperative, the implication is that the agitation ought to have been suppressed. So, too, great numbers who were moved by the terrible forecasts of *The Standard* and the melancholy wailings of *The Herald*, would fain have put down the free-trade propaganda; and had it been requisite to maintain their sense of security, they should have had their way. And similarly with removal of Catholic disabilities. Prophecies were rife of the return of papal persecutions with all their horrors. Hence the speaking and writing which brought about the change ought to have been forbidden, had the maintenance of a sense of security been held imperative.

Evidently such proposals to limit the right of free speech, political or religious, can be defended only by making the tacit assumption that whatever political or religious beliefs are at the time established, are wholly true; and since this tacit assumption has throughout the past proved to be habitually erroneous, regard for experience may reasonably prevent us from assuming that the current beliefs are wholly true. We must recognize free speech as still being the agency by which error is to be dissipated, and cannot without papal assumption interdict it.

Beyond the need, in past times unquestioned, for restraints on the public utterance of political and religious beliefs at variance with those established, there is the need, still by most people thought unquestionable, for restraining utterances which pass the limits of what is thought decency, or are calculated to encourage sexual immorality. The question is a difficult one—appears, indeed, to admit of no satisfactory solution. On the one hand, it seems beyond doubt that unlimited license of speech on these matters, may have the effect of undermining ideas, sentiments, and institutions which are socially beneficial; for, whatever are the defects in the existing domestic regime, we have strong reasons for believing that it is in most respects good. If this be so, it may be argued that publication of doctrines, which tend to discredit this regime, is undoubtedly injurious and should be prevented. Yet, on the other hand, we must remember that in like manner it was, in the past, thought absolutely certain that the propagators of heretical opinions ought to be punished, lest they should mislead and eternally damn those who heard them; and this fact suggests that there may be danger in assuming too confidently that our opinions concerning the relations of the sexes are just what they should be. In all times and places people have been positive that their ideas and feelings on these matters, as well as on religious matters, have been right; and yet, assuming that we are right, they must have been wrong. Though here in England we think it clear that the child marriages in India are vicious, yet most Hindus do not think so; and though among ourselves the majority do not see anything wrong in mercantile marriages, yet there are many who do. In parts of Africa not only is polygamy regarded as proper but monogamy is condemned, even by women; while in Tibet polyandry is not only held right by the inhabitants but is thought by travelers to be the best arrangement practicable in their poverty-stricken country. In presence of the multitudinous differences of opinion found even among civilized peoples, it seems scarcely reasonable to take for granted that we alone are above criticism in our conceptions and practices; and unless we do this, restraints on free speech concerning the relations of the sexes may possibly be hindrances to something better and higher.

Doubtless there must be evils attendant on free speech in this sphere as in the political and religious spheres; but the conclusion above implied is that the evils must be tolerated in consideration of the possible benefits. Further, it should be borne in mind that such evils will always be kept in check by public opinion. The dread of saying or writing that which will bring social ostracism, proves in many cases far more effectual than does legal restriction.

323. Though it is superfluous to point out that, in common with other rights, the rights of free speech and publication, in early times and most places either denied or not overtly recognized, have gradually established themselves; yet some evidence may fitly be cited with a view to emphasizing this truth.

Various of the facts instanced in the last chapter might be instanced afresh here; since suppression of beliefs has, by implication, been suppression of free speech. That the anger of the Jewish priests against Jesus Christ for teaching things at variance with their creed led to his crucifixion; that Paul, at first a persecutor of Christians, was himself presently persecuted for persuading men to be Christians; and that by sundry Roman emperors preachers of Christianity were martyred; are familiar examples of the denial of free speech in early times. So, too, after the Christian creed became established, the punishment of some who taught the nondivinity of Christ, of others who publicly asserted predestination, and of others who spread the doctrine of two supreme principles of good and evil, as well as the persecutions of Huss and Luther, exemplify in ways almost equally familiar the denial of the right to utter opinions contrary to those which are authorized. And so, in our country, has it been from the time when Henry IV enacted severe penalties on teachers of heresy, down to the 17th century when the nonconforming clergy were punished for teaching any other than the church doctrine and Bunyan was imprisoned for open-air preaching—down, further, to the last trial for propagating atheism, which is within our own recollection. But gradually, during recent centuries, the right of free speech on religious matters, more and more asserted, has been more and more admitted; until now there is no restraint on the public utterance of any religious opinion, unless the utterance is gratuitously insulting in manner or form.

By a parallel progress there has been established that right of free speech on political questions, which in early days was denied. Among the Athenians in Solon's time, death was inflicted for opposition to a certain established policy; and among the Romans the utterance of proscribed opinions was punished as treason. So, too, in England centuries ago, political criticism, even of a moderate kind, brought severe penalties. Later times have witnessed, now greater liberty of speech and now greater control: the noticeable fact being that during the war period brought on by the French revolution, there was a retrograde movement in respect of this right as in respect of other rights. A judge, in 1808, declared that "it was not to be permitted to any man to make the people dissatisfied with the government under which he lives." But with the commencement of the long peace there began a decrease of the restraints on political speech, as of other restraints on freedom. Though Sir F. Burdett was imprisoned for condemning the inhuman acts of the troops, and Leigh Hunt for commenting on excessive flogging in the army, since that time there have practically disappeared all impediments to the public expression of political ideas. So long as he does not suggest the commission of crimes, each citizen is free to say what he pleases about any or all of our institutions: even to the advocacy of a form of government utterly different from that which exists, or the condemnation of all government.

Of course, with increasing recognition of the right of free speech there has gone increasing recognition of the right of free publication. Plato taught that censors were needful to prevent the diffusion of unauthorized doctrines. With the growth of ecclesiastical power there came the suppression of writings considered heretical. In our own country under Queen Elizabeth, books had to be officially authorized; and even the Long Parliament reenforced that system of licensing against which Milton made his celebrated protest. But for these two centuries there has been no official censorship, save of public plays. And though many arrangements for shackling the press have since been made, yet these have gradually fallen into disuse or been repealed.

324. But in this case, as in cases already noticed, it follows from the precedence which the preservation of the society has over the claims of the individual, that such restraints may rightly be put on free speech and free publication as are needful during war to prevent the giving of advantage to the enemy. If, as we have seen, there is ethical justification for subordinating the more important rights of the citizen to the extent requisite for successfully carrying on national defense, it of course follows that these less important rights may also be subordinated.

And here, indeed, we see again how direct is the connection between international hostilities and the repression of individual freedom. For it is manifest that throughout civilization the repression of freedom of speech and freedom of publication, has been rigorous in proportion as militancy has been predominant; and that at the present time, in such contrasts as that between Russia and England, we still observe the relation.

After recognizing the justifiable limitations of these rights, that which it concerns us to note is that they, in common with the others severally deduced from the law of equal freedom, have come to be recognized in law as fast as society has assumed a higher form.

CHAPTER 19

A Retrospect with an Addition

325.   Where men's natures and their institutions are incongruous, there exists a force tending to produce change. Either the institutions will remold the nature or the nature will remold the institutions, or partly the one and partly the other; and eventually a more stable state will establish itself.

In our own case the action and reaction between our social arrangements and our characters, has produced a curious result. Compromise being an essential trait of the one has become agreeable to the other; so that it is not only tolerated but preferred. There has grown up a distrust of definite conclusions, and a positive aversion to system. Naturally, statesmen and citizens who, on the one hand, unite in declaring the sovereignty of the people, and who, on the other hand, dutifully write and complacently read royal speeches which address Lords and Commons as servants, and speak of the people as "my subjects," must be impatient of any demand for consistency in their political ideas. If, while they assert the right of private judgment in religious matters, they tacitly authorize Parliament to maintain a creed for them, they must be restive when asked how they reconcile their theory with their practice. Hence, in presence of the many instances in which they have to accept contradictory doctrines, they become averse to exact thinking, resent all attempts to tie them down to precise propositions, and shrink from an abstract principle with as much alarm as a servant girl shrinks from something she takes for a ghost.

An ingrained way of thinking and feeling thus generated by social conditions, is not to be changed by any amount of reasoning. Beliefs at variance with it cannot gain much acceptance. Readers in whom the separate arguments contained in foregoing chapters have failed to produce changes of opinions, will not have their opinions changed by bringing together these arguments and showing that they converge to the same conclusion. Still, before proceeding, it will be as well to show how strong are the united proofs of the propositions from which inferences are presently to be drawn.

326. We have no ethics of nebular condensation, or of sidereal movement, or of planetary evolution; the conception is not relevant to inorganic actions. Nor, when we turn to organized things, do we find that it has any relation to the phenomena of plant life: though we ascribe to plants superiorities and inferiorities, leading to successes and failures in the struggle for existence, we do not associate with them praise and blame. It is only with the rise of sentiency in the animal world, that the subject matter of ethics originates. Hence ethics, presupposing animal life, and gaining an appreciable meaning as animal life assumes complex forms, must, in its ultimate nature, be expressible in terms of animal life. It is concerned with certain traits in the conduct of life, considered as good or bad respectively; and it cannot pass judgments on these traits in the conduct of life while ignoring the essential phenomena of life.

In the chapter "Animal Ethics" this connection was shown under its concrete form. We saw that, limiting our attention to any one species, the continuance of which is held to be desirable, then, relatively to that species, the acts which subserve the maintenance of the individual and the preservation of the race, are classed by us as right and regarded with a certain approbation; while we have reprobation for acts having contrary tendencies. In the next chapter, "Subhuman Justice," we saw that, for achievement of the assumed desirable end, a condition precedent is that each individual shall receive or suffer the good or evil results of its own nature and consequent actions. We saw, also, that throughout the lower animal world, where there exists no power by which this condition precedent can be traversed, it eventuates in survival of the fittest. And we further saw that, since this connection between conduct and consequence is held to be just, it follows that throughout the animal kingdom what we call justice, is the ethical aspect of this biological law in virtue of which life in general has been maintained and has evolved into higher forms; and which therefore possesses the highest possible authority.

Along with the establishment of gregarious habits there arises a secondary law. When a number of individuals live in such proximity that they are severally apt to impede one another's actions, and so to prevent one another from achieving desired results; then, to avoid antagonism and consequent dispersion, their actions have to be mutually restrained: each must carry on its actions subject to the limitation that it shall not interfere with the like actions of others more than its own actions are interfered with. And we saw that among various gregarious creatures considerable observance of such restraints is displayed.

Finally, in the chapter "Human Justice" it was shown that among men, the highest gregarious creatures, this secondary law, prefigured in a vague way among lower gregarious creatures, comes to have more pronounced, more definite, and more complex applications. Under the conditions imposed by social life, the primary principle of justice, when asserted for each individual, itself originates the secondary or limiting principle by asserting it for all other individuals; and thus the mutual restrictions which simultaneous carrying on of their actions necessitates form a necessary element of justice in the associated state.

327. Adaptation, either by the direct or by the indirect process, or by both, holds of cerebral structures as of the structures composing the rest of the body; and mental functions, like bodily functions, tend ever to become adjusted to the requirements. A feeling which prompts the maintenance of freedom of action is shown by all creatures, and is marked in creatures of high organization; and these last also show some amount of the feeling which responds to the requirement that each shall act within the limits imposed by the actions of others.

Along with greater power of "looking before and after," there exist in mankind higher manifestations of both of these traits—clear where the society has long been peaceful and obscured where it has been habitually warlike. Where the habits of life have not entailed a chronic conflict between the ethics of amity and the ethics of enmity, a distinct consciousness of justice is shown; alike in respect of personal claims and the correlative claims of others. But where men's rights to life, liberty, and property, are constantly subordinated by forcibly organizing them into armies for more effectual fighting, and where by implication they are accustomed to trample on the rights of men who do not inhabit the same territory, the emotions and ideas corresponding to the principles of justice, egoistic and altruistic, are habitually repressed.

But subject to this qualification, associated life, which in a predominant degree fosters the sympathies, and while it gives play to the sentiment of egoistic justice exercises also the sentiment of altruistic justice, generates correlative ideas; so that in course of time, along with a moral consciousness of the claims of self and others, there comes an intellectual perception of them. There finally arise intuitions corresponding to those requirements which must be fulfilled before social activities can be harmoniously carried on; and these intuitions receive their most abstract expression in the assertion that the liberty of each is limited only by the like liberties of all.

Hence we get a double deductive origin for this fundamental principle. It is primarily deducible from the conditions precedent to complete life in the associated state; and it is secondarily deducible from those forms of consciousness created by the molding of human nature into conformity with these conditions.

328. The conclusions thus reached by deduction agree with the conclusions which induction has led us to. Accumulated experiences have prompted men to establish laws harmonizing with the various corollaries which follow from the principle of equal freedom.

Though disregarded during war, life during peace has acquired sacredness; and all interferences with physical integrity, however trivial, have come to be regarded as offenses. The slavery which in early stages almost everywhere existed, has, with the advance of civilization, been gradually mitigated; and, in the most advanced societies, restraints on motion and locomotion have disappeared. Men's equal claims to unimpeded use of light and air, originally ignored, are now legally enforced; and, though during great predominance of militant activity the ownership of land by the community lapsed into ownership by chiefs and kings, yet now, with the development of industrialism, the truth that the private ownership of land is subject to the supreme ownership of the community, and that therefore each citizen has a latent claim to participate in the use of the earth, has come to be recognized. The right of property, invaded with small scruple in early times, when the rights to life and liberty were little regarded, has been better and better maintained as societies have advanced; and while law has with increasing efficiency maintained the right to material property, it has more and more in modern times recognized and maintained the rights to incorporeal property: patent laws, copyright laws, libel laws, have been progressively made more effectual.

Thus while, in uncivilized societies and in early stages of civilized societies, the individual is left to defend his own life, liberty, and property as best he may, in later stages the community, through its government, more and more undertakes to defend them for him. Consequently, unless it be asserted that primitive disorder was better than is the comparative order now maintained, it must be admitted that experience of results justifies the assertion of these chief rights, and endorses the arguments by which they are deduced.

329. Of kindred nature and significance is an accompanying endorsement. While the community in its corporate capacity has gradually assumed the duty of guarding the rights of each man from aggressions by other men, it has gradually ceased from invading his rights itself as it once did.

Among uncivilized peoples, and among the civilized in early times, the right of bequest has been either denied (here by custom and there by law) or else greatly restricted; but with the growth of industrialism and its appropriate social forms, restrictions on the right of bequest have diminished, and in the most industrially organized nations have almost disappeared. In rude societies the ruler habitually interferes with the right of free exchange—monopolizing, restraining, interdicting; but in advanced societies internal exchanges are much less interfered with, and in our own society very little interference even with external exchanges remains. During many centuries throughout Europe, the state superintended industry, and men were told what processes they must adopt and what things they must produce; but now, save by regulations for the protection of employees, their rights to manufacture what they please and how they please are uninterfered with. Originally, creeds and observances were settled by authority; but the dictations have slowly diminished, and at present, in the most advanced societies, every one may believe or not believe, worship or not worship, as he likes. And so, too, is it with the rights of free speech and publication: originally denied and the assumption of them punished, they have gradually acquired legal recognition.

Simultaneously, governments have also ceased to interfere with other classes of private actions. Once upon a time they prescribed kinds and qualities of food and numbers of meals. To those below specified ranks they forbade certain colors for dresses, the wearing of furs, the use of embroideries and of lace; while the weapons they might wear or use were named. Those who might, and those who might not, have silver plate were specified; as also those who might wear long hair. Nor were amusements left uncontrolled. Games of sundry kinds were in some cases prohibited, and in other cases exercises were prescribed. But in modern times these interferences with individual freedom have ceased: men's rights to choose their own usages have come to be tacitly admitted.

Here again, then, unless it be maintained that sumptuary laws and the like should be reenacted, and that freedom of bequest, freedom of exchange, freedom of industry, freedom of belief, and freedom of speech, might with advantage be suppressed; it must be admitted that the inferences drawn from the formula of justice have been progressively justified by the discovery that disregard of them is mischievous.

330. Yet another series of inductive verifications, not hitherto named, has to be set down—the verifications furnished by political economy.

This teaches that meddlings with commerce by prohibitions and bounties are detrimental; and the law of equal freedom excludes them as wrong. That speculators should be allowed to operate on the food markets as they see well is an inference drawn by political economy; and by the fundamental principle of equity they are justified in doing this. Penalties upon usury are proved by political economists to be injurious; and by the law of equal freedom they are negatived as involving infringements of rights. The reasonings of political economists show that machinery is beneficial to the people at large, instead of hurtful to them; and in union with their conclusions the law of equal freedom forbids attempts to restrict its use. While one of the settled conclusions of political economy is that wages and prices cannot be artificially regulated with advantage, it is also an obvious inference from the law of equal freedom that regulation of them is not morally permissible. On other questions, such as the hurtfulness of tamperings with banking, the futility of endeavors to benefit one occupation at the expense of others, political economy reaches conclusions which ethics independently deduces.

What do these various instances unite in showing? Briefly, that not only *harmony* of cooperation in the social state, but also *efficiency* of cooperation, is best achieved by conformity to the law of equal freedom.

331. Two deductive arguments and three inductive arguments thus converge to the same conclusion. By inference from the laws of life as carried on under social conditions, and by inference from the dicta of that moral consciousness generated by the continuous discipline of social life, we are led directly to recognize the law of equal freedom as the supreme moral law. And we are indirectly led to such recognition of it by generalizing the experiences of mankind as registered in progressive legislation; since by it we are shown that during civilization there has been a gradual increase in the governmental maintenance of the rights of individuals, and that simultaneously there has been a gradual decrease in the governmental trespasses on such rights. And then this agreement is reinforced by the proofs that what is theoretically equitable is economically expedient.

I am by no means certain that acceptance of this quintuply rooted truth will be rendered any the more likely by thus showing that the *a posteriori* supports of it furnished by history are joined with the *a priori* supports furnished by biology and psychology. If there are *a priori* thinkers who obstinately disregard experiences at variance with their judgments; there are also *a posteriori* thinkers who obstinately deny all value to intuitive beliefs. They have faith in the cognitions resulting from the accumulated experiences of the individual, but no faith in the cognitions resulting from the accumulated experiences of the race. Here, however, we avoid both kinds of bigotry. The agreement of deduction with induction yields the strongest proof; and where, as in this case, we have plurality of both deductions and inductions, there is reached as great a certainty as can be imagined.

CHAPTER 20

The Rights of Women

332.   When in certain preceding chapters the fundamental principle of justice was discussed, a relevant question which might have been raised, I decided to postpone, because I thought discussion of it would appropriately introduce the subject matter of this chapter.

"Why," it might have been asked, "should not men have rights proportionate to their faculties? Why should not the sphere of action of the superior individual be greater than that of the inferior individual? Surely, as a big man occupies more space than a little man, so too does he need larger supplies of the necessaries of life; and so, too, does he need greater scope for the use of his powers. Hence it is unreasonable that the activities of great and small, strong and weak, high and low, should be severally restrained within limits too narrow for these and too wide for those."

The first reply is that the metaphors which we are obliged to use are misleading if interpreted literally. Though, as above, and as in previous chapters, men's equal liberties are figured as spaces surrounding each, which mutually limit one another, yet they cannot be truly represented in so simple a manner. The inferior man, who claims as great a right to bodily integrity as the superior man, does not by doing this trespass on the bodily integrity of the superior man. If he asserts like freedom with him to move about and to work, he does not thereby prevent him from moving about and working. And if he retains as his own whatever his activities have gained for him, he in no degree prevents the superior man from retaining the produce of his activities, which, by implication, are greater in amount.

The second reply is that denying to inferior faculty a sphere of action equal to that which superior faculty has, is to add an artificial hardship to a natural hardship. To be born with a dwarfed or deformed body, or imperfect senses, or a feeble constitution, or a low intelligence, or ill-balanced emotions, is in itself a pitiable fate. Could we charge nature with injustice, we might fitly say it is unjust that some should have natural endowments so much lower than others have, and that they should thus be in large measure incapacitated for the battle of life. And if so, what shall we say to the proposal that, being already disadvantaged by having smaller powers, they should be further disadvantaged by having narrower spheres for the exercise of those powers? Sympathy might contrariwise urge that, by way of compensation for inherited disabilities, they should have extended opportunities. But, evidently, the least that can be done is to allow them as much freedom as others to make the best of themselves.

A third reply is that, were it equitable to make men's liberties proportionate to their abilities, it would be impracticable; since we have no means by which either the one or the other can be measured. In the great mass of cases there is no difficulty in carrying out the principle of equality. If (previous aggression being supposed absent) A kills B, or knocks him down, or locks him up, it is clear that the liberties of action assumed by the two are unlike; or if C, having bought goods of D, does not pay the price agreed upon, it is clear that the contract having been fulfilled on one side and not on the other, the degrees of freedom used are not the same. But if liberties are to be proportioned to abilities, then the implication is that the relative amounts of each faculty, bodily and mental, must be ascertained; and the further implication is that the several kinds of freedom needed must be meted out. Neither of these things can be done; and therefore, apart from other reasons, the regard for practicability would require us to treat men's freedoms as equal, irrespective of their endowments.

333. With change of terms these arguments are applicable to the relation between the rights of men and the rights of women. This is not the place for comparing in detail the capacities of men and women. It suffices for present purposes to recognize the unquestionable fact that some women are physically stronger than some men, and that some women have higher mental endowments than some men—higher, indeed, than the great majority of men. Hence it results, as above, that were liberties to be adjusted to abilities, the adjustment, even could we make it, would have to be made irrespective of sex.

The difficulty reappears under another form, if we set out with the proposition that just as, disregarding exceptions, the average physical powers of women are less than the average physical powers of men, so too are their average mental powers. For we could not conform our plans to this truth: it would be impossible to ascertain the ratio between the two averages; and it would be impossible rightly to proportion the spheres of activity to them.

But, as above argued, generosity prompting equalization would direct that were any difference to be made it ought to be that, by way of compensation, smaller faculties should have greater facilities. Generosity aside, however, justice demands the women, if they are not artificially advantaged must not, at any rate, be artificially disadvantaged.

Hence, if men and women are severally regarded as independent members of a society, each one of whom has to do the best for himself or herself, it results that no restraints can equitably be placed upon women in respect of the occupations, professions, or other careers which they may wish to adopt. They must have like freedom to prepare themselves, and like freedom to profit by such information and skill as they acquire.

But more involved questions arise when we take into account the relations of women to men in marriage, and the relations of women to men in the state.

334. Of those equal liberties with men which women should have before marriage, we must say that in equity they retain after marriage all those which are not necessarily interfered with by the marital relation—the rights to physical integrity, the rights to ownership of property earned and property given or bequeathed, the rights to free belief and free speech, &c. Their claims can properly be qualified only in so far as they are traversed by the understood or expressed terms of the contract voluntarily entered into; and as these terms vary in different places and times, the resulting qualifications must vary. Here, in default of definite measures, we must be content with approximations.

In respect of property, for instance, it may be reasonably held that where the husband is exclusively responsible for maintenance of the family, property which would otherwise belong to the wife may equitably be assigned to him—the use, at least, if not the possession; since, if not, it becomes possible for the wife to use her property or its proceeds for her personal benefit only, and refuse to contribute towards the expenses of the joint household. Only if she is equally responsible with him for family maintenance, does it seem right that she should have equally unqualified ownership of property. Yet, on the other hand, we cannot say that the responsibilities must be entirely reciprocal. For though, rights of ownership being supposed equal, it would at first sight appear that the one is as much bound as the other to maintain the two and their children; yet this is negatived by the existence on the one side of onerous functions which do not exist on the other, and which largely incapacitate for active life. Nothing more than a compromise, varying according to the circumstances, seems here possible. The discharge of domestic and maternal duties by the wife may ordinarily be held a fair equivalent for the earning of an income by the husband.

Respecting powers of control over one another's actions and over the household, the conclusions to be drawn are still more indefinite. The relative positions of the two as contributors of monies and services have to be taken into account, as well as their respective natures; and these factors in the problem are variable. When there arise conflicting wills of which both cannot be fulfilled, but one of which must issue in action, the law of equal freedom cannot, in each particular case, be conformed to; but can be conformed to only in the average of cases. Whether it should be conformed to in the average of cases must depend on circumstances. We may, however, say that since, speaking generally, man is more judicially minded than woman, the balance of authority should incline to the side of the husband; especially as he usually provides the means which make possible the fulfillment of the will of either or the wills of both. But in respect of this relation reasoning goes for little: the characters of those concerned determine the form it takes. The only effect which ethical considerations are likely to have is that of moderating the use of such supremacy as eventually arises.

The remaining question, equally involved or more involved, concerns the possession and management of children. Decisions about management have to be made daily; and decisions about possession must be made in all cases of separation. What are the relative claims of husband and wife in such cases? On the one hand, it may be said of the direct physical claims, otherwise equal, that that of the mother is rendered far greater by the continued nutrition before and after birth, than that of the father. On the other hand, it may be urged on the part of the father, that in the normal order the food by which the mother has been supported and the nutrition of the infant made possible, has been provided by his labor. Whether this counterclaim be or be not equivalent, it must be admitted that the claim of the mother cannot well be less than that of the father. Of the compromise respecting management which justice thus appears to dictate, we may perhaps reasonably say that the power of the mother may fitly predominate during the earlier part of a child's life, and that of the father during the later part. The maternal nature is better adjusted to the needs of infancy and early childhood than the paternal nature; while for fitting children, and especially boys, for the battle of life, the father, who has had most experience of it, may be considered the best guide. But it seems alike inequitable and inexpedient that the power of either should at any time be exercised to the exclusion of the power of the other. Of the respective claims to possession where separation takes place, some guidance is again furnished by consideration of children's welfare; an equal division, where it is possible, being so made that the younger remain with the mother and the elder go with the father. Evidently, however, nothing is here possible but compromise based on consideration of the special circumstances.

Concerning the claims of women, as domestically associated with men, I may add that here in England, and still more in America, the need for urging them is not pressing. In some cases, indeed, there is a converse need. But there are other civilized societies in which their claims are very inadequately recognized: instance Germany.*

335. As in other cases, let us look now at the stages through which usage and law have grown into conformity with ethics.

Save among the few primitive peoples who do not preach the virtues called Christian but merely practice them—save among those absolutely peaceful tribes here and there found who, while admirable in their general conduct, treat their women with equity as well as kindness, uncivilized tribes at large have no more conception of the rights of women than of the rights of brutes. Such regard for women's claims as enables mothers to survive and rear offspring, of course exists;

---

* With other reasons prompting this remark, is joined the remembrance of a conversation between two Germans residing in England, in which, with contemptuous laughter, they were describing how they had often seen, on a Sunday or other holiday, an English artisan relieving his wife by carrying the child they had with them. Their sneers produced in me a feeling of shame—but not for the artisan.

since tribes in which it is less than this disappear. But, frequently, the regard is not greater than is needful to prevent extinction.

When we read of a Fijian that he might kill and eat his wife if he pleased; of the Fuegians and wilder Australians that they sacrificed their old women for food; and of the many peoples among whom women are killed to accompany their dead husbands to the other world; we see that they are commonly denied even the first of all rights. The facts that in these low stages women, leading the lives of slaves, are also sold as slaves, and, when married, are either stolen or bought, prove that no liberties are recognized as belonging to them. And on remembering that where wives are habitually considered as property, the implication is that independent ownership of property by them can scarcely exist, we are shown, that this further fundamental right is at the outset but very vaguely recognized. Though the matter is in many cases complicated and qualified by the system of descent in the female line, it is certain that, speaking generally, in rude societies where among men aggression is restrained only by fear of vengeance, the claims of women are habitually disregarded.

To trace up in this place the rising status of women is out of the question. Passing over those ancient societies in which descent in the female line gave to women a relatively high position, as it did among the Egyptians, it will suffice to note that in societies which have arisen by aggregation of patriarchal groups, the rights of women, at first scarcely more recognized than among savages, have, during these two thousand years, gradually established themselves. Limiting our attention to the Aryans who overspread Europe, we see that save where, as indicated by Tacitus, women, by sharing in the dangers of war, gained a better position (a connection of facts which we find among various peoples), they were absolutely subordinated. The primitive Germans bought their wives; and husbands might sell and even kill them. In the early Teutonic society, as in the early Roman society, there was perpetual tutelage of women, and consequent incapacity for independent ownership of property. A like state of things existed here in the old English period. Brides were purchased: their wills counting for nothing in the bargains. Mitigations gradually came. Among the Romans the requirement that a bride should be transferred to the bridegroom by legal conveyance, ceased to be observed. The life and death power came to an end: though sometimes reappearing, as when the early Angevin ruler, Fulc the Black, burnt his wife. Generalizing the facts we see that as life became less exclusively militant, the subjection of women to men became less extreme. How that decline of the system of status and rise of the system of contract, which characterizes industrialism, ameliorated, in early days, the position of women, is curiously shown by the occurrence of their signatures in the documents of guilds, while yet their position outside of the guilds remained much as before. This connection has continued to be a general one. Both in England and in America, where the industrial type of organization is most developed, the legal status of women is higher than on the Continent, where militancy is more pronounced. Add to which that among ourselves, along with the modern growth of free institutions characterizing predominant industrialism, the positions of women have been with increasing rapidity approximated to those of men.

Here again, then, ethical deductions harmonize with historical inductions. As in preceding chapters we saw that each of those corollaries from the law of equal freedom which we call a right, has been better established as fast as a higher social life has been reached; so here, we see that the general body of such rights, originally denied entirely to women, has, in the course of this same progress, been acquired by them.

336. There has still to be considered from the ethical point of view, the political position of women as compared with the political position of men; but until the last of these has been dealt with, we cannot in a complete way deal with the first. When, presently, we enter on the consideration of what are commonly called "political rights," we shall find need for changing, in essential ways, the current conceptions of them;

and until this has been done the political rights of women cannot be adequately treated of. There is, however, one aspect of the matter which we may deal with now or less conveniently than hereafter.

Are the political rights of women the same as those of men? The assumption that they are the same is now widely made. Along with that identity of rights above set forth as arising from the human nature common to the two sexes, there is supposed to go an identity of rights in respect to the direction of public affairs. At first sight it seems that the two properly go together; but consideration shows that this is not so. Citizenship does not include only the giving of votes, joined now and again with the fulfillment of representative functions. It includes also certain serious responsibilities. But if so, there cannot be equality of citizenship unless along with the share of good there goes the share of evil. To call that equality of citizenship under which some have their powers *gratis,* while others pay for their powers by undertaking risks, is absurd. Now men, whatever political powers they may in any case possess, are at the same time severally liable to the loss of liberty, to the privation, and occasionally to the death, consequent on having to defend the country; and if women, along with the same political powers, have not the same liabilities, their position is not one of equality but one of supremacy.

Unless, therefore, women furnish contingents to the army and navy such as men furnish, it is manifest that, ethically considered, the question of the equal "political rights," so-called, of women, cannot be entertained until there is reached a state of permanent peace. Then only will it be possible (whether desirable or not) to make the political positions of men and women the same.

It should be added that of course this reason does not negative the claims of women to equal shares in local governments and administrations. If it is contended that these should be withheld, it must be for reasons of other kinds.

CHAPTER 21

The Rights of Children

337. The reader who remembers that at the outset we recognized a fundamental distinction between the ethics of the family and the ethics of the state, and saw that welfare of the species requires the maintenance of two antagonist principles in them respectively, will infer that the rights of children must have a nature quite different from that of the rights of adults. He will also infer that since children are gradually transformed into adults, there must be a continually changing relation between the two kinds of rights, and need for a varying compromise.

Preservation of the race implies both self-sustentation and sustentation of offspring. If, assuming preservation of the race to be a good end, we infer that it is right to achieve these two sustentations; and if, therefore, the conditions precedent, without which they cannot be achieved, become what we call rights; it results that children have rights (or rather, for distinction sake, let us say rightful claims) to those materials and aids needful for life and growth, which, by implication, it is the duty of parents to supply. Whereas during mature life, the rights are so many special forms of that general freedom of action which is requisite for the procuring of food, clothing, shelter, &c.; during immature life the rightful claims are to the food, clothing, shelter, &c., themselves, and not to those forms of freedom which make possible the obtainment of them. While yet its faculties are undeveloped the child cannot occupy various parts of the sphere of activity occupied by the adult. During this stage of inability, such needful benefits as are naturally to be gained only within these unusable regions of activity, must come to it gratis. And, deduced as its claims to them are from the same primary requirement (preservation of the species), they must be considered as equally valid with the claims which the adult derives from the law of equal freedom.

I use the foregoing verbal distinction between the rights of adults and the rightful claims of children, because, in the general consciousness, rights are to so large an extent associated with activities and the products of activities, that some confusion of thought arises if we ascribe them to infants and young children, who are incapable of carrying on such activities and obtaining such products.

338. Still regarding preservation of the species as the ultimate end, we must infer that while in large measure children's rightful claims are to the products of activities, rather than to the spheres in which those activities are carried on, children have, at the same time, rightful claims to such parts of those spheres of activity as they can advantageously use. For if the desideratum is preservation of the species, then, to achieve it, the members of each generation have not only to be supplied by parents with such food, clothing and shelter as are requisite, but have also to receive from them such aids and opportunities as, by enabling them to exercise their faculties, shall produce in them fitness for adult life. By leading their young ones to use their limbs and senses, even inferior creatures, however unconsciously, fulfill this requirement to some extent. And if for the comparatively simple lives of birds and quadrupeds such needful preparation has to be made, still more has it to be made for the complex lives of mankind, and still more does there follow the responsibility of providing for it and furthering it.

How far the lives of parents must, in the due discharge of these responsibilities, be subordinated to the lives of children, is a question to which no definite answer can be given. In multitudinous kinds of inferior creatures, each generation is completely sacrificed to the next: eggs having been laid the parents forthwith die. But among higher creatures, which have to give much aid to their offspring while they grow, or which rear successive broods of offspring, or both, this of course is not the case. Here the welfare of the species demands that the parents shall continue to live in full vigor, that they may adequately nurture their offspring during their periods of immaturity. This is of course especially the case with mankind; since the period over which aid has to be given to offspring is very long. Hence, in estimating the relative claims of child and parent, it is inferable that parental sacrifices must not be such as will incapacitate for the full performance of parental duties. Undue sacrifices are eventually to the disadvantage of the offspring, and, by implication, to the disadvantage of the species. To which add that, since the well-being and happiness of parents is itself an end which forms part of the general end, there is a further ethical reason why the self-subordination of parents must be kept within moderate limits.

339. From the rightful claims of children on parents, we pass now to the correlative duties of children to parents. As before we must be content with a compromise which changes gradually during the progress from infancy to maturity.

Though, as we have seen, the child has a rightful claim to food, clothing, shelter, and other aids to development, yet it has not a right to that self-direction which is the normal accompaniment of self-sustentation. There are two reasons for not admitting this right—the one that exercise of it would be mischievous to itself, and the other that it would imply an ignoring of the claim of parent on child which is the reciprocal of the claim of child on parent. The first is self-evident, and the second scarcely needs exposition. Though here there can be made no such measurement of relative claims as that which the law of equal freedom enables us to make between adults; yet, if we guide ourselves by that law as well as may be, it results that for sustentation and other aids received there should be given whatever equivalent is possible in the form of obedience and the rendering of small services.

Meanwhile, in view of the ultimate end—the welfare of the species—this reciprocal relation between mature and immature should be approximated to the relation between adults as fast as there are acquired the powers of self-sustentation and self-direction. To be fitted for independent or self-directed activities there must be practice in such activities; and to this end a gradually increased freedom. As a matter of equity, too, the same thing is implied. Where a child becomes in a considerable degree self-sustaining before the adult age is reached, there arises a just claim to a proportionate amount of freedom.

Of course, essentially at variance as are the ethics of the family and the ethics of the state, the transition from guidance by the one to guidance by the other, must ever continue to be full of perplexities. We can expect only that the compromise to be made in every case, while not forgetting the welfare of the race, shall balance fairly between the claims of the two who are immediately concerned: not sacrificing unduly either the one or the other.

340. Still more in the case of children than in the case of women, do we see that progress from the lower to the higher types of society is accompanied by increasing recognition of rightful claims. Alike in respect of life, liberty, and property, the change is traceable.

In every quarter of the globe and among all varieties of men, infanticide exists, or has existed, as a customary or legalized usage—carried sometimes to the extent of one-half of those born. Especially where, the means of subsistence being small, much increase of the tribe is disastrous, the sacrifices of the newly born are frequent: the females being those oftenest killed because they do not promise to be of value in war. The practices of the Greeks, as well as those of the early Romans, among whom a father might kill his child at will, show that regard for the rights of the immature was no greater in law, though it may have been greater in usage. Of the early Teutons and Celts the like may be said: their habit of exposing infants, and in that way indirectly killing them, continued long after denunciation of it by the Christian church. Of course, with disregard for the lives of the young has everywhere gone disregard for their liberties. The practice of selling them, either for adoption or as slaves, has prevailed widely. Not only among the Fuegians, the people of New Guinea, the New Zealanders, the Dyaks, the Malagasy, and many other uncivilized peoples, is there barter of children, but children were similarly dealt with by the forefathers of the civilized. Hebrew custom allowed sale of them, and seizure for debt. The Romans continued to sell them down to the time of the emperors, and after the establishment of Christianity. By the Celts of Gaul the like traffic was carried on until edicts of the Roman emperors suppressed it; and the Germans persisted in it till the reign of Charlemagne. Of course, if the liberties of the young were disregarded in this extreme way, they were disregarded in minor ways. No matter what age a Roman had attained, he could not marry without his father's consent. Of course, too, along with nonrecognition of the rights of life and liberty went nonrecognition of the right of property. If a child could not possess himself, he clearly could not possess anything else. Hence the fact that by legal devices only did the son among the Romans acquire independent ownership of certain kinds of property, such as spoil taken in war and certain salaries for civil services.

Through what stages there has been eventually reached that large admission of children's rightful claims now seen in civilized societies, cannot here be described. Successive changes have gradually established for the young large liberties—liberties which are, indeed, in some cases, as in the United States, greater than is either just or politic. That which it concerns us here chiefly to note is that recognition of the rights of children has progressed fastest and farthest where the industrial type has most outgrown the militant type. In France, down to the time of the revolution, children continued to be treated as slaves. Sons who, even when adults, offended their fathers, could be, and sometimes were, put in prison by them; and girls were thrust into convents against their wills. Only after the revolution were the rights of sons "at last proclaimed," and "individual liberty was no longer at the mercy of *lettres de cachet* obtained by unjust or cruel fathers." But though among ourselves in past centuries the treatment of children was harsh, a father had not the power of imprisoning his son simply on his own motion. Though, up to recent generations, parental interdicts on the marriages of children, even when of age, were to a large extent voluntarily recognized, they were not legally enforced. And while at the present time, on the Continent, parental restraints on marriage to a great extent prevail, in England marriage contrary to parental wishes, quite practicable, does not even excite much reprobation: oftentimes, indeed, no probation.

Thus an extreme contrast exists between those early states in which a child, like a brute, could be killed with impunity, and modern states in which infanticide is classed as murder and artificial abortion as a crime, in which harsh treatment or inadequate sustentation by a parent is punishable, and in which, under trust, a child is capable of valid ownership.

341. Yet once more, then, we meet with congruity between theory and practice—between ethical injunctions and political ameliorations—between deductions from fundamental principles and inductions from experience.

When we keep simultaneously in view the ethics of the family and the ethics of the state, and the necessity for a changing compromise between the two during the progress of children from infancy to maturity—when we pay regard at the same time to the welfare of the individual and the preservation of the race, we are led to approximately definite conclusions respecting the rightful claims of children. These conclusions, reached *a priori*, we find verified *a posteriori* by the facts of history; which show us that along with progress from lower to higher types of society there has gone increasing conformity of laws and usages to moral requirements.

CHAPTER 22

Political Rights—So-Called

342. $\mathbf{E}$very day yields illustrations of the way in which men think only of the proximate and ignore the remote. The power of a locomotive is currently ascribed to steam. There is no adequate consciousness of the fact that the steam is simply an intermediator and not an initiator—that the initiator is the heat of the fire. It is not perceived that the steam engine is in truth a heat engine, differing from other heat engines (such as those in which gas is employed) only in the instrumentality employed to transform molecular motion into molar motion.

This limitation of consciousness to direct relations and ignoring of indirect relations, habitually vitiates thinking about social affairs. The primary effect produced by one who builds a house, or makes a road, or drains a field, is that he sets men to work; and the work, more prominent in thought than the sustenance obtained by it, comes to be regarded as itself a benefit. The imagined good is not increase in the stock of commodities or appliances which subserve human wants, but the expenditure of the labor which produces them. Hence various fallacies—hence the comment on destruction by fire that it is good for trade; hence the delusion that machinery is injurious to the people. If instead of the proximate thing, labor, there were contemplated the ultimate thing, produce, such errors would be avoided. Similarly is it with currency fallacies. Coins, which may be exchanged for all kinds of desired things, come themselves to be connected in men's minds with the idea of value, rather than the things they will purchase; which, as satisfying desires, are the truly valuable things. And then promises to pay, serving in place of coins, intrinsically valueless though they are, are, by daily experience of their purchasing power, so associated with the idea of value that abundance of them becomes identified in thought with wealth; and there results the belief that it only needs a profusion of banknotes to insure national prosperity: errors which would be avoided were the reasoning carried on in terms of commodities, instead of being carried on in terms of these symbols. This usurpation of consciousness by the proximate and expulsion from it of the remote—this forgetting of the ends and erecting the means into ends, is again shown us in education. The time was when knowledge anciently acquired having ceased to be current, the learning of Latin and Greek, in which that knowledge was recorded, became indispensable as a means to acquirement of it; and it was then regarded as a means. But now, long after this ancient knowledge has been rendered accessible in our language, and now, when a vastly larger mass of knowledge has been accumulated, this learning of Latin and Greek is persisted in; and, moreover, has come to be practically regarded as the end, to the exclusion of the end as originally conceived. Young men who are tolerably familiar with these ancient languages, are supposed to be educated; though they may have acquired but little of what knowledge there is embodied in them and next to nothing of the immensely greater amount of knowledge and immensely more valuable knowledge which centuries of research have established.

343. With what view is here made this general remark, thus variously illustrated? With the view of preparing the way for a further illustration which now concerns us. Current political

thought is profoundly vitiated by this mistaking of means for ends, and by this pursuit of the means to the neglect of the ends. Hence, among others, the illusions which prevail concerning "political rights."

There are no further rights, truly so-called, than such as have been set forth. If, as we have seen, rights are but so many separate parts of a man's general freedom to pursue the objects of life, with such limitations only as result from the presence of other men who have similarly to pursue such objects, then, if a man's freedom is not in any way further restricted, he possesses all his rights. If the integrity of his body is in no way or degree interfered with; if there is no impediment to his motion and locomotion; if his ownership of all that he has earned or otherwise acquired is fully respected; if he may give or bequeath as he pleases, occupy himself in what way he likes, make a contract or exchange with whomsoever he wills, hold any opinions and express them in speech or print, &c., &c., nothing remains for him to demand under the name of rights, as properly understood. Any other claims he may have must be of a different kind—cannot be classed as rights. Many times and in various ways we have seen that rights, truly so called, originate from the laws of life as carried on in the associated state. The social arrangements may be such as fully recognize them, or such as ignore them in greater or smaller degrees. The social arrangements cannot create them, but can simply conform to them or not conform to them. Such parts of the social arrangements as make up what we call government, are instrumental to the maintenance of rights, here in great measure and there in small measure; but in whatever measure, they are simply instrumental, and whatever they have in them which may be called right, must be so called only in virtue of their efficiency in maintaining rights.

But because of this tendency to occupation of the mind by the means and proportionate exclusion of the ends, it results that those governmental arrangements which conduce to maintenance of rights come to be regarded as themselves rights—nay, come to be thought of as occupying a foremost place in this category. Those shares of political power which in the more advanced nations citizens have come to possess, and which experience has shown to be good guarantees for the maintenance of life, liberty, and property, are spoken of as though the claims to them were of the same nature as the claims to life, liberty, and property themselves. Yet there is no kinship between the two. The giving of a vote, considered in itself, in no way furthers the voter's life, as does the exercise of those various liberties we properly call rights. All we can say is that the possession of the franchise by each citizen gives the citizens in general powers of checking trespasses upon their rights: powers which they may or may not use to good purpose.

The confusion between means and ends has in this case been almost inevitable. Contrasts between the states of different nations, and between the states of the same nation at different periods, have strongly impressed men with the general truth that if governmental power is in the hands of one, or in the hands of a few, it will be used to advantage the one or the few; and that the many will be correspondingly disadvantaged. That is to say, those who have not the power will be subject to greater restraints and burdens than those who have the power—will be defrauded of that liberty of each, limited only by the like liberties of all, which equity demands—will have their rights more or less seriously infringed. And as experience has shown that a wider distribution of political power is followed by decrease of these trespasses, maintenance of a popular form of government has come to be identified with the maintenance of rights, and the power of giving a vote, being instrumental to maintenance of rights, has come to be regarded as itself a right—nay, often usurps in the general apprehension the place of the rights properly so-called.

How true this is we shall learn on observing that where so-called political rights are possessed by all, rights properly so-called are often unscrupulously trampled upon. In France bureaucratic despotism under the Republic, is as great as it was under the Empire. Exactions and compulsions are no less numerous and peremptory; and, as was declared by English trade-union delegates to a congress in Paris, the invasion of citizens' liberties in France goes to an extent which "is a disgrace to, and an anomaly in, a Republican nation." Similarly in the United States. Universal suffrage does not prevent the corruptions of municipal governments, which impose heavy local taxes and do very inefficient work; does not prevent the growth of general and local organizations by which each individual is compelled to surrender his powers to wire-pullers and bosses; does not prevent citizens from being coerced in their private lives by dictating what they shall not drink; does not prevent an enormous majority of consumers from being heavily taxed by a protective tariff for the benefit of a small minority of manufacturers and artisans; nay, does not even effectually preserve men from violent deaths, but, in sundry states, allows of frequent murders, checked only by law officers who are themselves liable to be shot in the performance of their duties. Nor, indeed, are the results altogether different here. Far from having effected better maintenance of men's rights properly so-called, the recent extensions of the franchise have been followed by increased trespasses on them—more numerous orders to do this and not to do that, and greater abstractions from their purses.

Thus both at home and abroad the disproof is clear. From the extreme case in which men use their so-called political rights to surrender their power of preserving their rights properly so called, as by the plebiscite which elected Napoleon III, to the cases in which men let themselves be coerced into sending their children to receive lessons in grammar and gossip about kings, often at the cost of underfeeding and weak bodies, we find none of the supposed identity. Though the so-called political rights may be used for the maintenance of liberties, they may fail to be so used, and may even be used for the establishment of tyrannies.

344. Beyond that confusion of means with ends, which as we here see is a cause of this current misapprehension, there is

a further cause. The conception of a right is composite, and there is a liability to mistake the presence of one of its factors for the presence of both.

As repeatedly shown, the positive element in the conception is liberty; while the negative element is the limitation implied by other's equal liberties. But the two rarely coexist in due proportion, and in some cases do not coexist at all. There may be liberty exercised without any restraint; resulting in perpetual aggressions and universal warfare. Conversely, there may be an equality in restraints which are carried so far as practically to destroy liberty. Citizens may be all equally coerced to the extent of enslaving them, by some power which they have set up—may, in pursuance of philanthropic or other ends, be severally deprived by it of large parts of that freedom which remains to each after duly regarding the liberties of others. Now the confusion of thought above pointed out, which leads to this classing of so-called political rights with rights properly so-called, arises in part from thinking of the secondary trait, equality, while not thinking of the primary trait, liberty. The growth of the one has so generally been associated with the growth of the other, that the two have come to be thought of as necessary concomitants, and it is assumed that if the equality is obtained the liberty is ensured.

But, as above shown, this is by no means the case. Men may use their equal freedom to put themselves in bondage; failing as they do to understand that the demand for equality taken by itself is fulfilled if the equality is in degrees of oppression borne and amounts of pain suffered. They overlook the truth that the acquirement of so-called political rights is by no means equivalent to the acquirement of rights properly so-called. The one is but an instrumentality for the obtainment and maintenance of the other; and it may or may not be used to achieve those ends. The essential question is—How are rights, properly so-called, to be preserved—defended against aggressors, foreign and domestic? This or that system of government is but a system of appliances. Government by representation is one of these systems of appliances; and the choosing of representatives by the votes of all citizens is one of various ways in which a representative government may be formed. Hence voting being simply a method of creating an appliance for the preservation of rights, the question is whether universal possession of votes conduces to creation of the best appliance for preservation of rights. We have seen above that it does not effectually secure this end; and we shall hereafter see that under existing conditions it is not likely to secure it.

But further discussion of this matter must be postponed. We must first deal with a more general topic—the nature of the state.

CHAPTER 23

The Nature of the State

345. The study of evolution at large makes familiar the truth that the nature of a thing is far from being fixed. Without change of identity, it may at one time have one nature and at a subsequent time quite a different nature. The contrast between a nebulous spheroid and the solid planet into which it eventually concentrates, is scarcely greater than the contrasts which everywhere present themselves.

Throughout the organic world this change of nature is practically universal. Here is a *Polyp* which, after a period of sedentary life, splits up into segments which severally detach themselves as free-swimming *Medusæ*. There is a small larva of Annulose type which, moving about actively in the water for a time, fixes itself on a fish, loses its motor organs, and, feeding parasitically, grows into little more than stomach and egg bags; and there is another which ends the wanderings of its early life by settling down on a rock and, developing into what is popularly known as an acorn shell, gets its livelihood by sweeping into its gullet minute creatures from the surrounding water. Now the case is that of a wormlike form which, living and feeding for a long time in the water, finally, after a period of rest, bursts its pupa shell and flies away as a gnat; and again it is that of the maggot and flesh fly, or grub and moth, which everyday experience makes so familiar. Strangest and most extreme of all, however, are those metamorphoses presented by some of the low aquatic *Algæ* which, moving about actively for a brief period and displaying the characters of animals, presently fix themselves, sprout out, and become plants.

Contemplation of such facts, abundant beyond enumeration and wonderfully various, warns us against the error likely to arise everywhere from the tacit assumption that the nature of a thing has been, is, and always will be, the same. We shall be led by it, contrariwise, to expect change of nature—very possibly fundamental change.

346. It is tacitly assumed by nearly all that there is but one right conception of the state; whereas if, recognizing the truth that societies evolve, we learn the lessons which evolution at large teaches, we shall infer that probably the state has, in different places and times, essentially different natures. The agreement between inference and fact will soon become manifest.

Not to dwell on the earliest types, mostly characterized by descent in the female line, we may consider first the kind of group intermediate in character between the family and the society—the patriarchal group. This, as illustrated in the nomadic horde, forms a society in which the relationships of the individuals to one another and to their common head, as well as to the common property, give to the structure and functions of the incorporated whole a nature quite unlike the natures of bodies politic such as we now know. Even when such a group develops into a village community, which, as shown in India, may have "a complete staff of functionaries, for internal government," the generality (though not universality) of relationships among the associated persons gives to it a corporate nature markedly different from that of a society in which ties of blood have ceased to be dominant factors.

When, ascending to a higher stage of composition, we look at communities like those of Greece, in which many clusters of relations are united, so that members of various families, *gentes* and *phratries*, are interfused without losing their identities, and in which the respective clusters have corporate interests independent of, and often antagonistic to, one another; it is undeniable that the nature of the community as a whole differs greatly from that of a modern community, in which complete amalgamation of component clusters has destroyed the primitive lines of division; and in which, at the same time, individuals, and not family clusters, have become the political units.

Once more, on remembering the contrast between the system of status and the system of contract, we cannot fail to see an essential unlikeness of nature between the two kinds of body politic formed. In sundry ancient societies "the religious and political sanction, sometimes combined and sometimes separate, determined for every one his mode of life, his creed, his duties, and his place in society, without leaving any scope for the will or reason of the individual himself." But among ourselves neither religious nor political sanction has any such power; nor has any individual his position or his career in life prescribed for him.

In presence of these facts we cannot rationally assume unity of nature in all bodies politic. So far from supposing that the general conception of the state framed by Aristotle, and derived from societies known to him, holds now and serves for present guidance, we may conclude that, in all likelihood, it is inapplicable now and would misguide us if accepted.

347. Still more shall we be impressed with this truth if, instead of contrasting societies in their natures, we contrast them in their actions. Let us observe the several kinds of life they carry on.

As evolution implies gradual transition, it follows that extremely unlike as incorporated bodies of men may become, sharp divisions are impracticable. But bearing in mind this qualification, we may say that there are three distinct purposes for which men, originally dispersed as wandering families, may associate themselves more closely. The desire for companionship is one prompter: though not universal, sociality is a general trait of human beings which leads to aggregation. A second prompter is the need for combined action against enemies, animal or human, or both—cooperation, now to resist external aggression and now to carry on external aggression. The third end to be achieved is that of facilitating sustentation by mutual aid—cooperation for the better satisfying of bodily wants and eventually of mental wants. In most cases all three ends are subserved. Not only, however, are they theoretically distinguishable, but each one of them is separately exemplified.

Of social groups which satisfy the desire for companionship only, those formed by the Esquimaux may be named. The men composing one of them are severally independent. Having no need to combine for external offense or defense, they need no leaders in war and have no political rule: the only control exercised over each being the display of opinion by his fellows. Nor is there any division of labor. Industrial cooperation is limited to that between man and wife in each family. The society has no further incorporation than that which results from the juxtaposition of its parts: there is no mutual dependence.

The second class is multitudinous. Instances of its pure form are furnished by hunting tribes at large, the activities of which alternate between chasing animals and going to war with one another; and instances are furnished by piratical tribes and tribes which subsist by raids on their neighbors, like the Masai. In such communities division of labor, if present at all, is but rudimentary. Cooperation is for carrying on external defense and offense, and is to scarcely any extent for carrying on internal sustentation. Though when, by conquest, there are formed larger societies, some industrial cooperation begins, and increases as the societies increase, yet this, carried on by slaves and serfs, superintended by their owners, suffices in but small measure to qualify the essential character. This character is that of a body adapted for carrying on joint

action against other such bodies. The lives of the units are
subordinated to the extent needful for preserving (and in
some cases extending) the life of the whole. Tribes and nations
in which such subordination is not maintained must, other
things equal, disappear before tribes and nations in which it is
maintained; and hence such subordination must, by survival
of the fittest, become an established trait. Along with the
unquestioned assumption appropriate to this type, that war is
the business of life, there goes the belief that each individual is
a vassal of the community—that, as the Greeks held, the
citizen does not belong to himself, or to his family, but to his
city. And naturally, along with this merging of the individual's
claims in the claims of the aggregate, there goes such coercion
of him by the aggregate as makes him fit for its purposes. He is
subject to such teaching and discipline and control as are
deemed requisite for making him a good warrior or good
servant of the state.

To exemplify societies of the third class in a satisfactory way,
is impracticable; because fully developed forms of them do
not yet exist. Such few perfectly peaceful tribes as are found in
some Papuan islands, or occupying parts of India so malari-
ous that the warlike races around cannot live in them, are
prevented by their unfit environments from developing into
large industrial societies. The Bodo, the Dhimál, the Kocch
and other aboriginal peoples who, living by agriculture, cluster in villages of from ten to forty houses, and shift to new
tracts when they exhaust the old, show us, beyond the division of labor between the sexes, no further cooperation than
rendering mutual assistance in building their houses and
clearing their plots. Speaking generally, it is only after conquest has consolidated small communities into larger ones,
that there arise opportunities for the growth of mutual dependence among men who have devoted themselves to
different industries. Hence throughout long periods the industrial organization, merely subservient to the militant
organization, has had its essential nature disguised. Now,
however, it has become manifest that the most developed

modern nations are organized on a principle fundamentally unlike that on which the great mass of past nations have been organized. If, ignoring recent retrograde changes throughout Europe, we compare societies of ancient times and of the middle ages, with societies of our own times, and especially with those of England and America, we see fundamental differences. In the one case, speaking broadly, all free men are warriors and industry is left to slaves and serfs; in the other case but few free men are warriors, while the vast mass of them are occupied in production and distribution. In the one case the numerous warriors become such under compulsion; while in the other case the relatively few warriors become such under agreement. Evidently, then, the essential contrast is that in the one case the aggregate exercises great coercion over its units; while in the other case it exercises coercion which is small and tends to become less as militancy declines.

What is the meaning of this contrast reduced to its lowest terms? In either case the end to be achieved by the society in its corporate capacity, that is, by the state, is the welfare of its units; for the society having as an aggregate no sentiency, its preservation is a desideratum only as subserving individual sentiencies. How does it subserve individual sentiencies? Primarily by preventing interferences with the carrying on of individual lives. In the first stage, death and injury of its members by external foes is that which the incorporated society has chiefly, though not wholly, to prevent; and it is ethically warranted in coercing its members to the extent required for this. In the last stage, death and injury of its members by internal trespasses is that which it has chiefly if not wholly to prevent; and the ethical warrant for coercion does not manifestly go beyond what is needful for preventing them.

348. This is not the place to consider whether with this last function any further function may be joined. Limited as our subject matter is to the nature of the state, it concerns us only to observe the radical difference between these two social

types. The truth to be emphasized is that a body politic which has to operate on other such bodies, and to that end must wield the combined forces of its component units, is fundamentally unlike a body politic which has to operate only on its component units. Whence it follows that political speculation which sets out with the assumption that the state has in all cases the same nature, must end in profoundly erroneous conclusions.

A further implication must be pointed out. During long past periods, as well as in our own day, and for an indefinite time to come, there have been, are, and will be, changes, progressive and retrograde, approximating societies now to one type and now to the other: these types must be both mixed and unsettled. Indefinite and variable beliefs respecting the nature of the state must therefore be expected to prevail.

CHAPTER 24

The Constitution of the State

349. **D**ifference of ends usually implies difference of means. It is unlikely that a structure best fitted for one purpose will be best fitted for another purpose.

If to preserve the lives of its units, and to maintain that freedom to pursue the objects of life which is ordinarily possessed by unconquered peoples, a society has to use its corporate action chiefly for dealing with environing societies; then its organization must be such as will bring into play the effectually combined forces of its units at specific times and places. It needs no proof that if its units are left to act without concert they will be forthwith subjugated; and it needs no proof that to produce concerted action, they must be under direction. Conformity to such direction must be insured by compulsion; the agency which compels must issue consistent orders; and to this end the orders must emanate from a single authority. Tracing up the genesis of the militant type (see *Principles of Sociology*, secs. 547–61) leads irresistibly to the conclusion that for efficient external action of a society against other societies, centralization is necessary; and that establishment of it becomes more decided the more habitual is such external action. Not only does the fighting body itself become subject to despotic rule, but also the community which supports it. The will of the aggregate, acting through the governing power it has evolved, overrides and almost suppresses the wills of its individual members. Such rights as they are allowed they hold only on sufferance.

Hence so long as militancy predominates, the constitution of the state must be one in which the ordinary citizen is subject either to an autocrat or to an oligarchy out of which an autocrat tends continually to arise. As we saw at the outset, such subjection, with its concomitant loss of freedom and contingent loss of life, has a quasi-ethical warrant when necessitated by defensive war. The partial suspension of rights is justifiable when the object is to prevent those complete obliterations and losses of them which result from death or subjugation. Ordinarily, however, the militant type of society is developed more by offensive wars than by defensive wars; and where this is the case, the accompanying constitution of the state has no ethical warrant. However desirable it may be that the superior races should conquer and replace the inferior races, and that hence during early stages aggressive wars subserve the interests of humanity; yet, as before said, the subserving of such interests after this manner must be classed with the subserving of life at large by the struggle for existence among inferior creatures—a species of action of which ethics takes no cognizance.

Here, that which we have to note is that when the surrounding conditions are such that a society is endangered bodily by other societies, its required coercive constitution is one which, far though it may be from the absolutely right, is yet relatively right—is the least wrong which circumstances allow.

350. When, ignoring intermediate forms, we pass from the militant type to the industrial type, considered as fully developed, we see that the required constitution of the state is quite different. To maintain the conditions under which life and its activities may be carried on, is in either case the end; but to maintain these conditions against external enemies, and to maintain them against internal enemies, are two

widely unlike functions calling for widely unlike appliances. Observe the contrasts.

In the one case the danger is directly that of the community as a whole and indirectly that of individuals; while in the other case it is directly that of individuals and indirectly that of the community as a whole. In the one case the danger is large, concentrated, and in its first incidence local; while in the other case the dangers are multitudinous, small, and diffused. In the one case all members of the community are simultaneously threatened with injury; while in the other case the injury threatened or experienced is now of one person, now of another; and the citizen at one time aggressed upon is at another time an aggressor. And while the vast evil to be dealt with in the one case is, when warded off, no longer to be feared for some time at least; the evils to be dealt with in the other case, though small, are unceasing in their occurrence. Evidently, then, having functions so unlike, the political appliances employed should be unlike.

For preventing murders, thefts, and frauds, there does not need an army; and an army, were it used, could not deal with transgressions which are scattered everywhere. The required administration must be diffused as are the wrongdoings to be prevented or punished; and its action must be continuous instead of being occasional. But in the absence of large combined forces required for military purposes, there does not need that coercive rule by which alone combined forces can be wielded. Contrariwise, there needs a rule adapted for maintaining the rights of each citizen against others, and which is also regardful of those rights in its own dealings with citizens.

What is the appropriate constitution of the state? At first sight it seems that since every citizen (supposing him not to be himself an aggressor) is interested in the preservation of life and property, the fulfillment of contracts, and the enforcement of all minor rights, the constitution of the state should be one in which each citizen has an equal share of power with his fellows. It appears undeniable that if, in pursuance of the law of equal freedom, men are to have equal rights secured to them, they ought to have equal powers in appointing the agency which secures such rights.

In the last chapter but one it was shown that this is not a legitimate corollary; and various illustrations made it clear that the approved means did not achieve the desired end. Here we have to observe why they are not likely to achieve them.

351. Of truths concerning human conduct none is more certain than that men will, on the average, be swayed by their interests, or rather by their apparent interests. Government is itself necessitated by the general tendency to do this; and every act of Parliament makes provisions to exclude its injurious effects. How universally operative and how universally recognized such tendency is, every will, every lease, every contract proves.

The working of this or that form of government is inevitably determined by this tendency. Of those who form parts of the political agency, and of those who directly or indirectly appoint them, it must be true, as of all others, that they will be swayed by their apparent interests. The laws of every country furnish proofs without end. And history having thus conclusively shown that those who have predominant power will use it to their own advantage, there has been drawn the inference that only by endowing all with power can the advantage of all be secured. But the fallacy is becoming obvious.

A generation ago, while agitations for the wider diffusion of political power were active, orators and journalists daily denounced the "class-legislation" of the aristocracy. But there was no recognition of the truth that if, instead of the class at that time paramount, another class were made paramount, there would result a new class legislation in place of the old. That it has resulted every day proves. If it is true that a generation ago landowners and capitalists so adjusted public arrangements as to ease themselves and to press unduly upon others, it is no less true that now artisans and laborers, through representatives who are obliged to do their bidding, are fast remolding our social system in ways which achieve their own gain through others' loss. Year after year more public agencies are established to give what seem gratis benefits, at the expense of those who pay taxes, local and general; and the mass of the people, receiving the benefits and relieved from the cost of maintaining the public agencies, advocate the multiplication of them.

It is not true, then, that the possession of political power by all ensures justice to all. Contrariwise, experience makes obvious that which should have been obvious without experience, that with a universal distribution of votes the larger class will inevitably profit at the expense of the smaller class. Those higher earnings which more efficient actions bring to the superior, will not be all allowed to remain with them, but part will be drafted off in some indirect way to eke out the lower earnings of the less diligent or the less capable; and in so far as this is done, the law of equal freedom must be broken. Evidently the constitution of the state appropriate to that industrial type of society in which equity is fully realized, must be one in which there is not a representation of individuals but a representation of interests. For the health of the social organism and the welfare of its members, a balance of functions is requisite; and this balance cannot be maintained by giving to each function a power proportionate to the number of functionaries. The relative importance of the different functions is not measured by the number of units occupied in discharging them; and hence the general welfare will not be achieved by giving to the various parts of the body politic, powers proportionate to their sizes.

352. Whether hereafter there will arise a form of society in which equal political powers may be given to individuals, without giving to classes powers which they will misuse, is an unanswerable question. It may be that the industrial type, perhaps by the development of cooperative organizations, which theoretically, though not at present practically, obliterate the distinction between employer and employed, may

produce social arrangements under which antagonistic class interests either will not exist, or will be so far mitigated as not seriously to complicate matters. And it may be that in times to come men's regard for others' interests will so far check undue pursuit of their own interests, that no appreciable class legislation will result from the equal distribution of political powers. But the truth we have to recognize is that with such humanity as now exists, and must for a long time exist, the possession of what are called equal political rights will not ensure the maintenance of equal rights properly so-called.

Moreover, that constitution of the state which relative ethics justifies must, for another reason, diverge widely from that justified by absolute ethics. The forms of government appropriate to existing civilized societies must be transitional forms. As implied throughout the argument, the constitution of a state devoted to militancy must be fundamentally unlike the constitution of a state devoted to industrialism; and during the stages of progress from the one to the other, mixed forms of constitution have to be passed through—variable forms which are adjusted now to the one set of requirements, now to the other, as contingencies determine. For, as I have shown elsewhere (*Principles of Sociology,* secs. 547–75), if we exclude those nonprogressive types of mankind which have evolved social organizations that are no longer changeable, and contemplate the more plastic types still evolving, individually and socially, we see that increase in either kind of social action begins soon to produce change of structure.

We must therefore conclude that there is a quasi-ethical warrant for these mixed constitutions of the state which are appropriate to these mixed requirements. To maintain the conditions under which individual life and its activities may be carried on, being the supreme end; and maintenance of these conditions being endangered, now by masses of external enemies and now by single internal enemies; it results that there is a quasi-ethical justification for such political constitution as is best adapted to meet both kinds of dangers at any particular time; and there must be tolerated such unfitness for the one end as is necessitated by fitness for the other.

353. The title of the chapter covers a further question, which must not be passed over—the use of political power by women. Already we have concluded that in militant societies, and partially militant societies, the possession of the franchise by women is not strictly equitable: they cannot justly have equal powers unless they have equal responsibilities. But here, supposing that with the cessation of militancy this obstacle should disappear, we have to ask whether, in that case, the giving of votes to women would be expedient. I say expedient, because, as we have seen, it is not a question of right in the direct and simple sense. The question is whether rights, properly so-called, are likely to be better maintained if women have votes than if they have not. There are some reasons for concluding that maintenance of them would be less satisfactory rather than more satisfactory.

The comparative impulsiveness of women is a trait which would make increase of their influence an injurious factor in legislation. Human beings at large, as at present constituted, are far too much swayed by special emotions, temporarily excited, and not held in check by the aggregate of other emotions; and women are carried away by the feelings of the moment still more than men are. This characteristic is at variance with that judicial mindedness which should guide the making of laws. Freedom from passions excited by temporary causes or particular objects, is an obvious prerequisite to good legislation. This prerequisite is at present but imperfectly fulfilled, and it would be more imperfectly fulfilled were the franchise extended to women.

This moral difference is accompanied by a kindred intellectual difference. Very few men, and still fewer women, form opinions in which the general and the abstract have a due place. The particular and the concrete are alone operative in their thoughts. Nine legislators out of ten, and ninety-nine voters out of a hundred, when discussing this or that mea-sure, think only of the immediate results to be achieved—do not think at all of the indirect results, or of the effect which the precedent will have, or of the influence on men's characters. Had women votes, this absorption of consciousness in the proximate and personal to the exclusion of the remote and impersonal, would be still greater; and the immense mischiefs at present produced would be augmented.

At the outset it was shown that there is a radical opposition between the ethics of the family and the ethics of the state, and that introduction of either into the sphere of the other is injurious—fatal, indeed, if extensive and continuous. Char-acter is that which eventually determines conduct: the intelli-gence joined with it simply serving as a minister, procuring satisfactions for those feelings which make up the character. At present, both men and women are led by their feelings to vitiate the ethics of the state by introducing the ethics of the family. But it is especially in the nature of women, as a con-comitant of their maternal functions, to yield benefits not in proportion to deserts but in proportion to the absence of deserts—to give most where capacity is least. The love of the helpless, which may serve as a general description of the parental instinct, stronger in women than in men, and sway-ing their conduct outside the family as well as inside more than it sways the conduct of men, must in a still greater degree than in men prompt public actions that are unduly regardful of the inferior as compared with the superior. The present tendency of both sexes is to contemplate citizens as having claims in proportion to their needs—their needs being habitu-ally proportionate to their demerits; and this tendency, stronger in women than in men, must, if it operates politically, cause a more general fostering of the worse at the expense of the better. Instead of that maintenance of rights which, as we have seen, is but a systematic enforcement of the principle that each shall receive the good and evil results of his own conduct, there would come greater and more numerous breaches of them than at present. Still more than now would the good which the superior have earned be forcibly taken away from them to help the inferior; and still more than now would evils which the inferior have brought upon themselves be shouldered on to the superior.

Another trait of nature by which women are distinguished, arises by adjustment, not to the maternal relation but to the marital relation. While their feelings have become molded into special fitness for dealing with offspring, they have also become adjusted to an appropriate choice of husbands—so far at least as conditions have allowed them to choose. Power, bodily or mental, or both, is, and ever has been, that masculine trait which most attracts women; and by doing so furthers multiplication to the stronger. Varieties in which this instinctive preference was least marked must, other things equal, have ever tended to disappear before other varieties. Hence in women a worship of power under all its forms; and hence a relative conservatism. Authority, no matter how embodied—politically, ecclesiastically, or socially—sways women still more than it sways men. Evidence of this is furnished by societies of all grades. Sanctified by the injunctions of ancestry, customs are adhered to by women more than by men, even where instinctive feelings might have been expected to produce an opposite effect; as instance the adhesion by the women among the Juangs to something less than Eve's dress after the men had taken to loincloths. Religious fanaticism, which is the expression of extreme subordination to a power conceived as supernatural, has always been carried further by women than by men. The difference was remarked among the Greeks; observers have noticed it in Japan; instances are supplied by the Hindoos; and it is at present manifest throughout Europe. This sentiment, then, which power and the trappings of power under all forms excite, must, if votes were given to women, strengthen all authorities, political and ecclesiastical. Possibly it may be thought that under present conditions a conservative influence of this kind would be beneficial; and did there not exist the trait above described, this might be so. But cooperating with the preference for generosity over justice, this power worship in women, if allowed fuller expression, would increase the ability of public agencies to override individual rights in the pursuit of what were thought beneficent ends.

Whether in time to come, when the existing political complications caused by our transitional state have disappeared, such evils would result, is another question. It is quite possible that the possession of votes by women would then be beneficial.

But the immediate enfranchisement of women is urged on the ground that without it they cannot obtain legal recognition of their equitable claims. Experience does not countenance this plea. During the last thirty years various disabilities of women have been removed with but little resistance from men. Comparing the behavior of men to men with the behavior of men to women, it is manifest that in modern times the sentiment of justice has been more operative in determining the last than in determining the first. Ill-treated classes of men have had to struggle far longer before they obtained from the classes who ill treated them, the concessions they demanded, than women as a class have had to struggle before obtaining from men as a class, the various freedoms they asked. They have obtained these without political power; and there is no reason to doubt that such further injustice as they complain of—chiefly in respect of the custody of children— may be similarly removed without making the gigantic constitutional change which some of them seek.

That this probability amounts, indeed, to certainty, will be manifest if we look at the expectations in their simplest form. When it is openly contended that women must have the suffrage because otherwise they cannot get from men their just claims, it is practically contended that men will concede the suffrage knowing that with it they concede these claims, but will not concede the claims by themselves. A, the suffrage, involves the establishment of B, the claims; and the proposition is that though men will surrender A plus B, they will not surrender B by itself!

354. Under the head of the constitution of the state, something must be said concerning the distribution of state burdens as well as the distribution of state power. Clearly there is as much reason for insisting on equitable sharing in the costs of government as for equitable sharing in the direction of government.

In the abstract the question does not appear to present any great difficulty. The amounts individually paid should be proportionate to the benefits individually received. So far as these are alike, the burdens borne should be alike; and so far as they are unlike, the burdens borne should be unlike. Hence arises a distinction between the public expenditure for protection of persons and the public expenditure for protection of property. As life and personal safety are, speaking generally, held equally valuable by all men, the implication appears to be that such public expenditure as is entailed by care of these should fall equally on all. On the other hand, as the amounts of property possessed at the one extreme by the wage earner and at the other extreme by the millionaire differ immensely, the implication is that the amounts contributed to the costs of maintaining property rights should vary immensely—should be proportionate to the amount of property owned, and vary to some extent according to its kind. In respect to the costs of internal protection an approximately just distribution seems indicated by these considerations; but in respect of external protection a just distribution is more difficult to conceive. Invasion endangers both property and person. The citizen may be robbed, or he may be injured in body, or he may lose more or less freedom. A just distribution depends on the relative values put by each on these; and no expression of such values, either special or general, seems possible. Hence we must say that while militancy, or partial militancy, continues, nothing more than a rude approximation to a just incidence of public burdens can be made.

One conclusion, however, is clear. State burdens, however proportioned among citizens, should be borne by all. Every one who receives the benefits which government gives should pay some share of the costs of government, and should directly and not indirectly pay it.

This last requirement is all-important. The aim of the politician commonly is to raise public funds in such ways as shall leave the citizen partly or wholly unconscious of the deductions made from his income. Customs duties and excise duties are not unfrequently advocated for the reason that through them it is possible to draw from a people a larger revenue than could be drawn were the amount contributed by each demanded from him by the tax gatherer. But this system, being one which takes furtively sums which it would be difficult to get openly, achieves an end which should not be achieved. The resistance to taxation, thus evaded, is a wholesome resistance; and, if not evaded, would put a proper check on public expenditure. Had each citizen to pay in a visible and tangible form his proportion of taxes, the sum would be so large that all would insist on economy in the performance of necessary functions and would resist the assumption of unnecessary functions; whereas at present, offered as each citizen is certain benefits for which he is unconscious of paying, he is tempted to approve of extravagance; and is prompted to take the course, unknowingly if not knowingly dishonest, of obtaining benefits at other men's expense.

During the days when extensions of the franchise were in agitation, a maxim perpetually repeated was—"Taxation without representation is robbery." Experience has since made it clear that, on the other hand, representation without taxation entails robbery.

CHAPTER 25

The Duties of the State

355. Whether or not they accept the ethical principles set forth in the opening chapters of this part, most readers will agree with the practical applications of them made in subsequent chapters. Some, indeed, are so averse to deductive reasoning that they would gladly reject its results, even though they are verified by induction, could they do so. But the results in this case reached deductively, have one after another proved to be beliefs empirically established among civilized men at large, and, with increasing experience, have been more and more authoritatively formulated in law; so that rejection is scarcely practicable.

But here we are about to enter on topics concerning which there are divers opinions. To avoid raising prejudices against the conclusions reached, as being reached by a disapproved method, it will be best to proceed by a method which cannot be disapproved; and which, however insufficient taken by itself, all must admit to be good as far as it goes. Let us, then, commence inductively our inquiries concerning the duties of the state.

If the admired philosopher Hobbes, instead of deducing his theory of the state from a pure fiction, had prepared himself by ascertaining the facts as they are actually presented in

221

groups of primitive men, or men in the first stages of social life, he never would have propounded it. Had he known something more of savages as they really exist, he would not have ascribed to them those ideas of social order and its benefits, which are the products of developed social life; and he would have learned that subordination to a ruling power is at the outset not in the least prompted by the motive he assigns. Instead of proceeding *a priori* as he did, let us proceed *a posteriori*—let us contemplate the evidence.

356. The first fact is that where there neither is, nor has been, any war there is no government. Already it has been pointed out that among the Esquimaux, in the absence of intertribal conflicts, there are scarcely any of those conflicts between members of the tribe which Hobbes assumes must necessarily arise among ungoverned men. If, as occasionally happens, one Esquimo is ill used by another, his remedy is an appeal to public opinion through a satirical song. The Fuegians, who gather in tribes of from twenty to eighty, have no chiefs; "nor did they seem to require one for the peace of their society," says Weddell. Of the Veddahs, again, we read that the small clans have divisions of the forest which "are always honorably recognized"; and the head man of each, who is simply the most influential person, according to Tennant, "exercises no sort of authority beyond distributing at a particular season the honey captured by the various members of the clan."

The second fact is that when between tribes ordinarily peaceful there occur wars, leading warriors acquire predominant influence. In each case there arises some man distinguished from others by greater strength, courage, skill or sagacity; and who, consequently deferred to, becomes acknowledged leader. But at first, as shown us by the Tasmanians, the man who thus acquires predominance during war, loses it when peace is reestablished: there returns the state of equality and absence of government. As, however, the wars between tribes commonly become chronic, it usually happens that the man who acts as leader, now in one war and presently in another, gains permanent authority. The deference shown to him extends over the interval between the wars, as well as during the wars; and chieftainship is initiated. The Shoshones or Snakes of North America, which fall into three divisions, well illustrate these relationships of structure. The Mountain Snakes, scattered and wandering bands of men, who make no combined efforts to defend themselves against their hostile kindred, have no government. Among the War-are-aree-kas, or Fish-eaters, there is no trace of social organization, "except during salmon time"; when, resorting to the rivers in numbers, there arises temporarily "some person called a chief," whose advice is accepted rather than obeyed. And then the Shirry-dikas, who hunt buffaloes and are better armed, show us more pronounced chieftainship; though authority still depends on "the personal vigor of the chief" and is readily transferred to another. Among the Comanches, who are relatively warlike, chiefs have more power; though the office is not hereditary, but results from "superior cunning, knowledge, or success in war." And from these stages upwards we may trace the rise of definite chieftainship as a concomitant of chronic hostilities with other tribes.

The third fact is that where the enterprising leader in war subdues adjacent tribes, and, by successive conquests, forms a larger consolidated society, his supremacy becomes settled; and with increase of his power goes the imposing of his will in other than militant actions. When, by this process, nations are formed and chiefs grow into kings, governmental power, becoming absolute, becomes also coextensive with social life. Still it is to be observed that the king is above all things the leader in war. The records of the Egyptians and Assyrians, equally with the records of European nations, show that the ruler is primarily the head soldier.

And then, grouping several minor facts under the head of a fourth fact, we see that where, as in modern nations, the head of the state no longer commands his armies in battle, but deputes this function, he nevertheless is nominally a soldier—receives a military or naval education. Only in republics do there arise civil headships, and these are apt to lapse back into military ones. It needs only continued war to transform the government into its primitive type of a military dictatorship.

Thus induction puts beyond doubt the truth that government is initiated and developed by the defensive and offensive actions of a society against other societies. The primary function of the state, or of that agency in which the powers of the state are centralized, is the function of directing the combined actions of the incorporated individuals in war. The first duty of the ruling agency is national defense. What we may consider as measures to maintain intertribal justice, are more imperative, and come earlier, than measures to maintain justice among individuals.

357. While we are thus taught that the subordination of citizens to rulers has at first no such purpose as that which Hobbes fancied, we are also taught that for a long time the fulfillment of such purpose is not even attempted. Many simple societies exist permanently, and many complex societies have existed for long periods, without any measures being taken by the ruler to prevent aggressions of individuals on one another.

While the necessity for combined action against enemies of the tribe is obvious and peremptory, and prompts obedience to the leader, no obvious necessity exists for defending one member of the tribe against another: danger to tribal welfare is either not recognized or not thought great enough to call for interference. While there was no headship at all, and during times when headship existed only as long as war lasted, each member of the tribe maintained his own claims as well as he could: when injured, he did his best to injure the aggressor. This rude administration of justice, which we see among gregarious animals as well as among primitive hordes of men, having been a recognized custom before any political rule existed, long survived the establishment of political rule, as being a custom accepted from ancestry and sanctified by tradition. Hence in all early societies we find the *lex talionis* in force—now independently of the ruler, and now recognized by the ruler.

Beginning with the North American Indians we read of the Snakes, the Creeks, the Dacotahs, that private wrongs were avenged by the injured individuals or their families; that among the Comanches this system of retaliation was habitual, though councils sometimes interfered without success; and that among the Iroquois, with a comparatively well-developed government, the private righting of wrongs was permitted. So in South America, the Uaupes, the Patagonians, the Araucanians may be named as showing us degrees, more or less marked, of political subjection coexisting with primitive administration of justice by each man for himself, or by his family for him. In Africa, containing peoples in various stages of advance, we meet with various mixtures of systems. A Bechuanas king or chief makes little use of his power for punishment of any other crimes than those committed against himself or his servants. An injured man among the East Africans sometimes revenges himself and sometimes appeals to the chief. Some tribes of coast Negroes have judicial punishments, while in others murder is avenged by deceased's kindred; and there is a like variation in Abyssinia. Turning to Asiatics, we find that among the Arabs the prevalence of one or other of these modes of checking aggressions, depends on the state of the group as wandering or settled: where wandering, private retaliation and enforced restitution is the practice, but punishment by a ruler is usual in Arab towns. By the Bheels is shown a ratio between the chief's punitive action and that of the individual, which changes according to the chief's power; and by the Khonds, who pay little respect to authority, justice is enforced by private action. The custom of the Karens, too, is for each man to take the law into his own hands: the principle being that of equal damage.

That kindred states of things existed among the Aryan tribes which peopled Europe in early days, is a familiar fact.

Private vengeance and public punishment were mingled in various proportions: the one decreasing and the other increasing along with progress to a higher state. Says Kemble: "The right of feud . . . lies at the root of all Teutonic legislation . . . each freeman is at liberty to defend himself, his family and his friends; to avenge all wrongs done to them." Instead of being, as at first, his own judge respecting the extent of retaliation, the injured man presently came to have restraints put upon him by custom; and there grew up established rates of compensation for injuries, varying according to rank. When political authority gained strength, the first step was that of enforcing the customary fines, and, in default, permitting private rectification—"Let amends be made to the kindred, or let their war be borne." During this transitional stage, which is traceable among some of the German tribes when first described, part of the compensation went to the man or family injured, while part went to the ruler. Under feudalism the system of private rectification of wrongs slowly yielded to the public rectification only as the central government gained power. The right of private war between nobles continued among ourselves down to the 12th and 13th centuries, and in France even later. So deeply rooted was it that in some cases, feudal lords thought it a disgrace to maintain their rights in any other ways than by force of arms. With all which we must join the long survival of judicial duels and of private duels.

The facts have to be contemplated under two other aspects. Not only is the primary function of government that of combining the actions of the incorporated individuals for war, while its secondary function of defending its component members against one another is step by step established; but this secondary function arises by differentiation from the primary one. Even in the earliest stages the private rectification of wrongs is in part the business of the individual wronged and in part the business of his family or relatives. The progress which brings development of the family organization, at the

same time that it brings aggregation of clusters of families or
clans into a society, develops the doctrine of family responsibility. That is to say, the private wars between family groups
come to be of the same nature as the public wars between
societies; and the enforcement of private justice is akin to the
enforcement of intertribal justice. Hence arises the idea,
which seems to us so strange, that if, when a member of one
group has been murdered, a member of the group to which
the murderer belongs is killed, it is indifferent whether the
victim be the murderer or not. The group is injured to an
equivalent extent, and that is the essential requirement.

The other noticeable aspect of the facts is that this rude
enforcing of justice by private wars, is changed into public
administration of justice, not because of the ruler's solicitude
to maintain equitable relations, but much more because of his
solicitude to prevent that weakening of his society which
internal dissensions must produce. Be he primitive chief, or
be he captain of banditti, a leader must check fights among his
followers; and what is by these shown on a small scale was
shown on a larger scale when, in feudal times, kings forbade
private wars between nobles during the times when international wars were going on. Manifestly a king's desire to maintain a social order which conduces to fighting efficiency,
prompts the practice of arbitrating between antagonist followers; and manifestly appeals made to him by the injured,
recognizing as they do his authority, and responded to for this
reason, tend more and more to establish his judicial and
legislative powers.

Once established, this secondary function of the state goes
on developing; and becomes a function next in importance to
the function of protecting against external enemies. The truth
to be specially emphasized here, is that while other kinds of
governmental action diminish, this kind of governmental action increases. Militant activities may become gradually less,
and political agency may retire from various regulative actions
previously exercised over citizens. But with the progress of

civilization, the administration of justice continues to extend and to become more efficient.

358. And now, having reached these conclusions inductively, let us see whether corresponding conclusions cannot be reached deductively. Let us see whether from the natures of men as socially conditioned, it is not inferable that these two state duties are the essential ones.

At the outset it was shown that the prosperity of a species is achieved by conformity to two opposite principles, appropriate to the young and to the adult respectively: benefits being inversely proportioned to worth in the one case and directly proportioned to worth in the other. Confining our attention to the last of these principles, which now alone concerns us, it is clear that maintenance of those conditions under which each one's efforts bring their rewards is, in the case of a society, liable to be traversed by external foes and by internal foes. The implication is that for the prosperity of a species, or in this case of a society, these conditions must be maintained by a due exercise of force; and for the exercise of such force the corporate action of the society is demanded—imperatively in the one case and with something approaching to imperativeness in the other. To such exercise of force, citizens at large (excluding criminals) have good reasons to assent. Observe their motives.

Such contingent loss of life and partial loss of liberty as are entailed on soldiers, and such deductions from their earnings as other citizens have to contribute to support soldiers, are felt by each to be justified as instrumental to the supreme end of enabling him to carry on his activities and to retain the reward for them—sacrifice of a part to ensure the remainder. Hence he tacitly authorizes the required state coercion.

Though the need for corporate guardianship against internal foes is less urgently felt, yet from the pursuit of his ends by each there arises a resultant desire for such guardianship. As in every community the relatively strong are few, and the relatively weak are many, it happens that in the majority of cases purely private rectification of wrongs is impracticable. If beyond the aid of family and friends, often inadequate, there can be obtained the aid of some one more powerful, it is worth buying—at first by a bribe, and presently by tribute. Eventually, all find it answers best to pay for security rather than suffer aggressions.

Thus these primary and secondary duties of the state are implied by those fundamental needs which associated men experience. They severally desire to live, to carry on their activities, and reap the benefits of them. All have motives to maintain against external enemies the conditions under which these ends may be achieved, and all, save aggressors of one or other kind, have motives to maintain these conditions against internal enemies. Hence at once the duty of the state and the authority of the state.

359. If these duties devolve upon the state, then the state is under obligation to take such measures as are needful for efficiently discharging them.

That defensive appliances sufficient to meet imminent dangers must be provided, every one admits. Even where no attack by foreign foes seems likely, there should be maintained adequate forces to repel invasion; since total unpreparedness may invite attack. Though in this part of the world, and in our days, descents made without excuse by plundering hordes may not have to be guarded against; yet the readiness shown by peoples called civilized to hurl large armies upon one another with but small provocation, makes it manifest that even the most advanced nations cannot prudently trust their neighbors. What amount of military power is needful for safeguarding, of course depends on circumstances, and is a matter of judgment in each case.

But while the need for maintaining such an organization as is requisite for duly discharging the first duty of the state is fully recognized, the need for maintaining such an organization as is requisite for duly discharging its second duty is far from fully recognized. As we have seen above, the defense of citizens one against another, not at first a business of the government, has been undertaken by it but gradually; and even in the most civilized societies its discharge of this business is still but partial, and the propriety of full discharge of it is denied. I do not of course mean that the responsibility of the state for guarding citizens against offenders classed as criminal, is not admitted and fulfilled; but I mean that the state neither admits, nor is supposed by citizens to have, any responsibility for guarding them against offenders classed as civil. Though, if one who receives a rude push invokes the agents of the state, they will take up his case and punish the assailant; yet if he is defrauded of an estate they turn deaf ears to his complaint, and leave him either to bear the loss, or run the risk of further and perhaps greater loss in carrying on a suit and possibly appeals.

Not by lawyers only, but by most other people this condition of things is defended; and the proposition that it is the duty of the state to administer justice without cost, in civil as well as in criminal cases, is ridiculed: as, indeed, every more equitable arrangement is ridiculed before successful establishment of it proves its propriety. It is argued that did the state arbitrate between men gratis, the courts would be so choked with cases as to defeat the end by delay: to say nothing of the immense expense entailed on the country. But this objection proceeds upon the vicious assumption that while one thing is changed other things remain the same. It is supposed that if justice were certain and could be had without cost, the number of trespasses would be as great as now when it is uncertain and expensive! The truth is that the immense majority of civil offenses are consequent on the inefficient administration of justice—would never have been committed had the penalties been certain.

But when we come to contemplate it, it is a marvelous proposition, this which the objection implies, that multitudinous citizens should be left to bear their civil wrongs in silence or risk ruin in trying to get them rectified; and all because the state, to which they have paid great sums in taxes, cannot be at the trouble and expense of defending them! The public evil of discharging this function would be so great, that it is better for countless citizens to suffer the evils of impoverishment and many of them of bankruptcy! Meanwhile, through the officers of its local agents, the state is careful to see that their stink traps are in order!

360. One further duty of the state, indirectly included in the last but distinguishable from it, must be set down, and its consequences specified. I refer to its duty in respect of the inhabited territory.

For employments of the surface other than those already established, and tacitly authorized by the community through its government, there require state authorizations. As trustee for the nation the government has to decide whether a proposed undertaking—road, canal, railway, dock &c.—which will so change some tract as to make it permanently useless for ordinary purposes, promises to be of such public utility as to warrant the alienation; and has to fix the terms for its warrant: terms which, while they deal fairly with those who stake their capital in the enterprise, and while they protect the rights of the existing community, also keep in view the interests of future generations, who will hereafter be supreme owners of the territory. For the achievement of these several ends, the equitable arrangement would seem to be, not a permanent alienation of the required tract; nor an unscrupulous breaking of the contract by the state at will, as now; but an alienation for a specified period, with the understanding that the conditions may, at the termination of that period, be revised.

In discharge of its duties as trustee, the ruling body has to exercise a further control—allied but different. If not itself, then by its local deputies, it has to forbid or allow the breaking up of streets, roads, and other public spaces for the establishment or repair of water, gas, telegraph, and kindred appliances. Such supervisions are required for protecting each and all members of the community against the aggressions of particular members or groups of members.

That like considerations call for oversight by the state of rivers, lakes, or other inland waters, as also of the adjacent sea, is sufficiently clear. On the uses made of these and their contents, there may rightly be put such restraints as the interests of the supreme owner, the community, demand.

361. And now what are these duties of the state considered under their most general aspect? What has a society in its corporate capacity to do for its members in their individual capacities? The answer may be given in several ways.

The prosperity of a species is best subserved when among adults each experiences the good and evil results of his own nature and consequent conduct. In a gregarious species fulfillment of this need implies that the individuals shall not so interfere with one another as to prevent the receipt by each of the benefits which his actions naturally bring to him, or transfer to others the evils which his actions naturally bring. This, which is the ultimate law of species life as qualified by social conditions, it is the business of the social aggregate, or incorporated body of citizens, to maintain.

This essential requirement has to be maintained by all for each, because each cannot effectually maintain it for himself. He cannot by himself repel external invaders; and on the average, his resistance to internal invaders, if made by himself or with the aid of a few, is either inefficient, or dangerous, or costly, or wasteful of time, or all of these. To which add that universal self-defense implies chronic antagonisms, either preventing or greatly impeding cooperation and the facilitations to life which it brings. Hence, in distinguishing between things to be done by corporate action and things to be done by individual action, it is clear that, whether or not it does anything else, corporate action may rightly be used to prevent interferences with individual action beyond such as the social state itself necessitates.

Each citizen wants to live, and to live as fully as his surroundings permit. This being the desire of all, it results that all, exercising joint control, are interested in seeing that while each does not suffer from breach of the relation between acts and ends in his own person, he shall not break those relations in the persons of others. The incorporated mass of citizens has to maintain the conditions under which each may gain the fullest life compatible with the fullest lives of fellow citizens.

Whether the state has other duties is a question which remains now to be discussed. Between these essential functions and all other functions there is a division which, though it cannot in all cases be drawn with precision, is yet broadly marked. To maintain intact the conditions under which life may be carried on is a business fundamentally distinct from the business of interfering with the carrying on of the life itself, either by helping the individual or directing him, or restraining him. We will first inquire whether equity permits the state to undertake this further business; and we will then inquire whether considerations of policy coincide with considerations of equity.

CHAPTER 26

The Limits of State Duties

362. During those early stages in which the family and the state were not differentiated, there naturally arose the theory of paternal government. The members of the group were "held together by common obedience to their highest living ascendant, the father, grandfather, or great-grandfather." Ignoring those still earlier social groups of which Sir Henry Maine takes no account, we may accept his generalization that among Aryan and Semitic peoples, the despotic power of the father over his children, surviving more or less as his children became heads of families, and as again their children did the same, gave a general character to the control exercised over all members of the group. The idea of government thus arising, inevitably entered into the idea of government which became established as compound families grew into communities; and it survived when many of such small communities, not allied in blood or but remotely allied, became consolidated into larger societies.

The theory of paternal government originating in this way is a theory which tacitly asserts the propriety of unlimited government. The despotic control of the father extends to all acts of his children; and the patriarchal government growing out of it, naturally came to be exercised over the entire lives of those who were subject. The stage was one in which distinctions and limitations had not yet arisen; and while the group retained something like its original constitution, having in the main a common origin and holding in partial if not entire community the inhabited tract and its produce, the conception of government as unlimited in range was probably one best adapted to the requirements.

But this ancient social idea, like ancient religious ideas, survives, or continually reappears, under conditions utterly unlike those to which it was appropriate. The notion of paternal government is entertained in a vague sentimental way, without any attempt being made definitely to conceive its meaning; and consequently without any perception of the inapplicability of the notion to develop societies. For none of the traits of paternal government as it originally arose, exists now, or is possible. Observe the contrasts.

Fatherhood habitually implies ownership of the means by which children and dependents are supported; and something like such ownership continued under the patriarchal form of rule. But in developed nations not only is this trait absent, but the opposite trait is present. The governing agent does not now support those over whom it exercises authority, but those over whom it exercises authority support the governing agent. Under paternal rule, truly so called, the possessor of the power, being possessor of everything else, was benefactor to his children as well as controller of them; whereas a modern government, along with a power which is in chief measure given by those who are supposed to stand in the place of children, cannot be in such sense a benefactor, but has to receive from the children the means which enable it to do anything for them. Again, in simple and compound family groups there is an approach to identity of interests between rulers and ruled: the bonds of blood relationship go far to ensure a regulative action conducive to the general welfare. But in advanced societies there enter into the political relations no such emotions as those arising from family feeling and kinship, which serve to check the self-seeking of the ruling agent, be it king, oligarchy, or such democratic body as the United States show us. Once more, the supposed parallel fails in respect of knowledge and wisdom. With the primitive paternal power, and the patriarchal power derived from it, there generally went wider experience and deeper insight than were possessed by the descendants who were ruled. But in developed societies no such contrast exists between the mental superiority of those supposed to stand in the position of father, and the mental inferiority of those supposed to stand in the position of children. Contrariwise, among those figuratively spoken of as children, there exist many who are at once better informed and intellectually stronger than the ruling head, single or multiple, as the case may be. And where, the head being multiple, the so-called children have to choose from among themselves those who shall constitute it, they habitually ignore the best fitted: the result being that rule is exercised not so much by the collective wisdom as by the collective folly—the paternal and filial relation is in another way reversed.

Hence that theory of the functions of the state which is based on this assumed parallelism is utterly false. The only justification for the analogy between parent and child and government and people is the childishness of the people who entertain the analogy.

363. A conception of state duties which is connate with the last but gradually diverges from it, must next be noticed. I refer to the conception generated by experiences of those governmental actions needful for carrying on wars, which, up to recent times, have been its chief actions.

In social groups to types preceding the patriarchal, head-ship becomes established by frequent wars; and in the patriarchal group the head of the warriors is ordinarily head of the state. This identity, continuing through subsequent stages, determines the nature of government at large. That men may be good soldiers they must not only be subordinate, grade under grade, and must not only be drilled in warlike exercises, but must have their daily habits regulated in ways conducive to efficiency. More than this: the soldier-king, regarding the whole community as a body from which soldiers and supplies are to be drawn, extends his control over the entire lives of his subjects. And since nations in general have been, as many of them still are, predominantly militant, this idea of governmental power, with its concomitant idea of the duties of the state, has been almost universal.

In the most militant of Greek states, Sparta, preparation for war was the business of life, and the whole of life was regulated with a view to this preparation. Though in Athens no such strenuous efforts to achieve this end were made, yet there was a recognition of this end as the predominant one. Plato's ideal republic was one in which, by education, citizens were to be molded into fitness for social requirements, of which the chief was national defense; and this power of the incorporated community over its units was to go to the extent of regulating the procreation of them, both by selection of parents and by due adjustment of their ages. So, too, in Aristotle's *Politics*, it is urged that education should be taken out of the charge of parents, and that the different classes of citizens, differently educated, should be respectively adapted to public needs: authority being also assigned to the legislator to regulate marriage and the begetting of children. Thus the conception of governmental functions developed by militancy, and appropriate to a fighting body, becomes the conception of governmental functions at large.

Here, as before, we see that ideas, sentiments, and habits appropriate to early stages of development survive throughout later stages, to which they are no longer appropriate; and pervert the prevailing beliefs and actions. For by many the conception of state duties that was fit for Greek societies, is supposed to be fit for modern societies. Though the best social organization as conceived by Socrates and approved by Plato, was one in which the industrial classes were to be absolutely subject to the classes above them—though, in his *Politics*, Aristotle, regarding the family as normally consisting of freemen and slaves, taught that in the best regulated states no mechanic should be a citizen, and that all tillers of the ground should be serfs; yet it is believed that we may with advantage adopt the accompanying theory of state duties! One whose conceptions of right and wrong were shown in the belief that it is impossible for a man who lives the life of a mechanic or hired servant to practice virtue, is supposed to be one to whose conceptions of right and wrong in social affairs we may wisely defer! It is thought that the ideas appropriate to a society organized throughout on relations of *status*, are adapted to a society organized throughout on relations of contract! A political ethics belonging to a system of compulsory cooperation applies also to a system of voluntary cooperation!

364. There is indeed the excuse that to some extent among ourselves, and to a much larger extent among Continental peoples, the militant life, potential when not actual, still forms so considerable, and in many cases so great, a part of the social life as to render these traditional doctrines appropriate.

Compromise between old and new, which has perpetually to be made in practice, has to be made also in theory; for this must, on the average, conform itself to practice. It is therefore out of the question that there can be generally entertained the belief that governmental action should be subject to certain imperative restraints. The doctrine that there is a limited sphere within which only state control may rightly be exercised, is a doctrine natural to the peaceful and industrial type of society when fully developed; and is not natural either to the militant type or to types transitional between militancy and industrialism. Just relations between the community and its units cannot exist during times when the community and its units are jointly and severally committing injustices abroad. Men who hire themselves out to shoot other men to order, asking nothing about the equity of their cause, are not men by whom there can be established equitable social arrangements. While the nations of Europe are partitioning among themselves parts of the earth inhabited by inferior peoples, with cynical indifference to the claims of these peoples, it is foolish to expect that in each of these nations the government can have so tender a regard for the claims of individuals as to be deterred by them from this or that apparently politic measure. So long as the power to make conquests abroad is supposed to give rights to the lands taken, there must of course persist at home the doctrine that an act of Parliament can do anything—that the aggregate will may rightly impose on individual wills without any limit.

It may indeed be contended with reason that under existing conditions belief in the unrestricted authority of the state is necessary. The tacit assumption that the controlling agency which a community appoints or accepts, is subject to no restraints, has the defense that without it there could not be ensured that combined action from time to time required for meeting emergencies. As in war lack of faith in a leader may be a cause of defeat, so in war skepticism respecting governmental authority may produce fatal hesitations and dissensions. So long, therefore, as the religion of enmity so largely qualifies the religion of amity, the doctrine of unlimited state authority must prevail.

365. And now, having seen how the current conception of state duties originated, and how it has survived into modern conditions for which it is but partially adapted, we are the better prepared to entertain the true conception of state duties. After recognizing the probability, if not the certainty, that a theory concerning the proper sphere of government which was fit for societies organized on the principle of compulsory cooperation, must be unfit for societies organized on the principle of voluntary cooperation, we may proceed to ask what is the theory appropriate to these.

Each nation constitutes a variety of the human race. The welfare of humanity at large will be achieved by the prosperity and spread of the best varieties. After there has ended the predatory stage of progress—after there has come the stage in which the competition among societies is carried on without violence, there will, other things equal, be an increasing pre-dominance of societies which produce the greatest numbers of the best individuals. Production and maintenance of the best individuals is achieved by conformity to the law that each shall receive the good and evil results of his own nature and consequent conduct; and in the social state, the conduct of each bringing to him these results, must be restrained within the limits imposed by the presence of others similarly carrying on actions and experiencing results. Hence, other things equal, the greatest prosperity and multiplication of efficient individuals will occur where each is so constituted that he can fulfill the requirements of his own nature without interfering with the fulfillment of such requirements by others.

What, then, becomes the duty of the society in its corporate capacity, that is, of the state? Assuming that it is no longer called on to guard against external dangers, what does there remain which it is called on to do? If the desideratum, alike for the individuals, for the society, and for the race, is that the individuals shall be such as can fulfill their several lives sub-ject to the conditions named; then it is for the society in its corporate capacity to insist that these conditions shall be con-formed to. Whether, in the absence of war, a government has or has not anything more to do than this, it is clear it has to do this. And, by implication, it is clear that it is not permissible to do anything which hinders the doing of this.

Hence the question of limits becomes the question whether, beyond maintaining justice, the state can do anything else without transgressing justice. On consideration we shall find that it cannot.

366. For if the state goes beyond fulfillment of its duty as above specified, it must do this in one or both of two ways which severally or jointly reverse its duty.

Of further actions it undertakes, one class comes under the definition of actions which restrain the freedom of some indi-viduals more than is required by maintenance of the like freedom of other individuals; and such actions are themselves breaches of the law of equal freedom. If justice asserts the liberty of each limited only by the like liberties of all, then the imposing of any further limit is unjust; no matter whether the power imposing it be one man or a million of men. As we have seen throughout this work, the general right formulated, and all the special rights deducible from it, do not exist by authority of the state; but the state exists as a means of preserving them. Hence if, instead of preserving them, it trenches upon them, it commits wrongs instead of preventing wrongs. Though not in every society, yet in our society, the killing of all infants which do not reach the standard of goodness required by public authority, would probably be regarded as murder, even though committed by many individuals instead of one; and though not in early times, yet in our time, the tying of men to the lands they were born on, and the forbidding any other occupations than prescribed ones, would be considered as intolerable aggressions on their liberties. But if these larger inroads on their rights are wrong, then also are smaller inroads. As we hold that a theft is a theft whether the amount stolen be a pound or a penny, so we must hold that an aggression is an aggression whether it be great or small.

In the other class of cases the wrong is general and indirect, instead of being special and direct. Money taken from the citizen, not to pay the costs of guarding from injury his person, property, and liberty, but to pay the costs of other actions to which he has given no assent, inflicts injury instead of preventing it. Names and customs veil so much the facts, that we do not commonly see in a tax a diminution of freedom; and yet it clearly is one. The money taken represents so much labor gone through, and the product of that labor being taken away, either leaves the individual to go without such benefit as was achieved by it or else to go through more labor. In feudal days, when the subject classes had, under the name of *corvées,* to render services to their lords, specified in time or work, the partial slavery was manifest enough; and when the services were commuted for money, the relation remained the same in substance though changed in form. So is it now. Taxpayers are subject to a state *corvée,* which is none the less decided because, instead of giving their special kinds of work, they give equivalent sums; and if the *corvée* in its original undisguised form was a deprivation of freedom, so is it in its modern disguised form. "Thus much of your work shall be devoted, not to your own purposes, but to our purposes," say the authorities to the citizens; and to whatever extent this is carried, to that extent the citizens become slaves of the government.

"But they are slaves for their own advantage," will be the reply, "and the things to be done with the money taken from them are things which will in one way or other conduce to their welfare." Yes, that is the theory—a theory not quite in harmony with the vast mass of mischievous legislation filling the statute books. But this reply is not to the purpose. The question is a question of justice; and even supposing that the benefits to be obtained by these extra public expenditures were fairly distributed among all who furnish funds, which they are not, it would still remain true that they are at variance with the fundamental principle of an equitable social order. A man's liberties are none the less aggressed upon because those who coerce him do so in the belief that he will be benefited. In thus imposing by force their wills upon his will, they are breaking the law of equal freedom in his person; and what the motive may be matters not. Aggression which is flagitious when committed by one is not sanctified when committed by a host.

Doubtless most persons will read with astonishment this denial of unrestricted state power, and this tacit assertion that the state commits an offense when it exceeds the prescribed limits. In all places and times the beliefs which accompany the established institutions and habits, seem to those who hold them uncontrovertible. The fury of religious persecution has everywhere had behind it the conviction that dissent from the current creed implied deliberate wickedness or demoniacal possession. It was thought monstrous to question the authority of the church in days when the Pope was supreme over kings; and at the present time, in parts of Africa, how monstrous it is thought to reject the local creed is shown by the remark concerning disbelieving Europeans—"What fools these white men are!" So has it been politically. As in Fiji where, until recently, a man stood unbound to be killed, himself declaring that "whatever the king says must be done," it was held impossible to doubt the unbounded power of the ruling man—as throughout Europe, while the doctrine of the divine right of kings was universally accepted, the assertion that the many ought not to obey the one was re- garded by nearly all as the worst of crimes—as, even but a century ago, a church-and-king mob were ready to take the life of a preacher who publicly dissented from the established forms of government, political and ecclesiastical; so is it in a measure even still. One who denies the unlimited authority of the state is sure to be regarded by men at large as a fool or a fanatic. Instead of that "divinity which doth hedge a king," we have now the divinity which doth hedge a Parliament. The many-headed government appointed by multitudes of igno- rant people, which has replaced the single-headed govern- ment supposed to be appointed by heaven, claims, and is accorded, the same unrestricted powers. The sacred right of the majority, who are mostly stupid and ill informed, to coerce the minority, often more intelligent and better informed, is supposed to extend to all commands whatever which the majority may issue; and the rectitude of this arrangement is considered self-evident.

Hence, just as among those who uphold the "sacred duty of blood-revenge," the injunction to forgive injuries is unlikely to meet with much acceptance; so it is not to be expected that among party politicians, eagerly competing with one another to gain votes by promising state aids of countless kinds, any attention will be paid to a doctrine of state duties which excludes the great mass of their favorite schemes. But in face of all the contemptuous reprobation coming from them, it must still be asserted, as above, that their schemes are at variance with the fundamental principle of a harmonious social life.

367. Here, if kept strictly within its limits, this division of the *Principles of Ethics* should be brought to a close. Having seen what is the dictum of absolute ethics respecting the duties of the state, and having seen what qualifications are implied by that relative ethics which takes cognizance of the requirements generated by international aggressiveness—having further seen that during the transition between the militant and industrial forms of social life, an unduly exalted conception of state authority (which is natural and in large measure necessary) fosters a multiplicity of unjust state actions; there remains, from an ethical point of view, no more to be said. But it will be desirable here to devote some space to the proofs that these actions which are unjust in theory are also impolitic in practice.

The subject is a vast one, and cannot of course be fully dealt with in the space available. It will not be practicable to do more than present in outline the various divisions of the argument, with such few illustrations as are needful to indicate their bearings.

We will first deal with the state considered generally as an instrumentality, in contrast with other instrumentalities. We will examine next the assumption that it has a nature fitting it to remedy other evils than those entailed by aggression, external or internal. We will then consider the validity of the reasons for ascribing to it the duty and the power of achieving positive benefits. And we will end by inquiring whether the ultimate purpose—a higher development of human nature—is likely to be aided or hindered by its extended activities.

NOTE. Respecting the conclusions set forth in the following three chapters, it seems proper to say that their validity must not be measured solely by the evidence given, and the arguments used, in support of them. For the full vindication of these conclusions, and for the multitudinous facts which justify them, the reader is referred to various essays from time to time published, and now republished in the library edition of my essays. The titles of them are: "Over-Legislation"; "Representative Government—What Is it Good for?" "State-Tamperings with Money and Banks"; "The Collective Wisdom"; "Political Fetishism"; and "Specialized Administration." To these may be added sundry chapters forming the latter part of *Social Statics*, at present withdrawn from circulation, but selected portions of which I hope presently to republish.

CHAPTER 27

The Limits of State Duties—Continued

368. We saw (in chap. 23) that at a later stage of evolution a society may acquire a nature fundamentally unlike the nature it had at an earlier stage; and we drew the corollary that a theory of state duties appropriate when it had one nature must be inappropriate when it has the other nature. Here we have to draw a further corollary. The implied change of nature absolves the state from various functions for which it was at first the best agent; and generates for these functions other and better agents.

While war was the business of life, while militant organization was imperative, and while coercive rule was needful for disciplining improvident men and curbing their antisocial natures, agencies of a nongovernmental kind could not develop. Citizens had neither the means, nor the experience, nor the characters, nor the ideas, needed for privately cooperating in extensive ways. Hence all large purposes devolved on the state. If roads had to be made, if canals had to be cut, if aqueducts had to be built, the only instrumentality was governmental power exercised over slaves.

But with decline of militancy and rise of industrialism—the decay of the system of status and growth of the system of contract—there have gradually become possible, and have gradually arisen, multitudinous voluntary associations among citizens for discharging numerous kinds of functions. This result has been consequent on modifications of habits, dispositions, and modes of thought, which have been, generation after generation, produced by the daily exchange of services under agreement, in place of the daily enforcing of services. One result is that there can now be achieved without governmental power, various ends which in early days governmental power alone could achieve.

In discussing the sphere of state action we must take into account this profoundly significant fact. More than this: we must take into account a manifest inference. The changes above indicated are far from being ended; and we are justified in concluding that with further progress of them there may rightly go further relinquishment of functions which the state once discharged.

369. That such relinquishment of functions by the state, and assumption of them by other agencies, constitutes a progress, should be manifest to all who know anything about the laws of organization: though, unhappily, this truth seems no more appreciated by them than by those who began their school days with making nonsense verses and pass their mature years in pushing forward *ad captandum* legislation. For concerning individual organisms and social organisms, nothing is more certain than that advance from lower to higher, is marked by increasing heterogeneity of structures and increasing subdivision of functions. In both cases there is mutual dependence of parts, which becomes greater as the type becomes higher; and while this implies a progressing limitation of one function to one part, it implies also a progressing fitness of such part for such function.

When, some fifty years ago, Milne-Edwards gave to this principle of development in animals the name "physiological division of labor," he recognized the parallelism between vital economy and social economy; and this parallelism has been since growing ever clearer. But though among the cultured few, there is now some vague recognition of it; and though more especially the increasing division of labor which the industrial part of the social organism displays, has been made familiar by political economists, and the advantages of it duly insisted upon; there is little or no perception of the truth that the principle holds also within the controlling part, and throughout its relations to the other parts. Even without the facts which illustrate it, we might be certain that specialization, with consequent limitation, normally takes place in the regulative structures of a society as in all its other structures; that advantage is achieved by such specialization and limitation; and that any reverse change constitutes a retrogression.

The implication is therefore the same as before. All-embracing state functions characterize a low social type; and progress to a higher social type is marked by relinquishments of functions.

370. Most readers will feel little faith in these general conclusions. It will be needful to enforce them by arguments more readily appreciated.

In section 5 I named the fact that the welfare of any living body depends on the due proportioning of its several parts to their several duties; and that the needful balance of power among the parts is effected by a constant competition for nutriment, and the flowing to each of a quantity corresponding to its work. That competition throughout the industrial parts of a society achieves a kindred balance in a kindred way, needs no proof; and that social needs at large are best subserved by carrying out, wherever possible, this relation between effort and benefit, is manifest.

Now in all those nongovernmental cooperations constituting the greater part of modern social life, this balancing is spontaneously effected. I need not dwell on the principle of supply and demand as displayed throughout our industrial organization; and I need not do more than hint that this same principle holds throughout all other nongovernmental agencies—bodies for voluntary religious teaching, philanthropic associations, trades unions. Among all such, activity and growth, or quiescence and decay, occur according as they do or do not fulfill wants that are felt. Nor is this all. A truth which cannot be too much emphasized is that under this stress of competition, each of these agencies is impelled to perform the greatest amount of function in return for a given amount of nutrition. Moreover, competition constantly impels it to improve; to which end it not only utilizes the best appliances but is anxious to get the best men. The direct relation between efficiency and prosperity obliges all voluntary cooperations to work at high pressure.

Contrariwise, the compulsory cooperations by which governmental actions are effected, instead of direct relations between function and nutrition, show us highly indirect relations. Public departments, all of them regimented after the militant fashion, all supported by taxes forcibly taken, and severally responsible to their heads, mostly appointed for party reasons, are not immediately dependent for their means of living and growing on those whom they are designed to benefit. There is no fear of bankruptcy to prompt efficient and rapid performance of duty; there is no taking away of business by an opponent who does work more economically; there is no augmenting of profits by adopting improvements, still less by devising them. Every kind of defect results. As was lately said to me by one official concerning another, on whose remissness I was commenting, "Oh, he gets good pay and doesn't want to be bothered." In consequence of this indirectness of relation between benefits yielded and payments received, governmental agencies may continue to exist and draw funds for years, and sometimes for generations, after they have ceased to be of service; and when they are weak, or careless, or slow, the inefficiency has to be rectified by pressure exercised through the governmental machine—a machine so cumbrous and complex that only great pressure exercised with great patience can effect the needful change.

371. Every day's papers thrust illustrations of these truths before the world, in relation even to those essential functions which we have no alternative but to devolve on the state. The ill-working of the appliances for national protection and individual protection is a ceaseless scandal.

Army administration is exemplified by the retention of a royal duke as commander-in-chief, by the multiplicity of generals made in satisfaction of class interests, by promotion that is only in small measure determined by merit. It is again exemplified by keeping our own officers in ignorance of improvements which foreign officers are allowed to see; and by the repeated leaking out of secrets through employees in the arsenals. And it is yet again exemplified by the astounding disclosures respecting stores—bayonets that bend, swords that break, cartridges that jam, shells of wrong sizes; so that, as said by the Inquiry Commission of 1887: "The present system is directed to no definite object; it is regulated by no definite rules; it makes no regular stated provision, either for the proper supply and manufacture of warlike stores, or for enforcing the responsibility of those who fail to make them properly, or for ascertaining the fact that they are made improperly."

That the navy keeps the army in countenance, complaint, inquiry, and exposure, continually remind us. All remember the story of the naval evolutions on the occasion of the Jubilee, when, without the stress of a sea fight, more than a dozen vessels, great and small, came to grief in one way or other—collisions, explosions, breakdowns of engines, and so forth. And then there were the smaller but equally significant disasters which, in the same year, attended the cruise of twenty-four torpedo boats down channel and back; during which eight of the twenty-four were more or less disabled. Vessels that will not steer, guns that burst, ships that run aground, are

frequently reported; and then, furnishing a significant contrast, when a first-class man-of-war, the *Sultan*, after running
on a rock, sinks and is regarded by the Admiralty as lost, it is
raised again and saved by a private company. To which add
that the report concerning Admiralty administration issued in
March 1887 showed that "such management as is here dis-
closed would bring any commercial firm into the Bankruptcy
Court in a few months."

Similarly is it with the making and administration of laws.
So constant is the exposure of folly and failure, that the public
sense of them is seared. In parliamentary procedure we meet
with the extremes of utter recklessness and irrational careful-
ness: now a bill is hurried through all its stages without
debate, and now, after careful consideration has delayed its
enactment, it is dropped and has to pass through the whole
process again next session. While we see the amending and
reamending of clauses aimed to meet every contingency, we
see the whole act when passed thrown on to the immense
chaotic heap of preceding legislation, making its confusion
worse confounded. Complaint and denunciation lead to
nothing. Here, in 1867, is the report of a commission formed of
leading lawyers and statesmen—Cranworth, Westbury,
Cairns, and others—urging the need for a digest as a preparation for a code; and urging that it is a national duty to provide
citizens with a means of knowing the laws they have to
conform to. Yet, though the question has been occasionally
raised, nothing has been done—nothing, that is, by the state,
but something by private individuals: Chitty's *Equity Index*
and Sir James Stephen's *Digest of the Criminal Law,* have to
some extent taught legislators what has been done by themselves and their predecessors. Then there is the fact, to the
monstrosity of which custom blinds us, that even lawyers do
not know what the bearings of a new act are until judges have
made decisions under it; while the judges themselves exclaim
against the bungling legislation they have to interpret: one
judge saying of a clause that he "did not believe its meaning

was comprehended either by the draftsman who drew it" or "the parliament that adopted it," and another declaring that "it was impossible for human skill to find words more calculated to puzzle everybody." As a natural consequence we have every day appeals and again appeals—decisions being reversed and re-reversed, and the poorer litigants being compelled to submit by the wealthier ones, who can ruin them by going from court to court. The incredible disproportion of sentences, too, is a daily scandal. Here a hungry harvester is sent to prison for eating a pennyworth of the field beans he was cutting, as happened at Faversham; and there a rich man who has committed a violent assault has to pay a fine which to him is trivial. Still more disgraceful is the treatment of men charged with unproved offenses, and men who have been proved innocent: these being kept in prison for months before trials which show them to be guiltless, and those, after bearing long punishments before their innocence is shown, being granted "free pardons" and no compensation for inflicted sufferings and damaged lives.

Even the smallest daily transaction—the paying of a cabman or the purchase of a necktie—serves to remind one of official bungling; for how can it be better shown than by the coinage? In this we have frequent changes where changes are undesirable. We have mixed systems: decimal, duodecimal, and nondescript. Until recently we had two scarcely distinguishable pieces for threepence and fourpence; we had, four years since, the Jubilee sixpence withdrawn because it stimulated a half-sovereign so exactly that it needed only to be gilt to pass for one. We have the lately introduced four-shilling piece, only by deliberate inspection distinguishable from a five-shilling piece. In most cases there lacks the one needful piece of information—the declared value of the coin. And once more there are no proper adjustments to the demands: everywhere there is an unsatisfied cry for small change.

So that the inference which the general laws of organization compel us to draw, is inductively verified in respect of the three all-essential departments of the state, as well as in a subordinate department, by evidence which every day increases.

372. There are two leading implications of this general truth above exhibited in the abstract, and above exemplified in the concrete.

If people at large tolerate the extravagance, the stupidity, the carelessness, the obstructiveness, daily exemplified in the military, naval, and legal administrations; much more will they tolerate them when exemplified in departments which are neither so vitally important nor occupy so large a space in the public mind. The vices of officialism must exist throughout public organizations of every kind, and may be expected to go to greater extremes where the necessity for checking them is less pressing. Not only, then, may we rationally conclude that when, beyond its essential functions, the state undertakes nonessential functions, it will perform these equally ill, but we may rationally conclude that its performance of them will be still worse.

The second implication is that the ill-performance of essential functions is itself made more extreme by the absorption of attention and energy in discharging nonessential functions. It cannot but be that the power to conduct a few businesses is diminished by the addition of many other businesses to be conducted: and it cannot but be that when public criticism is directed to shortcomings of many kinds it must be less efficient than when directed to shortcomings of few kinds. If, instead of being almost wholly occupied with other things, Parliament were occupied almost wholly with the administrations for external protection and internal protection, no one will dare to deny that these would be more efficient than now; and no one will dare to assert that, if discussions on the platform and in the press were almost wholly about these administrations instead of being almost wholly about other things, the public would tolerate such inefficiency of them as it now does.

Thus whether we wish to avoid the multiplication of ill-performed functions, or whether we wish to have the essential functions better performed, the requirement is the same—limitation. Specialization of functions directly improves the discharge of each function by adjusting the organ to it, and indirectly improves the discharge of other functions by permitting each to acquire an appropriate organ.

373. The foregoing reasons for concluding that in the administration of social affairs the just is also the politic, will weigh but little with the majority. The beliefs in natural law and the universality of causation are not very strong even in the scientific world when vital phenomena are in question; and they are very feeble in the outer world. Only such of the above arguments as are based on facts daily published are likely to tell; and the adequacy of even these will be denied by most.

It will, therefore, be needful to reinforce them by others drawn from evidences directly relevant. Let us devote a chapter to these.

CHAPTER 28

The Limits of State Duties—Continued

374. "In simple matters direct perception cannot be trusted: to insure trustworthy conclusions we must use some mode of measurement by which the imperfections of the senses may be corrected. Contrariwise, in complex matters unaided contemplation suffices: we can adequately sum up and balance the evidences without reference to any general truth."

Does anyone smile at this absurd proposition? Why should he do so? The probabilities are ten to one that, under a disguised form, this proposition forms part of his tacitly accepted creed. If he hears of an artisan who pooh-poohs thermometers, and says he can tell better by his hand what is the right temperature for the liquid he uses, the reader, knowing that the sensation of heat or cold which anything yields varies greatly according to the temperature of the hand, sees how absurd is this self-confidence resulting from want of knowledge. But he sees no absurdity in the attempt to reach without any guiding principle a right conclusion respecting the consequences of some action affecting in multitudinous ways millions of people: here there needs no kind of meter by which to test the correctness of direct impressions. If, for instance, the question is whether he shall advocate the system of payment by results in state-aided schools, he thinks it obvious that the stimulus given by it to teachers cannot fail to be beneficial to pupils. It does not occur to him that perhaps the induced pressure will be too great; that perhaps it will foster a mechanical receptivity; that mere cram may end in ultimate aversion to learning; that there may be prompted special attention to clever pupils whose success will profit the teacher, and consequent neglect of dull ones; that a system which values knowledge for gaining money grants, and not for its own sake, is unlikely to produce healthy intelligence; and that even the teachers under such a system are likely to become mere machines. Seeing, as he thinks quite clearly, the immediate results, and either not perceiving at all the remote results or making light of them, he has no doubt that the plan will be a good one. And then when, after some twenty years the effects of the plan are found to be so injurious that it is abandoned, after having damaged the healths of millions of children and inflicted an immeasurable amount of physical and mental pain, he is not in the least the wiser for his disastrous misjudgment, but is ready next day to decide about some newly proposed scheme in the same way—by simple inspection and balancing probabilities. That is, as above said, though the aid of general principles is thought needful in simple matters, it is thought not needful in the most complex matters.

And yet a minute's thought should make it clear to every one not only that these unguided judgments are very likely to be wrong, but also that there must exist some guidance by which correct judgments may be reached. For what can be more nonsensical than the belief that there is no natural causation in social affairs? And how can anyone evade the charge of folly who, admitting that there must be natural causation, devises laws which take no account of it? As argued in a preceding chapter, if there is no causation then one law is as good as another, and lawmaking ridiculous. If one law is not as good as another, it must be that on men socially aggregated one law will operate more beneficially than another; and its more beneficial operation implies some adaptation to the natures of the men and their modes of cooperation. Concerning these there must exist some general truths, some deepest uniformities; and the ultimate effect of any legislation must depend on its recognition of such uniformities and its subordination to them. How, then, can there be anything more senseless than to proceed before inquiring what they are?

375. Pursuit of happiness without regard to the conditions by fulfillment of which happiness is to be achieved, is foolish socially as well as individually—nay, indeed, more foolish; since the evils of disregarding the conditions are not unfrequently evaded by the individual, but, in consequence of the averaging of effects among many individuals, cannot be evaded by the society.

Estimating the probable results of each act apart from any general sanction other than the pursuit of happiness, is the method pursued by every criminal. He thinks the chances are in favor of gaining pleasures and escaping pains. Ignoring those considerations of equity which should restrain him, he contemplates the proximate results and not the ultimate results; and, in respect of the proximate results, he is occasionally right: he has the gratifications which his ill-gotten gains bring and does not suffer the punishment. But in the long run it turns out that the evils are greater than the benefits; partly because he does not always avoid the penalties, and partly because the kind of nature fostered by his actions is incapable of the higher kinds of happiness.

The policy thus pursued with egoistic ends by the lawbreaker is pursued with altruistic ends by the expediency politician. He, too, not for his own good, but, as he thinks, for the good of others, makes calculations of probable pleasures and pains; and, ignoring the dictates of pure equity, adopts such methods as he thinks will achieve the one and avoid the other. If it is a question of providing books and newspapers in so-called free libraries, he contemplates results which he makes no doubt will be beneficial; and practically ignores the inquiry whether it is just to take by force the money of A, B, and C, to pay for the gratifications of D, E, and F. Should his aim be the repression of drunkenness and its evils, he thinks exclusively of these ends, and, determined to impose his own beliefs on others, tries to restrict men's freedom of exchange and to abolish businesses in which capital has been invested with legal and social assent. Thus, as above said, the altruistic aggressor, like the egoistic aggressor, disregards all other guidance than that of estimated proximate results—is not restrained by the thought that his acts break the first principle of harmonious social life.

Clearly this empirical utilitarianism, which makes happiness the immediate aim, stands in contrast with the rational utilitarianism, which aims at fulfillment of the conditions to happiness.

376. The upholders of political empiricism cannot object if we bring their own method to the empirical test. If, ignoring abstract principles, we are to be guided by results, either as calculated beforehand or as ascertained by experience, then, clearly, we cannot do better than judge in like manner of the empirical method itself. Let us do this.

In a discussion on socialistic legislation which took place in the House of Lords on May 19, 1890, our Prime Minister said, "We no more ask what is the derivation or philosophical extraction of a proposal before we adopt it than a wise man would ask the character of a footman's grandfather before engaging the footman."

After thus ridiculing the supposition that there are any general laws of social life to which legislation should conform, he went on to say, "We ought first to discuss every subject on its own merits." And Lord Salisbury's method thus distinctly avowed, is the method universally followed by politicians who call themselves practical and sneer at "abstract principles."

But unhappily for them their method is the method which has been followed by those legislators who, throughout past thousands of years, have increased human miseries in multitudinous ways and immeasurable degrees by mischievous laws. Regard for "the merits of the case" guided Diocletian when he fixed the prices of articles and wages of workers, and similarly guided rulers of all European nations who, century after century, in innumerable cases, have decided how much commodity shall be given for so much money, and in our own country guided those who, after the Black Death, framed the Statute of Labourers, and presently caused the peasant revolt. The countless acts which, here and abroad, prescribed qualities and modes of manufacture, and appointed searchers to see that things were made as directed, were similarly prompted by consideration of "the merits of the case": evils existed which it was obviously needful to prevent. Doubtless, too, the orders to farmers respecting the proportions of their arable and pasture lands, the times for shearing sheep, the number of horses to a plough, as well as those which insisted on certain crops and prohibited others, had "the merits of the case" in view. Similarly was it with the bounties on the exports of some commodities and the restrictions on the imports of others; and similarly was it with the penalties on forestallers, and the treatment of usury as a crime. Each one of those multitudinous regulations enforced by swarms of officials, which in France nearly strangled industry, and was a part-cause of the French revolution, seemed to those who established it, a regulation which "the merits of the case" called for; and no less did there seem to be called for the numberless sumptuary laws which, generation after generation, kings and their ministers tried to enforce. Out of the 14,000-odd acts which, in our own country, have been repealed, from the date of the Statute of Merton down to 1872—some because of consolidations, some because they proved futile, some because they were obsolete—how many have been repealed because they were mischievous? Shall we say one-half? Shall we say one-fourth? Shall we say less than one-fourth? Suppose that only 3,000 of these acts were abolished after proved injuries had been caused, which is a low estimate. What shall we say of these 3,000 acts which have been hindering human

man he stole them from." Here, consideration of "the merits of the case" was the avowed way of judging: the relative degrees of happiness of the thief and the person robbed were estimated and the decision justified the theft. "But the rights of property must be maintained," Lord Salisbury would reply. "Society would dissolve if men were allowed to take other men's goods on the plea that they had more need of them than the owners." Just so. But this is not judging by "the merits of the case"; it is judging by conformity to a general principle. That philosophy at which Lord Salisbury sneers, shows that social cooperation can be effectively and harmoniously carried on, only if the relations between efforts and benefits are maintained intact. And, as we have seen, it is the same with all those laws the enforcement of which constitutes the administration of justice, and which it is part of Lord Salisbury's essential business to uphold: all of them are embodied corollaries from the philosophy he scorns.

The essential difference is that though the lessons of thousands of years show that society improves in proportion as there is better and better conformity to these corollaries; and though it is to be inferred that it will be best to conform to them in each new case which arises; Lord Salisbury thinks that nonconformity to them is proper if a majority decides that "the merits of the case" demand it.

377. That anyone who has before him the facts daily set forth in newspapers, should suppose that when measures are taken to meet "the merits of the case," the consequences can be shut up within the limits of the case, is astonishing. That, after seeing how a change set up in some part of a society initiates other changes unforeseen, and these again others, anyone should think he is going to produce by act of Parliament certain effects intended and no unintended effects, shows how possible it is to go on reading day by day without getting wiser. In any aggregate formed of mutually dependent parts, there comes into play what I have elsewhere described as fructifying causation. The effects of any cause become

themselves causes, often more important than their parent; and their effects, again, become other causes. What happened when a great rise in the price of coals occurred some years ago? The expenditure of every household was affected, and the poor were especially pinched. Every factory was taxed, and either the wages lowered or the price of the commodity raised. The smelting of iron became more expensive, and the cost of all those things, such as railways and engines, into which iron enters largely, was increased. The ability to compete with various classes of foreign manufactures was diminished; fewer vessels were chartered for carrying products abroad; and the shipbuilding trade flagged with all the dependent trades. Similarly throughout in directions too numerous to follow. See, again, what has resulted from the late dock strike—or rather, from the ill-judged sympathy which, guided by "the merits of the case," led public and police to tolerate the violence employed by dockers to achieve their ends. Successful use in this case of assaulting, bullying, and boycotting, prompted elsewhere strikes enforced by like means—at Southampton, Tilbury, Glasgow, Nottingham, &c. Other classes followed the lead—painters, leather workers, cabinetmakers, scalemakers, bakers, carpenters, printers, sandwich men, &c. And there were prompted like movements, still more unscrupulous, in Australia and America. Then, as secondary results, came the stoppages and perturbations of businesses, and through them of connected businesses, with consequent decrease of employment. Among tertiary results we have encouragement of the delusion that it only requires union for workers to get what terms they please, prompting suicidal demands. And, among still remoter results, we have the urging on of meddling legislation and the fostering of socialistic ideas.

The indirect effects, multiplying and again multiplying, are often in the long run the reverse of those counted on. Past and present alike supply instances. Among those from the past may be named the Act of 8th Elizabeth, which, to protect the inhabitants of Shrewsbury against strangers, forbade all save freemen to trade in Welsh cottons, and which, six years afterwards, the Shrewsbury people begged should be repealed, because "of the impoverishing and undoing of the poor artificers and others, at whose suit the said act was procured": an experience paralleled in later days by that of the Spitalfields weavers. Then of striking examples which present times furnish, we have the results of certain laws in the Western states of America. In his message to the Colorado legislature, January 8, 1885, Governor Grant says: "These laws were designed to exterminate the hawks, wolves, and loco weeds . . . the hawks and wolves have steadily increased under the auspices of these bounty laws"; that is, as measured by the amount paid. Kindred results have been experienced in India.

From the times when vagrants swarmed round monasteries to the old Poor Law days when many parishes were nearly swamped by paupers, experience has continually shown that measures guided by the apparent "merits of the case," have done exactly the reverse of that which was proposed to be done—have increased distress instead of diminishing it. And recent facts have continued to illustrate the same thing. The chairman of the Bradfield Union, writing to the *Spectator* of April 19, 1890, points out that seventeen years' administration led by principle instead of impulse, had reduced the indoor paupers from 259 to 100, and the outdoor paupers from 999 to 42: the conviction with which he ends his letter being that "the majority of paupers are created by out-relief." And this warning against being guided by the seeming necessities, has been since emphasized by Mr. Arnold White, writing from Tennyson Settlement, Cape Colony, to the *Spectator* for January 10, 1891, in which he says: "Any colonizing scheme that does not distinctly include death to the willfully idle if they choose to die, is predestined to failure. . . . the lesson has been burned into me by long and bitter years of hard-earned experience." Which is to say that if, in respect of charity, we let ourselves be swayed by the apparent "merits of the case," we shall eventually exacerbate the evils instead of curing them.

The judgments of the legislator who derides philosophy,

and thinks it needful only to look at the facts before him, are equally respectable with those of the laborer who joins his fellows in vociferous advocacy of some public undertaking, for the reason that it will give employment—thus looking, as he does, at "the merits of the case" as directly to be anticipated, and thinking nothing of the remoter consequences: not asking what will be the effect of expending capital in doing something that will not bring adequate returns; not asking what undertakings, probably more remunerative and therefore more useful, the capital would have been otherwise devoted to; not asking what other trades and artisans and laborers would then have had employment. For though the legislator may contemplate effects somewhat more remote, yet he is practically as far as the laborer from conceiving the ultimate waves of change, reverberating and re-reverberating throughout society.

378. Which is the more misleading, belief without evidence, or refusal to believe in presence of overwhelming evidence? If there is an irrational faith which persists without any facts to support it, there is an irrational lack of faith which persists spite of the accumulation of facts which should produce it; and we may doubt whether the last does not lead to worse results than the first.

The average legislator, equally with the average citizen, has no faith whatever in the beneficent working of social forces, notwithstanding the almost infinite illustrations of this beneficent working. He persists in thinking of a society as a manufacture and not as a growth: blind to the fact that the vast and complex organization by which its life is carried on, has resulted from the spontaneous cooperations of men pursuing their private ends. Though, when he asks how the surface of the earth has been cleared and made fertile, how towns have grown up, how manufactures of all kinds have arisen, how the arts have been developed, how knowledge has been accumulated, how literature has been produced, he is forced to recognize the fact that none of these are of governmental origin, but have many of them suffered from governmental obstruction; yet, ignoring all this, he assumes that if a good is to be achieved or an evil prevented, Parliament must be invoked. He has unlimited faith in the agency which has achieved multitudinous failures, and has no faith in the agency which has achieved multitudinous successes.

Of the various feelings which move men to action, each class has its part in producing social structures and functions. There are first the egoistic feelings, most powerful and most active, the effects of which, as developing the arrangements for production and distribution, have been above adverted to, and which, whenever there is a new sphere to be profitably occupied, are quick to cause new growths. From the cutting of a Suez Canal and the building of a Forth Bridge, to the insurance of ships, houses, lives, crops, windows, the exploration of unknown regions, the conducting of travelers' excursions, down to automatic supply boxes at railway stations and the loan of opera glasses at theaters, private enterprise is ubiquitous and infinitely varied in form; and when repressed by state agency in one direction buds out in another. Reminding us of the way in which, in Charles II's time, there was commenced in London a local penny post, which was suppressed by the government, we have, in the Boy Messengers' Company and its attempted suppression, illustrations of the efficiency of private enterprise and the obstructiveness of officialism. And then, if there needs to add a case showing the superiority of spontaneously formed agencies we have it in the American Express Companies, of which one has 7,000 agencies, has its own express trains, delivers 25,000,000 parcels annually, is employed by the government, has a money-order system which is replacing that of the Post Office, and has now extended its business to Europe, India, Africa, South America, and Polynesia.

Beyond those egoistic feelings by the combined forces of which the sustaining organization of every society has been developed, there are in men the ego-altruistic and altruistic feelings—the love of approbation and the sympathy—which prompt them to various other single and combined actions, and generate various other institutions. It is needless to go back into the past to exemplify the operation of these in the endowments for charitable and educational purposes. The present day furnishes ample evidence of their potency. Here, and still more in America, we have vast sums left for founding colleges, and, in more numerous cases, sums for endowing professorial chairs and scholarships; we have gifts of immense sums to build and fill public libraries; we have parks and gardens given to towns by private individuals; we have museums bequeathed to the nation. In *The Standard* for April 11, 1890, is given an account showing that the bequests to hospitals, asylums, missions, societies, for 1889 amounted to £1,080,000; and that for the first quarter of 1890 they amounted to £300,000. Then, in *The Nineteenth Century*, for January, 1890, Mr. Huish has pointed out that during the last few years, the gifts of private individuals for the support of art, have been respectively, for buildings £347,500, and in pictures or money £559,000; to which may be added the more recent donation of £80,000 for a gallery of British Art.

Nor must we forget the daily activities of multitudinous philanthropic people in urging one or other movement for the benefit of fellow citizens. Countless societies, with an enormous aggregate revenue, are formed for unselfish purposes: all good in design if not in result. And the motives, largely if not wholly altruistic, which prompt the establishment and working of these, far from showing any decrease of strength, become continually stronger.

Surely, then, if these forces have already done so much and are continually doing more, their future efficiency may be counted upon. And it may be reasonably inferred that they will do many things which we do not yet see how to do.

379. So that even if we disregard ethical restraints, and even if we ignore the inferences to be drawn from that progressing specialization which societies show us, we still find

strong reasons for holding that state functions should be restricted rather than extended.

Extension of them in pursuit of this or that promised benefit, has all along proved disastrous. The histories of all nations are alike in exhibiting the enormous evils that have been produced by legislation guided merely by "the merits of the case"; while they unite in proving the success of legislation which has been guided by considerations of equity.

Evidence thrust before us every morning shows throughout the body politic a fructifying causation so involved that not even the highest intelligence can anticipate the aggregate effects. The practical politician so-called, who thinks that the influences of his measure are to be shut up within the limits of the field he contemplates, is one of the wildest of theorists.

And then, while his faith in the method of achieving artificially this or that end, is continually discredited by failures to work the effects intended and by working unintended effects, he shows no faith in those natural forces which in the past have done much, are at present doing more, and in the future may be expected to do most.

to be here discussed. Let us now enter on the discussion of them systematically.

381. Upwards from hordes of savages to civilized nations, countless examples show that to make an efficient warrior preparation is needed. Practice in the use of weapons begins in boyhood; and throughout youth the ambition is to be a good marksman with the bow and arrow, to throw the javelin or the boomerang with force and precision, and to become an adept in defense as well as in attack. At the same time speed and agility are effectually cultivated, and there are trials of strength. More relevant still to the end in view comes the discipline in endurance; sometimes going to the extent of submission to torture. In brief, each male of the tribe is so educated as to fit him for the purposes of the tribe—to fit him for helping it in maintaining its existence, or subjugating its neighbors, or both. Though not a state education in the modern sense, the education is one prescribed by custom and enforced by public opinion. That it is the business of the society to mold the individual is asserted tacitly if not openly.

With that social progress which forms larger communities regularly governed, there goes a further development of state education. Not only are there now deliberately cultivated the needful strength, skill, and endurance, but there is cultivated that subordination which is required for the performance of military evolutions, and that further subordination to leaders and to rulers without which the combined forces cannot be used in the desired ways. It is needless to do more than name Greece, and especially Sparta, as exemplifying this phase.

With this practice went an appropriate theory. From the belief that the individual belonged neither to himself nor to his family but to his city, there naturally grew up the doctrine that it was the business of his city to mold him into fitness for its purposes. Alike in Plato and in Aristotle we have elaborate methods proposed for the due preparation of children and youths for citizenship, and an unhesitating assumption that in a good state, education must be a public business.

Evidently, then, while war is the chief business of life, the training of individuals by governmental agency after a pattern adapted to successful fighting, is a normal accompaniment. In this case experience furnishes a tolerably correct ideal to be aimed at, and guidance in the choice of methods productive of the ideal. All free men have to be made as much as may be into military machines, automatically obedient to orders; and a unifying discipline is required to form them. Moreover, just as in the militant type the coercive system of rule which regimentation involves, spreads from the fighting part throughout the whole of the ancillary parts which support it; so, there naturally establishes itself the theory that not soldiers only, but all other members of the community, should be molded by the government into fitness for their functions.

382. Not recognizing the fundamental distinction between a society which, having fighting for its chief business, makes sustentation subordinate, and a society which, having sustentation for its chief business, makes fighting subordinate, there are many who assume that a disciplinary policy appropriate to the first is appropriate to the last also. But the relations of the individual to the state are in the two cases entirely different. Unlike the Greek, who, not owning himself was owned by his city, the Englishman is not in any appreciable degree owned by his nation, but in a very positive way owns himself. Though, if of fit age, he may on great emergency be taken possession of and made to help in defending his country; yet this contingency qualifies to but small extent the private possession of his body and the self-directing of his actions.

Throughout a series of chapters we saw that the progressive establishment by law of those rights which are deduced by ethics, made good the free use of himself by each individual, not only against other individuals but, in many respects, against the state: the state, while defending him against the aggressions of others, has in various directions ceased to aggress upon him itself. And it is an obvious corollary that in a state of permanent peace this change of relation would be complete.

How does this conclusion bear on the question at issue? The

implication is that whereas the individual had to be molded by the society to suit its purposes, the society has now to be molded by the individual to suit his purposes. Instead of a solidified body politic, wielding masses of its units in combined action, the society, losing its coercive organization, and holding together its units with no other bonds than are needed for peaceful cooperation, becomes simply a medium for their activities. Once more let me emphasize the truth that since a society in its corporate capacity is not sentient, and since the sentiency dwells exclusively in its units, the sole reason for subordinating the sentient lives of its units to the unsentient life of the society, is that while militancy continues the sentient lives of its units are thus best preserved; and this reason lapses partially as militancy declines, and wholly as industrialism becomes complete. The claim of the society to discipline its citizens disappears. There remains no power which may properly prescribe the form which individual life shall assume.

"But surely the society in its corporate capacity, guided by the combined intelligences of its best members, may with advantage frame a conception of an individual nature best fitted for harmonious industrial life, and of the discipline calculated to produce such a nature?" In this plea there is tacitly assumed the right of the community through its agents to impose its scheme—an assumed right quite inconsistent with the conclusions drawn in foregoing chapters. But not here dwelling on this, let us ask what fitness the community has for deciding on the character to be desired, and for devising means likely to create it.

383. Whether the chosen ideal of a citizen, and the chosen process for producing him, be good or bad, the choice inevitably has three implications, any one of which condemns it.

The system must work towards uniformity. If the measures taken have any effect at all, the effect must in part be that of causing some likeness among the individuals: to deny this is to deny that the process of molding is operative. But in so far as uniformity results advance is retarded. Everyone who has studied the order of nature knows that without variety there can be no progress—knows that, in the absence of variety, life would never have evolved at all. The inevitable implication is that further progress must be hindered if the genesis of variety is checked.

Another concomitant must be the production of a passive receptivity of whatever form the state decides to impress. Whether submissiveness be or be not part of the nature which the incorporated society proposes to give its units, it cannot enforce its plans without either finding or creating submissiveness. Whether avowedly or not, part of the desired character must be readiness in each citizen to submit, or make his children submit, to a discipline which some or many citizens determine to impose. There may be men who think it a trait of high humanity thus to deliver over the formation of its nature to the will of an aggregate mostly formed of inferior units. But with such we will not argue.

One further necessary implication is that either there exists no natural process by which citizens are in course of being molded, or else that this natural process should be superseded by an artificial one. To assert that there is no natural process is to assert that, unlike all other beings, which tend ever to become adapted to their environments, the human being does not tend to become adapted to his environment—does not tend to undergo such changes as fit him for carrying on the life which circumstances require him to lead. Anyone who says this must say that the varieties of mankind have arisen without cause; or else have been caused by governmental action. Anyone who does not say this must admit that men are in course of being naturally adjusted to the requirements of a developed social state; and if he admits this, he will hesitate before he asserts that they may be better adjusted artificially.

384. Let us pass now from these most abstract aspects of the matter to more concrete aspects.

It is decided to create citizens having forms fit for the life of their society. Whence must the conception of a fit form be derived? Men inherit not only the physical and mental constitutions of their ancestors, but also, in the main, their ideas and beliefs. The current conception of a desirable citizen must therefore be a product of the past, slightly modified by the present; and the proposal is that past and present shall impose their conception on the future. Anyone who takes an impersonal view of the matter can scarcely fail to see in this a repetition, in another sphere, of follies committed in every age by every people in respect of religious beliefs. In all places and in all times, the average man holds that the creed in which he has been brought up is the only true creed. Though it must be manifest to him that necessarily in all cases but one, such beliefs, held with confidence equal to that which he feels, are false; yet, like each of the others, he is certain that his belief is the exception. A confidence no less absurd, is shown by those who would impose on the future their ideal citizen. That conceived type which the needs of past and present times have generated, they do not doubt would be a type appropriate for times to come. Yet it needs but to go back to the remote past, when industrial life was held contemptible and virtue meant fortitude, valor, bravery; or to the less remote past when noble meant highborn while laborer and villein were equivalents; or to the time when abject submission of each grade to the grade above was thought the primary duty; or to the time when the good citizen of every rank was held bound to accept humbly the appointed creed; to see that the characters supposed to be proper for men were unlike the characters we now suppose proper for them. Nevertheless, the not very wise representatives of electors who are mostly ignorant, are prepared, with papal assumption, to settle the form of a desirable human nature, and to shape the coming generation into that form.

While they are thus confident about the thing to be done, they are no less confident about the way to do it; though in the last case as in the first, the past proves to them how utter has been the failure of the methods century after century pursued.

Throughout a Christendom full of churches and priests, full of pious books, full of observances directed to fostering the religion of love, encouraging mercy and insisting on forgiveness, we have an aggressiveness and a revengefulness such as savages have everywhere shown. And from people who daily read their Bibles, attend early services, and appoint weeks of prayer, there are sent out messengers of peace to inferior races, who are forthwith ousted from their lands by filibustering expeditions authorized in Downing Street; while those who resist are treated as "rebels," the deaths they inflict in retaliation are called "murders," and the process of subduing them is named "pacification."

At the same time that we thus find good reason to reject the artificial method of molding citizens as wrong in respect alike of end and means, we have good reason to put faith in the natural method—the spontaneous adaptation of citizens to social life.

385. The organic world at large is made up of illustrations, infinite in number and variety, of the truth that by direct or indirect processes the faculties of each kind of creature become adjusted to the needs of its life; and further, that the exercise of each adjusted faculty becomes a source of gratification. In the normal order not only does there arise an agent for each duty, but consciousness is made up of the more or less pleasurable feelings which accompany the exercise of these agents. Further, the implication is that where the harmony has been deranged, it gradually reestablishes itself—that where change of circumstances has put the powers and requirements out of agreement, they slowly, either by survival of the fittest or by the inherited effects of use and disuse, or by both, come into agreement again.

This law, holding of human beings among others, implies that the nature which we inherit from an uncivilized past, and which is still very imperfectly fitted to the partially civilized present, will, if allowed to do so, slowly adjust itself to the requirements of a fully civilized future. And a further implication is that the various faculties, tastes, abilities, gradually established, will have for their concomitants the satisfactions felt in discharging the various duties social life entails. Already there has been gained a considerable amount of the needful capacity for work, which savages have not; already the power of orderly cooperation under voluntary agreement has been developed; already such amounts of self-restraint have been acquired that most men carry on their lives without much impeding one another; already the altruistic interests felt by citizens in social affairs at large are such as prompt efforts, individual and spontaneously combined, to achieve public ends; and already men's sympathies have become active enough to generate multitudinous philanthropic agencies—too multitudinous in fact. And if, in the course of these few thousand years, the discipline of social life has done so much, it is folly to suppose that it cannot do more—folly to suppose that it will not in course of time do all that has to be done.

A further truth remains. It is impossible for artificial molding to do that which natural molding does. For the very essence of the process as spontaneously carried on, is that each faculty acquires fitness for its function by performing its function; and if its function is performed for it by a substituted agency, none of the required adjustment of nature takes place; but the nature becomes deformed to fit the artificial arrangements instead of the natural arrangements. More than this: it has to be depleted and dwarfed, for the support of the substituted agencies. Not only does there result the incapable nature, the distorted nature, and the nature which misses the gratifications of desired achievement; but that the superintending instrumentalities may be sustained, the sustentation of those who are superintended is diminished: their lives are undermined and their adaptation in another way impeded.

Again, then, let me emphasize the fundamental distinction. While war is the business of life, the entailed compulsory cooperation implies molding of the units by the aggregate to serve its purposes; but when there comes to predominate the voluntary cooperation characterizing industrialism, the molding has to be spontaneously achieved by self-adjustment to the life of voluntary cooperation. The adjustment cannot possibly be otherwise produced.

386. And now we come round again at last to the general principle enunciated at first. All reasons for going counter to the primary law of social life prove invalid; and there is no safety but in conformity to that law.

If the political meddler could be induced to contemplate the essential meaning of his plan, he would be paralyzed by the sense of his own temerity. He proposes to suspend, in some way or degree, that process by which all life has been evolved—to divorce conduct from consequence. While the law of life at large is to be partially broken by him, he would more especially break that form of it which results from the associated state. Traversing by his interference that principle of justice common to all living things, he would traverse more especially the principle of human justice, which requires that each shall enjoy the benefits achieved within the needful limits of action: he would redistribute the benefits. Those results of accumulated experiences in each civilized society which, registered in laws, have, age after age, established men's rights with increasing clearness, he proposes here or there to ignore, and to trespass on the rights. And whereas in the course of centuries, the ruling powers of societies, while maintaining men's rights against one another more effectually, have also themselves receded from aggressions on those rights, the legislative schemer would invert this course, and decrease that freedom of action which has been increasing. Thus his policy, setting at nought the first principle of life at large and the first principle of social life in particular, ignores also the generalized results of observations and experiments gathered during thousands of years. And all with what warrant? All for certain reasons of apparent policy, every one of which we have found to be untrustworthy.

But why needs there any detailed refutation? What can be a more extreme absurdity than that of proposing to improve social life by breaking the fundamental law of social life?

PART V
THE ETHICS OF SOCIAL LIFE: NEGATIVE BENEFICENCE

CHAPTER 1

Kinds of Altruism

387. One division of an earlier work in this series of works—*The Principles of Psychology*—was devoted to showing that all intellectual operations are ultimately decomposable into recognitions of likeness and unlikeness, with mental grouping of the like and separation of the unlike. The process of intelligence as there analyzed, was shown to be a differentiation in perception and thought, of the impressions produced on us by surrounding things and actions, and the integration of each series of similar impressions into a general conception: the result being the formation of as many different general conceptions as there are objects and acts and combined groups of them, which the particular type of intelligence is able to distinguish. In its lower stages, the process is one which we may call unconscious classification; and through many gradations, it rises to conscious classification, such as we see carried on by men of science.

The mental action by which from moment to moment we thus, in ways commonly too rapid to observe, class the objects and acts around, and regulate our conduct accordingly, has been otherwise named by some, and especially by Professor Bain, "discrimination." Intelligence is, in its every act, carried on by discrimination; and has advanced from its lowest stages to its highest by increasing powers of discrimination. It has done this for the sufficient reason that during the evolution of life under all its forms, increase of it has been furthered by practice or habit as well as by survival of the fittest; since good discrimination has been a means of saving life, and lack of it a cause of losing life. Let us note a few marked stages of its increase.

Look out towards the sky; shut your eyes; and pass your hand before them. You can discriminate between the presence and absence of an opaque object in front. If, being passive, an object is moved before your closed eyes by some one else, you cannot say whether it is a hand, or a book, or a lump of earth; and cannot say whether it is a small object close to, or a larger object farther off. This experience exemplifies to us the smallest degree of visual discrimination, such as that which is achieved by low creatures possessing nothing more than eye specks—minute portions of sensitive pigment in which light produces some kind of change. Evidently a creature having only this nascent vision is at great disadvantage—cannot distinguish between the obscuration caused by the moving frond of a weed in the water it inhabits, and the obscuration caused by a passing creature; cannot tell whether it results from a small creature near at hand or a larger one at a distance; cannot tell whether this creature is harmless and may serve for prey or is predacious and must be avoided. Thus one of the appliances for maintaining life is deficient, and early loss of life is apt to occur.

Passing over all intermediate grades, observe next the results of presence or absence among herbivorous creatures of the power to discriminate between plants of different kinds and qualities. By appearance, or odor, or taste, one animal is warned off from a poisonous herb, which another animal, less keenly perceptive, eats and dies. As intelligence develops, complex groups of attributes are separated in consciousness from other complex groups to which they are in many respects similar, and survival results from the discrimination; as when the fatal Monkshood is distinguished from the harmless Larkspur.

As we rise to creatures of relatively great intelligence, increasingly complicated clusters of attributes, relations and actions have to be distinguished from one another, under heavy penalties. Instance the ordinary case in which the shape and color and movements of a distant animal are mentally united into a perception of an enemy, or else are discriminated as forming some not unlike perception of a harmless animal: the result being now a successful flight and now a successful chase.

388. A much higher degree of discrimination is reached in creatures capable of appreciating the differences not only between objects perceived or presented, but also between objects conceived or represented—between the imaginations of them. The degree of mental power required for this is occasionally shown in small measure by the higher animals; as when a dog recognizes in idea the difference in length between a road that goes round the angle of a field and a short cut across the field, and takes the last. But generally it is only among men that the ability to discriminate between imagined clusters of things and properties and relations becomes appreciable. Even among men the discriminations often fail in consequence either of inaccuracy of such observations as have been made, or of imperfect ability to reproduce in thought the things observed. The contrast between Monkshood and Larkspur may serve again. Able as they are, when these two plants are before them, to see that though the two are similar in their sizes, modes of growth, deeply cut leaves, colors of flowers, &c., yet the structures of their flowers are unlike, the majority of people, even those having gardens, cannot so compare their ideas of these plants as to be able to say what the points of difference are.

If, then, between their imaginations of objects of but moderate degrees of complexity, most ordinarily disciplined minds fail to discriminate, still more will they fail to discriminate where the clusters of related attributes and properties and actions are immeasurably involved. Especially will they fail if, while many of the components are coexistent, many of them are sequent; and if, too, the groups of ideas which have to be distinguished from one another, include not only forms, colors, motions, sounds, and the feelings implied in those who make them; but include both the immediate effects wrought by a particular kind of action and the effects to be hereafter wrought by it. When the combinations of thoughts which must be simultaneously kept in mind reach these degrees of involution, the ability to discriminate either from the other, which is like it in many respects but differs in some essential respect, fails even in many highly cultured minds. Let us take instances.

Here is a geometrical problem—say, how to erect a perpendicular at the end of a straight line. Following the established routine, an ordinary teacher either shows his pupil how to solve this problem or tells him what he must do to solve it: the result being that the perpendicular is drawn as directed, and the pupil, not much interested in the proceeding, thenceforth knows how to draw it. Here is another teacher who, disapproving of this mechanical culture, adopts a different method. His pupil having been initiated through simpler problems, severally solved by his persevering efforts, takes to the new problem with zest; and, trying various experiments, in no very long time succeeds. In doing this he receives a relatively strong impression, due partly to the strained attention required, and partly to the pleasurable excitement of success. At the same time he acquires increased aptitude and increased courage; enabling him to deal by and by with more complex problems. Here, then, are two clusters of actions and acquisitions and feelings, which are in sundry respects alike. The problem is the same, the method of solution is the same, the knowledge acquired is the same; and the mechanical teacher, recognizing nothing more, does not discriminate between the two clusters of mental actions, and thinks it just as well to teach by instruction as by discovery.

Of more complex cases, one is furnished by a recent incident—the case of the Eastbourne salvationists. Most of the townspeople object to their processions headed by noisy bands; while these boisterous Christians say that they are simply maintaining that religious liberty which all now admit. But here comes the lack of discrimination. It is forgotten that while, in the interests of religious liberty, each citizen or group of citizens may rightly perform ceremonies ancillary to his belief; in the interests of general liberty, individual citizens or groups of them, may rightly resist intrusions upon that peaceful course of life they are pursuing. There is inability to separate in thought those assertions of religious freedom which do not involve aggressions on others, from those which do involve aggressions on others, in the form of nuisances. And not only do these fanatics fail to distinguish between religious liberty and religious license, but even our legislators (if we suppose them to be acting sincerely instead of seeking votes) also fail.

One more instance furnished by the politics of the day may be added—the failure, alike by legislators and people, to discriminate between the effects of moral injunctions on those having natures with which they are congruous, and their effects on those having natures with which they are incongruous. Here is a set of precepts, printed, read, explained, emphasized; and here are children's minds with their clusters of ideas, powers of understanding, and groups of feelings. The prevalent assumption is that since certain effects result where there is intellectual apprehension of these precepts *plus* responsive sentiments, like effects will result where there is the same intellectual apprehension *minus* the responsive sentiments. People think it needs only to teach children what is right and they will do what is right! They expect that by education—nay, even by mere acquisition of a knowledge which is not related to conduct—they will diminish crime!

Discrimination, then, characterizing intelligence from its lowest to its highest forms, is certain to be still very incomplete where the things to be discriminated are not visible objects and actions, but are mental representations of complex aggregates of things and actions and feelings, and causes and effects; part of them belonging to the passing time, and part of them to the time coming. After observing the stretch of imagination required for proper recognition of differences in this wide and obscure field, we may feel certain that alike in sociology and in ethics, failures to discriminate must be many and disastrous.

389. But why this long psychological disquisition? The answer is foreshadowed in the title of the chapter—"Kinds of Altruism." That altruistic conduct has divisions which must be distinguished is obviously implied. That the conceptions of these respective divisions, made up of represented things, acts, relations, and results, present and future, are among those complex things which are difficult to part from one another, has been above shown by analogy. That only those who are at once observant, critical, and have great powers of mental representation, can adequately make the discriminations, is a further implication. And that grave evils result from the prevalent inability is a corollary.

As distinguished from egoistic actions, altruistic actions include all those which either negatively by self-restraint, or positively by efforts for their benefit, conduce to the welfare of fellow men: they include both justice and beneficence. As we have seen in the last part, the first of these great divisions of altruism implies a sympathetic recognition of others' claims to free activity and the products of free activity; while the other great division implies a sympathetic recognition of others' claims to receive aid in the obtainment of these products, and in the more effectual carrying on of their lives. In section 54 I pointed out that the highest form of life, individual and social, is not achievable under a reign of justice only; but that there must be joined with a reign of beneficence. Here is a part of the argument:

> A society is conceivable formed of men leading perfectly inoffensive lives, scrupulously fulfilling their contracts, and efficiently rearing their offspring, who yet, yielding to one another no advantages beyond those agreed upon, fall short of that highest degree of life which the gratuitous rendering of services makes possible. Daily experiences prove that every one would suffer many evils and lose many goods, did none give him unpaid assistance. The life of each would be more or less damaged had he to meet all contingencies single-handed. Further, if no one did for his fellows anything more than was required by strict performance of contract, private interests would suffer from the absence of attention to public interests. The limit of evolution of conduct is consequently not reached, until, beyond avoidance of direct and indirect injuries to others, there are spontaneous efforts to further the welfare of others.

Throughout the past there has been slowly growing into clearness the distinction between these two primary divisions of altruism. But though justice and generosity have in recent days come to be fairly well discriminated, the changes now going on are confusing them again. The universal dissolution by which the old order of things is being abolished while a new order is being established, is bringing with it a dissolution of old conceptions: many of them wrong but some of them right. Among the last is this distinction between justice and beneficence. On the one side the many, eagerly expecting good, and on the other side the few, anxious to do good to them, agree in practically disregarding the line of demarcation between things which are to be claimed as rights and things which are to be accepted as benefactions; and while the division between the two is being obliterated, there is ceasing to be any separation made between means appropriate to the one and means appropriate to the other. Hotheaded philanthropy, impatient of criticism, is, by helter-skelter legislation, destroying normal connections between conduct and consequence; so that presently, when the replacing of justice by generosity has led to a redistribution of benefits irrespective of deserts, there will be reached a state having for its motto the words: It shall be as well for you to be inferior as to be superior.

390. The two great divisions of altruism, justice and benefi- cence, are to be discriminated as the one needful for social equilibrium, and therefore of public concern, and the other as not needful for social equilibrium, and therefore only of pri- vate concern. Observe why the two must be kept separate.

We have seen that justice in its primordial form, as seen throughout the animal kingdom at large, requires that each creature shall take the consequences of its own conduct; and among all ungregarious creatures this law operates without any qualification.

Along with gregariousness, especially when it reaches the degree which the human race exhibits, there arises a further requirement. While, as before, the relation between conduct and consequence has to be so maintained that actions shall be restrained by experience of results, actions have to be further restrained by the necessity of so limiting them that the inter- ference of each citizen with others shall not be greater than is implied by the associated state.

But, as shown in the above quotation, before life, individual and social, can reach their highest forms, there must be ful- filled the secondary law, that besides exchange of services under agreement there shall be a rendering of services beyond agreement. The requirements of equity must be supple- mented by the promptings of kindness.

And here we come upon the truth above hinted, and now to be emphasized, that the primary law of a harmonious social cooperation may not be broken for the fulfillment of the sec- ondary law; and that therefore, while enforcement of justice must be a public function, the exercise of beneficence must be a private function. A moment's thought will make this impli- cation manifest.

Beneficence exercised by a society in its corporate capacity, must consist in taking away from some persons parts of the products of their activities, to give to other persons, whose activities have not brought them a sufficiency. If it does this by force it interferes with the normal relation between conduct and consequence, alike in those from whom property is taken and in those to whom property is given. Justice, as defined in the foregoing pages, is infringed upon. The principle of harmonious social cooperation is disregarded; and the disregard and infringement, if carried far, must bring disasters. There are three, which we may contemplate separately.

391. If, that the inferior may have benefits which they have not earned, there are taken from the superior benefits which they have earned, it is manifest that when this process is carried to the extent of equalizing the positions of the two, there ceases to be any motive to be superior. Long before any such extreme is reached, there must result an increasing discouragement of the industrious, who see the surplus products of their industry carried away; and there must result among these better citizens an intensifying dissatisfaction, tending ever towards revolution. There must be a decline towards an unprosperous state and an unstable state.

A further result must be a slow degeneracy, bodily and mental. If, by an indiscriminate philanthropy, means of subsistence are forcibly taken from the better for the improved maintenance of the worse, the better, most of whom have means already insufficient for the good nurture of offspring, must have those means made still further deficient; while the offspring of the worse must, to a like extent, be artificially fostered. An average deterioration must be caused.

An equally disastrous, or still more disastrous, effect remains to be named. The policy, if persistently pursued, leads on to communism and anarchism. If society in its corporate capacity undertakes beneficence as a function—if, now in this direction and now in that, the inferior learn by precept enforced by example, that it is a state duty not simply to secure them the unhindered pursuit of happiness but to furnish them with the means to happiness; there is eventually formed among the poorer, and especially among the least deserving, a fixed belief that if they are not comfortable the government is to blame. Not to their own idleness and misdeeds is their misery ascribed, but to the badness of society in not doing its duty to them. What follows? First there grows up among numbers, the theory that social arrangements must be fundamentally changed in such ways that all shall have equal shares of the products of labor—that differences of reward due to differences of merit shall be abolished: there comes communism. And then among the very worst, angered that their vile lives have not brought them all the good things they want, there grows up the doctrine that society should be destroyed, and that each man should seize what he likes and "suppress," as Ravachol said, everyone who stands in his way. There comes anarchism and a return to the unrestrained struggle for life, as among brutes.

Such then are the ultimate results of not discriminating between justice and beneficence, and between the instrumentalities proper for carrying on the two.

392. But now we come to a question, no doubt existing unshaped in the minds of many, the right answer to which clears up, in another way, the prevailing confusion. Let me put this question in the form most favorable to those whose illusions I am seeking to dissipate.

"You say that justice in its primordial form requires that each creature shall receive the results of its own nature and consequent conduct. Of human justice, however, you say that while, as before, it demands that actions shall bring their natural consequences, the actions which do this must be limited to such as do not interfere with the similarly limited actions of others. Obviously the result is that while, under the reign of brute justice, each individual takes advantage of his powers, to the extent of injuring or destroying not only prey but also competitors, under the reign of human justice he may not do this—he is forbidden to injure competitors. What happens? Being protected by the incorporated society, the inferior members are enabled to carry ȯn their activities and reap all the benefits; which they could not have done had the superior used their superiorities without control. May it not be, then, that under the reign of human justice raised to a higher form, the inferior, thus partially saved from the results of their inferiority, shall be still further saved from them—shall not only be equalized with the superior by preserving for them their spheres of activity, but shall also be equalized with them in respect of the benefits they obtain within their spheres of activity?"

Doubtless, as I have elsewhere admitted, it seems, from one point of view, unjust that the inferior should be left to suffer the evils of their inferiority, for which they are not responsible. Nature, which everywhere carries on the struggle for life with unqualified severity, so as even to prompt the generalization—"the law of murder is the law of growth," cares not for the claims of the weaker, even to the extent of securing them fair play; and if it be admitted that this severity of nature may, among associated men, rightly be mitigated by artificially securing fair play to the inferior, why ought it not to be further mitigated by saving them from all those evils of inferiority which may be artificially removed?

Here we reach the place of divergence. Here we see the need for discrimination among complex conceptions. Here we see how important is recognition of the difference between justice and beneficence, and consequent difference between the instrumentalities appropriate to the two. For with the admission that that ferocious discipline of brute justice which issues in survival of the fittest, has, in societies of men, to be much qualified, not only by what we distinguish as human justice, but also by what we distinguish as beneficence, there must go the assertion that while the first may rightly be enforced, the second must be left to voluntary action. Denial that the second as well as the first should be attended to by the state, by no means involves denial that the second should be attended to; but merely implies that it should be otherwise attended to. It is admitted that the evils caused by inferiority should be mitigated in both ways; but it is asserted that while mitigations of the one kind should be public and general, those of the other kind should be private and special. For, as we have seen, the primary law of harmonious cooperation may not be broken for the purpose of fulfilling the secondary law; since, if it is so broken to any great extent, profound mischiefs result.

393.   For the discrimination thus demanded by a due regard for social stability, social prosperity, and social health, yet a further reason must here be urged. Only by maintaining this discrimination can the reciprocal benefits of beneficence, "blessing him that gives and him that takes," be preserved. When any of the evils which their inefficiencies or other defects bring on the inferior, are diminished by aid which some of the superior voluntarily furnish, these are made better by the exercise of their fellow feeling; but if, to mitigate them, funds are taken by force from the superior, none of this moralization results: often a demoralization—an excitement of ill feeling. Not only, as the poet says, "the quality of mercy is not strained," but also the quality of beneficence in general. If it is strained it ceases to be beneficence.

At the same time there is a corresponding difference between the effects produced on the beneficiaries. Kindly acts spontaneously done, usually excite in them emotions of gratitude and attachment; and a community containing beneficiaries thus related to benefactors, is one in which not only are the feelings of the lower favorably exercised as well as those of the higher, but one in which there is thereby produced an increased coherence and stability.

394. Having, too elaborately perhaps, discriminated between the primary altruism we call justice and the secondary altruism we call beneficence, and emphasized the need for the discrimination, we may now deal with the different kinds of beneficence. Let us first group these under certain subdivisions.

There comes first the species of beneficent conduct which is characterized by passivity in deed or word, at times when egoistic advantage or pleasure might be gained by action. Many forms of self-restraint, not commonly regarded as ethically enjoined, ought nevertheless to be so regarded; and have here to be pointed out and emphasized. These, which we have first to consider, fall under the general title—negative beneficence.

After them there come to be dealt with those kinds of actions alone recognized in the ordinary conception of beneficence, but which are here distinguished as positive beneficence. Under this head are comprised all actions which imply sacrifice of something actually or potentially possessed, that another or others may be benefited—sacrifice, it may be, of strength which would otherwise be economized, sacrifice of the product of efforts actually obtained, or of the forthcoming product of efforts made in the past. In all these there is a proximate loss of pleasure or means to pleasure; though there may be an immediate or remote compensation in sympathetic pleasure.

To complete preliminaries it needs to add that there is a cross-classification by which both of these groups have to be divided. The most conspicuous, though not the most familiar, kinds of beneficent actions, positive and negative, are those shown towards individuals who are inferior, or unfortunate, or both. But there are also beneficent actions, usually small but very numerous, which benefit those who are neither inferior nor unfortunate—actions which further the gratifications of persons around, and raise the tide of happiness in all.

In treating these divisions and subdivisions of beneficence in the order here indicated, we shall have to consider three sets of effects produced: 1, the reactive effects upon the benefactor, upon his dependents, and upon all who have claims on him; 2, the immediate effects on the beneficiary, as conducive to increase of his pleasure or diminution of his pain, and the remote effects as conducive to one or other change of character; and 3, the effects upon society at large, as influencing its stability, its immediate prosperity, and its remote prosperity.

CHAPTER 2

Restraints on Free Competition

395. **B**eyond those limits to the actions of individuals which it is the business of the state to maintain, individuals have to impose on themselves further limits, prompted by sympathetic consideration for their struggling fellow citizens. For the battle of life as carried on by competition, even within the bounds set by law, may have a mercilessness akin to the battle of life as carried on by violence. And each citizen, while in respect of this competition not to be restrained externally, ought to be restrained internally.

Among those who compete with one another in the same occupation, there must in all cases be some who are the more capable and a larger number who are the less capable. In strict equity the more capable are justified in taking full advantage of their greater capabilities; and where, beyond their own sustentation, they have to provide for the sustentation of their families, and the meeting of further claims, the sanction of strict equity suffices them. Usually, society immediately benefits by the putting out of their highest powers, and it also receives a future benefit by the efficient fostering of its best members and their offspring.

In such cases then—and they are the cases which the mass

of society, constituted chiefly of manual workers, presents us with—justice needs to be but little qualified by beneficence.

396. This proposition is indeed denied, and the opposite proposition affirmed, by hosts of workers in our own day. Among the trade unionists, and among leading socialists, as also among those of the rank and file, there is now the conviction, expressed in a way implying indignant repudiation of any other conviction, that the individual worker has no right to inconvenience his brother worker by subjecting him to any stress of competition. A man who undertakes to do work by the piece at lower rates than would else be paid, and is enabled by diligence long continued to earn a sum nearly double that which he would have received as wages, is condemned as "unprincipled"! It is actually held that he has no right thus to take advantage of his superior powers and his greater energy; even though he is prompted to do this by the responsibilities a large family entails, and by a desire to bring up his children well: so completely have the "advanced" among us inverted the old ideas of duty and merit.

Of course their argument is that the man who thus "outdoes" his fellow workers, and gets more money than they do, displaces by so much the demand for the labor of those who would else have been employed; and they further argue that, by executing the work at a smaller cost to the employer, he tends to lower the rate of wages: both of them regarded by these neo-economists, now so vociferous, as unmixed evils.

With them, as with nearly all thinkers about social and political affairs, the proximate result is the sole thing considered. Work and wages are alone thought of, and there is no thought given to the quantity of products, the concomitant prices of products, and the welfare of the consumers. Laborers and artisans conceived only as interested in getting high wages, are never conceived as interested in having cheap commodities; and there appears to be no conception that gain in the first end may involve loss in the second. When enlarging on the hardships entailed on those who, by cheaper piecework, are deprived of dearer day work, they ignore as irrelevant the fact that the article produced at less cost can be sold at less price; and that all artisans and laborers, in their capacity of consumers, benefit to that extent. Further they forget that the workers displaced become, after a time, available for other kinds of production: so benefiting the community as a whole, including all other workers.

We have here, in fact, but a new form of the old protest against machinery, always complained of by those immediately affected, as robbing them of their livelihoods. Whether through human machinery or the machinery made of wood and iron, every improvement achieves an economy and dispenses with labor previously necessary; and if that change in the human machinery constituted by adoption of piecework, and the gaining of larger earnings by greater application, is to be reprobated because of the displacement of labor implied, so also must be reprobated every mechanical appliance which from the beginning has facilitated production. He was an "unprincipled" man who substituted ploughs for spades, who replaced the distaff by the spinning jenny, who brought into use steam pumping engines in place of hand pumps, or who outran horses on roads by locomotives on railways. It matters not whether we contemplate the living agents of production or the dead implements they use; every more economical arrangement eventually lowers prices and benefits people at large. The so-called unprincipled man does good to humanity, though he inflicts temporary evils on a small number; which in fact, every improvement inevitably must.

But there remains to note the marvelous inversion of thought and sentiment implied by this socialistic trade-union idea. The man who is superior in ability or energy is thought "unprincipled" in taking advantage of his superiority; while it is not apparently thought "unprincipled" on the part of the inferior to obtain benefit by preventing the superior from benefiting himself. If in any occupation the majority, who are less able, insist that the minority, who are more able, shall not be paid higher wages than they are, and shall not discredit them by doing more or better work, it is undeniable that the majority, or less able, do this for their own advantage. Either by requiring that the more skilled and the less skilled shall be paid at equal rates, they ensure for themselves higher average wages than they would have were there discriminating payments, or else, by excluding the keener competition of the more skilled, they escape the pressure or strain which would otherwise be brought to bear on them; and in one or both of these ways the majority advantage themselves at the cost of the minority. Now if the word "unprincipled" is to be rationally applied, it is to be applied to the man who does this; for no high-principled man wishes to obtain a benefit by tying another's hands. If they are conscientious in the proper sense of the word, those who form the majority, or inferior, will never dream of requiring that the minority, or superior, shall diminish their earnings by not using their powers; and still less will they dream of trying to gain by such a course. Contrariwise, each among them, regretting though he may his relative inferiority, and wishing though he may that he had the powers of those few more favored by nature, will resolve to make the best of his smaller powers; and so far from asking to have given to him the benefits which the greater powers of others yield, he will insist that he shall have none of such benefits—will refuse point-blank to have any benefits beyond those which his nature brings him: content if the better endowed yield not material but moral benefits to the less happily constituted. This is the truly principled man, and the unprincipled man is the one who does the reverse.

And then the high-principled man, prompted to this course by a sense of equity, will be further thus prompted by a beneficent regard for the race. If he is adequately endowed with the human ability to "look before and after," he will see that a society which takes for its maxim, "It shall be as well for you to be inferior as to be superior," will inevitably degenerate and die away in long-drawn miseries.

397. But on passing from the working part of the industrial organization to the regulating part, we pass into a sphere in which a beneficent limitation of activity is sometimes called for. While the advantage which superiority gives to an artisan over his fellow artisans is relatively small, and may properly be appropriated without limit, the advantage which superiority gives to the director of many artisans over other such directors, may become very great; and it may, in the absence of a sympathetic self-restraint, be used by him to the ruin of his competitors. Such an one, so long as he does not break the law directly or indirectly, is commonly thought warranted in pushing his advantage to the extreme; but an undeveloped ethical consciousness is thus shown.

Not many years since there lived in New York a man named Stewart, who, carrying on a wholesale and retail business on a vast scale, acquired a colossal fortune. A common practice of his was suddenly to lower his prices for a certain class of goods to an unremunerative rate, seriously damaging, if nothing more, numerous small traders, and greatly hampering, if he did not ruin, sundry large ones. Another practice was to encourage and aid some manufacturer in apparently a friendly spirit, and then, when he was largely indebted, come down upon him for immediate payment; selling him up and often buying his stock when he could not at once pay.

Competitive warfare carried on in this style, might not unfitly be called commercial murder; and were its flagitiousness to be measured by the pain inflicted, it might be held worse than murder, originally so called: the amount of suffering eventually caused among the ruined men and their families, being greater than that which many an assassin visits on his victims and others.

Such utter lack of negative beneficence is to be condemned not only because of the intense evils thus directly inflicted, but is also to be condemned in the interests of society, as defrauding it of those advantages which competition, normally carried on, yields. For though, while competitors are being forced to sell at unremunerative prices, the public benefits; yet, after competitors have been thrust to the wall and a practical monopoly achieved, there comes a more than compensating rise of prices, by which the public suffers. In brief, the forms of competition are employed to destroy competition.

And then, as we shall see hereafter under another head, the transgressing trader himself, and his belongings, do in the long run suffer indirectly. They are led into a type of life lower than they might otherwise have led.

In its application to cases of this kind, the popular maxim "Live and let live" may, then, be accepted as embodying a truth. Anyone who, by command of great capital or superior business capacity, is enabled to beat others who carry on the same business, is enjoined by the principle of negative beneficence to restrain his business activities, when his own wants and those of his belongings have been abundantly fulfilled; so that others, occupied as he is, may fulfill their wants also, though in smaller measure.

398. What is to be said in this connection concerning competition among professional men—especially among doctors and lawyers?

An eminent physician who gives advice to all patients asking it, including patients who have left the physicians they previously consulted, cannot be blamed for doing this; even though he has already an amply sufficient income. For, supposing his reputation to be deserved, the implication is that, by giving the advice asked, he diminishes suffering and perhaps saves life; and this he cannot well refuse to do out of regard for competing physicians. It may rightly be held, too, that he is justified in raising his fees. Did he not by doing this diminish the number of his patients, two evils would happen. The swarm would become so great that no one would get proper attention; and his own health would speedily so greatly suffer that he would become incapacitated. But negative beneficence may properly require that he shall send to some of his brother physicians patients suffering from trivial maladies, or maladies concerning the treatment of which there can be no doubt.

On turning from the consulting room to the law court, we meet with cases in which professional competition needs restraining, not by negative beneficence only, but by justice. A system under which a barrister is prepaid for services he may or may not render, as it chances—a system under which another barrister in less repute is also retained, and feed to do the work for him should he fail to appear—a system which proceeds by quasi-contract which is closed on the side of the one who pays but not closed on the side of the one who works, is clearly a vicious system. But such restraints on the taking of cases by counsel, as would result either from regard for the equitable claims of clients or from consideration for competitors, is said to be impracticable. We are told that at the bar a man must either take all the business which comes to him or lose his business. Now this plea, though perpetually repeated, may reasonably be doubted until the assertion that such *would* be the result had been verified by the proof that such *has been* the result. It requires a large faith to believe that one whose conscientiousness determines him to take no more work than he can efficiently perform, or else, from regard for his fellows, refuses cases that they may have them, cannot do this without losing all his cases. For since one who thus limited the number of his clients would, as a matter of course, deny himself to those whose causes he thought bad, the mere fact of his appearance in any cause would become a preliminary assurance that it was a good cause—an assurance weighing much with a jury; and how, under such circumstances, implying increased anxieties to obtain his services, the demand for them should decrease beyond the degree he desired, it is difficult to see.

Clearly in this case, such negative beneficence as is implied by relinquishment of business that competitors may benefit, is a concomitant of that justice which demands that pay shall not be received unless services are rendered, and is a concomitant of that social benefit which results if good causes have good advocates. Moreover, it is a concomitant of that normal regard for self which forbids excess of work.

399. Yet another form of competition must be dealt with, though it is difficult to deal with it satisfactorily. I refer to the competition between one who has, by discovery or invention, facilitated some kind of production, and those who carry on such production in the old way.

Here, if he undersells competitors, he does so not, as in the cases instanced, to drive them out of the business; but he does so as a collateral result of giving a benefit to society. As already said (sec. 306), he has made a new conquest over nature, and giving, as he inevitably does, the greater part of the advantage to the community, he may rightly retain for himself something more than is obtained by carrying on production as before. Still there comes the question—How far shall he push his advantage? Should not negative beneficence restrain him from ruining his competitors by underselling them too much? But to this the answer is that if he does not undersell them in a decided manner, he does not give to the public the advantage which he might give. Out of regard for the few he disregards the many.

One way only does there seem to be in which, while consulting the welfare of the community, and while justly maintaining his own claim to a well-earned reward, he may also show due consideration for those whose businesses he of necessity diminished or destroyed. He may either offer them the use of his improved appliance at a moderate royalty, or may make them his agents for the sale of his products: giving them, in either case, a great advantage over any others who may wish to stand in the like positions, and may thus at any rate diminish the injury to them if he does not even cancel it.

400. It is needless in this place to illustrate further the operation of negative beneficence in putting restraints on competition, in addition to those which justice maintains.

With a population ever pressing on the means of subsistence, and amid struggles to attain higher positions and so be able, among other things, to rear offspring better, there must arise multitudinous cases in which natural capacities, or circumstances, or accidents, give to some great advantages over others similarly occupied. To what extent such advantages may be pushed, individual judgments, duly influenced by sympathy, must decide.

By refraining from certain activities which are at once legitimate and profitable, competitors may be benefited; and the question whether they should be so benefited must be answered by considering whether the wants of self and belongings have not been sufficiently regarded, and whether the welfare of competitors, as well as the welfare of society as a whole, do not enjoin desistance.

CHAPTER 3

Restraints on Free Contract

401. Society in its corporate capacity cannot be blamed for enforcing contracts to the letter—is often, indeed, to be blamed because it does not enforce them, but deliberately countenances the breaking of them, or itself breaks them; as when, after the houses forming a street have been taken on lease at high rents, because few vehicles pass, it authorizes the turning of this quiet street into a noisy thoroughfare; or as when, having given parliamentary titles to buyers of encumbered estates on certain terms, it, by subsequent laws, alters those terms; or as when it allows a proprietary agreement, entered into for one purpose, to be extended by a two-thirds majority so as to cover another purpose.

Contracts, then, must be strictly adhered to and legally enforced; save, as before pointed out, in cases where a man contracts himself away. And this necessity for severity in the enforcement of contracts, will be manifest on observing that if there grew up the system of judicially qualifying them, out of beneficent regard for defaulters, this beneficent regard would promptly be counted upon; and reckless contracts would be made in the expectation that, in cases of failure, the worst consequences would be staved off.

But while it is not for the state to relax contracts or mitigate their mischievous results, it remains open for those between whom they are made, voluntarily to modify the operation of them. Negative beneficence may still enjoin an entire or partial relinquishment of such undue advantage as a contract, literally interpreted, has given. Of merciless enforcement of contracts, and unscrupulous disregard of claims which have arisen under contracts, the treatment of tenants by landlords, especially in Ireland, furnish numerous instances. Where a barren tract—stony or boggy—taken on a short lease at a small rent, has by persistent labor been reclaimed, and the resulting fertility has given it some value, it not uncommonly happens that the landlord offers to this industrious tenant the option of either surrendering his occupancy at the end of his lease, or else of paying a greatly raised rent, proportionate to this raised value which his own toil has given to it. The contract not having been of a kind to exclude this disastrous result, the law can say nothing; but the landlord, if duly swayed by the sentiment of negative beneficence, will refrain from taking advantage of his tenant's position—will, indeed, feel that in this case what is here distinguished as negative beneficence does but enjoin a regard for natural justice, as distinguished from legal justice.

Kindred cases there are, as those of the Skye-crofters, in which the making of contracts, though nominally free, is not actually free—cases in which the absence of competing landlords gives to a local landlord an unchecked power of making his own terms, and in which the people, having little or no choice of other occupations and being too poor to emigrate, are compelled to accept the terms or starve. Here, where the conditions under which equitable exchange can be carried on are suspended, it remains for the promptings of negative beneficence to supplement those of equity, which are rendered inoperative. The landlord is called on to refrain from actions which the restraints of technically formulated justice fail to prevent.

There are cases of a more familiar kind in which sympathy demands, and often with success, that contracts shall be but partially enforced. During recent years of agricultural depression, the requirements of leases have been in multitudinous instances voluntarily relaxed, in ways which negative beneficence suggested. Landlords have returned parts of the rents agreed upon, when tenants have been impoverished by bad harvests to an extent which could not reasonably have been expected when the lease was made.

402. In the transactions of businessmen, there occur sundry allied classes of cases in which compromises between self-regard and regard for others, imply desistance from actions which justice does not interdict. Let us take three such.

Here is a grazier who, with numerous cattle at the end of a long drought, has scarcely anything for them to eat, and who, because other graziers are similarly circumstanced, cannot sell his cattle without great loss; and here is his neighbor who happens to have reserved large stacks of hay. What shall this neighbor do? If he pushes his advantage to the uttermost, he will either entail on the unfortunate grazier immense loss by the sale of his cattle, or impoverish him for years by an enormous expenditure in fodder. Clearly negative beneficence requires him to moderate his terms.

Another instance is that of a contractor who has undertaken an extensive work on terms which, to all appearance, will leave him only a fair remuneration, making due allowance for ordinary contingencies—say a heavy railway cutting, or a tunnel a mile or two long. No one suspected when the contract was made, that in the hill to be tunneled there existed a vast intrusion of trap. But now where the contractor expected to meet with earth to be excavated he finds rock to be blasted. What shall be done? Unless he is a man of large capital, strict enforcement of the contract will ruin him; and even if wealthy he will do the work at a great loss instead of at a profit. It may be said that even justice, considered not as legally formulated but as reasonably interpreted, implies that there should be a mitigation of the terms; since the intention of the contract was to make an exchange of benefits; and still more is mitigation of the terms required by negative beneficence—by abstention from that course which the law would allow. But clearly it is only where a disastrous contingency is of a kind greatly exceeding reasonable anticipation, that negative beneficence may properly come into play.

Under pressure entailed by a commercial crisis, a trader, while unable to get further credit from his bank, is obliged to meet a bill immediately falling due. One who has capital in reserve is asked for a loan on the security of the trader's stock. He may make either a merciful or a merciless bargain. He may be content with a moderate gain by the transaction, or, taking advantage of the other's necessities, may refuse except on conditions which will involve immense loss, or perhaps eventual bankruptcy. Here, again, there is occasion for the self-restraint which sympathy prompts.

Since, in cases such as these three, there is voluntary action on both sides, insistence, on ruinously hard terms cannot be classed under the head of injustice; but we are led to recognize the truth that in such cases the injunctions of negative beneficence are scarcely less stern than those which justice utters. Though in the first and the last instances, the taking of a pound of flesh is not under a contract previously made, it is under a contract to which there is practically no alternative; and in the last case as in the first, if the contract is fulfilled the patient may be left to bleed to death.

Let it be added that not only does the sympathetic regard for others' welfare which we here class as negative beneficence, forbid the unscrupulous carrying out of certain transactions which strict justice does not forbid, but regard for public welfare does the same thing. Any course which needlessly ruins those who are on the whole carrying on well their occupations, entails an injury to the social organization.

403. A still larger sphere throughout which the requirements of justice have to be qualified by the requirements of negative beneficence, is presented by the relations between

employers and employed—the contracts between those who yield services and those who pay for them.

How far ought an employer to take advantage of the competition among workers, who often greatly exceed in number the number wanted, and are some of them willing to accept low payments rather than starve? This question is much less easy to answer than at first appears; since it is complicated by other questions than those which concern the qualification of justice by negative beneficence. People who blame, often in the strongest language, masters who do not give higher wages than the market rate obliges them to give, think only of the fates of those who are employed, and forget the fates of those who remain unemployed. Yet obviously a master who, in an overfull market of wage earners, gives more than he is obliged, rejects the offers of those who would have taken less. Hence the most needy go without work, while the work is given to those whose needs are not so extreme—those who would not accept such low pay. Now while contemplating the benefits derived by these less necessitous, it will not do to leave out of consideration the exacerbated distress of the more necessitous. It seems a necessary implication that a seemingly generous employer, who looks only at direct results, may, by his generosity, intensify the miseries of the most miserable, that he may mitigate the miseries of the less miserable.

A further disastrous effect may be entailed. The competition in each business is keen, and the margin of profit on transactions is often thereby made so narrow, that much increase in the cost of production consequent on payment of higher wages, must cause inability to meet competitors in the market. Bankruptcy, by no means uncommon even among traders who economize in wages as much as they can, must therefore be the fate of those who do not economize. Only one whose capital is greatly in excess of his immediate wants, can behave thus generously for a time; and even on him bankruptcy must come if he persists. To the reply that he might distribute among his work-people his surplus returns when these were greater than usual, the rejoinder is that disaster would follow were he ordinarily to do this. Though, during a time of prosperity, an employer makes large profits, yet when there presently comes a time of depression, he is not unfrequently obliged to continue working without profit, or even at a loss, that he may keep his staff employed and his machinery in order; and had he not allowed himself to accumulate while prosperous, he could not do this.

Once more there is the fact, either overlooked or deliberately ignored by those who foster the antagonism between employers and employed, that a universal rise in wages is of no use if there occurs simultaneously a universal rise in the prices of commodities. The members of each trade union, thinking only of themselves as producers, and of the advantage to be gained by forcing masters to pay them more, forget that, other things equal, the price of the article they produce must presently rise in the market to a proportionate extent. They forget that if the members of each other trade union do the like, the things they severally produce will also rise in price; and that since, in respect of the more important commodities, the chief consumers are the masses of producers, or the people at large, these will have to pay more for all the things they buy. A broad view of the matter would show them that the factors are these: 1. A quantity of labor expended by all workers. 2. A quantity of capital required for the producing appliances, for stocks of raw materials, and for stocks of the articles produced. 3. A proportion of brainwork for regulating the labor and carrying on the financial operations—purchase and sale. 4. A resulting supply of products, which, in one way or other, has to be divided out among members of the community. As this supply is for the time being fixed, an increased share awarded to bodily labor implies a decreased share to capital, or mental labor, or both. Reduction of the interest on capital is restrained, since, if it is great, capital will go elsewhere; and if, by combination, the reduction is universally pushed below a certain limit, capital will cease to be accumulated. There is also a limit to the lowering of the payment for mental labor. Business capacity will go abroad if ill paid at home; and if everywhere the remuneration is inadequate, the stock of it will diminish. Men will not undergo the intellectual labor and the discipline needed to make them good managers, if they are not tempted by the prospect of considerable rewards. Thus the margin within which, under ordinary circumstances, negative beneficence may mitigate the usually hard terms of the labor market, is but narrow; and even within this margin, it may, as we have seen, involve unintentional cruelty with intentional kindness.

In so far as pecuniary contracts for services are concerned, the only cases in which negative beneficence operates, with undoubted advantage, are cases in which an employer whose returns are being so rapidly augmented as to give him more than the needful reserve, does not continue passively to take advantage of the change until he is forced to raise wages by the increased demand for labor—declines to use his power of monopolizing all the profit which circumstances give him. But here we verge upon the province of positive beneficence.

404. While, in the treatment of the employed by the employer, there is recognized scope for negative beneficence, in the treatment of an employer by the employed many suppose there is none. But this is untrue.

Every now and then the newspapers report some case in which a large contract for works, which have to be completed before a specified time under heavy penalty, is rendered unprofitable, or even ruinous, by workmen who seize the opportunity of demanding higher wages: believing that the contractor will have no alternative but to comply. If they give the required notices of termination of their engagements with the employer, they cannot be charged with injustice. They simply propose terms more favorable to themselves and decline continuing to work on the less favorable terms. How far the sentiment of negative beneficence ought to qualify their action, must depend on the circumstances of the particular case. Perhaps they have good reason to know that the contract has been taken at very profitable rates, and that payment of the higher wages demanded will still leave the contractor a sufficient return; and in this case the taking advantage of his necessity is consistent with a reasonable altruism. Perhaps, though not likely to gain largely by this particular contract, he has, during previous years, accumulated vast sums and has been a hard taskmaster; and in which case, too, sympathy with him does not indicate such regard for his interests as may prevent him from losing. But in other cases the treatment of an employer as one whose interests are to be entirely disregarded is indefensible. And not only does due consideration for him forbid this indirect coercion, but it is forbidden by regard for society. If, being frequently thus treated, a contractor is ruined, the society loses a useful functionary; and, at any rate for a time, the employed themselves find a diminished demand for their services.

But the endeavors of workers thus to better themselves by taking advantage of an employer's necessities, are in most cases not only unrestrained by the promptings of negative beneficence, but they are unrestrained by the promptings of justice. For while they refuse to work any longer on the terms previously agreed upon, the strikers commonly use their violence, or threats of violence, to prevent others from accepting those terms. They thus break the law of equal freedom. While they assert the right to enter into, or to refuse, contracts themselves, they deny to their fellows the same right. They may without ethical transgression try to persuade others to join them—may without doing wrong argue with those who propose to take their places, and frown on them if they persist; but any course which either forcibly hinders them from taking the places, or puts them in fear of evil consequences other than unpopularity, is morally forbidden: doubly forbidden, since negative beneficence joins with justice in reprobating their course. Those who would accept the terms they refuse (frequently good terms) are often impelled to do so by their responsibilities; and to prevent them is to entail distress not only on them but on their families.

If, as happens not only in the cases indicated but in cases of other kinds, both masters and nonunionist workers are coerced by some form of the system now called boycotting—if, as commonly happens, a united body of men refuse to work along with a man who is not a member of their union; or if, as in Ireland, a political combination enforces social outlawry against those who do not join them; we may see, as before, that the wrongs done are primarily injustices. Whatever the law may at present say about the matter, it is clear that men may, both individually and in combination, refuse to work with, or trade with, or hold any communication with, a certain person, so long as they do not in any way interfere with his activities. Their combination cannot properly be called a conspiracy, unless the thing which they conspire to do is wrong; and there is no breach of the law of equal freedom in declining to work along with one who is disapproved, or in declining to do business with him. The wrong done usually consists in the use of coercion to form and maintain the boycotting organization, and in inflicting penalties on those who do not obey it. No appreciable evil would result if each person remained not nominally but actually free to join or not to join the combination. Even without the checks which negative beneficence imposes the checks which justice imposes would suffice.

I may remark, in passing, that by their disregard of such checks, we are shown how far the mass of men are from fitness for free institutions. A society in which it has become a vice to maintain personal independence, and a virtue to submit to a coercive trade organization and to persecute those who do not, is a society which will rapidly lose again the liberties it has, in recent times, gained. Men who so little understand what freedom is will inevitably lose their freedom.

405. On contracts which justice does not restrain, the restraints put by negative beneficence which have been thus far considered, are those which forbid unduly pressing against

another an advantage which circumstances give. A higher form of negative beneficence operating in business transactions has to be considered.

Here and there may be found one who not only declines to sacrifice another's interests for his own benefit, but who goes further, and will not let the other make a sacrifice—will not let the other injure himself by a bad bargain. While not disregarding his own claims, he will not let his client or friend make bad terms for himself; but volunteers to give more, or to do more, than is asked. In a fully developed industrial society, formed of units having natures moulded to its requirements, such a mode of action will be normal. Beyond observance of that justice which consists in fulfillment of contract, there will be observance of that negative beneficence which forbids making a contract unduly advantageous to self.

Conduct thus guided is at present necessarily rare. People whose newspapers record in detail the betting transactions by which one receives pleasure through another's pain, are not people likely to refrain from hard bargains. The qualifying of contracts by sympathetic anxiety for another's welfare, cannot be prevalent in a nation which is given over to gambling throughout all its grades, from princes down to potboys.

CHAPTER 4

Restraints on Undeserved Payments

406. Still limiting ourselves to transactions in which money, or some equivalent, plays a part, we have here to consider a kind of negative beneficence which at first sight seems wholly unbeneficent. In daily occurring instances, immediate sympathy prompts certain actions which sympathy of a more abstract and higher form interdicts. I refer to refusals to do or to give things which are expected or asked.

This is a form of negative beneficence so unprepossessing, and so apt to be misinterpreted, that it is little practiced. The cases in which a selfish motive causes resistance to a claim made by another, enormously predominate in number; and hence most people find it nearly impossible to believe that such resistance may be instigated by an unselfish motive. Proximate effects exclusively occupy their thoughts; and they cannot see that recognition of remote pains may prevent actions which yield immediate pleasures. Usually there is scope for self-denial in doing a kind thing; but in some cases there is scope for self-denial in refusing to do what seems a kind thing, but is not so.

These are mostly cases in which regard for social interests, or the welfare of the many, ought to override regard for the welfare of individuals, or of the few. Let us contemplate instances.

407. "Poor fellows! I must give them something," says a softhearted lady, as she opens the window to hand out sixpence to the leader of a worthless band, which, for some ten minutes, has been disturbing the neighborhood by discordant playing of miserable music; and so saying she thinks she has done a good act, and ascribes lack of feeling to one who disapproves the act.

In the discussion which follows it is of little avail to point out that money given in return for something done, is properly given only when this something done is in one or other way beneficial—that it is right to pay for the receipt of pleasure, but not right to pay for the receipt of pain; and that if the principle of equally paying for pleasure and pain were pursued generally, social relations would dissolve. This is too abstract a conclusion for her. Nor is it of much use to dwell on the obvious fact that every payment of incapable bandsmen, induces them to perambulate other streets, inflicting upon other people their intolerable noises. The evils do not end here. If money can be got by bad playing, good playing will not be to the same extent cultivated; and besides a diffused infliction of pain there results a deprivation of pleasure. Yet one more evil happens. The unmusical musicians, if they were not paid, would abandon the occupation for which they are unfit and take to occupations for which they are fit; and society would then profit by their efforts instead of being injured by them. But, as I have implied, these remoter results are commonly never thought of; and, if pointed out, are too faintly imagined to operate as restraints.

Here a superior negative beneficence is shown by bearing the several pains which refusal entails—The pain which denying the immediate promptings of sympathy implies, and the pain caused by misinterpretation of motives.

408. Among the daily incidents of town life, as carried on by those who have means, may be named another in respect of which an unthinking generosity should be kept in check,

and sometimes a considerable annoyance borne. I refer to dealings with cabmen.

The question of regulated cab fares versus cab fares left, like omnibus fares, to open competition, checked only by due announcement of the rates charged, must here be left aside. The established system has adjusted itself in respect of the numbers of cabs and rates of profit of masters and men; and the question is what are the effects of not abiding by the prescribed rates. In the great majority of cases cabmen, a fairly well-behaved class, are content with their due. Here, however, is one who asks more. You know the distance well—have perhaps daily paid the same fare with the certain knowledge that it covers the claim and leaves a wide margin. But the man demands another sixpence; threatens a summons; and even when you have entered the house keeps his cab standing at the door, thinking to alarm you by his persistence. What will you do? It is a disagreeable business; and you feel inclined to pay the extra sixpence, about which you care next to nothing, and thus end the dispute. Moreover you perceive that some of those around think you mean in refusing; so that perhaps, after all, it will be better to do the generous thing as it seems. But if you are swayed by that higher negative beneficence which takes into account distant effects as well as near ones, and the benefit of the many as well as the benefit of the few, you will continue your refusal. Observe the various justifications.

If it is proper for you to yield, then it is proper for all others similarly overcharged, and similarly threatened, to yield; and it is proper that, by this process, the daily profits of cabmen should be raised. What do we learn respecting the effects, from political economy—the "dismal science," as Mr. Carlyle called it, much as a child might call its arithmetic dismal because of a like repugnance? The first effect would be a great increase in the number of cabdrivers: a pleasant occupation for idle fellows, of whom there is always no lack. The body of cabdrivers would be augmented partly by influx of these, and partly by recruits from other occupations which did not yield such good daily returns. Supposing the number of hirings of cabs remained the same (which it would not, since higher rates would lessen the demands of customers) what would be the subsequent effects on the enlarged body of cabdrivers? The same number of drives having to be divided among a larger number of drivers, it would result that, though each received more from every fare, he would have fewer fares. The reduction of his abnormally raised returns in this way, would go on until the profits of cabdriving no longer caused an influx into the occupation—until, that is, it had been brought down in its desirableness to the same level as before. A concomitant effect would be an increase in the number of cabs built; for an extra demand for them made by cabdrivers, would be met by an extra supply of cabs, and an extra rate charged for them: part of the total extra payments for cabs would go into the pockets of cab masters. Yet another evil sequence must be named. There would come a superfluous number of cabs and of horses drawing them—a wasteful investment of capital. A supply of cabs and horses in excess of the need implies a national loss. Nor have we even now got to the end of the mischief. To the wealthier of those who hire cabs, the payment of fares in excess of the authorized rates would be of no consequence, pecuniarily considered; but it would be of consequence to the less wealthy and more numerous, who are in some cases obliged to hire them, and who in other cases would be prevented from hiring them when fatigue or hurry prompted.

Of course it is not meant that through the mind of one who refuses the unwarranted demand, there suddenly pass thoughts of all these ultimate results. It is meant, rather, that if he has occasionally traced out the ramifying effects of men's actions, he is immediately conscious that breach of the understanding tacitly entered into when he took the cab, tends towards evil. He is aware, for instance, that the giving of considerable gratuities to the servants at hotels, had the effect of making their places so profitable that they had to buy them from the landlords; and he is aware that since the system of charging for servants in the bill has been established, the practice has been growing up afresh, and being presently taken account of by the landlords, will end in giving lower wages. That is, he recognizes the general truth that deviations from the normal relation of payments proportioned to services, are sure, after many mischievous perturbations, to end in reestablishment of the relation; and, being possessed by this general truth, he declines in the interests of all those who will in the long run be injuriously affected, to encourage a vicious system.

409. Other acts which appear to be beneficent but are essentially unbeneficent, are committed every hour at every railway station in the "tipping" of guards and porters. Organizations when first formed are healthy, and time is required for corruptions to gain entrance and spread. In early railway days, boards of directors were pure, and the administrations they presided over were pure. There were no share traffickings, no floatings of bad schemes for the sake of premiums, no cooking of accounts; and officials of all grades down to the lowest were paid due wages, for which they were expected to perform prescribed duties without further payments. At first, and for many years, the taking of fees by those who came in contact with passengers, was peremptorily forbidden: punishment being threatened, and occasionally inflicted, for breach of the regulation. But slowly and insidiously the feeing of porters and bribing of guards crept in, and has now become so general that even those who long resisted it as a mischievous abuse, have had to yield. To fee has become proper, and not to fee contemptible. Scarcely anyone recognizes the truth that the system arose not from generosity but from selfishness, and that it works out in various disastrous ways. Here are some of them.

Originally the contract between passenger and company was one under which the company for a certain sum agreed to carry the passenger to a specified place, giving him prescribed accommodation; and part of the accommodation was taking charge of his baggage, to do which it employed and paid certain attendants. Every passenger had a claim to the services of these attendants, and no one could take more than his share without diminishing the share equitably due to others. From the beginning, however, some passengers to whom small sums were of no moment, secretly gave these in return for extra promptness or nonessential aid: not remembering that the gaining of these attentions was at the cost of others who equally needed them—often needed them more. While the porter, expecting sixpence from some wealthy-looking man entering a first class, is fussing about in the compartment arranging his bundle of rugs, and parcels, and umbrella, in the rack, or is coming back from the van to tell him his portmanteau and gun case have been duly placed in it, two or three others are kept waiting—a shabby-looking person with bag in hand, from whom probably not a penny will come, or a widow with a cluster of children and miscellaneous belongings, who is agitated lest the train should start without her. So that the richer passenger's seeming generosity to the porter, involves ungenerosity to other passengers.

Much more serious results arise. These passengers from whom nothing is to be expected, have eventually to be accommodated. The train must wait until they, too, have been seated and their things taken charge of. What necessarily happens? The time spent in doing needless things for the paying passenger, and in telling him that his baggage is safe, and in waiting for a fee, is time in which other passengers could have been attended to. The postponed attention to these now keeps the train waiting. This effect, which I have myself repeatedly observed, and have led friends to observe, recurs at every large station, producing delay upon delay; and the general result is—chronic unpunctuality. That some passengers may have an undue share of the services for which every one paid when he took his ticket, all passengers must lose time. Fifty or a hundred people get to their journeys' ends long after the announced hours: occasionally to their great inconvenience. Nor is this all. The great majority of railway accidents are caused by unpunctuality. Collisions never occur between trains which are where they should be at the appointed times.

Collateral mischiefs have followed. From the feeing of porters has grown the bribing of guards; and to this are due sundry evils. That a gentleman—or one dressed as such—who has given or promised a shilling, may have partial or entire monopoly of a compartment, other compartments are inconveniently crowded. Worse happens. Here is one who, seeking a place, looks in where there are but two persons, with coats and rugs on the seats to represent others, and hurriedly seeks elsewhere in vain. At length he asks the guard whether these seats are occupied, and, forcing out the reply that they are not, only after stern demand has the locked door opened: a transaction which shows clearly how the system of gratuities initiates a selfish habit of getting extra advantage by taking from others the advantages they have paid for. Still worse is a concomitant evil—the bribing of guards to allow smoking in nonsmoking compartments. This abuse has now grown to the extent that guards carry in their pockets labels with the printed word "Smoking," which they fasten on the window of this or that compartment, as their paying clients inside request. It has actually come to this, and the company condones practices by which all first-class compartments are being made to stink like the taproom of a pothouse.

Here, then, are illustrations of the mode in which an apparently innocent yielding to the tacit expectations of porters, leads the way to grave abuses: some of them occasionally entailing great loss of property and even loss of life. We are shown how that kind of negative beneficence which takes account of general and remote welfare, sometimes enjoins resistance to the instigations of immediate sympathy, and enjoins also the bearing of odium.

410. Generalizing these conclusions, we may say that exchange of benefits should always conform as nearly as pos-

sible to actual or tacit contract where there is one; or, where there is no contract, to such a conceived one as might have been reasonably made.

One of the traits of evolution is increasing definiteness, and, in the course of social progress, we find increasing definiteness in the transactions among citizens. Originally there were no wages or salaries, no specified agreements, no avowed prices for commodities. The regime was one of compulsory services, of presents, of bribes; and exchanges of benefits were vague and uncertain. Hence the implication is that deviations from cooperation under contract, are retrograde changes—tend towards a lower type of society, and should be resisted.

That social life may be carried on well without gratuities, we have clear proof. A generation ago, while there still continued much of the purity which at first characterized American institutions, employees, and among others the servants in hotels, looked for nothing beyond the wages they had contracted to have for services rendered. In England, too, at the present time, there are to be found, even among the more necessitous, those who will not accept more than they have bargained to receive. I can myself recall the case of a poor workwoman who, seeming to be underpaid by the sum she asked, declined to receive the extra amount I offered her. So that, evidently, it is quite possible to have on both sides resistance to a retrograde form of social cooperation.

In such a state the function of negative beneficence, in so far as it concerns the relations of employers and employed, is that of seeing that the employed do not, when the agreement is made, underestimate the values of their services. Clearly, under the rule of the implied sentiments, that which is lost by the cessation of irregular payments will, in the long run, be gained by the raising of regular payments.

CHAPTER 5

Restraints on Displays of Ability

411. Beyond the material advantages which men give and receive under the system of social cooperation, they give and receive nonmaterial advantages. These are the benefits, or satisfactions, or pleasures, obtained during social intercourse; and which may or may not be apportioned in the most desirable ways. Here the office of negative beneficence is that of so restraining the actions which bring such gratifications to self, as to allow others to obtain their shares.

The superiorities, bodily or mental or both, which enable one citizen to exceed others in gaining wealth, but which, as we have seen, he ought not to utilize to the extreme, regardless of others' welfare, are superiorities which may also bring to him an unusually large share of approbation. Or an unusually large share of approbation may come to one who has superiorities of another order, conducive, say, not to material prosperity but to popularity. In such cases there arises the question—How far shall the superior push his advantages? To what extent shall he refrain from using his greater faculties; so that others may obtain applause, or may not experience the pain of defeat?

Difficult questions grow out of these. The battle of life through which all higher powers, subhuman and human, have arisen, may rightly be carried out of that activity which has sustentation for its end, into that activity which has for its end the pleasures given by superfluous play of the faculties. In the absence of this competition, partly bodily but mainly mental, social intercourse would lose its salt. And yet in this field, as in the other, sympathy ought to produce a self-restraint limiting the pleasures of success.

412. A form of selfishness occasionally displayed, and rightly condemned, is that of men who display without bounds their remarkable conversational powers. Of various brilliant talkers we read that on some occasions the presence of others who vied with them, raised obvious jealousies; and that on other occasions, in the absence of able competitors, they talked down everyone, and changed what should have been conversation into monologue. Contrariwise, we sometimes hear of those who, though capable of holding continuously the attention of all, showed solicitude that the undistinguished or the modest should find occasions for joining in the exchange of thoughts: even going to the extent of "drawing them out." Men of these contrasted types exemplify the absence and presence of negative beneficence; and they exemplify, too, the truth, commonly forgotten, that undue efforts to obtain applause often defeat themselves. One who monopolizes conversation loses more by moral reprobation than he gains by intellectual approbation.

Over the dinner table, or in groups of persons otherwise held together, there frequently occur cases in which an erroneous statement is made or an invalid argument urged. One who recognizes the error may either display his superior knowledge or superior logic, or he may let the error pass in silence: not wishing to raise the estimate of himself at the cost of lowering the estimate of another. Which shall he do? A proper decision implies several considerations. Is the wrong statement or invalid argument one which will do appreciable mischief if it passes uncorrected? Is the person who utters it vain, or one whose self-esteem is excessive? Is he improperly regarded as an authority by those around? Does he trample down others in the pursuit of applause? If to some or all of these questions the answer is—Yes, the correction may fitly be made; alike for the benefit of the individual himself and for the benefit of hearers. But should the error be trivial, or should the credit of one who makes it, not higher than is proper, be unduly injured by the exposure, or should his general behavior in social intercourse be of a praiseworthy kind, then sympathy may fitly dictate silence—negative beneficence may rightly restrain the natural desire to show superiority.

Of course much of what is here said respecting the carrying on of conversation or discussion, applies to the carrying on of public controversy. In nearly all cases the intrusion of personal feeling makes controversy of small value for its ostensible purpose—the establishment of truth. Desire for the *éclat* which victory brings, often causes a mercilessness and a dishonesty which hinder or prevent the arrival at right conclusions. Negative beneficence here conduces to public benefit while it mitigates private injury. Usually the evidence may be marshaled and a valid argument set forth, without discrediting an opponent in too conspicuous a manner. Small slips of statement and reasoning, which do not affect the general issue, may be generously passed over; and generosity may fitly go to the extent of admitting the strength of the reasons relied on, while showing that they are inadequate. A due negative beneficence will respect an antagonist's *amour propre*; save, perhaps, in cases where his dishonesty, and his consequent endeavor to obscure the truth, demand exposure. Lack of right feeling in this sphere has disastrous public effects. It needs but to glance around at the courses of political controversy and of theological controversy, to see how extreme are the perversions of men's beliefs caused by absence of that sympathetic interpretation which negative beneficence enjoins.

413. A few words may be added respecting more special motives which should occasionally prevent the superior from manifesting his superiority.

A game of skill is being played with one whose little boy is a spectator. The father's play is such as makes his antagonist tolerably certain of victory, should he put out his strength. But if he is adequately swayed by the sentiment of negative beneficence, he will, not obtrusively but in a concealed way, play below his strength, so as to let the father beat him. He will feel that such small pleasure as triumph might bring, would be far more than counterbalanced by sympathy with the annoyance of the father at being defeated in presence of his son, and by sympathy with the son on finding his father not so superior as he supposed. Though in this course some insincerity is implied, yet that evil is trivial in comparison with the evils otherwise entailed.

In like manner none will doubt that one who, in a discussion or in a wit combat, might be easily overcome, may, even though at other times unworthy of consideration, be rightly let off under particular circumstances. Say, for instance, that his fiancée is present. To show that he is ignorant, or that he is illogical, or to utter a witticism at his expense, would be cruel. All but the unusually callous will see that to shame him before a witness with whom he stands in such a relation, would be an improper exercise of intellectual power. An interlocutor who is swayed by due fellow feeling, will, in such a case, consent to see himself ill-informed or stupid, rather than inflict the pain which would follow any other course.

414. Here, then, are ways in which negative beneficence should operate by voluntarily making a conscious superiority, and thus harmonizing social intercourse.

Perhaps in such cases we see more clearly than in others, the propriety of mitigating, so far as we can, the pains caused by inequalities of faculty. As admitted on a previous occasion, the harsh discipline of nature, which favors the well-endowed and leaves the ill-endowed to suffer, has, from the human point of view, an aspect of injustice; and though, as we have seen, it is not permissible so to traverse the normal relation between conduct and consequence, as to equalize the fates of the well-endowed and the ill-endowed, it is permissible to modify its results where this may be done without appreciably interfering with the further progress of evolution. Though many difficulties stand in the way of thus qualifying the material effects which severally come to the efficient and the inefficient in the battle of life, yet comparatively little difficulty stands in the way of qualifying the mental effects, as socially manifested.

There are doubtless cases in which display of mental power in conversation or controversy, conduces to pecuniary benefit, and may hence be regarded as rightly to be taken advantage of in the struggle for life; but in the cases above instanced, which typify the average cases, the more skilled player, or better talker, or keener logician, may hold his greater powers in check without endangering the prosperity of the superior, and may avoid discrediting a competitor without appreciably furthering the prosperity of the inferior. He may here diminish the evils caused by nature's unfairness, without entailing other evils.

And restraint of the desire for triumph, thus inculcated by negative beneficence, is the restraint of a barbarous desire appropriate to early stages of human evolution. For the pride taken in victory over an opponent, is of like kind whether the opponent fights with hand or with tongue—wields the sword or wields the pen. The militant nature which throughout social progress has gloried in successful bodily encounters, is essentially the same militant nature which glories in successful mental encounters. In the interests of a higher civilization, therefore, there should be practiced this self-restraint which prevents a needless discrediting of the mentally inferior.

CHAPTER 6

Restraints on Blame

415.   The subject matter of this chapter joins naturally on to that of the last chapter—is, in fact, scarcely to be parted from it: since criticisms passed in conversation and controversy necessarily imply a kind of blame. But blame, specially so called, is sufficiently distinguishable to be separately treated.

Neither sympathy alone, nor judgment alone, serves rightly to regulate the utterance of blame, either in respect of occasion or degree. Sometimes it is a duty to withhold censure, and sometimes censure cannot be withheld without breach of duty. For right guidance many things must be borne in mind. There are the relative positions of the two, as being in some cases parent and child, in some cases employer and employed, in some cases elder and younger; while in some cases they stand in relations of equality and independence. There are the characters of the person reproving and the person reproved, as being relatively superior or inferior, either to the other; and there are the effects as liable to be beneficial or injurious, immediately or remotely or both. The presence or absence of witnesses, too, must be taken into account; as also the degree and manner of the blame.

To adjust behavior in such ways as duly to regard all the

facts and circumstances, there needs active fellow feeling and also quick perception and much foresight. Wherever possible, it is desirable that time should be taken for consideration.

416. Blame of the most familiar kind is that which the relation of parent and child leads to. In countries where the imperative need for having a son results from the belief that only by a son can proper sacrifices be made to a father's ghost, we see clearly implied the conception, which has prevailed down to comparatively modern times, that children exist mainly for the benefit of parents. Along with the prevalence of this conception and along with the enjoining of punishment, which accompanied it, the blaming of children could not well be checked by careful thought for their welfare. In modern times, however, characterized if not by entire inversion of this conception, yet by partial inversion of it, so that very often parents exist chiefly for the benefit of children, the blaming of them has come to be qualified by considerations touching the effects wrought. The better natured among parents in our days, find scope for negative beneficence in often restraining themselves from those faultfindings which irritation prompts.

Insight and sympathy will, at the cost of some self-sacrifice, cause tolerance of that restlessness, mental and bodily, characterizing early life; and will, within reasonable limits, prompt submission to that cross-questioning which children are prone to. The aim will be to find pleasure in giving the desired information; and when the questioning becomes too troublesome, to end it, not by words of blame but in some indirect way.

Constant recognition of the truth that from an undeveloped nature there must not be expected conduct which only a developed nature is capable of, will stop many scoldings. The higher regulative emotions, later than others in coming into play, must not be counted upon as though fully operative. Remembering this a parent of well-balanced feelings will not harshly condemn minor transgressions. Not that faults are to be passed over in silence, but that disapproval is to be expressed in a moderated way.

Negative beneficence will check a too-frequent blame because of remote effects as well as because of immediate effects. Perpetual infliction of moral pain produces callousness and eventually alienation. Both of these conflict with salutary discipline. A parent who passes over small faults without comment, or at most visits them with disapproving looks, and reserves open reprobation for serious transgressions, will, other things equal, obtain a control not to be obtained by a harsh parent; for the harsh parent fails to bring into play those motives from which good conduct should have proceeded, and substitutes for them those lower motives which dread of him generates.

Of course much that is here said of the family circle may be said also of the school. The measures used, punitive in a kindly way, should have in view not only the control of present conduct but the permanent moulding of character; and should form parts of a government which though mild is not lax.

417. Primarily, the relations of employer and employed, or of master and servant, must be such as are implied by conformity to contract. Justice takes precedence of beneficence; and here, therefore, considerations touching blame are subordinate to considerations touching duty. Fulfillment of the understanding made, may rightly be insisted on, and reproof for nonfulfillment may rightly be uttered—should, indeed, be uttered; for as healthy social cooperation depends on discharge of engagements, failure in the discharge (unless it is due to adequate unforeseen causes) should not be passed over in silence.

Ethical judgments on questions hence arising, are complicated by the consciousness that in the relation between employer and employed, and especially in that between master and servant, there is an element scarcely recognizable by absolute ethics. Though the agreement to render specified services for specified sums, is perfectly consistent with pure equity; yet, since fulfillment of one side of the contract, payment of money, occurs only at intervals while fulfillment of the other side by obedience to orders is continuous, there clings to it a feeling not wholly different from that which clings to the obedience of slave to owner (see sec. 169). Whether, under a reign of absolute ethics, social organization may become such as practically to eliminate this feeling, we cannot say; but under such social organizations as we now know, elimination is not possible, and a system of relative ethics has to make the best of forms of conduct which subordination gives rise to. One way of making the best of these forms is to restrain blame in amount and manner; so as to keep out of view, as much as may be, this undesirable relation.

Of the several nonfulfillments of duty, those which have their origin in the dishonest disregard of contracts entered into, are, as above implied, those on which blame may with least hesitation be visited. The withholding of blame in such cases, though it may be suggested by immediate sympathy, is not approved by that higher beneficence which recognizes distant results—the reform of the erring individual and the welfare of society. For the individual who, by lack of reproof, is encouraged in lax discharge of functions, is less likely to prosper than if his laxity is checked; and those with whom he may afterward be engaged will be advantaged by whatever improvement is made in him.

A mode of discipline to be used as much as possible in cases of the above class, may be used also with advantage in cases of another class—those in which the cause of failure in duty is forgetfulness. In the treatment of servants as in the treatment of children, the discipline of the natural reaction should be allowed to act where practicable. If they continually find that what has been left undone has eventually to be done, neglect, whether due to idleness or to carelessness, is not unlikely to be prevented. When one who in winter cannot remember to shut the door, is required to come back and shut it, there may be produced a certain amount of irritation; but the irritation will probably be less than that produced by perpetual scolding, and the desire to avoid trouble will often be effectual.

Faults which result from stupidity or awkwardness are

those which, though frequently visited with the sharpest re-
proofs, deserve the mildest. Such faults more manifestly than
most others arise from inherited defects of organization. A
scarcely credible slowness of apprehension, even of simple
things, is often found among children of the poor; and those
in whom unintelligence is innate or superinduced by ill-
nurture, are to be dealt with tenderly. If it is a function of
beneficence to mitigate, so far as consists with other ends, the
injustices of nature, then the lowly endowed should not have
those injustices of nature from which they suffer, made harder
to bear by the needlessly harsh treatment of men. Negative
beneficence requires that such blame as their failures call for,
shall be sparing in amount and gentle in kind.

Not for altruistic reasons only, but also for egoistic reasons,
should the tendency to blame be kept under restraint. For
beyond the direct self-injury caused by excess of it, there is the
indirect self-injury arising from failure of its purpose. Those
whose faultfinding is perpetual cease to be regarded; and
those who, though in authority, but rarely blame, produce
unusual effects.

418. What is to be said about the expression of blame when
the persons concerned are independent of one another—
either friends or strangers? The question is one to which there
seems no general answer. Each case must be separately considered.

Misbehavior on the part of a stranger, if not great in degree,
may often be best ignored, or at any rate be noticed only by
look or manner; since more evil than good is likely to result
from words—especially if the misbehavior is towards one-
self. But if it is of a grave kind, both immediate and remote
reasons call for notice of it. Everyone is bound to resist distinct
aggression, alike in his own interests and in the interests of
other men; for if no one resists an aggressor he is encouraged
in his aggressiveness. If the misbehavior is towards others,
the utterance of blame is not therefore uncalled for, but is in
some respects more called for; since self-interest is no longer a

factor. Interference, even by words, is in such cases often resented. Among the vulgar there is commonly vented the exclamation "What is it to you?" and the vulgar-minded in any class usually entertain the thought thus expressed. In such cases negative beneficence has no place. Any desire there may be not to give pain to the transgressor, is a desire which should be overridden by sympathy with the injured. Positive beneficence comes into play. For the transgressor who in such case makes the common rejoinder "Mind your own business" needs to be told that it is the business of everyone to aid in maintaining harmonious social life, and to defend those who are ill-treated by word or deed.

If it is a friend who has misbehaved, toward either self or others, the desire not to give pain by utterance of a reproach, is often so far enforced by the desire not to lose a friend, or not to decrease friendly feeling, that it operates unduly. The negative beneficence which in such case prompts passivity is not always to be obeyed. Blame may rightly be uttered in defense of personal claims, and still more may rightly be uttered in defense of the claims of third persons, when these have been disregarded. Contemplation of remote effects as well as immediate effects, will then show that the disagreeable thing must be said, even at the cost of giving serious offense.

But when those concerned are intimate, expression of blame may often fitly be limited to change of behavior. For while coldness of manner frequently conveys a reproof as distinctly as words, and sometimes even more forcibly, since it leaves play to the imagination of the person reproved, it has the advantage that it does not inflict pain in the same overt way, and gives much less specific reason for complaint and possible alienation.

419.   Along with insufficient restraints on blame in some cases, there go, in other cases, restraints that are too great. The utterance of condemnation, or of statements which would lead to condemnation, is often withheld where it is not only deserved but demanded.

In countries where the moral tone is low, we see antagonism to the law and sympathy with the criminal. The law is regarded by citizens as the common enemy rather than as the common friend. A feeling of kindred nature is shown among ourselves at public schools, with the result that it is a point of honor to shield a transgressor from punishment and a disgrace to inform against him. This feeling goes even to the extent that a smaller boy who has been seriously ill treated by a bigger boy, dare not say anything about his grievance to those in authority. If he does, he is sent to Coventry: the result being that no blame comes on him who has deserved it, while blame comes on him who has not deserved it.

Influenced very much as they are by school ethics, many men betray in the afterlife sentiments like these of schoolboys; so that not unfrequently they take the side of one who has seriously misbehaved, while they frown on one who exposes his misbehavior. Often, indeed, it seems better to have done wrong than to have drawn attention to the wrongdoing. The strangest anomalies occasionally arise from this reluctance to express blame where it is called for. A chairman of directors was discovered in treasonable negotiations, injurious to the interests of the company he presided over. His colleagues forced him to resign; and then, by way of "letting him down easily," as the phrase goes, gave him a testimonial—a testimonial which was subscribed to by the member of the board who informed me of the fact.

Now, as rightly understood, negative beneficence does not require such withholdings of blame: quite the contrary. There can be no ethical justification for practice which enables demerit to prosper, and makes it dangerous to bring on demerit its normal results.

420. Much that has been said in this chapter applies, with change of terms, to punishment—the blame which takes the form of hard deeds instead of hard words. Here, as elsewhere, the principle of the natural reaction should be acted upon whenever it is possible. For instance, though sympathy will

rightly cause the occasional unpunctuality of an employee to be passed by in silence, yet if the unpunctuality is chronic, maintenance of contract, in which all citizens are concerned, requires that there shall be experienced the natural reaction, by losing, in some way, part of the sum agreed upon for services. If an employer has workmen who constantly come behind time, he is defrauded of a certain amount of the work which was to be given in return for the sum to be paid; and he may rightly deduct an equivalent amount—may impose fines. Unhappily there are in our present phase of progress, many natures on which neither sense of duty, nor mild expostulation, nor strong words, have any appreciable effects; and in dealing with them the normal punishment constituted by loss of benefit, is called for by justice, and must not be interdicted by negative beneficence.

Respecting punitive deeds as well as punitive words, we may say that where decisive blame is deserved, the function of negative beneficence is that of preventing the undue severity which anger—even a legitimate anger—is apt to prompt. The sympathy which in some cases checks a direct infliction of pain, and in others suggests mitigation of reproof, may in all cases rightly rein in the excited feelings.

Moderation not abstinence is the word. There is a general notion, taking for its formula "Never lose your temper," which assumes that under all circumstances anger is improper. This is quite a mistake. Anger is a normal, and in some cases a needful, mode of displaying feeling. Were anger never shown by those who are aggressed upon, aggressions would be multitudinous. Mankind are at present not sufficiently civilized to dispense with the check which fear puts upon them. Negative beneficence can do no more than keep anger within due bounds.

CHAPTER 7

Restraints on Praise

421. How that form of altruism which we here distinguish as negative beneficence, should put any check on praise, is not obvious: to most, indeed, will appear incomprehensible.

They see at once that regard for truth should in many cases suppress the wish to give pleasure by applause. They do not doubt that when, even if there is no thought of gaining favor, there is professed an admiration which is not felt, a fault has been committed. The ancient Egyptian Ptah-hotep declared that "he who departs from truth to be agreeable is detestable"; and in the intervening five thousand years there have continued to be reprobations of flattery. In our own day the untruthfulness of one who utters insincere eulogies, excites a little contempt, even in the person eulogized. All feel, if they do not say, that there is something wrong in a kindness which prompts undeserved compliments.

But the avoidance of falsehood is in such cases the implied requirement. From veracity, and not from negative beneficence, the interdict is supposed exclusively to come. The withholding of laudations when they are not merited, cannot, it is thought, be referred to that form of altruism which refrains from acts and words productive of pain. Surely it must be a mistake to include restraints on praise under the head of negative beneficence?

No, there are other restraints besides those which truthfulness imposes. Even supposing the applause uttered or displayed arises from genuine admiration, there are circumstances under which it should be kept back. The desire to give immediate pleasure has often to be suppressed by the desire to further ultimate welfare; now of the individual, now of society.

It is difficult to deal separately with these checks to laudation, shown sometimes in look and manner, sometimes in words, which are demanded sometimes by sincerity, and sometimes by consideration of remote effects instead of proximate effects. There will be no harm in massing together the variously required withholdings of praise, which often involve considerable self-sacrifice for others' benefit.

422. Admiration for the child is by implication reflected on to the mother; and, consciously or unconsciously desiring this admiration, the mother summons her little boy from the nursery to be seen by a visitor. Already vanity, dominant enough in existing humanity at large, has been made specially active in the little urchin by daily ministrations—by special attentions to pretty clothes, to carefully curled hair, and by flattering remarks of the nursemaid. Shall you please the child and gratify the mother by some complimentary remark—shall you encourage her still more to foster the child's self-consciousness and appetite for approbation? Not to do this will cause disappointment to both, and will perhaps diminish the mother's friendly feeling. Yet a far-seeing regard for both will arrest the expected eulogy.

Here again is a handsome young lady accustomed to tribute in words and looks. She is constantly thinking of the admiration she excites and is looking for signs of it. Unquestionably her beauty is great—so great that you can scarcely avoid showing that you recognize it. Shall you give her the pleasure she seeks by letting your glances be seen? If you think only of proximate results you may; but not if you think also of remote results. If you recognize the fact that already her nature is in large measure deformed by vanity—if you watch the manifestations of her purely egoistic desire, and see how it excludes from consciousness altruistic desires, which should predominate; you will endeavor to avoid showing that you are thinking any more about her than about other persons.

Such self-restraint, called for by negative beneficence, will probably be thought by many needless or even absurd. If, however, they will consider that the mental attitude described often proves a deplorable one, eventually entailing unhappiness on self and others—if they remember that it is liable in after years to vitiate domestic life in various ways, even to the extent of making mothers jealous of their daughters; and if they remember that it has been developed year after year by the open and tacit flatteries of those around; they will see that the reticence here insisted on is not unimportant.

423. Kindred restraints, imposed now by sincerity and now by the wish to avoid doing injury, are called for in multitudinous cases where the applause expected is of something achieved—a book, a poem, or a speech, a painting or other work of plastic art, a song or a musical performance. In private life the spectator or auditor finds it difficult to act conscientiously. The wish not to disappoint prompts the utterance of approval which is not felt, and shuts out from thought the evils that may arise from uncandid speeches. Where encouragement is needed, there should of course be no greater restraint on praise than is required by truthfulness; and something may commonly be found in the way of partial approval which, serving to give pleasure without fostering vanity, may serve to excite further efforts. If the product is a sketch or a decorative work, there need to be no check caused by thought of remoter consequences; but if the product is of a literary kind—verses, an essay, or perhaps a volume—there should usually be a suppression of words which might encourage an unrealizable ambition. Silence, or adverse criticism gently

expressed, is in such cases kind: not alone as perhaps prevent-ing future disappointment of the aspirant, but also as tending to prevent public evil. Verses which have no true poetry in them, and books which contain neither facts nor thoughts of any value, do not simply entail loss to the community in paper and print thrown away, but help to smother things of true worth. The withholding of praise hence becomes in mul-titudinous cases a duty to the world at large. Negative benefi-cence commands silence.

Evils less widely diffused, but more conspicuous, arise from applauding those who have received the customary musical culture but have no considerable musical faculty, and who, on all available occasions, are invited to perform for the supposed pleasure of those around. The pestilent social system which aims to make every individual as like every other individual as possible, by passing all through the same educational mill, insists on giving to each young lady lessons in singing, and a course of instruction on the piano; even though she has not a tolerable ear, and is utterly averse to the practices she has to go through. Daily, for years, are caused weariness to the pupil and irritation to the teachers, annoyance to the household, nuisance to the neighbors; and all to achieve the result that when there comes an evening party, a song ill sung or an ill played piece on the piano, may be inflicted upon guests, who hypocritically say "Thank you." Manifestly the giving of praise, which sincerity forbids, is also here forbidden by re-gard for the general welfare. Negative beneficence of the wider kind interdicts utterances which, individually trivial though they may be, serve by their aggregate effect to main-tain a system that vitiates social intercourse.

It goes without saying that duty to society should still more imperatively forbid the public critic from giving currency to unmerited encomiums.

424. There is a form of praise allied to flattery which also needs to be restrained—the tacit flattery implied by constant agreement with another person's opinions. If, on the one hand, we must disapprove of that nature which always finds

reason to dissent, we must, on the other hand, disapprove of that nature which (moved perhaps in some measure by sympathy but often in a greater measure by a kind of servility) always finds reason to assent.

Of course regard for truth represses this undue tendency to coincide with others' views. Save in those who have got no ideas at all, there cannot but frequently arise convictions at variance with those they hear; and to utter words inconsistent with these convictions, everyone condemns as dishonest. Not only does sincerity require that the tacit praise taking this form shall be restrained, but a far-seeing negative beneficence also requires it. It is not a matter of indifference whether another continues to believe that which you see reason to think is untrue. A double evil may result from an expressed acquiescence in his statement or opinion. The error itself may have injurious consequences to him; and, further, a groundless self-esteem may be fostered. Moreover, as an ultimate effect of this acquiescent habit, social intercourse is rendered uninteresting by absence of mental conflict. Emerson somewhere reprobates the man who is "a mush of concession"; and it is clear that among those who are thus characterized, conversation must lose its point. All pronounced opinions and all individualities of character must disappear in a tame uniformity, if everybody is anxious to please everybody else by agreeing with him.

The restraint which, in this sphere, negative beneficence may rightly enjoin, is the maintaining of silence in cases where no good will be effected by avowed dissidence. Often it requires some tact to preserve the right attitude—neither to express difference when it is useless nor to profess agreement when it is not felt; but there are cases in which such tact comes in aid of kindly feeling.

425. The request to join in giving public honor to an individual who has probably done no more than perform well the duties before him, calls for another restraining action of negative beneficence.

Passive resistance to the getting up of testimonials, is seen by many to be needful to prevent further growth of an abuse. A presentation-portrait in recognition of services is proposed. If the man to be thus distinguished is actively sympathetic, he will prefer rather to go without such a mark of esteem than to have his friends taxed all round that he may receive it: knowing, as he does, that in most cases their contributions would be given under a kind of moral coercion. But if the beneficiary, not thus unusually sympathetic, countenances the subscription, then one who, under the ordinary circumstances refuses to subscribe, may do this simply from a beneficent regard for the general welfare.

Even where the applause takes the form of a costless testimonial, he may still often find good reason for refraining from joining in it. He may be restrained by the thought that the distribution of testimonials is ill adjusted to the merits of individuals: many of the more worthy being passed over while the less worthy are honored: the result being a misdirection of public opinion. And, further, he may be restrained by the belief that for the beneficiary to have done well what we had to do, should not be regarded as a reason for special eulogy; since everyone should do this as a matter of duty and not with a view to approbation.

And here, indeed, we come upon a final reason for being reticent of praise. As was pointed out in *The Principles of Psychology*, sections 519–23, the ego-altruistic sentiments have been, from early days down to our own, among the chief regulators of social conduct; and have been needful in the absence of anything like adequate amounts of the altruistic sentiments. Desires for reputation, fame, glory, have been the prompters; and not desires to do the appointed work, discharge obligations, behave kindly. Love of praise has in large measure served in place of love of rectitude. The proethical sentiments have had to rule because the ethical sentiments were not strong enough to take their places. But if so, it follows that a higher state, individual and social, will be one in which "the last infirmity of noble minds" will have greatly diminished; and in which, by implication, applause will be less sought for and less given. Men will be ruled by higher motives than love of approbation; and approbation being less demanded will be less yielded. From which conclusion it is a corollary that the appetite for praise should be discharged. A far-seeing desire to further human development, may rightly become a motive for often withholding applause—especially where it is greedily claimed.

CHAPTER 8

The Ultimate Sanctions

426. Though occasionally, in the foregoing chapters, I have briefly indicated the origin of the obligation to be beneficent, I have not under each head referred to this origin, but have thought it best here to emphasize it generally.

The admitted desideratum being maintenance and prosperity of the species, or that variety of the species constituting the society, the implication is that the modes of conduct here enjoined under the head of negative beneficence, have their remote justification in their conduciveness to such maintenance and prosperity. It was pointed out that certain restraints on free competition are demanded not only by regard for a competitor as likely to be needlessly ruined, but also by regard for society at large; injury of which would result from partial destruction of its producing and distributing organization. It was tacitly alleged that restraints on free contract are imposed by recognition of extreme damages to individuals, considerable damage to society, and consequent damage to the local variety of the species, which result if contracts are under all circumstances enforced to the letter. And kindred reasons were implied for reprobating various minor divergencies from the fundamental principle of social cooperation—that each individual shall, under ordinary circumstances, receive neither more nor less than a true equivalent for his services.

Here it should be added that the maintenance or prosperity of the race, or the variety, is the ultimate sanction also for those kinds of negative beneficence treated of as restraints on praise and blame. For the right restraints are in all cases such as have in view the eventual welfare of the individual blamed or praised—his eventual improvement. But improvement of the individual consists in the better fitting of him for social cooperation; and this, being conducive to social prosperity, is conducive to maintenance of the race.

427. The second sanction is a correlative of the first, or indeed, from one point of view, is the first; since, unless the race maintained is a recipient of happiness, maintenance of it ceases to be a desideratum. As was pointed out in section 16, "pessimists and optimists both start with the postulate that life is a blessing or a curse, according as the average consciousness accompanying it is pleasurable or painful. . . . The truth that conduct is considered by us as good or bad, according as its aggregate results, to self or others or both, are pleasurable or painful, we found on examination to be involved in all the current judgments of conduct: the proof being that reversing the applications of the words creates absurdities. And we found that every other proposed standard of conduct derives its authority from this standard"; for "perfection of nature," or "virtuousness of action," or "rectitude of motive," cannot be conceived without including the conception of happiness as an ultimate result, to self, or others or both. Hence the conclusion that the ultimate sanction for the conduct we call beneficent is conduciveness to maintenance of the species, simultaneously implies that its ultimate sanction is conduciveness to happiness, special or general: the two being different aspects of the same truth.

Their fundamental correlation is, as we before saw, necessary—has been inevitably established during the evolution of life at large. For as in all types of creatures lower than the human, there have been no prompters to performance of some actions and desistance from others, except the pleasurable and painful feelings produced respectively, it follows that through myriads of generations of creatures preceding the human, there have been in course of establishment, organic relations between pleasures and beneficial actions, and between pains and detrimental actions—now to the individual, now to the species, now to both. Of these organic relations, the essential ones, referring to the needs of the physical life, are inherited by the human race, savage and civilized; and are on the average efficient guides to the welfare of the individual and of the species. Though change from the requirements of savage life to the requirements of civilized life, has put many of the more complex among these relations out of gear; and though readjustment, already to some extent effected, has to continue through long future periods, before harmony between the feelings and the needs is fully reestablished; yet there cannot be an abolition of this primordial method of guidance. The requisite reorganization of the human being, must make him like inferior beings in the sense that not the lower parts of his nature only but the higher parts, will be adjusted to the conditions imposed by his mode of life—so adjusted that in him, as in them, all the actions conducive to self-welfare and the welfare of the species will be pleasurable.

Hence the two correlative sanctions of beneficence are conduciveness to happiness, immediate or remote, or both, and consequent conduciveness to maintenance of the species or the variety, regarded as hereafter the recipient of increased happiness. And this is implied vaguely if not clearly in the current conception of beneficence; since a mode of conduct which tends to increase the total of unhappiness, immediate or remote or both, is universally recognized as not beneficent but maleficent.

Of course these considerations touching the nature of beneficence at large, here appended as a commentary on the actions classed under the head of negative beneficence, equally apply, and indeed apply still more manifestly, to the actions classed under the head of positive beneficence, to which we now pass.

PART VI
THE ETHICS OF SOCIAL LIFE:
POSITIVE BENEFICENCE

CHAPTER 1

Marital Beneficence

428.   In the history of humanity as written, the saddest part
concerns the treatment of women; and had we before
us its unwritten history we should find this part still sadder. I
say the saddest part because, though there have been many
things more conspicuously dreadful—cannibalism, the tortur-
ings of prisoners, the sacrificings of victims to ghosts and
gods—these have been but occasional; whereas the brutal
treatment of women has been universal and constant. If,
looking first at their state of subjection among the semicivilized, we pass to the uncivilized, and observe the lives of
hardship borne by nearly all of them—if we then think what
must have gone on among those still ruder peoples who, for
so many thousands of years, roamed over the uncultivated
earth; we shall infer that the amount of suffering which has
been, and is, borne by women, is utterly beyond imagination.

As I have before pointed out, this ill-treatment of women
has been an unavoidable concomitant of the chronic struggle
for life among tribes, which is still going on in some places and
once went on universally (sec. 335). The brutality fostered in
men by their dealings with enemies, necessarily operated
throughout their daily lives. The weakest went to the wall
inside the tribe as well as outside the tribe. Utter absence of

sympathy made it inevitable that women should suffer from the egoism of men, without any limit save their ability to bear the entailed hardships. Passing this limit, the ill-treatment, by rendering the women incapable of rearing a due number of children, brought about disappearance of the tribe; and we may safely assume that multitudes of tribes disappeared from this cause: leaving behind those in which the ill-treatment was less extreme.

It must not be supposed, however, that the women who, throughout the past, had to bear all this misery, and in many places still have to bear it, were or are essentially better than the men. All along the brutality of nature has been common to the two; and, as we see in the love of torturing prisoners, is, among some of the North American tribes, even more pronounced in the women than in the men. The truth is simply that the unqualified and cruel egoism characterizing both, has worked out its evil results on those least able to resist. Hence the women have been compelled to carry all the burdens, do all the wearisome and monotonous work, remain unfed till their masters have satisfied themselves, and left to live on the remnants.

Only during these later periods of human history, in which the destructive passions have not been so constantly excited by the struggle for existence between societies, small and large, has the treatment of women slowly become less brutal; and only during this same period has there been growing up in men, a perception that women have certain special claims upon them, and a sentiment responding to the perception.

429. Perhaps, however, it is going too far to ascribe this softening of conduct to any consciousness of its propriety. Little by little character has changed; and the accompanying amelioration in the behavior of men to women, leading to gradual modifications of customs, has had no recognized sanction beyond the authority of these customs. Such and such privileges are now conceded to women, partly because immediate sympathy prompts, and partly because social con-

ventions direct; but there is recognized in no definite way the true ethical basis for this better treatment.

In preceding chapters we have several times seen that beyond the equalization which justice imposes upon us, by putting to the liberties of each limits arising from the liberties of all, beneficence exhorts us to take steps towards a further equalization. Like spheres of action having been established, it requires us to do something towards diminishing the inequalities of benefits which superior and inferior severally obtain within their spheres. This requirement has first to be fulfilled in the relations between men and women. Leaving aside all questions concerning mental powers, it is undeniable that in respect of physical powers, women are not the equals of men; and in this respect are disadvantaged in the battle of life. It is also unquestionable that, as the bearers of children, they are placed at a further serious disadvantage—are from time to time in considerable measure incapacitated for using whatever powers they have. Nor can it be doubted that though on the man devolves the business of providing sustenance for the family, yet the onerous duties of the woman, in unceasing attention to children from morning to night day after day, tie her more closely to home, and generally limit individual development to a greater degree. The inequalities thus necessarily arising between the lives of the two sexes, men have to rectify as much as they can—are called upon to make compensations.

Thus the observances which characterize the conduct of men to women in civilized societies, are not, as they at first seem, arbitrary conventions. If not consciously, still unconsciously, men have in modern times conformed their behavior to certain well-authorized dictates of positive beneficence.

430. The ideas and sentiments which should regulate the relations between men and women at large, find their special sphere in the marital relation. Here, more than elsewhere, it is the duty of the man to diminish, so far as may be, the disadvantages under which the woman has to live.

During the early stages of married life this duty is usually well fulfilled. Save in the utterly brutal, the sentiment which unites the sexes ensures on the part of the man, at any rate for a time, a recognition of the woman's claim. Her relative weakness forms one element of attraction; and, by implication, there results the desire to shield off such evils as the relative weakness entails. But though the nature inherited from a ruder type of humanity has been rendered less exclusively egoistic, it eventually reasserts itself to some extent in a large proportion of cases. Frequently the solicitude at first shown, diminishes; and, occasionally, even the acts of consideration which custom dictates, come to be disregarded—sometimes with assignable excuse, and sometimes without excuse.

It is consequently needful that there should be kept in mind the true ethical basis for the sympathetic self-sacrifices required of men to women in general, and especially required of husbands in their behavior to wives. So long as the code of conduct which regulates the general relations of the sexes, and more especially the marital relation, is thought of as conventional in its origin, it is more apt to be disregarded than when it is seen to originate in that form of beneficence which seeks to make less unequal the lives of those to whom Nature has given unequal advantages.

The incidents of female life during the childbearing period, are such as from time to time demand special consideration. Perturbations of health, more or less marked, are ordinary concomitants; and with these there sometimes go mental perturbations. When recognized as accompaniments of the functions which bear so heavily on women, these are of course to be tenderly dealt with. There is a further more general effect liable to be produced, which, in some cases being misunderstood, undermines affection. As before indicated, the antagonism between reproduction and individuation not unfrequently causes in women a sensible diminution in mental activity. Intellectual interests which before marriage were marked, diminish or cease; and a highly cultured man, who had hoped for a wife's sympathy in his aims, finds

himself disappointed. Hence, sometimes, an alienation leading to decrease of domesticity. But a beneficence of the enlightened kind, rightly construing this decline of brainpower,
will not regard it with impatience but with regret: accompanied even with some extra sympathy, in consideration of the
mental pleasures which are being lost.

431. Of course these self-sacrifices, small and large, which a
husband is called on to make for a wife, are not without limit.
While on the one hand the inherited moral nature, at present
so imperfect, frequently causes on the part of husbands a
neglect of those attentions which a due beneficence requires
of them; on the other hand, this same inherited moral nature
frequently causes insistence by women on undue claims.
Something much beyond the normal compensation for
feminine disadvantages is demanded and gained.

Not unfrequently a relation of this kind is established during a first pregnancy. At such a time *exigeante* behavior on the
part of a wife cannot well be resisted. Any considerable mental agitation might have disastrous consequences; and the
husband, fearful of such consequences, feels obliged to yield,
however unreasonable the demand may be. Once initiated
and continued for some months, the relative attitudes of the
two tend to become permanent. This result is evidently most
liable to occur where the wife is one for whom unusually large
sacrifices ought not to be made—one whose inferiority of
nature is shown by thus using her advantage.

What should be done in such cases it is difficult to say. The
answer must vary with the circumstances. While pronounced
supremacy of husband over wife is undesirable, still more
undesirable is pronounced supremacy of wife over husband—more undesirable because woman is less judicially
minded and more impulsive than man. Though the undue
assertions of claims on the part of a wife cannot well be
resisted under the circumstances in which they are probably
first made, yet they may be resisted afterward, when possible
mischiefs no longer threaten. And for the happiness of both

they should be resisted. For since the masculine trait which above all others attracts women, and gives permanence to their attachments, is the manifestation of power, the lack of power shown by constant yielding to aggression, eventually becomes a cause of declining affection and diminished conjugal happiness. The truth that a woman often loves more a strong man who ill treats her than a weak man who treats her well, shows how great a mistake it is for a husband to accept a position of subordination.

But all questions of this kind which take their rise in a human nature not yet sufficiently civilized for harmonious domestic life, any more than for harmonious social life, must remain with very indefinite answers. Active sympathy, and the beneficence resulting from it, are requisite in both husband and wife; and lack of them in either must have evil results, not in any way to be remedied. All one may say is that the needful beneficence on the part of a husband should err by excess rather than by defect.

432. Of course marital beneficence should be reciprocal. Though it is owed in chief measure by husband to wife, it is owed in large measure by wife to husband. While there have to be made by her no compensations for relative weakness and vital disadvantages, yet a return for benefits and sacrifices received, has to be made in such smaller benefits and sacrifices as domestic life affords place for.

Indebtedness to the bread-winner has to be recognized, and in some measure discharged: the tacit contract implies this as a matter of justice. But beyond fulfillment of the tacit contract by due performance of necessary household duties, there is scope for beneficence in the multitudinous small acts which help to make a home happy. If, on the one hand, we often see among the least civilized of our people, husbands utterly regardless of their wives' claims, burdening them with labors such as are fit only for men, we often see on the other hand slatternly wives who, lounging at doors and spending their time in gossip, so neglect household work as to bring on continual altercations and domestic misery. Even among the well-to-do classes there are not a few married women who, now occupied in novel reading, now in visiting, now in fancy work, scarcely ever go into their kitchens, and delegate all their duties to servants. Beyond the efficient household administration demanded alike by justice and by beneficence, there needs on the part of a wife sympathy in a husband's interests and aims and anxieties. That this is spontaneously given to a large extent is true; but it is also true that there is frequently little or no attempt made to participate in his leisure occupations and tastes. The way in which girls who daily practice music before marriage, give up their music after marriage, exemplifies the failure in those small beneficences which due reciprocity demands.

433. Respecting all that part of good conduct in the marital relation which goes beyond the demands of justice—the tacit contract for fostering and protection on the one side and discharge of domestic and maternal duties on the other—it may be remarked that it should be spontaneous. As before said, beneficence when constrained ceases to be beneficence.

Unfortunately many of the observances prompted by kindness, become mechanical as fast as they become established; and in so doing lose much of that beauty they originally had. When what were concessions come to be claimed as rights, the pleasurable feelings on both sides which at first accompanied them, disappear, and are sometimes replaced by opposite feelings—the claiming of the assumed rights implies egoism, and the yielding of them is without sympathy.

Hence alike in the social relations of men and women and in the marital relation, it is desirable to maintain, as much as may be, the distinction between justice and beneficence; so that the last may continue to bear about it the aspect of a freshly prompted kindness which has not been counted upon.

Full beneficence in the marital relation is reached only when each is solicitous about the claims of the other. So long as there continues that common attitude in which each maintains rights and resists encroachments, there can never be entire harmony. Only when each is anxious rather to make a sacrifice than to receive a sacrifice, can the highest form of the relation be reached.

CHAPTER 2

Parental Beneficence

434. A lready in the chapter "Parenthood," forming part of "The Ethics of Individual Life," much has been said which might equally well or better have been reserved for treatment under the above title. But the conduct of parents to children has still several aspects, not included in that chapter, which remain to be considered here.

Speaking generally, we may say that parental conduct exemplifies beneficence more than any other conduct. Though in the relation of parent to child egoism now and then becomes more pronounced than altruism, and though there is such a thing as the selfishness of affection which sacrifices the higher interests of a child to gain immediate pleasurable emotion, yet there is here less need for emphasizing beneficence than there is for emphasizing certain restrictions upon it.

Thoughtless beneficence has to be replaced by thoughtful beneficence. In cases where there is an ungrudging supply of everything needful for bodily development, and a furnishing by proxy of all the requisite aids to intellectual development, there is often but a niggardly expenditure of the reflection and attention required for good management.

435. To the mass of people nothing is so costly as thought. The fact that, taking the world over, ninety-nine people out of

a hundred accept the creed to which they were born, exemplifies their mental attitude towards things at large. Nearly all of them pursue mechanically the routine to which they have been accustomed, and are not only blind to its defects but will not recognize them as defects when they are pointed out. And the reluctance to think which they show everywhere else, is shown in their dealings with children. The tacit assumption is that when they have provided well for their physical needs, and delivered them over to teachers paid by themselves or by the public, they have done their duty.

But parental beneficence truly conceived includes more than this. Some parts of mental culture may rightly be deputed; other parts cannot. Though the later stages of intellectual education may with advantage be consigned to teachers, the earlier stages of it, as well as the education of the emotions during all stages, devolve on parents. They may here be aided by others but cannot properly be replaced by others. Even while yet in arms, the child looks for intellectual sympathy: thrusting something given to it into your face that you too may look at it; and when it reaches a conversational age, constantly adding to its statements the question "Isn't it?"—so showing its desire for agreement and verification. From parents more than from others should come the response to this intellectual need; and by parents more than by others should the normal process of instruction be based on the child's habits of inquiry. For parental affection, where it is joined with an observing and reasoning intelligence, will give an interest to this process of unfolding—a greater interest than can be felt by others. The eagerness for knowledge which every child shows by perpetual questions, parental beneficence will aim to satisfy: from time to time opening the way to new classes of inquiries concerning facts which a child's mind can appreciate. It may be said that a father after his business fatigues, or a mother in the midst of her domestic cares, cannot do this. But a very small amount of attention given daily, will suffice to aid and direct self-development; and rightly cultured parents will find interest in watching the progress.

Still more is home regulation required for the right molding of character, alike in the earlier and in the later stages of education. If parental conduct has been what it should be, the reciprocal affection produced gives to a parent a greater power of influencing the emotions than can be possessed by anyone else; and a good parent will regard it as a part of daily duty to use this influence to the best purpose. Not by coercive methods will he proceed; for if a right relation has been established these will rarely be needed, but he will proceed by influence—signs of approval and disapproval, of sympathy and repugnance, given to actions which are now above and now below the standard. Where from the beginning there has been pursued a proper course, and where there is a due amount of that inventive thought required for adjusting modes of control to peculiarities of nature, moral education will cease to be a trouble and may become a pleasure.

But whatever may be the difficulties in the way, parental beneficence includes ministration to the minds of children as well as ministration to their bodies. If the young are to be reared into fitness for life, it is absurd to suppose that parents are concerned with one factor in the fitness and not with the other.

436. While parental beneficence usually falls far short of the requirement in some ways, it greatly exceeds the requirement in other ways; or rather, let us say, in other ways it prompts the giving of immediate happiness without due regard for remote happiness. Of course I refer to the practice, everywhere recognized and condemned, of "spoiling" children.

If it is the business of education to produce fitness for adult life, then it should make the life of early days simulate the life to be led in later days, in so far as to maintain, if not the same proportion, yet some proportion, between its labors and its pleasures. Doubtless early life, as being the time for growth and development, should differ from later life in the respect that more should be given and less demanded, both physically and mentally. But, nevertheless, there should from the first be initiated that relation between efforts and benefits which is to become pronounced at maturity. There should not be a perpetual giving gratification out of all relation to industry. A thoughtful beneficence will avoid a profuse ministration to childish desires.

Besides the mischief caused by too great a dissociation of benefits from efforts, there is often in modern times an accompanying mischief—not among the poorer members of the community but among those who have means. Various social pleasures which should be reserved for adult life, are provided in large amounts for children; and a necessary consequence is that adult life has much less to give them than it should have. In a rationally conducted education, the surrounding world and the incidents of every day, may be made to yield pleasures quite sufficient to fill the leisure parts of a child's life, without having recourse to many artificial pleasures; and a wise beneficence, by taking care fully to utilize these, will avoid the evil now frequently inflicted by indulgent parents, who make a son blasé before life in its full form has been entered upon.

437. Often where parental beneficence is adequate in all other ways, there remains a way in which it falls short. There is a lack of proper self-control in the proportioning of kindnesses and attentions to different children. This causes much mischief, of which there seems but little consciousness.

It is in the nature of things that there cannot be equal amounts of affection felt by parents for all their children. The law of the instability of the homogeneous shows itself in this detail as everywhere else. There is inevitably a gravitation toward inequality, and more or less of favoritism. Even from birth some children commend themselves less to maternal affection than others do; and the differences in the feelings drawn out toward them, once established, are apt to be increased by the differences of treatment which result, and the different amounts of responsive affection.

Here we are shown the way in which blind instincts, even of

the altruistic kind, require to be checked and guided by the higher sentiments. For beneficence and justice alike dictate as near an approach as may be to equal treatment of children— that is, to equal participation in parental care and kindness. No one will question that, as a matter of justice, each child has as good a claim as another to those aids to development which parents are called on to yield; and it can scarcely be denied that such parts of parental conduct as exceed justice and pass into beneficence, should also be distributed with approximate fairness.

It is important that in this sphere the rule of the sentiments over the instincts should be strong; for immense mischiefs arise from favoritism in families. Parents in many respects high-minded, often inflict great cruelties on some of their children, to whom they show habitual indifference while daily lavishing affection on their brothers and sisters. It is no small thing to cast a gloom over all the years of a child's life. But beyond the direct evil there are indirect evils. The mental depression produced tends toward discouragement; and often causes intellectual inefficiency. The character is un-favorably modified by the awakening of antagonistic and jealous feelings. And there is a loss of that controlling power which is gained by a parent who has fostered sympathetic relations with a child.

In few directions is parental beneficence more called for than in resisting the tendency which inevitably arises to dis-tribute kindnesses to children unequally.

438. The most injurious kind of ill-regulated parental be-neficence remains to be named—an excess in one direction often associated with deficiencies in other directions. A father who has discharged his duties to children quite mechanically, taking no trouble about their mental culture, and giving to them throughout their early lives but little parental sympathy, has nevertheless devoted many years of untiring labor to accumulating a large fortune, which he bequeaths to them. Not, indeed, that he has been prompted wholly, or even

mainly, by the wish to leave them well provided for. Often the purely egoistic desire to obtain the honor which wealth brings, has been the chief motive. But joined with this there has been the desire that his children shall have bequests which will enable them to live without labor and anxiety. In so far as this shows beneficence, it shows a mistaken benefi-cence.

Our existing social regime, with its vast amounts of prop-erty in relatively few hands, though a regime appropriate to the existing type of humanity, and probably essential to it, is one which we may rightly regard as transitional. Just as modern times have seen a decrease in those great political inequalities, and accompanying inequalities of power, which characterized earlier times; so future times will most likely see a decrease in those great pecuniary inequalities which now prevail. Having emerged from the militant social type, we appear to be passing through a social type which may be distinguished as militant industrialism—an industrialism which, though carried on under the system of contract, in-stead of under the system of status, is in considerable measure carried on in the old militant spirit; as, indeed, it could not fail to be, seeing that men's characters and sentiments can be changed only in the course of long ages. Though pecuniary inequalities—some of them perhaps not inconsiderable—may be expected to characterize the future, reasserting themselves after socialisms and communisms have temporarily tri-umphed; yet we may infer that under higher social forms and a better type of humanity, they will be nothing like so marked as now. There will be neither the possibilities nor the desires for accumulating large fortunes: decrease in the desires being, in part, caused by recognition of the truth that parental benefi-cence, instead of enforcing them, interdicts them.

For a man's children are injuriously influenced both by the hope that they will be enabled to live without labor and by the fulfillment of that hope. As indicated in the chapter "Activity" and elsewhere, there can be no truly healthful life if benefits are dissociated from efforts. The principle on which human beings, in common with all other beings (save parasites) are organized, is that sustentation shall be effected by action; and detriment results if the sustentation comes without the action. There is initiated a relaxation of the organic adjustments which, if continued generation after generation, will cause decay. There is no need to emphasize this. The demoralization caused by "great expectations" is matter of common remark.

While parental beneficence when it exceeds the normal requirement—that of fully preparing children for complete living, and helping them to make a fair start in life— is disastrous in the way pointed out, it is disastrous in another way. It generates in children thoughts and feelings profoundly at variance with the filial relation. The scene between Henry V and his dying father, when to Prince Henry's excuse for taking away the crown, "I never thought to hear you speak again," the king replies, "Thy wish was father, Henry, to that thought"; may be taken as typical of the state of mind which is apt to arise where a father's death brings to a son great power or property or both. The well-recognized fact that between the existing owner of an entailed estate and the expectant owner, there commonly arises a certain silent jealousy, sufficiently proves this. Inevitably, therefore, one who accumulates a large fortune which at his death will pass to his children, who will simultaneously escape from tutelage, runs an imminent risk of raising in their minds the dreadful wish that he may die. Thoughts about the benefits which will come after his decease frequently suggest themselves; and though filial affection may be strong enough to repress them, they cannot be long absent, and must produce a chronic emotional conflict of a demoralizing kind.

In all ways is this common habit of providing largely for children maleficent rather than beneficent. Besides tempting them to inactivity and carelessness while they are young, and besides confirming these traits when they come into possession, thus making their lives abnormal ones, it is injurious alike to parent and to society. Entire absorption in business— an utter materialization of aims, while it dwarfs the parental life mentally, undermines it physically: bringing on ill-health, and an end earlier than is natural. At the same time the greed of property frequently prompts that merciless competition which, as we saw in a preceding chapter, not only inflicts misery on competitors needlessly, but entails social mischief.

Hence it is inferable that due regard for his own claims, for the claims of fellow citizens, and for social claims, should conspire with a far-seeing beneficence in preventing a parent from making his children independent.

CHAPTER 3

Filial Beneficence

439.   Many years of childhood have to pass before there can be entertained the thought of naturally derived obligations to parents—whether those which justice imposes or those which beneficence imposes. The obligation to obedience is indeed perpetually insisted upon; and while in some cases ignored, is, in other cases, duly recognized. But in any case it is conceived as established by arbitrary authority. There is little or no idea of its natural fitness.

Here and there, however, even before the teens have been reached, especially in families having narrow means, predominant sympathy produces a constant helpfulness—an endeavor to lighten the burdens which fall especially on the mother; and in such cases there perhaps arises the thought that such helpfulness is but a small return for the fostering care received in preceding years. But more generally this praiseworthy assistance is due to the direct promptings of affection, and resulting kind feeling, rather than to recognition of parental claims.

In many cases, however, and it is to be feared in the great majority, not even the approach to maturity brings any idea of filial gratitude, as sequent on the idea of filial indebtedness. Feeding, clothing, and education are accepted as matters of course for which no thanks are due; but rather there come half-uttered grumblings because many things desired are not supplied. When, occasionally during an expostulation, a father points out to a youth the sacrifices that have been made for his benefit, and indicates the propriety of recognizing them, and conforming to a reasonable parental wish if nothing more, silent admission on the youth's part of the undeniable fact, is often not accompanied by the feeling which should be produced. Parents are in most cases regarded as ordained fountains of benefits from whom everything is to be expected and to whom nothing is due.

And this is, indeed, the primitive relation. Throughout the animate creation in general, this is the connection between each generation and the next. With untiring energy and persistent care, parents rear offspring to maturity; and the offspring, incapable of conceiving what has been done for them, are also incapable of any responsive feeling. This brute form of the parental and filial relation, still, to a considerable degree, persists in the human race. Often at an age when they should be capable of complete self-maintenance, the young continually claim aid from the old; and express in no very respectful words their vexation if they do not get what they ask. Recognitions of the immense indebtedness of child to parent, and of the resulting duties, have indeed been occasionally expressed from the earliest ages; as witness the words of the Egyptian sage Ani:

> "Thou wast put to school, and whilst thou wast being taught letters she came punctually to thy master, bringing thee the bread and the drink of her house. Thou art now come to man's estate; thou art married and hast a house; but never do thou forget the painful labor which thy mother endured, nor all the salutary care which she has taken of thee. Take heed lest she gave cause to complain of thee, for fear that she should raise her hands to God and he should listen to her prayer." [*The Hibbert Lectures*, 1879, by P. Le Page Renouf, p. 102.]

But though theoretically admitted by all, the obligation of child to parent has been in fact but little felt, and is very inadequately felt still; and there is still a very inadequate consciousness of the duty of discharging it as far as possible.

440. Filial beneficence as currently conceived is not wide enough in its range. Except the utterly brutal, all feel that it is imperative to save parents from want or direct physical privations; but not many feel the imperativeness of those constant attentions, and small kindnesses, and manifestations of affection, which are really due. The reciprocity called for includes not material benefits only but moral benefits—such endeavors to make the old age of parents happy, as shall correspond with the endeavors they made to render happy the early days of their children.

In few directions is existing human nature so deficient as in this. Though, among the civilized, the aged are not left, as among various rude savages, to die of bodily starvation, yet they are often left to pine away in a condition that may be figuratively called mental starvation. Left by one child after another as these marry, they often come at length to lead lives which are almost or quite solitary. No longer energetic enough for the pleasures of activity, and not furnished with the passive pleasures which the social circle yields, they suffer the weariness of monotonous days. From time to time there comes, now from one child and now from another, a visit which serves nominally to discharge filial obligation, and to still the qualms of conscience in natures which are sympathetic enough to feel any qualms; but there is rarely such an amount of affectionate attention as makes their latter days enjoyable, as they should be. For in a rightly constituted order, these latter days should bring the reward for a life well passed and duties well discharged.

Insistence on filial beneficence is a crying need; and there is no saying in what way it is to be met. It cannot properly come from the aged themselves, since they are to be the beneficiaries. From the young we cannot expect it in adequate measure, since the need for it implies their deficiency in the sentiment which makes it needful. And by the official expounders of rectitude the subject is but rarely dealt with, or is dealt with ineffectually.

If those who are appointed to instruct men in the conduct of life, fail properly to emphasize filial beneficence in the interests of parents, still more do they fail to emphasize it in the interests of the children themselves. Neglecting to enforce the claims of fathers and mothers on their offspring, they leave these offspring to suffer, in declining life, from the consciousness of duties unperformed, when there is no longer a possibility of performing them—leave them a prey to painful thoughts about the dreary latter days of those they should have tenderly cared for: dreary days which they begin to realize when their own latter days have become dreary.

CHAPTER 4

Aiding the Sick and the Injured

441. Part of the subject matter of the preceding three chapters is included under the title of this chapter; for marital beneficence, parental beneficence, and filial beneficence, severally dictate solicitous care of any member of the family who is suffering from illness or from accident. In the natural order of things the house becomes at need a hospital and its inmates nurses.

Whether or not in respect of those outside the family group, beneficence requires that the sick and the hurt shall be succored, even at the risk of self-injury, it certainly requires that this shall be done inside the family group. If, as we see, the protecting of wife by husband is demanded as ancillary to continuance of species (since if the mother is unprotected the species must suffer), then, for the same reason, the care of wife when she is in any way prostrated is demanded. In like manner a reciprocal care of the breadwinner is called for as a condition to maintenance of the family. Still more obviously requisite is a diligent attendance on children who are ill: the obligation to nurse them being included in the general obligation to use all means of rearing them to maturity. Only in the case of afflicted parents having grown-up children, are we debarred from saying that the welfare of the species dictates the succoring of them. Here the fact that direct increase of happiness results from rendering the needful assistance, gives rise to the obligation.

As happens in the case of infectious diseases, obligations of this class have to be discharged, even at the risk of suffering and sometimes of death. Nature at large teaches us this lesson. Beyond the fact that among innumerable kinds of lower creatures, parental life is wholly sacrificed for the benefit of offspring, we see that among higher creatures the instincts are such as prompt, especially on the part of a mother, the facing of any danger for protection of the young: survival of the fittest has established this recklessness of evil. Hence it must be held that the risking of infection is ethically enjoined on a human mother: the only important check being the consideration that loss of life involves loss of ability to discharge obligations to the surviving members of the family. And there seems no reason why an equal obligation to meet the risk should not devolve on the father; unless it be that he has to provide the necessaries of life alike for the household at large and for its suffering member, and that his incapacity may bring starvation on all.

Are there any other checks to the self-sacrifices entailed on some of the family by the illness of another or others belonging to it? There are such other checks. A wise and duly proportioned beneficence does not countenance loss of the relatively worthy for preservation of the relatively worthless. Everyone can name persons wrecked in body and mind by cherishing invalid relatives—relatives who often thanklessly receive the sacrifices made for them. Here is a wife whose sole occupation for a decennium has been that of nursing a gouty husband; and who, as a result, dies of a worn-out physique before he does. Here is a daughter who, after many years' attendance on an invalid mother, is shortly after required to give similar attendance to an invalid aunt; and who, now that she has lived through these long periods of daily abnegations and wearisome duties, is becoming mentally unhinged. And here is a husband whose latter days are made miserable by the task of safeguarding, in his own house, an insane wife. Though in such cases (all of them occurring within my own small circle) beneficence demands great self-sacrifice, yet its dictates should be so far qualified as not to require that the lives of the healthy shall be lost in making the lives of the diseased more tolerable. Some compromise has to be made by which there may be achieved partial relief from the heavy burdens.

Especially is it proper that domestic invalids who make undue demands should receive a not unlimited attention. Often a whole household is subordinated to the exactions of a sickly member; and instead of gratitude there comes grumbling. This tyranny of the weak ought to be resisted. For the checking of their own egoism, as well as for the welfare of those around, the unreasonable sacrifices they continually ask should be refused. Such invalids are not only physically sick, but are morally sick also; and their moral sickness requires treatment as well as their physical sickness. Husbands in the decline of life who have married young wives, and presently make them little else than nurses—objecting even to have other nurses to share the labors with them—require awakening to a due sense not of others' duties to them but of their own duties to others. A man is not absolved from the obligations of beneficence because he is ill; and if he rightly feels these obligations he will insist that others shall not injure themselves for his benefit.

442. Concerning that wider beneficence which expends itself in care for sick persons not belonging to the family, it is difficult to say anything definite. Each case is rendered more or less special by the character of the patient and the circumstances; so that general propositions can scarcely find place. We may set down, however, the considerations by which judgment should be guided.

If, as all will admit, the care of one who is sick devolves primarily on members of the family group, and devolves secondarily on kindred, it devolves only in smaller measure on unrelated persons. These may rightly limit themselves to indirect aid, where this is needed and deserved. Only in cases where there are no relatives, or none capable of undertaking relatives' duties, does it seem that beneficence demands from unrelated persons the requisite attentions.

How far such attentions shall be carried must, again, be determined in part by thought of the claims arising from character and conduct. If, with Friendly Societies around him throughout life, the man who is at length taken ill, refused to make any provision against sickness, it cannot be held fit that his necessities as an invalid shall be ministered to as well as they might have been had he made such provision. If sympathy prompts an equal attention to the improvident as to the provident, the sentiment of justice puts a veto. Then, again, there is the question of character. If as much sacrifice is made for the sick good-for-nothing as is made for the sick good-for-something, there is abolished one of those distinctions between the results of good and bad conduct which all should strive to maintain. Further, there is the allied question of value. Much more may rightly be done for one whose abilities or energies promise public benefit, than for one who is useless to his fellow men, or is a burden on them.

Besides the beneficiaries, their characters and circumstances, there have to be considered the constitutions and circumstances of the benefactors. On those who have but little vitality and but small recuperative power after illness, a rational beneficence does not impose as heavy duties as it does on those in high vigor, who can bear disturbances of health without permanent mischief. Differences of claims hence arising, are seen to be greater on remembering that those with low blood pressure, are more liable to contract infectious diseases than those in whom the tide of life rises higher: especially when, as commonly happens, there is fear in the one case and not in the other. To the check which, for these reasons, a reasonable egoism puts upon altruism, must be joined a check of an altruistic kind; namely, consideration for those on whom evils will be entailed by contracting an infectious disease, or an illness caused by exhaustion. These evils are of several kinds. One who, engaged in nursing a stranger, comes home to the family group with a fever, risks their health and life as well as her own. Moreover, she entails on them the troubles and anxieties attendant upon nursing her, as well as the moral pains which her sufferings and perhaps her death, produce. Even when a fatal issue is escaped, there is necessarily for some time an inability to discharge such obligations as she has ordinarily to discharge; and, occasionally, a permanent inability to discharge them. Evidently, then, while beneficence prompts such aid to sick persons who have no claims of relationship, as may be given without considerable risk, it does not dictate the giving of such aid by those who have family ties and important duties.

Nevertheless we must not ignore the fact that such aid may be, and often is, given without injury by those who, if the above reason is valid, ought to hesitate in giving it. In a way somewhat remarkable, medical men (taking, however, in most cases some precautions) daily visit patients suffering from fevers or kindred diseases, and but rarely take them. We must suppose that use, and perhaps an acquired mental indifference, unite to give them immunity; and yet, even if so, it is not easy to see how, during the earlier stages of their professional lives, they escape. Hospital nurses, too, apparently become impervious. So that the risks of evil run by those whose sympathies prompt them to adopt nursing as an occupation, are not so great as at first appears; and where the nursing is of those suffering from other than infectious diseases, it may be consistent with fairly good health.

That strange emotion, so difficult to analyze, the luxury of pity, is an incentive to the sacrifices which nursing implies; and when with this there coexists a large share of the maternal instinct, which is in essence a love of the helpless, the care of the helpless sick becomes a source of subdued pleasure, which in large measure neutralizes the pain, and even makes the occupation a gratifying one. Without enjoining the beneficence which issues in these results, one may fitly look on and admire.

443. Though due regard for all circumstances puts some restraint on ministration to the sick who have no family claims, it puts no restraint on ministration to sufferers of another class—those who have met with accidents. Everyone is from time to time witness to injuries caused by falls, or by runaway horses, or by carriage collisions; and everyone is, in such cases, bound to render all possible assistance. None save those in whom the brutality of the barbarian still predominates, fail to feel contempt for the Pharisee in the parable and approval of the Samaritan.

But while the duty of caring for the injured is commonly recognized, as demanded even by the most ordinary beneficence, there is an ancillary duty which has only of late gained partial recognition—the duty of acquiring such knowledge and skill as shall make efficient the efforts to aid. Up to our own days, and even still in ninety-nine people out of a hundred, the wish to help the wounded or maimed is unaccompanied by instructed ability—nay, worse, is accompanied by an ignorance which leads to mischievous interferences. The anxiety to do something ends in doing harm; for there is commonly no adequate consciousness of the truth that there are many ways of going wrong to one way of going right.

Hence a provident beneficence suggests the acquirement of such surgical and medical knowledge as may be of avail to sufferers before professional aid can be obtained. Unqualified applause, then, must be given to those Ambulance Societies and kindred bodies, which seek to diffuse the requisite information and give by discipline the requisite skill. Unfortunately, when there come the demands for the acquired knowledge and aptitude, the hoped for benefits are not always forthcoming: nervousness or indecision, or perhaps perplexity amid the various lessons which have been learned, leads to failure. Still, the inference to be drawn is not that such preparations for aiding the injured should be abandoned, but rather that they should be more thorough, and should in fact form a part of the education given to all.

CHAPTER 5

Succor to the Ill-Used and the Endangered

444. In everyone who is capable of ethical ideas and senti-ments, more than one kind of motive prompts the defense of those who are aggressed upon: especially when they are weaker than the aggressors. There cooperate an im-mediate sympathy with the pains, mentally or bodily, in-flicted; a feeling of indignation against the person who inflicts them; a sense of justice which is irritated by the invasion of personal rights; and (where there is a quick consciousness of remote results) an anger that the established principles of social order should be broken. Whoever is civilized, not in the superficial sense but in the profound sense, will feel himself impelled to aid one who is suffering violence, either physical or moral; and will be ready to risk injury in yielding the aid.

The courage shown by one of those hired men who unite in conquering small semicivilized nations and weak, uncivilized tribes, is to be admired about as much as is the courage of a brute which runs down and masters its relatively feeble prey. The courage of one who fights in self-defense, or who as a soldier fights to defend his country when it is invaded, is respectable—is a proper manifestation of direct egoism in the one case, and in the other case a manifestation of that indirect egoism which makes it the interest of every citizen to prevent national subjugation. But the courage which prompts the succoring of one who is ill used, and which, against odds of superior strength, risks the bearing of injury that the weaker may not be injured, is courage of the first order—a courage backed, not as in many cases by base emotions, but backed by emotions of the highest kind.

One might have thought that even in a pagan society the ill-treatment of the weak by the strong would be universally reprobated. Still more might one have thought that in a professedly Christian society, general indignation would fall upon a bully who used his greater bodily powers to oppress a victim having smaller bodily powers. And most of all one might have felt certain that in educational institutions, governed and officered by professed teachers of Christianity, ever enjoining beneficence, ill-treatment of the younger and weaker by the elder and stronger would be sternly forbidden and severely repressed. But in our clerically administered public schools, the beneficence just described as of the highest order, finds no place; but, contrariwise, there finds place an established maleficence. Bullying and fagging, in past times carried to cruel extremes, still survive; and, as happened not long since, a resulting death is apologized for and condoned by one of our bishops. There is maintained and approved a moral discipline not inappropriate for those who, as legislators and military officers, direct and carry out, all over the world, expeditions which have as their result to deplete pagans and fatten Christians.

But though public-school ethics and, by transmission, the ethics of patriotism so-called, do not in practice (whatever they may do in theory) include that form of beneficence which risks injury to self in defending the weak against the strong, the ethics of evolution, as here interpreted, emphasize this form of beneficence; since the highest individual nature and the highest social type, cannot exist without a strength of sympathy which prompts such self-sacrificing beneficence.

445. And here, before considering the demands for self-sacrifice arising, not in the cases of injuries threatened by

maleficent human beings, but in the cases of injuries threatened by the forces of nature, something should be said concerning the courage required for the last as for the first; and, indeed, frequently more required, since the forces of nature are merciless.

Very generally the virtue of courage is spoken of as though it were under all circumstances worthy of the same kind of applause, and its absence worthy of the same kind of contempt. These indiscriminating judgments are indefensible. In large measure, though not wholly, the development of courage depends on personal experience of ability to cope with dangers. It is in the order of nature that one who perpetually fails, and suffers from his failures, becomes increasingly reluctant to enter into conflict with either organic or inorganic agencies; while, conversely, success in everything undertaken fosters a readiness to run risks—sometimes an undue readiness: each fresh success being an occasion of extreme satisfaction, the expectation of which becomes a temptation. Hence, to a considerable extent, timidity and courage are their own justifications: the one being appropriate to a nature which is physically, or morally, or intellectually defective in a greater or less degree; and the other being appropriate to a nature which is superior either in bodily power, or strength of emotion, or intellectual aptitude and quickness. Errors of estimation in this matter may be best excluded by taking a case in respect of which men's preconceptions are not strongly established— say the case of Alpine explorations. Here is one who has constitutionally so little strength that he is prostrated by climbing two or three thousand feet; or whose hands are not capable of a powerful and long-sustained grip; or whose vision is not keen enough to make him quite sure of his footing; or who cannot look down a precipice without feeling dizzy; or who so lacks presence of mind that he is practically paralyzed by an emergency. All will admit that any one of these physical or mental deficiencies rightly interdicts the attempt to scale a mountain peak, and that to make the attempt would be a mark not of courage but of folly. Contrariwise, one who to strength of limb adds power of lungs, and with these joins acute senses, a clear and steady head, and resources mental and bodily which rise to the occasion when danger demands, may be held warranted in a risky undertaking; as, for instance, descending into a *crevasse* to rescue one who has fallen into it. His courage is the natural accompaniment of his ability.

Such contrasts of natures should ordinarily determine such contrasts of actions; and estimates of conduct should recognize them—should, in large measure, take the form of pity for the incapacities of one or other kind which fear implies, and respect for the superiorities implied by courage. "In large measure," I say, because there are degrees of timidity beyond those which defects justify, and degrees of courage beyond those appropriate to the endowments; and while the first of these rightly deserves reprobation, the last may be duly admired, supposing it is not pushed to the extent of irrational imprudence.

Speaking generally, then, the sanction for courage must take into account the relation between the thing to be done and the probable capacity for doing it. The judgment formed must obviously vary according to the age—cannot be the same for the young or the old as for one in the prime of life; must vary with the state of health, which often partially incapacitates; must vary with what is called the "personal equation," since, when in danger, slowness of perception or of action is often fatal. The single fact that heart disease produces timidity—a timidity appropriate to that inability which failure of circulation involves—suffices alone to show that, both in self and in others, the estimated obligation to run a risk must always be qualified by recognition of personal traits.

Even without taking account of such special reasons, there is, indeed, a prevailing consciousness that some proportion should be maintained between the degree of danger and the ability to meet the danger. It is usual to condemn as "rash," conduct which disregards this proportion. The saying that "discretion is the better part of valor," though by implication referring only to the risks of battle, is applicable to other risks;

and implies that there should be not approval but disapproval if the danger is too great. Similarly the epithet "foolhardy," applied to one who needlessly chances death or great injury, is an epithet of reprobation; and implies, too, the perception that not unfrequently a large part of that which passes for courage is simply stupidity—an inability to perceive what is likely to happen. There is in fact generally felt a certain kind of obligation not to risk life too recklessly, even with a good motive.

While the injunction uttered by positive beneficence to succor those who are endangered by the merciless powers of nature, must be thus qualified, it must, as we shall presently see, be further qualified by recognition of the collateral results, should the effort to yield the succor prove fatal.

446. From the general we may turn now to the special. Let us ask what is the obligation imposed by beneficence to rescue one who is drowning. In what cases is the duty positive, and in what cases must it be doubtful or be negatived?

Clearly a man who, being a good swimmer, has the requisite ability, and yet makes no effort to save the life of one who, at no great distance, is in danger of sinking, is not only to be condemned as heartless but as worse. If at small risk to himself he can prevent another's death and does not, he must be held guilty of something like passive manslaughter. The only supposable excuse for him is his consciousness that one who is drowning is apt to grapple his rescuer in such way as to incapacitate him, and cause the deaths of both—a liability, however, which he might know is easily excluded by approaching the drowning person from behind.

But what are we to say when there is less fitness in strength, or skill, or both, to meet the requirements? What if weakness makes long-continued exertion impracticable? Or suppose that though he has general strength enough, the bystander has not acquired an ability to swim more than fifty yards, while the person to be rescued is considerably further off. Or suppose that, the scene of the threatened disaster being the sea, the power of the breakers is such that once in their grasp there is small chance of getting out again: even alone, much less when helping one who is drowning. Here it seems manifest that however much an unthinking beneficence may prompt running the risk, a judicial beneficence will forbid. An irrational altruism has in such cases to be checked by a rational egoism; since it is absurd to lose two lives in a hopeless effort to save one.

Other restraints have usually to be taken into account. A man who is without a wife or near relatives, so that his death will inflict no great amount of mental suffering—a man who is not responsible for the welfare of children or perhaps aged parents, may fitly yield to the immediate promptings of sympathy, and dare to do that which should not be done by one whose life is needful to other lives. In such cases beneficence urges and beneficence restrains. Quite apart from the instinct of self-preservation, the sense of duty to dependents may forbid the attempt to give that succor which fellow feeling instigates.

So that nothing definite can be said. Save in the instances first indicated, where the obligation is manifest, the obligation must be judged by the circumstances of each case: account being taken, not only of the qualifications named, but the value of the person for whom the effort is made; for the same risks should not be run on behalf of a criminal as on behalf of one who is noble in character, or one who is highly serviceable to his society.

447. Difficult as are the questions sometimes raised in presence of probable death from drowning, they are exceeded in difficulty by questions raised in presence of probable death from fire. In the one case the ability of the rescuer, resulting from his strength, skill, and quickness, counts for much; and the actions of the element, now quiet now boisterous, with which he has to contend, may be fairly well gauged by him; but, in the other case, he has to contend with an agent the destructive actions of which are much more terrible, much less calculable, and not to be overcome by strength.

From time to time we read of those who, at the peril of their lives, have rescued relatives and even strangers from burning houses; and again we read of others whose efforts of like kind have proved fatal. Are we then, under parallel circumstances, to say—Go thou and do likewise? Does beneficence demand disregard of self, carried to the extreme that it may very likely end in the sacrifice of a second life without the saving of a first? No general answer can be given. The incidents of the case and the special emotions—parental, filial, fraternal, or other—must decide. Often the question is one which cannot be answered even if there is absolute self-abnegation; as when, having brought out a child from one room which is in flames, a parent has to decide whether to rush into an upper room and rescue another child, at the same time that fire on the staircase threatens death to all. Evidently in such a chaos of conditions and feelings and obligations and risks, nothing can be said. And what is true in this extreme case is true in a large proportion of the cases. Ethics is dumb in presence of the conflicting requirements.

When not the life of the rescuer only is concerned, but when loss of his life must make other lives miserable, and leave grave obligations undischarged, interdict rather than injunction may be the ethical verdict.

448. Doubtless it is well for humanity at large to maintain the tradition of heroism. One whose altruistic promptings are so strong that he loses his own life in an almost hopeless effort to save another's life, affords an example of nobility which, in a measure, redeems the innumerable cruelties, brutalities, and meannesses, prevailing among men, and serves to keep alive hope of a higher humanity hereafter. The good done in occasionally putting egoism to the blush, may be counted as a setoff against the loss of one whose altruistic nature should have been transmitted.

But in all questions of the kind dealt with in this chapter, we may fitly fall back on the ancient doctrine of the mean. When throwing dice with death, the question whether death's dice

CHAPTER 6

Pecuniary Aid to Relatives and Friends

449.   A curious change of sentiments has accompanied a curious change of obligations, during the transition from that ancient type of social structure in which the family is the unit of composition to that modern type in which the individual is the unit of composition. The state of things still existing among the native Australians, under which the guilt of a murderer is shared in by all his kindred, who severally hold themselves subject to vengeance—the state of things which, throughout Europe in early days, made the family or clan responsible for any crime committed by one of its members, seems strange to us now that we have ceased to bear the burdens, criminal or other, not only of our remote relatives but even of our near relatives.

From one point of view the ancient system seems ethically superior—seems more altruistic. From another point of view, however, it is the reverse; for it goes along with utter disregard of, and very often enmity to, those not belonging to the family group. The modern system, while it does not recognize such imperative claims derived from community of blood, recognizes more than the old, claims derived from community of citizenship, and also claims derived from community of human nature. If we bear in mind that the primary ethical principle is that each individual shall experience the effects of his own nature and consequent conduct, and that under the ancient system sundry effects of his conduct were visited as readily on his relatives as on himself, whereas, under the modern system, they are visited on himself only; we shall infer that the modern system is the higher of the two. And we shall infer this the more readily on remembering that it is accompanied by a more equitable political regime, and consequent social ameliorations.

Acceptance of this inference will guide our judgments respecting obligations to assist relatives. The claims of immature children on parents, are directly deducible from the postulate that continuance of the species is a desideratum—a postulate from which, as we have seen, ethical principles in general originate. The reciprocal claims of parents on children are directly deducible from the position of indebtedness in which parental care has placed the children. But no other claims of relationship have anything like a fundamental authority. Community of blood arising from community of parentage, has not in itself any ethical significance. The only ethical significance of fraternity is that which arises from community of early life, and reciprocal affections presumably established by it. Brethren and sisters usually love one another more than they love those who are outside the family circle; and the accepted implication is that the stronger attachments which have arisen among them, originate stronger dictates to yield mutual aid. If, as is rightly said, relatives are ready-made friends, then children of the same parents must be regarded as standing in the first rank of such friends. But their obligations to one another must be held as consequent not on their common origin but on their bonds of sympathetic feeling—bonds made to vary in their strengths by differences of behavior, and which therefore generate different degrees of obligation.

This view, which will probably be dissented from by many, I enunciate before asking how far positive beneficence requires brothers and sisters to yield one another pecuniary aid. And I enunciate it the more emphatically because of the extreme mischiefs and miseries apt to result from the making and conceding of claims having no other warrant than community of parentage. Within these three years I have become personally cognizant of two cases in which, here impoverishment and there ruin, have been brought on sisters who have lent money to brothers. Ignorant of business, incapable of criticizing plausible representations, prompted by sisterly regard and confidence, they have yielded to pressure: being further led to yield by belief in a moral obligation consequent on the relationship. A rational beneficence countenances no such concessions. A brother who, in pursuit of his own advantage, wishes thus to hypothecate the property of sisters, who will grievously suffer should he not succeed, is a brother who proves himself devoid of proper fraternal feeling. The excuse that he feels sure of success is an utterly inadequate excuse. It is the excuse made by men who, to tide over emergencies, appropriate the funds they hold in trust, or by men who forge bills which they hope to be able to meet before they are due. And if in such cases it is recognized as criminal thus to risk the property of others on the strength of a hoped-for success, we cannot absolve from something like criminality a brother who, on the strength of a similar hope, obtains loans from trustful sisters. One who does such a thing should no longer be considered a brother.

But what is to be done when a loan is asked not from a sister but from a brother—a brother who has considerable means and is a competent judge? The answer here is of course indeterminate. The prospective creditor may in this case be capable of estimating the probable results—capable of estimating, too, his brother's business ability; and he may also rightly have such confidence in his own power of making money that he can reasonably risk a considerable loss. Especially if it is a case of difficulty to be met, sympathy may join fraternal affection in prompting assent. Even here, however, there may fitly be hesitation on both sides. Where there is in the matter an element of speculation, the one who needs money, if a conscientious man, will scarcely like to receive, much less to ask—will feel that it is bad enough to play with anyone the game "Heads I win, tails you lose"; and worse still with a brother.

450. Respecting those who are more remotely related or who are not related at all, much the same incentives and restraints may be alleged. If affection and fellow feeling, rather than common parentage or common ancestry, are the true prompters to needful monetary aids, then a friend with whom a long and kindly intercourse has established much sympathy, has a stronger claim than a little known relative, whose conduct has led now to disapproval now to dislike. Recognition of personal worth, or recognition of value as a citizen, may also rightly guide beneficent feeling to yield assistance where a difficulty, and especially an unforeseen difficulty, threatens evil. When it comes to the question of advancing means, not for preventing a probable disaster, but for entering upon some new undertaking, a longer pause for reflection is demanded. The worth and honesty of the borrower being taken for granted, there have still to be considered the amount of his energy, his appropriate knowledge, his proved capacity; and there have still to be considered the effects which will be felt should he fail. For the act must be considered from the egoistic side as well as from the altruistic side; and the degree of possible self-sacrifice may be greater than ought to be asked. Balanced judgments are in such cases hard to reach.

Much the same things may be said concerning that indirect hypothecation which consists in giving security. Here the difficulty of deciding is often greater; since there is no reply but either yes or no, and since the amount risked is usually large. Between a proper altruism and a reasonable egoism there is much strain in such cases. On the one hand, to negative the obtainment of some desirable post, which may be the first step towards a prosperous life, seems cruel. On the other hand, to risk the possible ruin which may come from yielding, seems something more than imprudent. A much greater power of judging character than is common must be possessed by one who can safely furnish a warrant for another's behavior. The incongruity between appearance and reality is often extreme; and there are but few adequately on their guard against it. Agreeableness and plausible professions usually attract a confidence which is repelled by a brusque sincerity that makes little effort to please; and trustworthiness is wrongly identified with the one rather than with the other.

But manifestly in such cases, as in preceding ones, the strongest restraint on a too easy beneficence is that which comes from due regard for the claims of dependents. One who, with exalted generosity, is ready to risk the wreck of his own life, is not warranted in risking the wreck of lives for which he is responsible. A judicial beneficence, weighing the possible future mischiefs to others against the present benefit to one, will usually see reason to resist the pressure.

In these days, however, such considerations scarcely need setting down; for now that the principle of insurance has been extended to the giving of security for good behavior on payment of an annual sum, no right-minded man will think of asking a friend to become security for him. Anyone who now asks another thus to endanger himself, is thereby proved to be unworthy of confidence.

451. To these counsels of kindness qualified by prudence, which are such as ordinary experience will suggest to most, there has to be added one other, which does not lie quite so much upon the surface. While desire for a friend's or relative's welfare may in some cases prompt the yielding of a large loan, a wise forethought for his welfare will often join other motives in refusing such aid.

For the beneficiary himself often needs saving from the disasters which his too sanguine nature threatens to bring on him. A large proportion of those who want loans may rightly be refused in their own interests. Anxiety to borrow so often goes along with incapacity to acquire, that we may almost say that money should be lent only to those who have proved their ability to make money. Hence, in many cases, the withholding of a desired accommodation is the warding off unhappiness from one who asks it.

I say this partly on the strength of a remark made in my hearing by a highly conscientious man who had carried on a business—a manufacture, I think—with borrowed capital. He said that the anxiety nearly killed him. The thought of the extent to which the welfare of others was staked, and the strain to fulfil his obligations, made his life a misery. Clearly, therefore, a far-seeing beneficence will in many cases decline, for the sake of the borrower, to furnish money, where a shortsighted beneficence would assent.

CHAPTER 7

Relief of the Poor

452.   We enter now upon the subject with which the conception of beneficence is almost wholly identified in some minds, and chiefly identified in many minds. With the word beneficence (or rather with the word benevolence, which commonly usurps its place) there usually springs up the idea of openhanded generosity to those in want. The giving of money or money's worth is so much the easiest and the most familiar mode of showing kindness, that by the unthinking, and especially by recipients, kindness is conceived as little else.

This species of beneficence, which, as we have seen, is one out of many, is daily presented to us in three different shapes. We have the law-established relief for the poor by distribution of money compulsorily exacted; with which may fitly be joined the alms derived from endowments. We have relief of the poor carried on by spontaneously organized societies, to which funds are voluntarily contributed. And then, lastly, we have the help privately given—now to those who stand in some relation of dependence, now to those concerning whose claims partial knowledge has been obtained, and now haphazard to beggars. We will consider these three kinds in the order here presented.

453. After all that has been said in preceding parts of this work, it is needless to argue at length that relief of the poor from public funds raised by rates, is, if considered apart from certain antecedents to be presently named, inconsistent with that limitation of state functions which ethics insists upon. If, as repeatedly pointed out, the true function of the state is that of guarding the aggregate of citizens and the individual citizen against aggressions, external and internal, so that each may be able to carry on his life with no greater hindrance than that which proximity of other citizens involves—if the state's only other function is that of so controlling the uses made of the inhabited territory, as to prevent sacrifice of the interests of the joint owner, the community; then it follows that if it taxes one class for the benefit of another, it exceeds its functions, and, in a measure contravenes the first of them.

This conclusion, however, holds as I have said "if considered apart from certain antecedents to be presently named." The antecedents referred to are those which become visible on going back to prefeudal and feudal times, when serfs, though bound to the soil, had certain established rights to some produce of the soil; and those further antecedents which, at a later period, after cessation of serfdom and accompanying divorce of the serf from the soil, eventually reinstituted his connection and his lien by a Poor Law. While, in a measure, again tying him to his locality, this, in a measure, again recognized his claim upon its produce.

So regarded, a Poor Law may be said to have an equitable basis, and the poor relief administered under it to be something more than a charitable dole. Entire usurpation of the land by the landlord, and entire expropriation of the laborer, were unjust; and the reestablishment of the old relation in a freer form, may be interpreted as a roundabout mode of admitting afresh a just claim. Not improbably the relative stability of English institutions during later times, has been indirectly due to absence of that disaffection which results where the classes having no property are wholly at the mercy of the classes who have property.

The beneficence which takes the form of relief administered by public agencies, is difficult to deal with not only because it is thus complicated by considerations of justice, but because it is further complicated by considerations of accompanying injustices. Though, in early days, the legally enforced aid to the poor was contributed almost wholly by those who, as landowners, were rightly called on to contribute it; yet, in later days, it has come to be in large measure contributed by others than landowners—others on whom there is no just claim. Hence nothing beyond empirical judgments concerning compulsory beneficence seem possible.

When, however, we remember that beneficence, properly so-called, loses its quality when it is made compulsory, and that both benefactor and beneficiary then cease to have those feelings which normally accompany it, we shall be inclined to think that could the just claims of each member of the community as a part owner of the land be otherwise recognized, and beneficence wholly dissociated from governmental force, it would be far better. Let us contemplate the evils of the present system.

454. While, as admitted above, the community as a whole is the ultimate owner of the territory inhabited, considered as unreclaimed (though not of that value which clearing and cultivation have given to it); and while each member of the community has a resulting lien upon it; yet no such "right to a maintenance out of the soil," irrespective of energy expended, as is often alleged, can be sustained. The land produces only in return for labor; and one who does not give the labor has no claim on its produce; or, at any rate, has a claim only to a share of the small amount it would yield if wild, which, with the existing population, would constitute nothing like a maintenance.

It is argued that the poor work for society while young and hale, and should be supported by society when sick and old. Under a socialist regime, which artificially apportioned payments for services, this would be a valid position; but, as it is, society gives to the laborer when young and hale as much as competition proves his work to be worth: so discharging its debt. Further, there is the reply that if, during his period of activity he has been underpaid, the underpayment has been in large part due to the fact that he has been burdened by having to help indirectly, if not directly, to support the idle and incapable. Giving necessaries of life to those who do not labor, inevitably takes away necessaries of life from those who do labor. The well-to-do are not pinched by this abstraction from the total supply of commodities. Those who are pinched are those who have but small margins. If they had not been thus depleted, they would have been able to provide for a period of unproductive life.

Apologists contend that rapid multiplication is ever producing a surplus of people for whom there is no work, but who must be supported. The first reply is that in proportion as provision is made for such a surplus, the surplus will go on continually increasing. The second reply is that only if the work to be done by the community is a fixed quantity, can the argument be sustained; since, otherwise, there must always be some further work which the surplus may be profitably employed on, in return for their maintenance. To say that some ought to do extra work that others may remain idle is absurd.

Occasionally it is urged that since there must always be a certain proportion of necessitous people—the diseased, the incapable, the unfortunate, the old—it is best that these should be relieved from funds administered by men appointed for the purpose, who will look carefully in each case and adjust the aid to the needs. This implies a faith in officialism at large which experience, repeated generation after generation, fails to dissipate. The assumption is that the agents employed, who in most cases aim to get their salaries with the least trouble, will be the best critics of the character, conduct, and wants of the recipients; and that guardians will administer public funds more wisely than private persons would administer their own funds. It ignores the enormous mass of evidence collected in Parliamentary Blue Books, as well as in special works on the subject, proving that under this system in past days corruptions and abuses of every kind were created and fostered, resulting in a universal demoralization.

Let us not forget that cruel injustice to individuals and mischief to the community, are caused by a heavy taxation of those who are but just able to maintain themselves and families, and are striving to do it. Numerous cases occur in which worthy and diligent men—sometimes thrown out of work by lack of demand and sometimes incapacitated for work by prolonged sickness—are compelled to pay rates; and even have their goods seized that money may be obtained for the maintenance of good-for-nothings. More than this; it not unfrequently happens that men who are employed in parishes at distances from their own, and could there maintain themselves but for the persecution of the poor-rate collector, have to abandon their places, return to their own parishes, get from it money to bring back their wives and children, and then apply for relief. So that there is a breaking up of healthy industrial relations to maintain a system which substitutes doles for wages.

Nor must we omit the fact that public administration of relief is doubly extravagant. It is extravagant in the sense that the distribution inevitably becomes lax, and, in the absence of personal interests, aid is given where aid is not required: often most lavishly to the least deserving. And it is extravagant in the sense that a large part of the total fund raised goes to maintain the machinery—goes in salaries of rate collectors, relieving officers, masters of workhouses and their subordinates, parish surgeons, &c.: a part amounting in extreme cases in Ireland to more than two-thirds, and in some cases in England at the present time to more than one-third—proportions which, if not paralleled generally, go along with high average proportions.

When we remember that law-enforced charity is, as already shown, inconsistent with justice, we are taught that in this as in all other cases, what is not just is in the long run not beneficent.*

455. Less objectionable than administration of poor relief by a law-established and coercive organization, is its administration by privately established and voluntary organizations—benevolent societies, mendicity societies, &c. "Less objectionable" I say, but still, objectionable: in some ways even more objectionable. For though the vitiating influences of coercion are now avoided the vitiating influences of proxy distribution remain. If we have not a machinery so rigid as that set up by the Poor Law, yet we have a machinery. The beneficiary is not brought in direct relation with the benefactor, but in relation with an agent appointed by a number of benefactors. The transaction, instead of being one which advantageously cultivates the moral nature on both sides,

---

* In treating of Poor Laws as above, I have been aided by the writings of one specially qualified judge—a late uncle of mine, the Rev. Thomas Spencer, of Hinton Charterhouse, near Bath. His antecedents and his experience gave his opinion a value which the opinion of scarcely one man in a hundred thousand could have. His special sympathy with his parishioners was proved by his having established in Hinton a parish school, a village library, a clothing club, and land allotments; by having also built model cottages; and by having at one time gone to the extent of giving every Sunday a meat dinner to a group of laborers. His general sympathy with the working classes was proved by the fact that he devoted a large part of his spare time to the diffusion of temperance by lectures and writings; by the fact that he joined in the Complete Suffrage Movement, which aimed to diffuse political power; and above all by the fact that he was the only clergyman who took an active part in the agitation for the repeal of the Corn Laws, and said grace at the first anti–Corn Law banquet as well as at the last. His philanthropic feeling, then, cannot be questioned. As to his experience, it was no less wide and complete. Though originally a pauper's friend—always on the side of the pauper against the overseer—he afterwards became convinced of the immense mischief wrought under the old Poor Law; and when the new Poor Law was enacted, he forthwith applied it to his parish (having, I believe, gained the assent of the Poor Law commissioners to do this before the Bath Union was formed), and very shortly reduced the rates from £700 a year to £200 a year; with the result of making the parish far more contented and prosperous. Then, on the formation of the Bath Union, he was appointed chairman of the Board of Guardians and held that office for several years: thereby being made familiar with a wide range of facts. The outcome was that he wrote four pamphlets under the title "Reasons for a Poor Law Considered"; of which the net result is a verdict against Poor Laws in general.

excludes culture of the moral nature as much as is practicable, and introduces a number of bad motives. Note the ill-workings of the system.

As with the Poor Law (especially the old Poor Law), those who were distressed but thrifty and well conducted got no help, while help came to the improvident and ill conducted; so with philanthropic societies in general. The worthy suffer rather than ask assistance; while the worthless press for assistance and get it. The Mansion House Fund of 1885–86, for instance, was proved to have gone largely for the support of "idlers, spendthrifts, and drunkards." "They did not see why they should not have some of the money going as well as their neighbors." In some cases applicants "*demanded* their share." Where, as in another case, employment was offered, less than one-fifth proved to be good for anything; showing that the unemployed, so generally pitied as ill used by society, are unemployed because they either cannot or will not work; and showing, by implication, that charitable agencies enable them to evade the harsh but salutary discipline of nature.

The encouragement of hypocrisy, which goes along with this neglect of the good poor who do not complain and attention to the bad poor who do, becomes conspicuous when religious professions are found instrumental to obtainment of alms. Clergy and pious women, easily deluded by sanctimonious talk, favor those who are most skilled in utterance of spiritual experiences, and in benedictions after receiving gifts. Hence a penalty on sincerity and a premium on lying; with resulting demoralization.

This evil is intensified by sectarian competition. There are competing missions which collect and distribute money to push their respective creeds, and bribe by farthing breakfasts and penny dinners. Nearly half the revenue of one mission is distributed in credit tickets, and "if the recipient wishes to cash his ticket, he cannot do so until after the evening service": this vicious system being carried even to the extent that the visitors try "to force its tickets on the most respectable and independent people"—pauperizing them to make hypocritical converts of them. Said one woman, poor but clean and tidy, who saw how the emissaries of the church favored the good-for-nothings: "I didn't want any of the good lady's tickets . . . but it's very 'urtful to the feelings to see that careless drinking people living like 'ogs gets all, and them as struggles and strives may go without." And not only does there result a discouragement of virtue and an encouragement of vice, but there results a subsidizing of superstitions. Unless all the conflicting beliefs thus aided are right, which is impossible, there must be a propagation of untruth as well as a rewarding of insincerity.

Another evil is that easygoing people are *exploité* by cunning fellows who want to make places for themselves and get salaries. A crying need is found; prospectuses are widely distributed; canvassers press those on whom they call; and all because A, B, C &c., who have failed in their careers, have discovered that they can get money by playing the parts of manager, secretary, and collector. Then, if the institution vehemently urged is established, it is worked in their interest. But it is not always established. As there are bubble mercantile companies, so there are bubble philanthropic societies—societies kept up for a time merely for the purpose of getting subscriptions. Nay, on good authority I learn that there are gangs of men who make it their business to float bogus charities solely to serve their private ends.

Not even now have we reached the end of the evils. There is the insincerity of those who furnish the funds distributed: flunkeyism and the desire to display being often larger motives than beneficent feeling. These swindling promoters when writing to wealthy men for contributions, take care to request the honor of their names as vice presidents. Even where the institutions are genuine, the giving of handsome subscriptions or donations, is largely prompted by the wish to figure before the world as generous, and as filling posts of distinction and authority. A still meaner motive cooperates. One of the *nouveaux riches,* or even one whose business is tolerably prosperous, takes an active part in getting up, or in carrying on, one of these societies supposed to be originated purely by benevolence, because he likes the prospect of sitting on a committee presided over by a peer, and perhaps side by side with the son of one. He and his wife and his daughters enjoy the thought of seeing his name annually thus associated in the list of officers; and they contemplate this result more than the benefits to be given.

There are kindred vitiations of other organizations having beneficent aims—orphanages, provisions for unfortunate and aged tradesmen, &c. Here again, the least necessitous, who have many friends, are usually those to benefit, and the most necessitous, who have no friends, are neglected. Then there is the costliness and corruption of the selecting process—expensive and laborious canvassing, exchange of votes, philanthropic logrolling. Evidently the outlay for working the system, in money and effort, is such as would be equivalent to a maintenance for many more beneficiaries, were it not thus wasted in machinery.

Nor is it otherwise with institutions thought by most people to be indisputably beneficial—hospitals and dispensaries. The first significant fact is that thirty percent of the people of London are frequenters of them; and the largeness of this proportion makes it clear that most of them, not to be ranked as indigent, are able to pay their doctors. Gratis medical relief tends to pauperize in more definite ways. The outpatients begin by getting physic and presently get food; and the system "leads them afterwards openly to solicit pecuniary aid." This vitiating effect is proved by the fact that during the forty years from 1830 to 1869, the increase in the number of hospital patients has been five times greater than the increase of population; and as there has not been more disease, the implication is obvious. Moreover the promise of advice for nothing, attracts the mean-spirited to the extent that "the poor are now being gradually ousted out of the consulting room by well-to-do persons." People of several hundreds a year, even up to a thousand, apply as outpatients, going in disguise: twenty percent of the outpatients in one large hospital having "given false addresses" for the purpose of concealing their identity. Swarming as patients thus do, it results that each gets but little attention: a minute being the average for each, sometimes diminished to forty-five seconds. Thus those for whom the gratis advice is intended get but little. Often "the assistance given is merely nominal"; and "is both a deception on the public and a fraud upon the poor." These gratuitous medical benefits, such as they are, "are conferred chiefly by the members of the unpaid professional staffs" of these charities. Some of them prescribe at the rate of 318 patients in three hours and twenty minutes—a process sufficiently exhausting for men already hard worked in their private practice, and sufficiently disheartening to men with little private practice, who thus give without payment aid which otherwise they would get payment for, very much needed by them. So that the £600,000 a year of the metropolitan hospitals, which, if the annual value of the lands and buildings occupied were added would reach very nearly a million, has largely the effect of demoralizing the patients, taking medical care from those it was intended for and giving it to those for whom it was not, and obliging many impecunious doctors and surgeons to work hard for nothing.*

These various experiences, then, furnished by societies and institutions supported by voluntary gifts and subscriptions, unite to show that whatever benefits flow from them are accompanied by grave evils—evils sometimes greater than the benefits. They force on us the truth that, be it compulsory or noncompulsory, social *machinery* wastes power, and works other effects than those intended. In proportion as beneficence operates indirectly instead of directly, it fails in its end.

456. Alike in the foregoing sections and in the foregoing parts of this work, there has been implied the conclusion that

---

* The evidence here summarized will be found in *Medical Charity: Its Abuses, and How to Remedy Them,* by John Chapman, M.D. Some of the sums and numbers given should be greatly increased; for since 1874, when the work was published, much hospital extension has taken place.

the beneficence which takes the form of giving material aid to those in distress, has the best effects when individually exercised. If, like mercy it "blesses him that gives and him that takes," it can do this in full measure only when the benefactor and beneficiary stand in direct relation. It is true, however, that individual beneficence often falls far short of the requirements, often runs into excesses, and is often wrongly directed. Let us look at its imperfections and corruptions.

The most familiar of these is the careless squandering of pence to beggars, and the consequent fostering of idleness and vice. Sometimes because their sympathies are so quick that they cannot tolerate the sight of real or apparent misery; sometimes because they quiet their consciences and think they compound for misdeeds by occasional largesse; sometimes because they are moved by that other-worldliness which hopes to obtain large gifts hereafter by small gifts here; sometimes because, though conscious of mischief likely to be done, they have not the patience needed to make inquiries, and are tempted to end the matter with a sixpence or something less; men help the bad to become worse. Doubtless the evil is great, and weighs much against the individual exercise of beneficence—practically if not theoretically.

The same causes initiate and maintain the begging-letter impostures. Occasional exposures of these in daily papers might serve as warnings; but always there is a new crop of credulous people who believe what they are told by cunning dissemblers, and yield rather than take the trouble of verification: thinking, many of them, that they are virtuous in thus doing the thing which seems kind, instead of being, as they are, vicious in taking no care to prevent evil. That the doings of such keep alive numbers of scamps and swindlers, every one knows; and doubtless a considerable setoff to the advantages of individual beneficence hence arises.

Then, again, there meets us the objection that if there is no compulsory raising of funds to relieve distress, and everything is left to the promptings of sympathy, people who have little or no sympathy, forming a large part of the community, will contribute nothing; and will leave undue burdens to be borne by the more sympathetic. Either the requirements will be inadequately met or the kindhearted will have to make excessive sacrifices. Much force though there is in this objection, it is not so forcible as at first appears. In this case, as in many cases, wrong inferences are drawn respecting the effects of a new cause, because it is supposed that while one thing is changed all other things remain the same. It is forgotten that in the absence of a coercive law there often exists a coercive public opinion. There is no legal penalty on a lie, if not uttered after taking an oath; and yet the social disgrace which follows a convicted liar has a strong effect in maintaining a general truthfulness. There is no prescribed punishment for breaking social observances; and yet these are by many conformed to more carefully than are moral precepts or legal enactments. Most people dread far more the social frown which follows the doing of something conventionally wrong, than they do the qualms of conscience which follow the doing of something intrinsically wrong.* Hence it may reasonably be concluded that if private voluntary relief of the poor replaced public compulsory relief, the diffused sentiment which enforces the one would go a long way toward maintaining the other. The general feeling would become such that few, even of the unsympathetic, would dare to face the scorn which would result did they shirk all share of the common responsibility; and while there would probably be thus insured something like contributions from the indifferent or the callous, there would, in some of them, be initiated, by the formal practice of beneficence, a feeling which in course of time would render the beneficence genuine and pleasurable.

---

* A most instructive and remarkable fact, which illustrates this general truth at the same time that it illustrates a more special truth, is that already cited in section 183, respecting the rudest of the Musheras of India, who have no form of marriage, but among whom "unchastity, or a change of lovers on either side, when once mutual appropriation has been made, is a thing of rare occurrence"; and, when it does occur, causes excommunication. So that among these simple people, public opinion in respect of the marital relation is more potent than law is among ourselves. (For account of the Musheras, see *Calcutta Review,* April 1888.)

A further difficulty presents itself. "I am too much occupied," says the man of business when exhorted to exercise private beneficence. "I have a family to bring up; and my whole time is absorbed in discharging my responsibilities, parental and other. It is impossible for me, therefore, to make such inquiries as are needful to avoid giving misdirected assistance. I must make my contribution and leave others to distribute." That there is force in the reply cannot be denied. But when we call to mind the common remark that if you want anything done you must apply to the busy man rather than to the man of leisure, we may reasonably question whether the busy man may not occasionally find time enough to investigate cases of distress which are forced on his attention. Sometimes there may even result, from a due amount of altruistic action, a mental gain conducive to efficiency in the conduct of affairs.

At any rate it must be admitted that individual ministration to the poor is the normal form of ministration; and that, made more thoughtful and careful, as it would be if the entire responsibility of caring for the poor devolved upon it, it would go a long way towards meeting the needs: especially as the needs would be greatly diminished when there had been excluded the artificially generated poverty with which we are surrounded.

457. But now, from this general advocacy of individual giving versus giving by public and quasi-public agencies, I pass to the special advocacy of the natural form of individual giving—a form which exists and which simply needs development.

Within the intricate plexus of social relations surrounding each citizen, there is a special plexus more familiar to him than any other, and which has established greater claims on him than any other. Everyone who can afford to give assistance, is brought by his daily activities into immediate contact with a cluster of those who by illness, by loss of work, by a death, or by other calamity, are severally liable to fall into a state calling for aid; and there should be recognized a claim possessed by each member of this particular cluster.

In early societies, organized on the system of status, there went, along with the dependence of inferiors, a certain kind of responsibility for their welfare. The simple or compound family group, formed of relatives standing in degrees of subordination, and usually possessing slaves, was a group so regulated that while the inferiors were obliged to do what they were told, and receive what was given to them, they usually had a sufficiency given to them. They were much in the position of domestic animals in respect of their subjection, and they were in a kindred position in respect of due ministration to their needs. Alike in the primitive patriarchal system and in the developed feudal system, we see that the system of status presented the general trait, that while dependents were in large measure denied their liberty, they were in large measure supplied with the means of living. Either they were directly fed and housed, or they were allowed such fixed proportion of produce as enabled them to feed and house themselves. Possession of them unavoidably brought with it care for them.

Along with gradual substitution of the system of contract for the system of status, this relation has been changed in such manner that while the benefits of independence have been gained the benefits of dependence have been lost. The poorer citizen has no longer any one to control him; but he has no longer any one to provide for him. So much service for so much money, has become the universal principle of cooperation; and the money having been paid for the service rendered, no further claim is recognized. The requirements of justice having been fulfilled, it is supposed that all requirements have been fulfilled. The ancient regime of protection and fealty has ceased, while the modern regime of beneficence and gratitude has but partially replaced it.

May we not infer, with tolerable certainty, that there has to be reinstituted something akin to the old order in a new form? May we not expect that without reestablishment of the ancient power of superiors over inferiors, there may be resumed something like the ancient care for them? May we not hope that without the formation of any legal ties between individuals of the regulating class, and those groups whose work they severally regulate in one or other way, there may come to be formed stronger moral ties? Already such moral ties are in some measure recognized. Already all householders moderately endowed with sympathy, feel bound to care for their servants during illness; already they help those living out of the house who in less direct ways labor for them; already from time to time small traders, porters, errand boys, and the like, benefit by their kind offices on occasions of misfortune. The sole requisite seems to be that the usage which thus shows itself here and there irregularly, should be called into general activity by the gradual disappearance of artificial agencies for distributing aid. As before implied, the sympathetic feelings which have originated and support these artificial agencies, would, in their absence, vitalize and develop the natural agencies. And if with each citizen there remained the amount now taken from him in rates and subscriptions, he would be enabled to meet these private demands: if not by as large a disbursement, yet by a disbursement probably as large as is desirable.

Besides reestablishing these closer relationships between superior and inferior, which during our transition from ancient slavery to modern freedom have lapsed; and besides bringing beneficence back to its normal form of direct relation between benefactor and beneficiary; thus personal administration of relief would be guided by immediate knowledge of the recipients, and the relief would be adjusted in kind and amount to their needs and their deserts. When, instead of the responsibility indirectly discharged through Poor Law officers and mendicity societies, the responsibility fell directly on each of those having some spare means, each would see the necessity for inquiry and criticism and supervision: so increasing the aid given to the worthy and restricting that given to the unworthy.

458. And here we are brought face to face with the greatest of the difficulties attendant on all methods of mitigating distress. May we not by frequent aid to the worthy render them unworthy; and are we not almost certain by helping those who are already unworthy to make them more unworthy still? How shall we so regulate our pecuniary beneficence as to avoid assisting the incapables and the degraded to multiply?

I have in so many places commented on the impolicy, and indeed the cruelty, of bequeathing to posterity an increasing population of criminals and incapables, that I need not here insist that true beneficence will be so restrained as to avoid fostering the inferior at the expense of the superior—or, at any rate, so restrained as to minimize the mischief which fostering the inferior entails.

Under present circumstances the difficulty seems almost insurmountable. By the law-established and privately established agencies, coercive and voluntary, which save the bad from the extreme results of their badness, there have been produced unmanageable multitudes of them, and to prevent further multiplication appears next to impossible. The yearly accumulating appliances for keeping alive those who will not do enough work to keep themselves alive, continually increase the evil. Each new effort to mitigate the penalties on improvidence, has the inevitable effect of adding to the number of the improvident. Whether assistance is given through state machinery, or by charitable societies, or privately, it is difficult to see how it can be restricted in such manner as to prevent the inferior from begetting more of the inferior.

If left to operate in all its sternness, the principle of the survival of the fittest, which, as ethically considered, we have seen to imply that each individual shall be left to experience the effects of his own nature and consequent conduct, would quickly clear away the degraded. But it is impracticable with our present sentiments to let it operate in all its sternness. No serious evil would result from relaxing its operation, if the degraded were to leave no progeny. A shortsighted beneficence might be allowed to save them from suffering, were a longsighted beneficence assured that there would be born no more such. But how can it be thus assured? If, either by public action or by private action, aid were given to the feeble, the unhealthy, the deformed, the stupid, on condition that they did not marry, the result would manifestly be a great increase of illegitimacy; which, implying a still more unfavorable nurture of children, would result in still worse men and women. If instead of a "submerged tenth" there existed only a submerged fiftieth, it might be possible to deal with it effectually by private industrial institutions, or some kindred appliances. But the mass of effete humanity to be dealt with is so large as to make one despair: the problem seems insoluble.

Certainly, if solvable, it is to be solved only through suffering. Having, by unwise institutions, brought into existence large numbers who are unadapted to the requirements of social life, and are consequently sources of misery to themselves and others, we cannot repress and gradually diminish this body of relatively worthless people without inflicting much pain. Evil has been done and the penalty must be paid. Cure can come only through affliction. The artificial assuaging of distress by state appliances, is a kind of social opium eating, yielding temporary mitigation at the eventual cost of intenser misery. Increase of the anodyne dose inevitably leads by and by to increase of the evil; and the only rational course is that of bearing the misery which must be entailed for a time by desistance. The transition from state beneficence to a healthy condition of self-help and private beneficence, must be like the transition from an opium-eating life to a normal life—painful but remedial.

CHAPTER 8

Social Beneficence

459. Is each person under obligation to carry on social intercourse? May he, without any disregard of claims
upon him, lead a solitary life, or a life limited to the family
circle? Or does positive beneficence dictate the cultivating of
friendships and acquaintanceships to the extent of giving and
receiving hospitalities? And if there is such a requirement,
what constitutes proper discharge of it?

Only vague replies to these questions seem possible. We
may indeed say that, peremptory claims permitting, some
amount of social intercourse is obligatory; since, without it,
general happiness would fall short. If a community of sol-
itaries, or of families leading recluse lives, would be relatively
dull—if gatherings for the interchange of ideas and mutual
excitation of emotions add, in considerable measure, to the
gratifications of each and all; then there seems to be imposed
on each the duty of furthering such gatherings.

Of course this duty is less peremptory than most other
duties; and when it can be fulfilled must be fulfilled in subordination to them. Receptions entailing appreciable cost have
no ethical sanction where there is difficulty in meeting family
claims, the claims of justice, and the claims arising from the
misfortunes of the worthy. Here that kind of social intercourse

which may be carried on without expense (often the best social intercourse) is alone ethically enjoined.

Moreover, such obligation to cultivate the society of our fellows as beneficence imposes, it imposes only on condition that more pleasure than pain is caused. No countenance is given by it to the mechanical process of gathering and dispersing, carried on by those who are "in society," or in the wider circles which adopt the habits of society. Beneficence tells no one to help in keeping up the movement of "the social treadmill." Only supposing that the persons brought together, derive from one another's company amounts of enjoyment well purchased by the entailed trouble and cost, can beneficence be said to dictate the bringing of them together.

And here, indeed, it may be said that instead of enjoining mechanical social intercourse, beneficence dictates efforts to restrict and abolish it. Everyone finds that most of the entertainments people give and attend, fail to yield the gratifications sought, while they involve troubles and vexations to hosts and guests: all because display and conformity to conventional requirements are far more thought of than the pleasures of friendship. Many have found, too, that most endeavors to reestablish the reality, at present supplanted by the sham, are futile. Some who, early in the century, desiring to have occasional visits from people they cared about, notified that they would be "at home" on specified evenings, hoped by this abandonment of formalities to get what they wanted. But as fast as the practice spread, the "at-homes" became conventionalized, like all other gatherings; and now are not distinguishable from the "routs" of earlier days. The like has happened even with a more recently attempted remedy—the "at-homes" which are distinguished as "small and early"; for a small and early party has now come to mean one which consists of a room full of people who arrive between ten and eleven.

Social beneficence, then, does not include participation in these kinds of social intercourse which lose the aim in the preparation, and the actuality in the show. Contrariwise, it enjoins unceasing resistance to a system which achieves pain while seeking pleasure.

460. Though the furthering of ordinary social intercourse of the genuine kind, will by many scarcely be classed under beneficence, there is another kind of social intercourse the furthering of which they will not hesitate so to class. I refer to the intercourse between those whose social positions are superior and those who hold inferior social positions.

At all times there has been more or less of this—in old days occasional feasts provided by feudal nobles for their retainers; and in later times entertainments given by squires to villagers at recurring periods, or on special occasions. After an interval during which such usages seem to have become less general, they have revived in new forms—garden parties at country residences to the neighboring poor people: gratis excursions of children and others from London into the country; village school treats, and so forth. Penny Readings, too, and concerts given by amateurs to listeners who are asked to pay little or nothing, are other forms taken by this species of social beneficence. They are in the main to be applauded; both for the immediate pleasures they give, and for their effects in cultivating good feeling between classes, with consequent increase of social cohesion. Usually they are genuine promptings of sympathy; and, in the better among those who are entertained, evoke some gratitude: both results being beneficial. Only in cases where the usage becomes mechanical—is given by routine on the one side and expected as a matter of course on the other, may we recognize a drawback. And only, in other cases, where such entertainments are got up in the interests of religious sects to gather adherents, may we recognize a further drawback. But the drawbacks are not greater, nor so great, as those attendant on the intercourse of the wealthier with one another; and we may safely say that social beneficence enjoins these various modes of bringing rich and poor together.

Not less to be approved, if not indeed more to be approved,

are the efforts made by some to give instruction, as well as pleasure, to fellow citizens who are not so well off as themselves. Those who, a century ago, strove to dissipate the ignorance of artisans and laborers by Sunday Schools, deserve far more to be remembered than many whose names are familiar; and the tens of thousands of the middle classes who, for generations after, devoted large parts of their Sundays to teaching—bearing for many years the reprobation of those who considered themselves their "betters"—ought to be remembered with gratitude: with much more gratitude than those who have busied themselves to coerce people into giving and receiving Board-School lessons. Though this Sunday School system, spreading first among the Dissenters and then adopted by the church to prevent loss of its members, has been in part subordinated to sectarian purposes; yet the original aim was good, and the self-sacrificing fulfillment of the aim has been in the main good. Social beneficence has been in this way well exemplified.

Voluntary teaching of another kind has in recent days taken a serviceable development. I refer to lectures given in towns and villages by nonprofessional lecturers. Sometimes employer and employed are thus associated in a way other than by business contracts. A late friend of mine, the number of whose work people exceeded a thousand, besides occasional entertainments and excursions into the country, gave them from time to time explanatory accounts of various classes of physical phenomena, with illustrative experiments. But whether by a master to his hands, or by some local man, who has cultivated a specialty, to an assemblage of his neighbors, this gratis yielding of information is a beneficence to be commended. Especially does there need volunteered teaching in respect of topics touching the conduct of life and social affairs. The state of society might now have been far better had men capable of doing it, enlightened those living around them on political and moral questions. Many wild ideas now prevailing would probably never have arisen.

But in all cases customs tend to become laws—concessions

to become rights; and these extensions of social intercourse giving instruction, as well as those giving pleasure, are apt to lose the quality of beneficence and fall into settled observances accompanied by little kindness on the one side or thanks on the other. How to prevent this usual decadence it is difficult to see.

461. Thus far the requirements of social beneficence specified, if not practically fulfilled by readers, will be theoretically admitted by them. But we come now to less obvious requirements—requirements which, indeed, will by most be denied, and by many will even be considered at variance with social obligations. I refer to actions which have for their ends to change habits and usages that are opposed to general well-being.

Though they do not contend that conformity to conventions is a moral duty, yet the majority of people think it a duty; and they speak in reprobation of those who break any of the rules which society has tacitly enacted for the regulation of life and behavior. They may be unable to give good reasons for these rules; they may admit that many of them entail trouble and annoyance for no beneficial purpose; they may even condemn some as absurd. Yet they hold that these rules, even down to the color of an evening necktie, should be respected. While they regard disobedience as a transgression to be frowned upon, they do not ask whether the observance does not entail grave evils, and whether they ought not to try and abolish those evils.

One who does not pick up his opinions ready made, but elaborates them himself, will see clearly enough that along with other duties to his fellow men, there goes the duty of seeking to increase their happiness by rationalizing their modes of life. He will see that beneficence, rightly understood, is not limited to the giving of money, the yielding of assistance, the manifestation of sympathy, the uttering of kind words; but that it includes also the doing of various things which, though proximately painful to others, are remotely beneficial to them; and which, instead of bringing him smiles, bring him frowns. In a degree far beyond what the mass of people conceive, their lives are vitiated by observance of the regulations—many needless and others injurious—imposed by an unseen social power. Let us contemplate some of the mischievous mandates which should be disobeyed.

462. Naturally there may be taken first in order those which concern dress. To denounce here the follies of fashion is superfluous: everyone recognizes them. No one however, or scarcely anyone, refuses to join in them. Not only do nearly all conform, but they defend their conformity. They laugh at the modes exhibited in old books of costume, and admit that were it not for habit they might think the current modes equally absurd. The needless expenditure entailed by discarding dresses which are still good, because they are no longer as is required, they recognize and even lament. They also complain occasionally of the amount of time and trouble and worry entailed by keeping their clothing up to date. Nevertheless the assertion that, alike on their own behalf and on behalf of others, they ought to resist a dictation which brings these mischievous results, they combat and even ridicule. Social beneficence, as conceived by them, includes submission rather than resistance.

Doubtless they may plead lack of courage. They dare not risk the deprecations of friends and the jeers of strangers. But, in the first place, the bearing of disagreeable consequences of right actions, is one of the forms which beneficence takes; and, in the second place, when a nonconformity which is intrinsically rational, obviously results neither from ignorance nor poverty but from independence, the world generally accepts the situation, and not only tolerates it but even secretly respects it.

Concerning dress, social beneficence has something more to say than to enjoin resistance to these perpetual changes from one absurd pattern to another. Beyond an improper obedience to an illegitimate control of dress, there is an undue regard for dress itself, considered apart from fashion. Here, again, protest is superfluous; since large expenditure of money and time in providing externals which shall evoke applause, is a stock subject for reprobation. What needs, perhaps, to be emphasized is the truth that undue devotion of life and thought to the gaining of admiration by personal adornment, often brings loss of admiration. The feeling with which an overdressed woman is regarded, shows this in a pronounced way; and this feeling is excited, if less strongly, by many who are not condemned as overdressed. For any such elaborate toilette as shows the beholder that desire for approbation has been dominant, causes in him a reactive emotion: disapproval of the moral trait being set against approval of the appearance achieved. Nobody thinks love of praise a fine characteristic.

To be beautiful without manifest cost, elegant without manifest thought, is that which dress should achieve. Such attention to appearance as implies a certain respect for those around is proper; and yet not an attention which implies great anxiety about their opinions. A dash of aesthetic genius, possessed by but few, is requisite for success in this compromise. But it may be approached by others; and the approach to it should be aided and approved by that social beneficence which aims at rationalizing social usages.

463. Allied to the undue regard for appearance in clothing is the undue regard for appearances in general. Time, among the women of the upper and middle ranks, is largely, and often mainly, spent in pursuit of the ornamental. To make things look pretty seems to have become with them the chief end of life; and they never ask whether there is any proper limit to aesthetic gratifications.

As was pointed out in the closing chapter of Part III, very much in the right conduct of life turns on a due proportioning of the various activities. Recognizing in a measure an ancient doctrine, we saw that concerning each kind of activity, judgment has to decide whereabouts between the two extremes lies the mean. And we also saw that, beyond this, judgment is called for to decide what is the proper ratio between each kind of activity and other kinds of activity. In contemplating the doings of people around, we see that this due proportioning is very little attended to; and, indeed, by many there seems to be no perception that it is needed. Here in respect of work, there in respect of amusement, now in respect of culture, and again in respect of a hobby, there is undue absorption of energy; and no one seems to pause and ask whether the pursuit of their particular aim does not unduly sacrifice the pursuit of other aims. It is especially thus with the pursuit of beauty, or that which is thought to be beauty. Into many minds, and especially feminine minds, there seems never to have entered the question whether the spending of time over ornamental surroundings may not be carried to excess. The tacit assumption is that achievement of the elegant and the decorative everywhere and always, is meritorious; and the consequent neglect of important ends is not recognized. In a degree which examination provides to be extreme, the mind is perverted and the body injured by this insane subordination of reality to show. While many things needful of satisfactory living are left undone, the mistress of the house spends much of her time in fancy work, in keeping ornamental things in order, in arranging flowers, &c.: much more time than she gives to procuring food of good quality and well cooked, and to superintending the education of her children.*

---

* For these many years I have wished to write an essay on aesthetic vices, and have accumulated illustrations of the way in which life is vitiated by making attractiveness of appearance a primary end, instead of a secondary end to be thought of only in subordination to usefulness. Here are a few out of multitudinous illustrations of the ways in which comfort and health are alike perpetually trenched on to achieve some real or fancied beauty in a thing which should make no pretensions to beauty. You take up a poker to break a lump of coal, and find that the ornamented brass handle, screwed on the steel shaft, is loose, making the poker rickety; and you further find that the filigree work of this brass handle hurts your hand if you give the lump a blow. Observing that the fire is low you turn to the coal scuttle, and, perceiving it to be empty, ring for more coal; and then, because the elegant coal scuttle, decorated perhaps with a photograph surrounded by elaborate gilding, may not be damaged in the cellar, you are obliged to hear the noise of pouring in coal from a black scuttle

Not only is all this to be ethically disapproved as putting the less important ends of life before the more important ends, but it is even to be aesthetically disapproved. The pursuit of beauty carried to excess defeats itself. In the first place many domestic objects are not fit for decoration. Between an elaborately ornamented coal scuttle and its black, dirty contents, there is an absurd incongruity; and the time spent in making imitation leaves and flowers to cover a pie crust, stands in ridiculous contrast with the trivial result: the crust being destroyed nearly as soon as seen. A large proportion of things in a house should be simply unobtrusive or inoffensive. In the second place, if beauty is aimed at only in objects which exist exclusively for it as their end, and in other permanent objects which may be made beautiful without diminishing their usefulness, there results an increased totality of aesthetic plea-

---

outside the door, accompanied by the making of dust and probably the scattering of bits: all which you are expected to be content with for the sake of the photograph and the gilding. Then, when you sit down, after having put the fire in order, some discomfort at the back of your head draws your attention to a modern antimacassar, made of string which is hardened by starch: the beauty of its pattern being supposed to serve you as compensation for the irritation of your scalp. So is it with a meal. At breakfast you are served with toast made from bread of an undesirable quality, but which has the advantage that its slices can be cut into triangles, much admired for their neatness. If you take a poached egg you discover that, for the sake of looking pretty, it has been cooked in shallow water; with the effect that while the displayed yolk in the center is only half done, the surrounding white is overdone and reduced to a leathery consistence. Should the meal be a more elaborate one you meet with more numerous illustrations. To name the sweets only, you observe that here is a tart of which the crust is bad, because the time that should have been devoted to making it has been devoted to making the filigree work decorating its outside; and here is another of which the paste, covered with a sugared glaze, has been made close and indigestible by the consequent keeping in of the steam. At one end of the table is a jelly which, that it may keep the shape of the elegant mould it was cast in (which the proper material often fails to do) is artificially stiffened; so that if you are unwise enough to take a mouthful, it suggests the idea of soluble India rubber. And then at the other end, you see the passion for appearance carried to the extent that to make a shaped cream attractive, it is colored with the crimson juice of a creature which, when alive, looks like a corpulent bug. Such is the experience all through the day, from the first thing in the morning, when while standing dripping wet, you have to separate the pretty fringes of the bathtowel which are entangled with one another, to the last thing at night, when the bootjack, which, not being an ornamental object is put out of sight, has to be sought for.

sure; for, to be fully appreciated, beautiful things must have as their foils things which make no pretensions to beauty. A graceful statuette, or a fine watercolor landscape, looks far better amid surroundings that are relatively plain and inconspicuous, than in a room crowded with multitudinous pretty things or things supposed to be pretty. Moreover while the room, if filled with pictures and sculptures and vases and numerous curiosities, loses its individuality, it may, when containing only a small number of beautiful objects artistically arranged, become itself a work of art.

Similarly rooted in an undue desire for display, goes the practice of accumulating needless appliances. As a typical instance may be named a silver butter knife. It is an implement utterly superfluous. There can be no pretense that there is any chemical action of the butter on steel; for a steel knife is used by each person to spread it. There can be no pretense that a steel knife is not equally effective as a tool: indeed the butter knife is mechanically ill adapted for its purpose. It has no *raison d'être* whatever, save to show the possession of money enough to purchase an appliance which society prescribes. With various other domestic superfluities it is the same. Needless original outlay and daily cost in cleaning, are entailed by useless articles which people buy lest silent criticisms should be passed in their absence.

Social beneficence, then, enjoins efforts to diminish the sacrifice of use to appearance, and the accompanying expenditure of time, energy, and money for secondary ends to the neglect of primary ends.

464. Endeavors to benefit fellow citizens by improvements in modes of life, have yet another sphere of action. There are various prescribed habits, and various social observances, which should be resisted, and modified or abolished, in the interests of men at large. Already philanthropy in some cases recognizes this duty.

We have, for example, the efforts made to check extravagant

outlays for funerals. It is seen that the demands of custom weigh heavily on necessitous families: perhaps seriously diminishing the small sum left to meet the immediate wants of a widow and her children. Lack of a certain display is thought to imply lack of respect for the dead; and hence the peremptory need for disbursements which cannot be borne without suffering. The evil is far more intense among some slightly-civilized peoples, as those of the Gold Coast, where, according to Beecham, "a funeral is usually absolute ruin to a poor family." For discouraging lavish expenditure, even though among us it is far less, there are the further reasons that, as the costly burial rites are equally accorded to the bad and to the good, they fail to be signs of respect; and that were they generally abandoned, no slight would be implied by the absence of them.

Kindred reasons may be given for trying to moderate sundry wedding customs. These have in some places gone to extremes beyond any known in this part of the world; and have entailed astonishing mischiefs. In one case among the partially civilized, if not in more, the marriage feast has become so ruinously costly to the bride's family, that female infanticide is practiced as a remedy: daughters being put out of the way while infants, because of the expense they would one day entail if reared. Here, though parental expenditures entailed by weddings are less serious, there are concomitant evils which cry aloud for remedy. In old times the making of presents to a newly married couple, had for its purpose to start them in housekeeping; and now, as of old, presents given with this end are justified. But out of this once rational custom has grown an irrational one. Presents are showered in upon brides who, as well as the bridegrooms, are wealthy enough to provide for themselves amply in all ways, by friends prompted less by feelings of friendship than by fears of criticism: a heavy tax on those who have many friends, being the consequence. And now, among the upper classes, the system has grown to the extent that, in an utterly shameless way, lists of the presents with the names of their donors are published in newspapers. So that we have a public boast of social position on the one side and generosity on the other.

A further group of observances may be named among those to be discouraged by everyone who has a far-seeing regard for social well-being. I refer to the various complimentary actions brought round by the seasons. It is said that in Paris the making of Easter presents has become so burdensome a usage, that not a few escape from it by going on a journey, for one or other alleged reason. People have created for themselves a system of mutual taxation. A feels bound to give to B, C, D, and the rest; B, to A, C, D, and the rest; and so on throughout the alphabet. Among ourselves have arisen in recent times, the less serious mischiefs accompanying distribution of Christmas cards and Easter cards. Beyond the expenditure of money and trouble and time, these entail both negative and positive evils—negative, because such customs, as fast as they grow general, lose their meaning and cease to give pleasure; and positive, because neglect of them produces ill-feeling. So long as these kindnesses are shown spontaneously to one or a few, specially liked or loved, they have their value; but as fast as they become matters of routine they become valueless or worse.

Let every one insist on reality and sincerity, and refrain as much as he can from complimentary usages which involve untruths. If each resolves to tell as few tacit lies as possible, social intercourse will be much healthier.

465. Doubtless most readers have been surprised to find the three foregoing sections included in a work on ethics: having been unaccustomed to contemplate acts of social conformity under their ethical aspects. But, as has been contended from the beginning, all conduct which issues in increase or decrease of happiness, has its ethical aspect; and it cannot be questioned that the observances imposed by society either conduce to happiness or the contrary.

But the social beneficence which enjoins resistance to in-

jurious customs, is by some disapproved because resistance is
followed by a reputation for eccentricity, and this diminishes
the ability to forward more important reforms: political and
religious, for example. The conclusion might be granted, were
the premise rightly admitted. It is not true that the reform of
social usages is less important than other reforms. Consider
the evil results of partially turning night into day, while
breathing the bad air generated by artificial lights. Consider,
too, the mischiefs entailed by ill-arranged meal hours—taking
the chief meal at a time when digestive power is flagging,
instead of at a time when it is greatest. Note, again, how this
irrational arrangement abridges social intercourse, and increases the formality of what remains. Remember to what an
extent, as shown in preceding sections, life, or at least the life
of the well-to-do classes, is absorbed in fulfilling usages—
now in needless changes of dress, in consulting dressmakers,
in discussing fashions with friends; now in buying, or producing, pretty things so named, which are mostly in the way; now
in making calls, often in the hope that those called on will not
be at home.* When there is added the unceasing trouble and
large cost entailed by parties yielding little satisfaction and
much annoyance, it will be seen that the evils to be combated
are anything but trivial. Those who diligently conform to the
requirements, instead of being happy are simply playing at
being happy.

Two illustrations occur to me as showing how, in social life
as carried on according to rule, the reality is lost in the show.
One of them was furnished by a lady pursuing the ordinary
upper-class routine, to whom I was expressing my aversion to
the weariness of railway traveling; and who said that, contrariwise, she always found it a great satisfaction to enter a

---

* An amusing satire on this system appeared some dozen years or so ago in *The
Owl*. The proposal was that there should be established a Ladies' Exchange (Clear-
inghouse it should have been named) to which their men-servants should every day
severally take the cards that were due from them to various friends, and receive the
cards owned them by other friends: so performing the mechanical process of distribution more economically.

train at Paris on the way to Algiers (where they had a resi-
dence), and to feel that for many hours she would be free from
her wearisome occupations—no parties, no calls, no letters.
The other was furnished by the testimony of some who have
contrasted the trammeled life in England with an untram-
meled colonial life. The early emigrants to New Zealand belonged to a more cultivated class than colonists generally do,
and carried with them those observances of civilized life
which originate in good feeling, while leaving behind those
which are merely conventional. After experiencing for years
the resulting pleasures, some who came back to England were
so disgusted by the artificiality of its ways, that they returned
to New Zealand. Two only of these colonists have I known,
and both decided to end their days there.

Far from being true, then, is the belief that the rationaliza-
tion of social observances is relatively unimportant. It may be
doubted whether, as measured by the effects on happiness, it
is not an end more important than any other. The simplifica-
tion of appliances and usages, with resulting decrease of the
friction of life, a well-wisher to his species will unceasingly
strive for. Social beneficence here finds an object to be kept
ever in view.

CHAPTER 9

Political Beneficence

466. The injunction ascribed to Charles I, "Touch no state matters," was one appropriately enough promulgated by a king; for a king naturally likes to have his own way. Ready conformity to the injunction, however, on the part of subjects, does not appear so natural; and yet throughout the past it has been general, and is not uncommon even now. There are many who, though they probably never heard of this rule of King Charles, unconsciously subordinate themselves to it, and seem to take a pride in their subordination. "I never meddle in politics," you may hear a tradesman say; and he says it in a way implying that he thinks the abstention creditable.

There have, indeed, been times—bad times—to which this mental attitude was fit. In days of exclusive militancy, when slavish submission was conducive to efficiency in war, individuality of thought and action was out of place. But under a political regime like that into which we have grown, taking a share in political life is the duty of every citizen; and not to do so is at once shortsighted, ungrateful, and mean: shortsighted, because abstention, if general, must bring decay of any good institutions which exist; ungrateful, because to leave uncared for these good institutions which patriotic ancestors established, is to ignore our indebtedness to them; mean, because to benefit by such institutions and devolve the maintenance and improvement of them entirely upon others, implies readiness to receive an advantage and give nothing in return.

For a free political organization to remain alive and healthy, all its units must play their parts. If numbers of them remain passive, the organization, in so far as they are concerned, is dead; and, in proportion as such numbers increase, must corrupt. Political beneficence includes the duty of preventing this. Let us glance at some of the evils arising from disregard of this duty, and the benefits which greater regard of it would bring, alike to self and to others.

467. When the system of status has passed into the system of contract, it becomes requisite that the system of contract shall be properly carried out. Protection of life and liberty being presupposed, the one requisite to a social life carried on by voluntary cooperation, is that agreements shall be fulfilled—that for a given amount of work the specified wages shall be paid; that for a definite portion of a commodity there shall be handed over its price in money or an equivalent; that when certain actions are undertaken on certain conditions, the actions shall be performed and the conditions observed. While criminal law has to yield protection against direct aggression, civil law has to yield protection against indirect aggression. And each citizen is, to the extent of his ability, responsible for the efficient performance of these functions.

Unfortunately at present each citizen has little or no consciousness of any such responsibility. If he feels called on to take any share in political life, it is a share in electioneering, or a share in some agitation for shortening hours, or diminishing the number of licenses, or empowering municipal bodies to buy up waterworks, make tramways, &c. As to maintenance of the primary condition to a healthy social life—that each citizen shall have the entire benefit his actions bring while he shall not be allowed to impose on others any evils his actions bring, and that to achieve these ends each shall be compelled to do all he has undertaken to do, and be entitled to receive all he bargained to receive—as to these essential things, the ordinary citizen thinks little or nothing about them. He thinks only of superficial questions and overlooks the fundamental question. He forgets the folly of a legislature which, generation after generation, does nothing to make it possible for citizens to know what the laws are. He looks on vacantly at the absurd actions every year committed by Lords and Commons in heaping a number of new acts on to the vast heap of old acts: making the confusion worse confounded. And just as though it were an unchangeable course of nature, he stands idly by while, in law courts, equity is defeated by technical error; sums gained are eaten up by sums lost in gaining them; poor suitors ruin themselves in fighting rich suitors who defy them by appeals; and the great mass of people aggressed upon, submit to injustice rather than run the risk of greater injustice.

Political beneficence of the rational kind will seek removal of these enormous evils more energetically than it will seek constitutional changes or extensions of state management. For, in countless ways, the lives of all are vitiated by non-fulfillment of this primary conditon to social cooperation. They eat adulterated food and wear clothes made of fabrics only partially genuine; all because there is no easy remedy for breach of contract in selling as one thing what is in part another thing. They pay more for every commodity than need be because, in each business, a certain average sum goes in law expenses which have to be met by extra rates of profit. And everyone is in danger of that grave loss which results when one with whom he has transactions suffers, perhaps to the extent of bankruptcy, from large dishonesties for which there is practically no redress. Were it not that in most cases the proximate hides from view the remote, men would see that in seeking a pure and efficient administration of justice, they are conducing to human happiness far more than in seeking the ends ordinarily classed as philanthropic.

468. Probably all will admit that political life is healthy only in proportion as it is conscientious; but few will admit that, as a corollary, political life carried on by party warfare is unhealthy; and that political beneficence may fitly seek to mitigate, and as far as possible abolish, such warfare. It is manifest to us here that in the United States, where the advent of Democrats or Republicans to power is followed by the turning out of officeholders of the one kind and putting in those of the other, and where both ins and outs are heavily taxed to provide funds for those electioneering campaigns which give them or take from them places and incomes, the governmental machinery is made to work ill by the substitution of private ends for public ends. But it is not generally perceived that in England party government, with its struggles for office, has vices which if less are still very great.

One of these vices, always manifest, is daily becoming more conspicuous—the dishonesty of candidates who profess what they do not believe, and promise to do that which they know ought not to be done: all to get support and to help their political leaders. In simple language they try to gain power by force of falsehood. And when, in the House of Commons, many of them say by their votes that they think one thing, while in fact they think the opposite thing, what, in plain words, shall we call them? Actually it has come to this, that a vote, which, on the face of it, is an expression of belief, perhaps on a matter affecting the happiness of millions of people, ceases to be an expression of such belief; and, instead, merely implies the desire that such and such men should fill such and such posts!

"But party loyalty necessitates this sacrifice of private convictions," is the excuse put in. Yes, party loyalty has come to be a fancied virtue to which the real virtue of veracity is sacrificed. Whence comes the alleged virtue of party loyalty? In what system of ethics does it find a place? It is simply a dishonest mode of conduct disguised by a euphemistic phrase. It is simply demerit assuming the garb of merit.

So utter is the vitiation of sentiments and ideas produced by the system, that the few who will not conform to it are vilified, and represented as hindering political action. In America, where party organization is more developed than here, whoever declines to surrender his convictions, and follow in the mob which is led by a "boss" to the polls, is labeled with the contemptuous name of "Mugwump"; and is condemned as pharisaic and as of an unsocial disposition. In "the land of liberty" it has become a political crime to act on your own judgment. Representative government, rightly so called, has become a sham; under the disguise of which there exists an oligarchy of officeholders, office seekers, and men who exercise irresponsible power.

So far is party government from being an appliance for carrying out the national will, it continually becomes an appliance for overriding the national will. A ministry raised to power by electors many of whom have been misled by promises never to be fulfilled, represents perhaps, the predominant opinion of the nation on some leading question. Once in office, the chiefs of the party backed by a compact majority, can for years do with a free hand many things they were never commissioned to do. By the aid of submissive supporters prompted by "party loyalty," a small knot of men, headed by one of great influence, enacts this or that law, which, were it put to a plebiscite, would be decisively rejected. Thus, in a second way too, party government defeats representative government. A single man with his troop of obedient servants can for some time impose his will on the nation, just as he might do were he a despotic king.

"But how can public life be carried on in any other way?" This question is thought to embody an unanswerable defense of party government. Says an American, whose advocacy of the system I have just been reading—"Every public measure must have one party in its favor and another against it. There never can be more than two parties on living, practical issues." Here the fallacy is transparent. The argument implies that a party has never more than one question to decide. It assumes that those who agree with its leaders on some issue which brought them into office, will agree with its leaders on all other issues which may arise during their term of office— an absurd assumption. But a further question is put—"How is a ministry to retain office unless its opinion subordinates the individual opinions of its supporters? and what must happen if ministries are perpetually thrown out by the votes of recalcitrant members of their parties?" Here we have one among countless illustrations of the errors caused by assuming one thing changed while other things remain unchanged. If politicians were conscientious; if, as a result, no one would vote for a thing which he did not believe good; and if, consequently, the body of representatives fell, as it must do, not into two large parties but into a number of small parties and independent members, no ministry could count upon anything like a constant majority. What would happen? A ministry would no longer be required to resign when in a minority; but would simply accept the lesson which a division gave it. It would not, as now, be for a time the master of the House, but would be always the servant of the House: not dictating a policy to it, but accepting that which was found to be its policy. Hence no measure could be carried unless it obtained the sincere support of the average of its many parties, and was thereby proved to be most likely in accordance with the national will. If, as may be contended, this would lead to great delay in the passing of measures, the reply is—So much the better. Political changes should never be made save after overcoming great resistances.

But apart from these considerations, the ethical *dictum* is clear. There are lies told by actions as well as lies told by words, and ethics gives no more countenance to the one than to the other. As originating from ultimate laws of right conduct, beneficence and veracity must go together; and political beneficence will be shown by insisting on political veracity.

469. Among the tasks enjoined by political beneficence are not only such general ones as enforcement of equitable laws made known to all, and sincerity of political conduct, but

there is also the maintenance of pure and efficient administration.

Manifestly included in this task is the choice of good representatives, general and local. Though there is some perception of the need for deliberate effort in this direction, the perception is an unenlightened one. There is no adequate consciousness of the share of duty which each elector has, not simply in giving his vote, but also in seeing that a good choice shall be made possible by a preceding good naming of candidates. At present, while there is a carefully devised machinery for choosing among nominated men, there is only a hole-and-corner machinery for deciding what men shall be nominated: this last function being really more important than the first. For it is of little use to have the overt power of deciding between A and B, when secret powers have picked out for choice an A and a B who are both undesirable. At present the local *caucus* of each party, more or less under direction of a central *caucus* in London, overrides the wills of electors by forcing them to say which of two or more they will have; often leaving them practically to say which they dislike least. Under this system there is very little regard for true fitness in a representative. Has he been a large local benefactor? Does he bind himself to support the head of the party? Is he in favor of this or that pet scheme? Can he bring to bear family influence or command votes by popularity of manner? These, and such as these, are the questions which determine his selection by the *caucus*, and therefore his selection by the constituency. Whether he has wide political knowledge; whether he has much administrative experience; whether he is far-seeing; whether he is conscientious and independent; whether he will promise nothing that he does not approve, or does not feel himself able to perform—these are questions scarcely asked. Of course the general result is a House of Commons made up of political incapables, popularity hunters, and time servers, who, believing in common with their constituents that a society is not a growth but a manufacture, carry on their legislative work under the profound delusion that things can be effectually arranged this way or that way at will; and in pursuit of their party and personal ends, do not inquire what may be the ultimate effects of their temporary expedients. Of course, political beneficence dictates strenuous exertions against this system; and enjoins the duty of seeking some way in which constituents may acquire a real instead of a nominal choice, and be led to choose men who will be fit lawmakers instead of fit tools of party.

Those on whom devolves the choice of men for county councils, municipal bodies, vestries, and the like, are spurred into activity by their leaders when members of such bodies are to be elected; but, forthwith lapsing into their usual quiescence, most of them give small attention to the doings of these bodies, or if they are made aware of inefficiency and corruption, are not prompted by a sense of public duty to seek remedies. A shopkeeper does not like to move because some of his customers, directly or indirectly interested in the misdoings he perceives, may be offended. Among a doctor's patients there are probably a few who, if not implicated with those whose carelessness or incapacity needs exposing, are on friendly terms with them; and he does not feel called upon to risk alienation of such. Even a man of means, whose pecuniary interests will not be endangered by any course he may take, hesitates lest he should make himself unpopular. He knows that enmities will be generated and no compensating friendships formed. And then there are many who, if not deterred by motives above indicated, do not see why they should give themselves trouble for no personal benefit. Abuses are consequently allowed to rise and grow.

Thus is it very generally with administrations. There is no conception that political beneficence requires of each man that he shall take his share in seeing that political machinery, general and local, does its work properly.*

---

* Let me here emphasize my meaning by giving an instance of maladministration which daily comes under the eyes of millions of people inhabiting London. I refer to the persistently bad state of the macadamized roads. What is the cause? After rain

470. "The price of liberty is eternal vigilance," said one of the early American statesmen; and eternal vigilance is also the price of well-working institutions. In proportion as human nature is defective, the organizations formed out of human beings must be defective too. And they will become far more defective than they would else be, if there are not constant detections of their defects and constant efforts to prevent increase of them.

Hence a proper sense of public duty will prompt endeavors to stop abuses the moment they become visible, without waiting for them to become serious. The misdoings which, in course of time, make useless or mischievous this or that administration, begin with trivial derelictions of duty, which no one thinks it worth while to protest against. Each increment of mischief, similarly small, is passed over as unimportant; until at length the evil is found to have grown great and perhaps

---

anyone who looks may see. Generally, if not always, each elevated portion of the surface has at its highest point a piece of broken stone larger than the average of the pieces forming the road—twice or thrice as large. Each of these large pieces, supported by several pieces below, has more power of resisting the impacts of carriage wheels than the smaller pieces around, and becomes relatively prominent. Every carriage wheel, when passing with speed over a prominent point, is jolted upwards, and instantly afterward comes down with a blow upon the succeeding part of the surface. By repetition of these blows a hollow is formed. More than this happens. In rainy weather each hollow becomes filled with water, which makes it softer than the prominent parts and more apt to yield. Hence a surface full of small hills and holes. The evils caused are various. Continuous shakings, uncomfortable to the strong and to the weak very injurious, have to be borne by hundreds of thousands of people in omnibuses, cabs, and carriages; vehicles wear out faster than they should do; horses are overtaxed, and have to be replaced by others sooner than would else be needful. And then the roads themselves wear out rapidly. How does all this happen? Simply because the road contractor profits by evading the regulation respecting the size of broken stones. And as the steamroller, of late years introduced, flattens down large and small to an even surface, the surveyor passes the work as all right. Why does he do this? Well, contractors are frequently rich men; and the salaries of surveyors are not very high.

Here then is an example of a conspicuous evil concerning which complaint seems useless. If you name it to a county councillor the reply is that the council has no power in the matter; and you get no satisfaction if you mention it to a vestryman. Among the many men who are in power, and the multitudes of men who ought to see that those in power do their duty, there are none who take a step toward remedying this great abuse.

incurable. A good illustration of the way in which ultimate disasters result from the disregard of trifling imperfections, has often struck me when watching the emptying of a canal lock. Here and there in the wall, as the water descends, may be observed a small jet issuing from a crevice—a crevice through which the water enters again when the lock is re-filled, and from which there again issues a jet when the water again falls. In an old and neglected lock, not only are these jets numerous but some have become very large. At every use of the lock, a cavity which has been gradually formed behind each of these, is charged and discharges itself; and the larger it becomes the more rapidly does the powerful ingoing and outgoing stream increase it and its channel. Eventually, if nothing is done, the joints of the stonework are so much eaten away, and the back of the wall so much hollowed, that one or other part collapses. In an analogous way the insignificant abuses in an institution, which are initiated by carelessness or self-interest, and tolerated by indifference, or what seems good nature, increases little by little until the whole structure becomes worthless or injurious.

The "eternal vigilance" required to maintain not only liberty but purity, should have for its guide a principle just opposite to the principle commonly followed. Most men, alike in public affairs and private business affairs, assume that things are going right until it is proved they are going wrong; whereas their assumption should be that things are going wrong until it is proved they are going right. Though in churches they continually hear asserted the ingrained wickedness of men, and though in every day's newspaper they find exposed various dishonesties and deceptions, not of simple kinds only but of those complex kinds which bubble companies and swindling syndicates practice; yet they seem to think that in the transactions of any political or social organization they are concerned with, there are, and will be, no corruptions. Though every receipt they take is a precaution against dis-honesty, though every law deed makes many provisions to prevent breaches of understanding, and though every act of

Parliament is full of clauses implying the belief that some will do wrong if there are any openings left for them to do wrong, people argue that unless evidence has raised it, there should be no suspicion respecting the doings of incorporated bodies or official organizations; and this notwithstanding the daily proofs that bank failures and company disasters arise from ill-grounded beliefs in the conscientiousness of all concerned, and the lack of checks against possible roguery.*

Political beneficence, then, prompting this "eternal vigilance," will, I say, be ever ready to detect possible modes of corruption; ever ready to resist insignificant usurpations of power; ever prepared to challenge transactions which in the smallest ways deviate from the proper order; and ever ready to bear the odium consequent on taking such courses.

---

* At the moment these pages are passing through the press, abundant warnings are furnished to those who can recognize the lesson they teach. Besides minor cases, there are now simultaneously reported in the papers, proceedings concerning the Liberator Building Society, the London and General Bank, Limited, the Hansard Union, Limited, Hobbs & Co., Limited, Barker & Co.'s Bank; in Italy the Banca Romana; and in France the gigantic Panama scandals, implicating directors, legislators, and even ministers. Nevertheless, we shall have tomorrow new schemes, which people will suppose are going right till some catastrophe proves they have been going wrong.

CHAPTER 10

Beneficence at Large

471. Most readers have been surprised by much which has, in the foregoing chapters, and especially the later ones, been included under the head of beneficence. Only special parts of social and political conduct are usually thought of as having ethical aspects; whereas here most parts of them have been dealt with as having such aspects. But the reader who bears in mind the doctrine laid down at the outset and recently reenunciated, that all conduct which in an indirect, if not in a direct way, conduces to happiness or misery, is therefore to be judged as right or wrong, will see that the various topics touched upon could not rightly be omitted. After the conduct which is of individual concern only, and affects others in but remote ways, if at all; and after the conduct comprehended under the head of justice, which sets forth restraints on individual life imposed by social life; nearly all the remainder of conduct becomes the subject matter of beneficence, negative or positive. For nearly all this remainder of conduct pleasurably or painfully affects others from hour to hour.

After thus conceiving the sphere of beneficence, it becomes obvious that even more has to be included than has yet been included. Large space would be required to treat in detail the incentives and restraints which should guide behavior to those around. There are words and tones and facial expressions which throughout daily intercourse continually excite disagreeable emotions, and others which excite agreeable emotions; and the amounts of happiness or of misery created by them, often far exceed the amounts created by maleficent or beneficent actions of conspicuous kinds. Not, indeed, that agreeableness or disagreeableness of behavior is to be wholly ascribed to the presence or absence of beneficent promptings. The presence or absence of a desire for approbation is commonly a chief cause. But the sweetness of manner which springs from sympathy, is in most cases easily distinguishable. Acted goodness of feeling rarely produces the same effect as real goodness of feeling.

Though beneficence of other kinds may be produced by general sense of duty, by desire to establish right human relations, by a high ideal of conduct, this kind of beneficence can be produced only by active fellow feeling. In a few finely constituted natures, this fellow feeling is dominant, and spontaneously shows itself: beneficence has in so far become with them organic. Everyone feels the better for their presence. They are natural centers of happiness. Those of inferior natures, forming the immense majority, can here fulfill the dictates of beneficence only in so far as they can subordinate themselves to an ideal of behavior; and even then in but a partial way. Occasionally, it may be possible for them to recognize in time some nascent manifestation of unamiable feeling and check it, or to perceive with sufficient quickness an opportunity of showing sympathy, and even of arousing it by a quick imagination of the circumstances. By keeping in mind the requirements of beneficence, some small amount of self-discipline may thus be achieved.

Beyond the beneficent regulation of conduct toward members of the family and towards friends, there is the beneficent regulation of conduct towards those who occupy positions of subordination, or of lower social status. A large sphere for the anodyne influence of sympathy is here opened. From the militant regime, with its graduated ranks and obedience coercively maintained, there have descended those modes of behavior which continually recall the relations of superior and inferior. Pervading social life they influence all in ways difficult to resist. Though, among the better natured on the one side, there is a dislike to usages which make others feel their inferiority, and though the more independent on the other side, vaguely resent such usages; yet it seems impossible to change forthwith the established manners, and to get rid of the unbeneficent emotions accompanying them. Doubtless, along with the substitution of the system of contract for the system of status, there has been a relaxation of those customs which remind men of their respective grades. This has gone so far that in modern days a true gentleman is described as aiming to make those who rank below him in the social scale, at ease in his presence: seeking, not to emphasize any distinction between himself and them, but rather to obliterate the consciousness of the distinction.

As regulating such intercourse, beneficence has the function of increasing the happiness of the less fortunate by raising them for the time being to the level of the more fortunate, and making them as much as possible forget the difference in position or in means.

472. The foregoing paragraphs will probably raise in many minds a silent protest, several times before raised, against the tacit acceptance of a social system which they reprobate. Impatient with the multitudinous evils which humanity at present suffers, and ascribing these to the existing organization of society, they reject indignantly all conclusions which take for granted that this organization is to continue. Let us hear what they say.

"Your conception of beneficence is a radically unbeneficent one. Your remarks about restraints on free competition, and on free contract, imply the belief that all men are hereafter, as now, to fight for individual gain. Services rendered by the ill-off to the well-off are taken for granted in your remarks about restraints on blame. The various modes of administering charity, condemned or approved by you, assume that in the future there must be rich and poor as at present. And some of the immediately foregoing exhortations concerning behavior, presuppose the continued existence of superior and inferior classes. But those who have emancipated themselves from beliefs imposed by the past, see that all such relations of men to one another are bad and must be changed. A true ethics—a true beneficence—cannot recognize any such inequalities as those you take for granted. If ethical injunctions are to be carried out, then all social arrangements of the kinds we now know must be abolished, and replaced by social arrangements in which there are neither caste differences nor differences of means. And, under the implied system, large parts of the actions you have classed as beneficent will have no place. They will be excluded as needless or impossible."

Unquestionably there is an *a priori* warrant for this protest. A society in which there are marked class distinctions cannot fulfill the conditions under which only the fullest happiness can be achieved. Though it is not within the range of possibility that all the units shall be equal in respect of their endowments (a dreadful state, could it be reached), yet it is possible that there may be reached such kind of equality as results from an approximately even distribution of different kinds of powers—those who are inferior in some respects being superior in others: so producing infinite variety with a general uniformity, and so excluding gradations of social position. Some such type of human nature, and consequent social type, are contemplated by absolute ethics.

But it is forgotten that during the stages through which men and society are slowly passing, we are chiefly concerned with relative ethics and not with absolute ethics. The dictates of absolute ethics being kept before us as the ideal, we have little by little to mold the real into conformity with them, as fast as the nature of things permits. Sudden transformation being impossible, sudden fulfillment of the highest ethical requirements is impossible.

473. Those who, not content with that progress through small modifications which is alone permanent, hope to reach by immediate reorganization a high social state, practically assume that the human mind can forthwith have its qualities so changed that its bad products will be replaced by good products. Old beliefs in the wonders to be worked by a beneficent fairy, were not more baseless than are these new beliefs in the wonders to be worked by a revolutionized social system.

A world which, from the far east of Russia to the far west of California and from Dunedin in the North to Dunedin at the Antipodes, daily witnesses deeds of violence, from the conquests of one people by another to the aggressions of man on man, will not easily find place for a social order implying fraternal regard of each for each. A nature which generates international hatreds and intense desires for revenge—which breeds duelists and a contempt for those who do not seek to wipe out a slight by a death, is not a nature out of which harmonious communities can be molded. Men who rush in crowds to witness the brutalities of football matches, who roar out ferocious suggestions to the players, and mob the umpires who do not please them, so that police protection is required, are not men who will show careful consideration of one another's claims when they have agreed to work together for the common good. Not by any ingenuity can there be framed well-working institutions for people who shoot those who will not enter the political combinations they form, who mutilate and torture the cattle of dissentients, who employ emissaries to blow up unconcerned persons and cause a panic, and who then, when the wretches have been convicted, are indignant that they are not released. Only to a wild imagination will it seem possible that a social regime higher than the present, can be maintained by men who, as railway employees, wreck and burn the rolling stock of companies which will not yield to their demands—men who, as ironworkers, salute with bullets those who come to take the wages they refuse, try by dynamite to destroy them along with the houses they inhabit and seek to poison them wholesale—men who, as miners, carry on a local civil war to prevent a competition they do not like. Strange, indeed, is the expectation that those who, unscrupulous as to means, selfishly strive to get as much as possible for their labor and to give as little labor as possible, will suddenly become so unselfish that the superior among them will refrain from using their superiority lest they should disadvantage the inferior!

Without having recourse to such extreme illustrations, we may see, on contemplating a widely diffused habit, how absurd is the belief that egoistic conduct may forthwith be changed into altruistic conduct. Here, throughout the whole community, from the halls of nobles and the clubs frequented by the upper ten thousand, down through the trading classes, their sons and daughters, and even to the denizens of kitchens and the boys in the street, we find gambling and betting; the universal trait of which is that each wishes to gain by his neighbor's loss. And now we are told that under a new social system, all those who have greater ability will submit to loss that those who have less ability may gain! Without any transformation of men's characters, but merely by transforming social arrangements, it is hoped to get the effects of goodness without the goodness!

474. While the majority believe that human nature is unchangeable, there are some who believe that it may rapidly be changed. Both beliefs are wrong. Great alterations may be wrought, but only in course of multitudinous generations: the small alterations, such as those which distinguish nation from nation, taking centuries, and the great alterations, molding an egoistic nature into an altruistic one, taking eras. Nothing but a prolonged discipline of social life—obtainment of good by submission to social requirements, and suffering of evil from disregard of them—can effect the change.

This would scarcely need saying were it not that the education received by the upper classes, and now diligently forced by them on the lower, leaves all with nature's open secrets unlearned. One of these is that there can be no social or political actions but what are determined by the minds, separate or aggregated, of human beings; that these human beings can have no mental processes and consequent activities which are not parts of their lives, subject to the laws of their lives; and that the laws of their lives are included within those most general laws to which life at large must conform. Could statesmen and politicians and philanthropists and schemers recognize this truth, which profoundly concerns them, they would see that all social phenomena, from the beginning down to the present, and onward through the future, must be concomitants of the readaptation of mankind to its new circumstances—the change from a nature which fitted men for the wandering and predatory habits of the savage, to a nature which fits them for the settled and industrial habits of the civilized. They would see that this long process, during which old aptitudes and desires have to dwindle, while new aptitudes and desires have to be developed, is necessarily a process of continued suffering. It would become manifest to them that this suffering, caused by the constant overtaxing of some powers and denying to others the activities they crave, cannot by any possibility be escaped. And they would infer, lastly, that to suspend the process by shielding individuals and classes from those stern requirements imposed by the social state, must not only fail to prevent suffering but must increase it; since the loss of adaptation consequent upon relaxation of the conditions, has eventually to be made good. The readaptation has to be gone through afresh, and the suffering borne over again.

Thus, along with those permanent functions of beneficence which will become more dominant in an ultimate social state, there must, for thousands of years, continue those temporary functions of it proper to our transitional state. After men's attempts to realize their ideals, and reform society without reforming themselves, have ended in disaster, and, sobered by sufferings, they submit themselves afresh to the hard discipline which has brought us thus far, further progress may be made. But there must be great changes before this progress can go on unimpeded. Over the greater part of the earth, men have ceased to devour one another, and to receive honor in proportion to their achievements in that way; and when societies shall have ceased to devour one another, and cease to count as glory their success in doing this, the humanization of the brute may become comparatively rapid. It is impossible that there can be much advance towards a reign of political justice internally, while there is maintained a reign of political burglary externally. But when the antagonism between the ethics of amity and the ethics of enmity has come to an end, there may go on without much check, the rise toward that high state vaguely foreshadowed by the distorted visions of our social schemes.

Meanwhile, the chief temporary function of beneficence is to mitigate the sufferings accompanying the transition; or rather, let us say, to ward off the superfluous sufferings. The miseries of readaptation are necessary; but there are accompanying unnecessary miseries which may, with universal advantage, be excluded. The beneficence which simply removes a pain must, considered apart from other effects, be held intrinsically good. The beneficence which yields present relief so far as consists with the individual's welfare, is better. But the beneficence which takes into account not only the immediate and remote results to the individual, but also the results to posterity and to society at large, is best. For this is the beneficence which is so dominated by the sense of responsibility, that it consents to bear immediate sympathetic pain, rather than be subject to the consciousness of having helped to entail greater and more widespread pains. The highest beneficence is that which is not only prepared, if need be, to sacrifice egoistic pleasures, but is also prepared, if need be, to sacrifice altruistic pleasures.

475. And here we come again to the conclusion once before reached, that these self-sacrifices imposed by the transitional state, gradually diminishing, must eventually occupy but small spaces in life; while the emotions which prompted

them, ceasing to be the mitigators of misery, will become the multipliers of happiness. For sympathy, which is the root of all altruism, causes participation in pleasurable feelings as well as in painful feelings; and in proportion as painful feelings become less prevalent, participation in pleasurable feelings must be its almost exclusive effect.

As was pointed out in section 93, quick and wide sympathies would intensify and multiply miseries, did they exist during stages in which the pains of average lives exceeded the pleasures. If the better constituted and the more fortunately circumstanced, were fully conscious of all which their fellow creatures have to bear, the result would be to make them as unhappy as the rest, and so increase the total unhappiness. Life would be intolerable to the highly sympathetic, could they vividly represent to themselves the tortures inflicted on Negroes by Arab slave catchers, the dreadful years passed by kidnapped Kanakas, who are slaves under another name, the daily sufferings of Hindu ryots, half-starved and heavily taxed, the dreary existence of Russian peasants, conscripted, or even in the midst of famine, bled to support conscripts. Acute fellow feeling would be a curse to its possessors, did it bring vividly before them the states of body and mind experienced even by the masses around—the long persistence in work under protesting sensations, the poor food often insufficient in quantity, the thin clothing, the insufficient fire, the scanty bedding, the crying children, the wife soured by privation and the husband occasionally brutalized by drink: all joined with hopelessness—with the consciousness that most of this has to be borne throughout the rest of life, and much of it to be intensified as old age comes on. Evidently the altruistic sentiments, while they serve in a measure to mitigate the sufferings accompanying the readaptation of the race, are continually repressed or seared by the presence of this irremediable misery, and can develop only in proportion as it diminishes. Slightly decreased suffering may be followed by slightly increased sympathy; and this, rightly directed, may further decrease the suffering; which, again, may make more sympathy possible; and so on *pari passu*. But only when the amount of suffering has become insignificant, can fellow feeling reach its full development.

When the pressure of population has been rendered small—proximately by prudential restraints and ultimately by decrease of fertility—and when long-range rifles, big guns, dynamite shells, and other implements for wholesale slaughter which Christian peoples have improved so greatly of late, are to be found only in museums; sympathy will probably increase to a degree which we can now scarcely conceive. For the process of evolution must inevitably favor all changes of nature which increase life and augment happiness: especially such as do this at small cost. Natures which, by the help of a more developed language of emotion, vocal and facial, are enabled to enter so fully into others' pleasurable feelings that they can add these to their own, must be natures capable of a beatitude far greater than is now possible. In such natures a large part of the mental life must result from participation in the mental lives of others.

Thus, along with increasing readaptation, altruism will become less and less the assuager of suffering and more and more the exalter of happiness.

476. To most this conclusion will not commend itself: dissent being in some intellectually prompted and in others emotionally prompted. The first constitute the class of men who, while believing in organic evolution, and knowing that many of the multitudinous transformations effected by it are so marvellous as to seem scarcely credible, nevertheless tacitly assume that no further transformations will take place—not even such relatively small ones as would raise the higher types of men to a type fitted for harmonious social cooperation. The second constitute the much larger class, to whom the future of humanity is not a matter of much interest; and who regard with indifference a conclusion which holds out no promise of benefit to themselves, either here or hereafter.

But there exist a few who differ intellectually from the one of these classes and morally from the other. To them it seems not only rational to believe in some further evolution, but irrational to doubt it—irrational to suppose that the causes which have in the past worked such wonderful effects, will in the future work no effects. Not expecting that any existing society will reach a high organization, nor that any of the varieties of men now living will become fully adapted to social life, they yet look forward through unceasing changes, now progressive now retrogressive, to the evolution of a humanity adjusted to the requirements of its life. And along with this belief there arises, in an increasing number, the desire to further the development. The anxieties which in many now go beyond the welfares of personal descendants, and include the welfare of the nation and its institutions, as well as, in some cases, the welfares of other nations and other races, will more and more become an anxiety for human progress at large.

Hereafter, the highest ambition of the beneficent will be to have a share—even though an utterly inappreciable and unknown share—in "the making of man." Experience occasionally shows that there may arise extreme interest in pursuing entirely unselfish ends; and, as time goes on, there will be more and more of those whose unselfish end will be the further evolution of humanity. While contemplating from the heights of thought, that far-off life of the race never to be enjoyed by them, but only by a remote posterity, they will feel a calm pleasure in the consciousness of having aided the advance towards it.

APPENDICES

APPENDIX A

The Kantian Idea of Rights

Among the tracks of thought pursued by multitudinous minds in the course of ages, nearly all must have been entered upon if not explored. Hence the probability is greatly against the assumption of entire novelty in any doctrine. The remark is suggested by an instance of such an assumption erroneously made.

The fundamental principle enunciated in the chapter entitled "The Formula of Justice," is one which I set forth in *Social Statics: The Conditions Essential to Human Happiness Specified and the First of Them Developed,* originally published at the close of 1850. I then supposed that I was the first to recognize the law of equal freedom as being that in which justice, as variously exemplified in the concrete, is summed up in the abstract. I was wrong, however. In the second of two articles entitled "Mr. Herbert Spencer's Theory of Society," published by Mr. F.W. Maitland (now Downing Professor of Law at Cambridge) in *Mind,* vol. viii. (1883), pp. 508–9, it was pointed out that Kant had already enunciated, in other words, a similar doctrine. Not being able to read the German quotations given by Mr. Maitland, I was unable to test his statement. When, however, I again took up the subject, and reached the chapter on

451

"The Formula of Justice," it became needful to ascertain definitely what were Kant's views. I found them in a recent translation (1887) by Mr. W. Hastie, entitled *The Philosophy of Law, An Exposition of the Fundamental Principles of Jurisprudence as the Science of Right*. In this, at p. 45, occurs the sentence: "Right, therefore, comprehends the whole of the conditions under which the voluntary actions of any one person can be harmonized in reality with the voluntary actions of every other person, according to a universal law of freedom." And then there follows this section:

Universal Principle of Right

Every action is *right* which in itself, or in the maxim on which it proceeds, is such that it can coexist along with the Freedom of the Will of each and all in action, according to a universal law.

If, then, my action or my condition generally can coexist with the freedom of every other, according to a universal law, anyone does me a wrong who hinders me in the performance of this action, or in the maintenance of this condition. For such a hindrance or obstruction cannot coexist with Freedom according to universal laws.

It follows also that it cannot be demanded as a matter of Right, that this universal Principle of all maxims shall itself be adopted as my maxim, that is, that I shall make it the *maxim* of my actions. For anyone may be free, although his Freedom is entirely indifferent to me, or even if I wished in my heart to infringe it, so long as I do not actually violate that freedom by *my external action*. Ethics, however, as distinguished from Jurisprudence, imposes upon me the obligation to make the fulfillment of Right a *maxim* of my conduct.

The universal Law of Right may then be expressed, thus: "Act externally in such a manner that the free exercise of thy Will may be able to coexist with the Freedom of all others, according to a universal Law." This is undoubtedly a Law which imposes obligation upon me; but it does not at all imply and still less command that I *ought*, merely on account of this obligation, to limit my freedom to these very conditions. Reason in this connection says only that it *is* restricted thus far by its Idea, and may be likewise thus limited in fact by others; and it lays this down as a Postulate which is not capable of further proof. As the object in view is not to teach Virtue, but to explain what right *is*, thus far the Law of Right, as thus laid down, may not and should not be represented as a motive-principle of action.

These passages make it clear that Kant had arrived at a conclusion which, if not the same as my own, is closely allied to it. It is, however, worth remarking that Kant's conception, similar though it is in nature, differs both in its origin and in its form.

As shown on a preceding page, his conclusion is reached by a "search in the pure reason for the sources of such judgments"—forms a part of the "metaphysic of morals"; whereas, as shown on pp. 67–68 of the original edition of *Social Statics*, the law of equal freedom, there shadowed forth and subsequently stated, is regarded as expressing the primary condition which must be fulfilled before the greatest happiness can be achieved by similar beings living in proximity. Kant enunciates an *a priori* requirement, contemplated as irrespective of beneficial ends; whereas I have enunciated this *a priori* requirement as one which, under the circumstances necessitated by the social state, must be conformed to for achievement of beneficial ends.

The noteworthy distinction between the forms in which the conception is presented is this. Though (on p. 56) Kant, by saying that "there is only one innate right, the birthright of freedom," clearly recognizes the positive element in the conception of justice; yet, in the passages quoted above, the right of the individual to freedom is represented as emerging by implication from the wrongfulness of acts which aggress upon this freedom. The negative element, or obligation to respect limits, is the dominant idea; whereas in my own case the positive element—the right to freedom of action—is represented as primary; while the negative element, resulting from the limitations imposed by the presence of others, is represented as secondary. This distinction may not be without its significance; for the putting of obligation in the foreground seems natural to a social state in which political restraints are strong, while the putting of claims in the foreground seems natural to a social state in which there is a greater assertion of individuality.

APPENDIX B

The Land Question

The course of nature, "red in tooth and claw," has been, on a higher plane, the course of civilization. Through "blood and iron" small clusters of men have been consolidated into larger ones, and these again into still larger ones, until nations have been formed. This process, carried on everywhere and always by brute force, has resulted in a history of wrongs upon wrongs: savage tribes have been slowly welded together by savage means. We could not, if we tried, trace back the acts of unscrupulous violence committed during these thousands of years; and could we trace them back we could not rectify their evil results.

Landownership was established during this process; and if the genesis of landownership was full of iniquities, they were iniquities committed not by the ancestors of any one class of existing men but by the ancestors of all existing men. The remote forefathers of living Englishmen were robbers, who stole the lands of men who were themselves robbers, who behaved in like manner to the robbers who preceded them. The usurpation by the Normans, here complete and there partial, was of lands which, centuries before, had been seized, some by piratical Danes and Norsemen, and some at an earlier time by hordes of invading Frisians or old English. And then the Celtic owners, expelled or enslaved by these, had in bygone ages themselves expropriated the peoples who lived in the underground houses here and there still traceable. What would happen if we tried to restore lands inequitably taken—if Normans had to give them back to Danes and Norse and Frisians, and these again to Celts, and these again to the men who lived in caves and used flint implements? The only imaginable form of the transaction would be a restoration of Great Britain bodily to the Welsh and the Highlanders; and if the Welsh and the Highlanders did not make a kindred restoration, it could only be on the ground that, having not only taken the land of the aborigines but killed them, they had thus justified their ownership!

The wish now expressed by many that landownership should be conformed to the requirements of pure equity, is in itself commendable; and is in some men prompted by conscientious feeling. One would, however, like to hear from such the demand that not only here but in the various regions we are peopling, the requirements of pure equity should be conformed to. As it is, the indignation against wrongful appropriations of land, made in the past at home, is not accompanied by any indignation against the more wrongful appropriations made at present abroad. Alike as holders of the predominant political power and as furnishing the rank and file of our armies, the masses of the people are responsible for those nefarious doings all over the world which end in the seizing of new territories and expropriation of their inhabitants. The filibustering expeditions of the old English are repeated, on a vastly larger scale, in the filibustering expeditions of the new English. Yet those who execrate ancient usurpations utter no word of protest against these far greater modern usurpations—nay, are aiders and abettors in them. Remaining as they do passive and silent while there is going on this universal land-grabbing which their votes could stop; and supplying as they do the soldiers who effect it; they are responsible for it. By deputy they are committing in this matter grosser and more numerous injustices than were committed against their forefathers.

That the masses of landless men should regard private landownership as having been wrongfully established, is natural; and, as we have seen, they are not without warrant. But if we entertain the thought of rectification, there arises in the first place the question—which are the wronged and which are the wrongers? Passing over the primary fact that the ancestors of existing Englishmen, landed and landless, were, as a body, men who took the land by violence from previous owners; and thinking only of the force and fraud by which certain of these ancestors obtained possession of the land while others of them lost possession; the preliminary question is—Which are the descendants of the one and of the other? It is tacitly assumed that those who now own lands are the posterity of the usurpers, and that those who now have no lands are the posterity of those whose lands were usurped. But this is far from being the case. The fact that among the nobility there are very few whose titles go back to the days when the last usurpations took place, and none to the days when there took place the original usurpations; joined with the fact that among existing landowners there are many whose names imply artisan-ancestors; show that we have not now to deal with descendants of those who unjustly appropriated the land. While, conversely, the numbers of the landless whose names prove that their forefathers belonged to the higher ranks (numbers which must be doubled to take account of intermarriages with female descendants) show that among those who are now without land, many inherit the blood of the land-usurpers. Hence, that bitter feeling towards the landed which contemplation of the past generates in many of the landless, is in great measure misplaced. They are themselves to a considerable extent descendants of the sinners; while those they scowl at are to a considerable extent descendants of the sinned-against.

But granting all that is said about past inequities, and leav-

ing aside all other obstacles in the way of an equitable rearrangement, there is an obstacle which seems to have been
overlooked. Even supposing that the English as a race gained
possession of the land equitably, which they did not; and even
supposing that existing landowners are the posterity of those
who spoiled their fellows, which in large part they are not;
and even supposing that the existing landless are the posterity
of the despoiled, which in large part they are not; there would
still have to be recognized a transaction that goes far to prevent rectification of injustices. If we are to go back upon the
past at all, we must go back upon the past wholly, and take
account not only of that which the people at large have lost by
private appropriation of land, but also that which they have
received in the form of a share of the returns—we must take
account, that is, of Poor Law relief. Mr. T. Mackay, author of
The English Poor, has kindly furnished me with the following
memoranda, showing something like the total amount of this
since the 43rd Elizabeth (1601) in England and Wales.

> Sir G. Nicholls [History of Poor Law, appendix to Vol. II] ventures
> no estimate till 1688. At that date he puts the poor rate at nearly
> £700,000 a year. Till the beginning of this century the amounts are
> based more or less on estimate.

1601–1630	say	3 millions.	
1631–1700	[1688 Nicholls puts at 700,000]	30	"
1701–1720	[1701 Nicholls puts at 900,000]	20	"
1721–1760	[1760 Nicholls says 1¼ millions]	40	"
1761–1775	[1775 put at 1½ millions]	22	"
1776–1800	[1784 2 millions]	50	"
1801–1812	[1803 4 millions; 1813 6 millions]	65	"
1813–1840	[based on exact figures given by Sir G. Nicholls]	170	"
1841–1890	[based on Mulhall's Dict. of Statistics and Statistical Abstract]	334	"
		734 millions.	

The above represents the amount *expended* in relief of the
poor. Under the general term "poor rate," moneys have al-

ways been collected for other purposes—county, borough, police rates, &c. The following table shows the annual amounts of these in connection with the annual amounts expended on the poor.

			Total levied	Expended on poor	Other purposes *balance*
Sir G. Nicholls	{	In 1803	5.348.000	4.077.000	1.271.000 ?
	}	" 1813	8.646.841	6.656.106	1.990.735 ?
	(	" 1853	6.522.412	4.939.064	1.583.341 ?
			Total spent		Sum spent
Statistical	{	" 1875	12.694.208	7.488.481	5.205.727
abstract	(	" 1889.	15.970.126	8.366.477	7.603.649

In addition, therefore, to sums set out in the first table, there is a further sum, rising during the century from 1¼ to 7½ millions per annum "for other purposes."

Mulhall on whom I relied for figures between 1853 and 1875 does not give "other expenditure."

Of course of the £734,000,000 given to the poorer members of the landless class during three centuries, a part has arisen from rates on houses; only such portion of which as is chargeable against ground rents, being rightly included in the sum the land has contributed. From a landowner, who is at the same time a Queen's Counsel, frequently employed professionally to arbitrate in questions of local taxation, I have received the opinion that if, out of the total sum received by the poor, £500,000,000 is credited to the land, this will be an underestimate. Thus even if we ignore the fact that this amount, gradually contributed, would, if otherwise gradually invested, have yielded in returns of one or other kind a far larger sum, it is manifest that against the claim of the landless may be set off a large claim of the landed—perhaps a larger claim.

For now observe that the landless have not an equitable claim to the land in its present state—cleared, drained, fenced, fertilized, and furnished with farmbuildings, &c.— but only to the land in its primitive state, here stony and there marshy, covered with forest, gorse, heather, &c.: this only, it is, which belongs to the community. Hence, therefore, the question arises—What is the relation between the original "prairie value" of the land, and the amount which the poorer among the landless have received during these three centuries. Probably the landowners would contend that for the land in its primitive, unsubdued state, furnishing nothing but wild animals and wild fruits, £500,000,000 would be a high price.

When, in *Social Statics*, published in 1850, I drew from the law of equal freedom the corollary that the land could not equitably be alienated from the community, and argued that, after compensating its existing holders, it should be reappropriated by the community, I overlooked the foregoing considerations. Moreover, I did not clearly see what would be implied by the giving of compensation for all that value which the labor of ages has given to the land. While, as shown in chap. 11, I adhere to the inference originally drawn, that the aggregate of men forming the community are the supreme owners of the land—an inference harmonizing with legal doctrine and daily acted upon in legislation—a fuller consideration of the matter has led me to the conclusion that individual ownership, subject to state suzerainty, should be maintained.

Even were it possible to rectify the inequitable doings which have gone on during past thousands of years, and by some balancing of claims and counterclaims, past and present, to make a rearrangement equitable in the abstract, the resulting state of things would be a less desirable one than the present. Setting aside all financial objections to nationalization (which of themselves negative the transaction, since, if equitably effected, it would be a losing one), it suffices to remember the inferiority of public administration to private administration, to see that ownership by the state would work ill. Under the existing system of ownership, those who manage the land, experience a direct connection between effort and benefit; while, were it under state ownership, those who managed it would experience no such direct connection. The vices of officialism would inevitably entail immense evils.

APPENDIX C

The Moral Motive

Some months after the first five chapters of this volume appeared in *The Nineteenth Century,* the Rev. J. Llewelyn Davies published in *The Guardian* for July 16, 1890, some criticisms upon them. Such of these criticisms as concern other questions I pass over, and here limit myself to one which concerns the sentiment of duty, and the authority of that sentiment. Mr. Davies says:

> To the best of my knowledge, Mr. Spencer, though often challenged, has never fully explained how, with his philosophy, he can take advantage of the ordinary language and sentiment of mankind about duty. . . . I have to repeat a criticism which I offered in my former paper. Mr. Spencer seems to me to imply what he professes not to recognize. To construct the idea and sentiment of justice, he implies a law having authority over the human mind and its conduct—viz., that the well-being of the species is to be desired, and an acknowledgment by the human mind of that law, a self-justifying response to it. Whilst he confines himself to tracing natural evolution, he has no right to use the terms of duty. What can be added to the *dictum* of Kant, and how can it be confuted?
>
> If we fix our eyes simply upon the course of nature, the *ought* has no meaning whatever. It is as absurd to ask what nature ought to be as to ask what sort of properties a circle ought to have. The only question we can properly ask is, What comes to pass in nature? just as we can only ask, What actually are the properties of a circle?

461

When Mr. Spencer inveighs with genuine moral vehemence against aggression and other forms of illdoing, when he protests, for example, against "that miserable *laissez-faire* which calmly looks on while men ruin themselves in trying to enforce by law their equitable claims"—he is borrowing *our* thunder, he is stealing fire from heaven.

And then, after further argument, Mr. Davies ends his letter by asking for "some justification of the use of ethical terms by one who professes only to describe natural and necessary processes."

As Mr. Davies forwarded to me a copy of *The Guardian* containing his letter, my reply took the form of a letter addressed to him, which appeared in *The Guardian* for August 6. With the exception of an omitted part, relating to another matter, it ran as follows:

Fairfield, Pewsey, Wilts, July 24, 1890

Dear Mr. Davies—The copy of the *Guardian* has just reached me, and I have read your criticism with much interest. Would that criticisms in general were written in the same spirit!

* * * * *

In asserting the illegitimacy of my use of the words "duty," "ought," "obligation," &c., you remind me of the criticisms of Mr. Lilly. By such community as exists between you, amid your differences, you are both led to the assumption that the idea of "duty" can have no other than a supernatural origin.

This assumption implies that men's actions are determined only by recognition of ultimate consequences, and that if recognition of ultimate consequences does not lead them to do right, they can have no motive to do right. But the great mass of men's actions are directly prompted by their likings, without thought of remote results; and among actions thus prompted are, in many cases, those which conduce to other men's welfare. Though, on reflection, such actions are seen to be congruous with the ends ranked as the highest, yet they are not prompted by thought of such ends.

The relation of direct to indirect motives is best seen in a familiar case. Any normally constituted parent spends much labor and thought in furthering the welfare of his children, and daily, for many years, is impelled to do this by immediate liking—cannot bear to do otherwise. Nevertheless, while he is not impelled to do what he does by the consciousness that he *ought* to do it, if you ask the reasons for his self-sacrificing conduct he will say that he is under obligation; and if you push your inquiries to the end, you will compel him to assign the fact that if men in general did not do the like the race would disappear. Though the consciousness of obligation may serve to justify, and perhaps in a small degree to strengthen, the promptings of his natural affections, yet these are quite sufficient of themselves.

Similarly is it with the idea of obligation in respect of conduct to our fellow men. As you must know from your personal experiences, such conduct may be effectually prompted by immediate desire, without thought of other consequence than the benefits given. And though these benefits are given from simple desire to give them, if the question be raised whether they should be given, there comes the answer that it is a duty to minister to human welfare.

You contend that my theory of moral guidance gives me no warrant for anger against aggression, or other ill doing: saying of me that, in such case, "he is borrowing *our* thunder." This implies the assertion that only those who accept the current creed have any right to feel indignant when they see other men wronged. But I cannot allow you thus to monopolize righteous indignation. If you ask what prompts me to denounce our unjust treatment of inferior races, I reply that I am prompted by a feeling which is aroused in me quite apart from any sense of duty, quite apart from any thought of Divine command, quite apart from any thought of reward or punishment here or hereafter. In part the feeling results from consciousness of the suffering inflicted, which is a painful consciousness, and in part from irritation at the breach of a law of conduct on behalf of which my sentiments are enlisted, and obedience to which I regard as needful for the welfare of humanity in general. If you say that my theory gives me no reason for feeling this pain, the answer is that I cannot help feeling it; and if you say that my theory gives me no reason for my interest in asserting this principle, the answer is that I cannot help being interested. And when analysis shows me that the feeling and the principle are such as, if cherished and acted upon, must conduce to the progress of humanity towards a higher form, capable of greater happiness, I find that though my action is not immediately prompted by the sense of obligation, yet it conforms to my idea of obligation.

That motives hence resulting may be adequately operative, you will find proof on recalling certain transactions, dating back some eight years, in which we were both concerned. You can scarcely fail to remember that those who were moved by feelings and ideas such as I have described, and not by any motives which the current creed furnishes, displayed more anxiety that our dealings with alien peoples should be guided by what are called Christian principles than is displayed by Christians in general.* I am, sincerely yours,

HERBERT SPENCER

P.S.—Should you wish to publish this letter as my response to your appeal, I am quite willing that you should do so. Other claims on my time will, however, prevent me from carrying the discussion further.

Along with this letter, when published in *The Guardian*, there appeared a rejoinder from Mr. Davies, which, omitting, as before, a part concerning a different question, ran thus:

Kirkby Lonsdale, July 28, 1890

Dear Mr. Spencer—I am much obliged to you for responding so kindly to the challenge which I ventured to address to you. You will not think it ungracious, I hope, if, notwithstanding the purpose which you intimate in your postscript, I make public some of the reflections which your letter suggests to me.

* * * * *

Most amply do I acknowledge the generous zeal for human welfare, the indignation against oppression, shown by yourself and others who recognize no supernatural sanction of morality. The Christianity of today owes much to—has, I hope, really gained much from—your own humane ardor and the bold protestations of the followers of Comte. A Christian's allegiance is not to the Christian world, not even to Christianity, but to the law of Christ and the will of the Heavenly Father; and he may as easily admit that Christians have been surpassed in Christian feeling and action by agnostics as that the priest and the Levite were put to shame by the Samaritan.

I have also no difficulty in acknowledging that the performance of good offices may arise out of sympathy and pleasure in doing them. I do not understand why "the assumption that the idea of 'duty' has a supernatural origin" should be supposed to imply "that men's actions are determined only by recognition of ultimate consequences, and that if recognition of ultimate consequences does not lead them to do right, they can have no motive to do right." I never thought of

---

* In my letter as originally written, there followed two sentences which I omitted for fear of provoking a controversy. They ran thus: "Even one of the religious papers recognized the startling contrast between the energy of those who do not profess Christianity and the indifference of those who do. I may add that on going back some years further you will find that a kindred contrast was implied by the constitution of the Jamaica Committee."

questioning that men act, in a great part of their conduct, from the motives you describe. What I wish to know is why, when the thought of duty comes in, a man should think himself *bound* to do, whether he likes it or not, what will tend to the preservation of the species. It is quite intelligible to me that you "cannot help" trying to protect other men from wrong: what I still fail to see clearly is how your philosophy justifies you in reproaching those who *can* help being good. It is nature, you say, that makes the thoughtful parent good, that makes the generous man sacrifice himself for the benefit of his fellow men. But nature also makes many parents selfishly regardless of the interests of their children; nature makes some men hardened freebooters. If they also cannot help being what they are, is there any sense, from your point of view, in saying that they act as they ought not to act? Would they feel that you were appealing to their sense of duty if you explained to them as a fact of nature that, should other men do as they are doing, the race would tend to disappear? To Mr. Huxley, as a philosopher, a taste for good behavior belongs to the same category as an ear for music—some persons have it and others are without it; the question which I cannot help asking is whether that is the ultimate word of your ethics. I cannot see how a man who is made aware that he acts only from natural impulse can reasonably consider whether he ought or ought not to do a certain thing, nor how a man who knows that he acts only for the gratification of his own desires can reasonably throw himself away for the sake of any advantage to be won for others.

As I do not quite know what "the current creed" may be on the questions at issue, I beg leave to sum up my own belief as follows: The Unseen Power is gradually creating mankind by processes of development, and the human consciousness is so made as to be responsive to the authority of this Power; justice is the progressive order which the Maker is establishing amongst human beings, and it is binding upon each man as he becomes aware of it, and is felt to be binding, because he is the Maker's creature. Believe me, very truly yours,

J. LLEWELYN DAVIES

Before proceeding to discuss further the special question at issue, I may remark, respecting the more general question involved in Mr. Davies' closing paragraph, that there is a curiously close kinship between his view and that which I have myself more than once expressed. In section 34 of *First Principles* I have said, in reference to the hesitating inquirer:

> It is not for nothing that he has in him these sympathies with some principles and repugnance to others. He, with all his capacities, and aspirations, and beliefs, is not an accident, but a product of the time. He must remember that while he is a descendant of the past, he is a parent of the future; and that his thoughts are as children born to him, which he may not carelessly let die. He, like every other man, may properly consider himself as one of the myriad agencies through whom works the Unknown Cause; and when the Unknown Cause produces in him a certain belief, he is thereby authorized to profess and act out that belief.

And then in the *Data of Ethics,* section 62, speaking of the different types of ethical doctrine as severally presenting one or other aspect of the truth, I have said:

> The theological theory contains a part. If for the divine will, supposed to be supernaturally revealed, we substitute the naturally revealed end towards which the Power manifested throughout Evolution works; then, since Evolution has been, and is still, working towards the highest life, it follows that conforming to those principles by which the highest life is achieved, is furthering that end.

Returning now to the special question, I have first to remark that Mr. Davies, and those who take kindred views, tacitly assume that the conception of "ought" is a universal and a fixed conception; whereas it is a variable conception, and is in large measure relevant to the social needs of the time being. In an article on "The Ethics of Kant," published in *The Fortnightly Review* for July 1888 and now contained in the third volume of my *Essays,* I have given seven authorities in support of the conclusion that "the lower races of men may be said to be deficient in the idea of right": they have no such feeling of "ought" as is general with us, and where it exists it is often quite otherwise directed. Among various savage peoples the *duty* of blood revenge is of all duties the most sacred. A Fijian slave tribe "said it was their *duty* to become food and sacrifices for the chiefs"; and Jackson tells of a Fijian chief who was thrown into religious frenzy from a belief that the god was angry with him for not killing more of the enemy. Nor is it among the inferior races that we meet with conceptions of *"ought"* utterly different from those which Mr. Davies assumes are recognized by men as of supreme authority. Among the Riff pirates of the Morocco coast, the greatest insult a man can receive is to be told that his father died in his bed—that he did not die fighting while engaged in robbery: the implication being that he *ought* to have so died. Similarly is it with European peoples in respect of duels. The aggrieved man is forced by a strong sense of *obligation* to challenge one who has injured him; and the injurer entertains no doubt that he *ought* to accept the challenge—feels, in common with all his associates, that it is his *duty* to do this thing which is condemned by the creed he professes. And in the German Emperor's recent applause of dueling clubs as giving to the youth "the true direction of his life," we see a deliberate advocacy of usages utterly at variance with the nominally accepted principles of right conduct.

These cases show, I think, that the conception of "ought" is relevant, partly to sentiments predominant in the individual, partly to the feelings and ideas instilled during education, and partly to the public opinion which prevails: all of them variable factors. The truth is that every desire, seeking as it does gratification, carries along with it the idea that its gratification is proper or right; and when it is a powerful desire it generates, when it is denied, the idea that the denial is wrong. So true is this that a feeling which prompted a wrong action, but was effectually resisted, will, in some cases, afterward generate regret that the act prompted was not committed; while, conversely, a good action at variance with the habitual bad actions may be followed by repentance: instance the miser who feels sorry that he was betrayed into a piece of generosity. Similarly the consciousness of "ought," as existing among men of superior types, is simply the voice of certain governing sentiments developed by the higher forms of social life, which are in each individual endorsed by transmitted beliefs and current opinion—a sanction much stronger than that which any of the inferior feelings have.

A full answer to the question put by Mr. Davies, presented in a different and much more elaborate form, has been already given in *The Data of Ethics*. In the chapter entitled "The Psychological View," and more especially in sections 42–46, the genesis of the feeling of obligation is explained at considerable length.

Perhaps he will still ask—Why, having the feeling of obligation, should a man yield to it? If so, the answer is of the same general nature as that which may be given to the question—Why, having an appetite for food, should a man eat? Though, in the normal order, a man eats to satisfy hunger, and without definite consciousness of remoter ends, yet, if you demand his justification, he replies that, as conducive to health, strength, and ability to carry on life and do his work, the yielding to his appetite is needful. And similarly one who performs an act which his sense of duty prompts, if asked for his reason, may fitly reply that though he yielded to the feeling without thought of distant consequences, yet he sees that the distant consequences of such conformity are, on the average of cases, beneficial not only to others but in the long run to himself. And here let me repeat a truth which I have elsewhere insisted upon, that just as food is rightly taken only when taken to appease hunger, while the having to take it when there is no inclination implies deranged physical state; so, a good act or act of duty is rightly done only if done in satisfaction of immediate feeling, and if done with a view of ultimate results, in this world or another world, implies an imperfect moral state.

[After the publication of the first edition of this work, I received from Mr. Davies a letter containing, among others, the following paragraph:

"Allow me to demur to one statement you make in the Appendix on *the moral motive*. I think I, for one, do *not* tacitly assume that the conception of 'ought' is 'a *fixed* conception.' I hold that the notions of what is right vary with the variations, and advance with the progress, of the social order."

Hence it appears that in a further respect Mr. Davies' views and my own diverge in a smaller degree than at first appeared.]

APPENDIX D

Conscience in Animals

Shortly after the publication in *The Guardian* of the correspondence reproduced in the preceding Appendix, I received from a gentleman residing in Devonshire the letter which I here quote:

Dear Sir—The following careful observations on animals other than man may be of interest to you as supporting your idea that the idea of "duty" or "ought" (owe it) may be of non-"supernatural" origin. ["Supernatural" is used in usual sense without committing the writer to any opinion.]

My dog has an aversion to injure living flesh or anything that is "shaped." He will not bite any animal except under the *greatest* provocation. If I press a sharp-pointed pen-knife against the skin of the back, he seizes my wrist between his hind teeth. The mechanical advantage is such, that if he closed his jaw he could crush flesh and bone. But no matter how I increase or prolong the pressure he *will* not close his jaw sufficiently to mark the flesh. I have repeated this and similar *experiments* may times. I can't find how the "ought" was established. It is not hereditary. The father was a good-tempered "fighting" dog—the mother *most vicious*; but I never allowed her to come into contact with the pup but in the dusk, in order to avoid imitation or unconscious education.

Until "Punch" was three yrs. old I never knew him give an angry growl. I sat down on his tail, doubling it under me accidentally one day, when I heard a growl of a totally different *timber* to what I had ever before. The odd thing was—when I rose the dog begged pardon for the unusual tone and temper in a way that could not be mistaken.

469

Evidently he recognized his own violation of an "ought" existing in his mind (conscience).

Further, if I tease him with a rough stick he seizes it and *crushes* it, but if with my crutch (I am lame) or my mahl stick, he seizes it; but will not leave the mark of his teeth in anything that has had "work" done on it to any extent.

The "ought" may be established as an obligation to a higher mind, in opposition to the promptings of the strongest feelings of the animal, e.g.

A bitch I had many years ago showed great pleasure at the attentions of male dogs, when in season. I checked her repeatedly, by *voice only*. This set up the "ought" so thoroughly, that tho' never tied up at such times, she died a virgin at 13½ yrs. old.* By the time she was 4 she resented strongly any attention from the male, and by seven she was a spiteful old maid, resenting even the presence of the males.

Dogs can form a standard of "ought" as to skill or powers of doing. This bitch was a powerful swimmer. A *young* smooth Scotch terrier was introduced into the house. They became playfellows, chasing and running all over the grounds. One day they were crossing the Prince's Street Ferry, Bristol. The bitch sprang from the ferry boat as usual into the water and the young dog followed; but began to drown. She saw his efforts, seized him by the back of neck and swam ashore with him. A few seconds after, she seized him and shook him violently for some time. Ever after, she bit or shook him if he attempted to play. [Contempt on discovery of want of power she apparently regarded before as normal?]

Further, "indignation" is not confined to human beings. I used to pretend to beat a younger sister and she feigned crying. The bitch flew at me. Reversing the conditions, the bitch growled and finally flew at my sister. We tried the experiment many times with other actors and same results. Her sympathies were always on the side *of the persons attacked,* unless she had a previous dislike to them.

Further observation showing her the attacks were feigned, she often joined in them with uproarious hilarity, but this state of mind did not arise till after repeated observation.

Pardon these records of observation if they appear trivial. Unfortunately I have only been able to make myself acquainted very partially with your works, and such facts may have come under your observation to a greater extent than under mine.

I am yours obdtly.,
T. Mann Jones

Northam, Devon,
14/8/90

---

* At least I have no cause to think otherwise.—T.M.J.

My response, thanking Mr. Jones and recognizing the value of the facts set forth in his letter, drew from him a second letter, in which he says:

> Pray make what use you like of the letter, but it is only right to say that some of the facts are in the possession of Prof. Romanes. You can depend upon the accuracy of the observations—I learned to observe from the Belfast naturalists, Pattison, the Thompsons and others—and I trained my wife, before marriage, to help me, and not run away with mere impressions.
>
> The idea of "ought" is abnormally strong in Punch, the dog I spoke of—his tastes too are unusual. He cares more for sweets than meat. When he was about 6 months old I found out some way he had gained the meaning of Yes and No. I have hundreds of times offered him a knob of sugar—when he was on the point of taking it said No! He draws back. If he has taken it in his mouth a *whispered* No! causes him to drop it. If he is lying down and I place sugar all round whispering No! the lumps remain untouched till a "Yes" is said. But—but—but—the dog differs from the human being! He will rarely accept a *first* Yes, tho' he does a first No! Experience has taught him the Yes *may* be followed by a No! and he waits expectantly. *There is no eagerness to set aside the "ought" when an excuse offers.* (Special probably, not general in dogs.) *The minds of dogs discriminate between great and small* departures from their standard of "ought." If I dropped a fair-sized piece of sugar, neither Fan (the bitch) nor Punch, considered they had the slightest right to touch it. If the piece were very small both hesitated—and if No! were not said, finally ate it. I have tried graduating the lumps to find out where the "ought" came in. The male has a finer conscience than the female. I need hardly say I carefully avoided loud tones and gesticulation.
>
> No! Oh! So! Go! are equivalents to a dog's ear, but the sibilant must be very soft. So also "Yes," "bess," "press," but they recognize various forms of expression as equivalent. "Yes," or "You may have it," are same value to Punch. My pony is nervously anxious to obey the "ought." Woh! Halt! Stop! &c., are of equal value. The dog appears to me to study the *tone* less than the pony and to pay more attention to sound and its *quantity.* Many of the acts of both strike me as possibly acts of "worship" in its simplest form, e.g., the fact I think I mentioned in my letter, of the dog's anxiety to "propitiate" on the occasion of his first angry growl, when three years old; though I had not recognized the "ought" in the dog's mind nor had I ever punished him.

Along with this letter Mr. Mann Jones inclosed a series of memoranda which, while they are highly interesting and instructive, also serve to show how carefully and critically his inquiries have been conducted, and how trustworthy, therefore, are his conclusions. With the omission of some paragraphs, they are as follows:

Recognition of duty or ought in a bitch—deliberate violation of the principle recognized—simulation of indignation at the ought being set at nought by a cat

Prior to '85 I had satisfied myself that domestic animals recognized duty. I was anxious, however, to procure as thoroughly degraded an animal as I could to test—1st, whether the "ought" might not proceed from two very different classes of motives, which I had been accustomed to distinguish as (A) the *Rectal-moral* and (B) the selfish or *conventional-moral*. 2ndly, I wanted to test whether the idea set forth by some theologians that the "most noxious animal was *innocent*," and that moral responsibility only attached to man, was true.

I observed a very handsome bitch at Mardock station repeatedly drive a large number of fowls belonging to the stationmaster off the line and platform so soon as she heard the distance signal.

I asked her history and found she had been accidentally left by a lady traveling in a first-class carriage some months before. I inferred she was likely to have been "spoiled" and as she was evidently aged, she would not easily lose any bad habits. Further, I ascertained she was gluttonous, passionate, yet sulky, lascivious, a coward, not fond of children, without any strong attachments, and dirty in her habits. She seemed so much like the worst specimen of "fallen humanity" the *putaine,* that I asked but one more question 'She is very intelligent, you have taught her to clear the station at proper time?' 'She *is* very sharp, but I did not teach her; she watched the boy a few times doing the work and then took it as her duty. Now, though she is very greedy, if we are late in the morning, she comes without her breakfast and has nothing till late in the day rather than not clear the line.' This trait decided me. I thought if I removed her from the stationmaster's house, she would drop the last "duty" that was at all unselfish, and be thoroughly "bad-all-round."

I took her home. She went willingly, shewing no fright and making herself at home on reaching my house. I kept her in a house and an outhouse 24 hours, feeding her well, then took her to the station when she showed little pleasure at seeing her master and little inclination for the old duty. By end of a fortnight she took no notice of either.

The third morning the stableboy, Ben, came to me. 'Sir, Judy is mad. I was sweeping near her over 2 hours ago and stooped to pat her. She first bit my hand and then my leg' (both wounds bled) 'and she has sat in the corner, with her back crushed into it, ever since.' I went to the stable, spoke kindly to her and then stooped to pat her. She snapt viciously. Letting the muscles of the hand balance so that the finger bones and metacarpals played loose on each other and the wrist, I struck her heavily over the eyes. She snapt again and I struck as she snapt. The contest continued 5 minutes, when I left her, nearly blind eyed and tired. I asked Ben two hours after how she was. 'Oh! I think she *is* mad. She is as sulky as ever and sits as she was in the corner.' When I went in, she came forward and fawned upon me. *From that day I never struck her.* She was most obedient, good tempered, gentle and anxious to please me. To a certain extent she showed the same character to my wife and to a servant, the cook, who was very decided, but to the boy and a younger servant she showed the old character and also to others. In fact henceforth she lived a double life, altering her apparent character the moment she heard my footstep. I saw here that her sense of duty and her obedience had no ethical value: they were simply effects of fear, or, in some degree, hope of gain. They formed no part of her real character.

I took care she was frequently and well fed, purposely with a large *variety* of food. I therefore left no motive for theft. About a fortnight after I bought her, the cook came to my wife—'Ma'm, I am constantly missing things off the kitchen table. Either one of the cats has turned thief or Judy takes the things, yet I can't tell how she gets at them. I don't leave a chair near enough the table for her to use—besides she is so stiff and long-backed that if she tries to get on the chair she slips over the other side.'

I give a diagram of kitchen and surroundings to make clear what follows. I caused a number of articles of food brought out of dining room, to be placed on the table: the chair being put too far off for use. Sending some of the family in the dining room with injunctions to keep still till I called I left the two cats and Judy at their plate, *f*. I then went into the garden but returned quietly to window *b*, which had a colored muslin half-blind that hid me from observation. As soon as all was quiet Judy left her dinner, went to door *d*, apparently listened intently and looked repeatedly up and down passage. She then went to *x* and reared herself on her hind legs, walking along so as to see the whole surface of table and going backward so as to get better view. She then went to one of the cats and hustled her to the chair. The cat at length understood Judy, jumped on chair, thence on to table and dragged a meat bone down to *f*. Judy shook her—took the bone and began to pick it. I gave the signal and a light-footed girl ran into the kitchen. *As soon as* Judy heard the footsteps, which was not till the girl got to the door, *she flew at the cat with a growl and worried her and finally chased her through a hedge 200 feet off.*

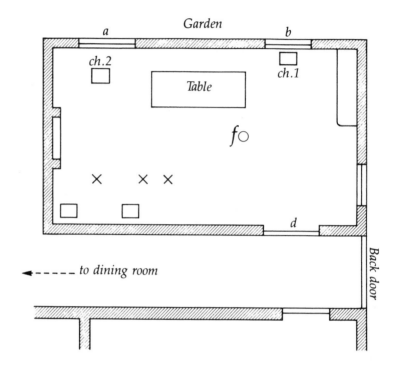

I saw the whole of this drama enacted on two occasions—parts on several; others saw parts many times. The same caution to ascertain the "coast was clear," the same employment of one or other of the cats and the same feigned indignation and attempt by gesture to fix the theft on the cat, occurred every time.

I don't think I am wrong in concluding that Judy recognized that the cat had no right to get on the table after the food; that she was instigating breach of duty, and that she simulated anger in order to shift responsibility which her mind acknowledged.

Space and time prevent my giving many more illustrations of her character. She was an extreme type, but I have had other animals like her, who recognized duty and "moral obligation" to a greater or less extent as something expected of them by a superior, but which they performed entirely from hopes of reward or fear of punishment generally, occasionally from liking (which was *not sympathy*) but that form arising from the object giving pleasure or profit to the subject so "liking." The idea of duty, justice, "ought," in all such cases arose from selfishness. I class them as "selfish-moral," conventional-moral, fashion-moral acts of duty, or shortly as "Judyism."

I now proceed briefly to consider the "sense of duty" or "ought" in another of my teachers—the dog Punch. I have given details before but briefly. He wills not to injure any living thing, nor anything that shows by its shape that work has been expended upon it. The most striking instance is that I have repeatedly purposely caused him severe and long continued pain by pressing upon and even cutting the subcutaneous loops of the nerves without ever being able to induce him to bite me or even snap at me. In the same way, when bitten by dogs, often severely, he will not bite them. There appears to me to be here a "sense of duty," or of "ought," which is specifically different from all those varieties I have styled Judyism.

I ask why does he not bite?

It may be said he is afraid of you. I think that if anyone saw the relations between us they would soon dismiss this as the motive. I appreciate him too much as a valuable "subject" to make the blunder of inspiring fear. I would as soon think of doing so as the electrician would think of using his most sensitive electroscope roughly. The dog and his pupil are so *en rapport* that if the former wants a door opened, or a thorn or insect removed, he comes to me, say I am at my desk, stands up, puts his right paw on my arm and taps my shoulder with the left repeatedly till I attend to him, when he clearly indicates what he wants, and if the want is to have thorn or insect removed he clearly indicates the surface, often to a square inch or nearer.

It may be urged that he will not hurt me because he has such trust or faith in me—he thinks I would not willingly hurt him. There appears something in this at first sight, and it gains color from the fact that when he was less than 12 months old, a gamekeeper shot at him when near, and deposited about 30 pellets of shot in his head and body, which I extracted. The memory of these operations might lead him to class my pressure of the knife point as something curative.

But then, where does such an explanation come in, in his behavior to my *mahl* stick, which he will not break under the same circumstances that cause him to crush an unshaped stick to splinters? It may be said that when bitten by another dog, he does not retaliate because he is a coward. The explanation won't do. He barks remonstratively, as he does when I hurt him when we are romping, but he *won't run away*. I can't get him away often, and he is frequently bitten more severely in consequence. An incident that occurred a few days back threw some more light on the idea of "right" in Punch's (or Monkey's) mind—he answers indifferently to both names. I was coming through the very narrow street of West Appledore when a much larger dog seized him, and bit Punch so severely about the face as to make him bleed. Punch then resisted for the first time, to my knowledge, not by biting, but by a Quaker-like defense that was most scientific. He seized the other dog firmly by the hind leg above the heel, and raised the leg so high off the ground as to throw the dog's body into unstable equilibrium. The dog stood still for some time, evidently afraid to move for fear of falling on his back and being at the mercy of his opponent. He was in no pain, for Punch was not biting but simply holding firmly. At length the attacking dog tried to get his head round to bite Punch again, but the latter frustrated this by lifting the leg higher and carrying it gradually round in the opposite direction to the dog's head, so as to preserve the original distance. At the end of about 2 minutes I was compelled to interfere, as a horse and cart were coming close. The dog slank off whilst Punch jumped vertically, bounding many times off the ground in a manner that I can only compare with the bounding of a football, barking merrily at the same time.

Hundreds of similar instances to the few I have given, convince me that this dog has in his mind a sense of duty totally *different* in *kind* from that which I have illustrated and characterized as *Judyism*. It is in fact "Do-as-you-would-be-done-by-ism." I have observed this spe-cies of sense of duty, of the "ought" (or morality) in a number of animals, and I have become accustomed to call this *kind* "Rectal sense of duty" and hence to divide "morality" into *selfish*, emotional, clique, "fashion" morality, or Judyism, and Rectal morality.

I never met with two such extreme types of the dominance of the two kinds of motive before. Most animals are actuated by the two species of sense of duty in varying ratio, many only by selfish or Fashion-morality; but some individuals appear affected little by either. These form the utterly "immoral." So far as my inductions from observations of animals go, the division into Rectal and con-ventional "sense of duty" is exhaustive and inclusive. All acts that recognize an "ought" appear to me to come under one or the other.

There is a remarkable difference in the animal according to which sense of duty is predominant—which species of morality rules its life. If *Rectal*, the animal is trustworthy and reliable. If *conventional*, un-trustworthy, changeable and shifty. So much for results in outward conduct. I apprehend that the results on the mind or ethical sense, of conventional morality is on the whole disintegrating. In fact I have observed this in animals, though I have not been able to pursue my observations so far as I could wish.*

---

* Query? I take it the "rectal" sense of duty is at the base of all reality of character, the conventional has more the character of an acquired mental habit.

On the other hand, the Rectal sense of duty in animals is, in the phraseology of the philosopher, a developing force. The Rectal morality of the animal increases with time. In the phraseology of some theologians it may perhaps be termed a regenerating or "saving" force. (Those who believe that a profession of a creed is the only saving force, would scarcely admit it had more value than the conventional "ought," or perhaps not as much in some cases.)

As to the origin of the Rectal sense of duty or rectal morality, so far as my observations go, the chief thing I can predicate is that it is unselfish. It seems to be closely connected with "sympathy," as distinguished from "feeling" of the kind before defined. The individuals among the higher animals who act from the rectal sense of duty appear to be remarkable, so far as my observations go, for ability to "put-yourself-in-his-place-edness" which is at the root of true "sympathy." The tendency is always "to do as they would be done by." In most cases that I have observed it appeared to be inborn, but developed as the animal got older.

The division I have been led to, by hundreds of observations on individuals of different species, of the "Idea of duty," and consequently all morality, into Rectal and conventional (*mores*) I have never seen formulated. *Probably other observers have made the distinction.* It is tacitly recognized, however, in most of the oldest writings I know anything of. The recognition of the value of the Rectal appears to me to run through many of the books collected as the Bible, and the O.T. and N.T. Apocrypha, like a vein of gold in quartz, and to be the very *protagon* or "nerve-center stuff" of most of Christ's teaching. I have seen the distinction tacitly admitted in many theological works, tho' I think I am right in asserting (I say it as the oratorians speak—under correction) there is a want of recognition of the fact that the chief (if not only) value of the conventional "sense of duty," or selfish "ought," is to prevent friction.

Not only do animals (other than man) act upon the "ought" in their minds, but some of the more intelligent act as if they expected or believed that it existed in the minds of some men

In August '86 I was driving Prince (my pony) and at the same time discussing an interesting point in science with my wife. I generally guided him entirely by the voice, but in the heat of the argument unthinkingly emphasized my points with the whip (which had had a new knotted lash on that day) on the pony's flanks. He stopped about the third blow and looked round. This attracted my wife's attention— "Prince is remonstrating: You struck heavily." Later on I must have struck him repeatedly. When he was loosed from the harness, I was standing *out of his direct line to the stable door.* Instead of going to the stable, as was usual, he walked up to me, and after repeated attempts to draw my attention, touched me with his nose and then approached his nose as closely as he could to the wales. This he repeated until I had the places bathed.

About two months later, on a similar occasion, he repeated the same actions.

In autumn '86 I was in Ware with my pony. Coming out of a shop, I was on the point of stepping into the carriage when I noticed the pony (Prince) watching me. (He was accustomed to my boy jumping up when the vehicle was in motion.) I told my wife to start him. She tried repeatedly, but he would not move till he saw I was seated, when he started at once. (The experiment was repeated many times subsequently.) The strange thing is the complicated train of thought that evolved an "ought" differing in the case of a lame man from the duty in other cases.

The same autumn, we were driving from Wearside to Hadham. On the road we met with a group of children with two perambulators. They were in awkward positions: several children being close to the lefthand hedge, a perambulator and children further to right, the second further still, as in diagram:

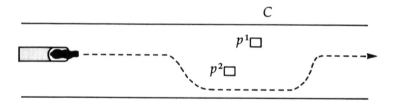

the distance between c.p^1, p^2 and right hedge being about equal. There was room to pass between p^1 and p^2 easily, but the children were confused and passed repeatedly between the two points. My wife said, "See if Prince will avoid the children." I dropped the reins on his neck. He went on at a smart trot till 7 or 8 yards from the children at *a*, when he fell into a walk, turned to the right, and passed them with the right wheel near the hedge, turning his head more and more to see whether he was clearing the right or outer perambulator. He left it about 3 yards in the rear, and then returned sharply to the left side of road and resumed his trot without any intimation he was to do so.

In Nov. '87, after the death of my wife, a relative came to live with me and she drove the same pony. She is so deaf, she cannot hear a vehicle overtaking her. Consequently I always went with her, and if she had the reins, signed with my left hand if a vehicle were coming up behind, for her to draw over to left.

As she was driving one day up a steep hill (therefore with slack reins) on road to Ware, I heard a brewer's cart coming behind. The man had been drinking and followed close in our wake, though there was plenty of room to pass if he had kept well to the right. I gave my relative no signal, as I wanted to observe the pony's actions. He appeared nervous and restless, turning his head as far as he could to the right to see what was wrong. The man drove the heavy cart very close behind but the pony could not see the horse or vehicle. After 3 or 4 minutes anxiety (I use the word advisedly: the working of the ears and the "twitching" of his muscles justifies me), receiving no sign, he deliberately drew as closely as possible into the *lefthand* hedge and waited. As soon as the waggon passed, he went off at a brisk trot.

After many experiments on different days I found that if I were driving and a vehicle overtook us, Prince waited for me to tighten the left rein, but if my relative were driving, he decided by the sound when to draw to the left. Even if she tightened the right rein—he disobeyed the sign. After many experiments I had full confidence he would always act, if she were driving, on the evidence of his own hearing; and she often subsequently drove without me, the pony evidently recognizing his new duties.

Examples of animals (other than men) initiating cooperation in duty. [Simultaneous occurrence of the idea of duty, suggested by same circumstances]

In the autumn of 1886, I started after 10 o'clock p.m. from my cottage at Baker's End to drive some friends homeward. On descending from the high ground, I passed into a dense fog, which the carriage lights failed to penetrate 6 feet—the fog reflected the light like a wall. Some distance past the Mardock Station road, my road turned almost at right angles. Here we so thoroughly failed to find the turning that the horse was driven against the bank, up which he reared crashing into the hedge at the top. We all alighted and my friends went on. I turned pony and carriage and got in, to drive back: the pony moved slowly, but almost dragging the reins out of my hands. I got out thinking the reins were caught on the shaft as the pony had always shown a liking for a very tight rein down hill and our road here was a descent. I could find nothing wrong with the reins. Taking out a lamp I went to the pony's head, which he was still holding as low as he could. Then I saw his nose was nearly on the back of my black dog Jack (the father of

Punch) who was standing in front with his nose near the ground, but pointing homeward. I got in; said "Go on"; did not use the reins, but as we went at a walking pace, tried frequently to measure with the whip handle the distances they kept from each hedge. They took me safely into the yard behind my house, and my measurements showed they kept the middle of the road the whole way; except at one place, where there is a deep gully on the right, separated from the road by a very slight fence. Here they kept within 18 inches of the left (or further side from the gully). Altho' the night was cold and the pace that of the Dead March, the horse was wet with perspiration and the dog panting with tongue out when we got into the yard, probably from the anxiety to do the duty they had undertaken. There are 6 turns in the road and three of them are right angles, narrow in all cases, but not more than the full length of horse and carriage, in two cases I think, and my memory is pretty clear.

There was a little episode when we got into the yard, illustrating the close analogy between the feelings of these animals and human feelings under similar circumstances. The horse rubbed his head repeatedly against Jack, whilst Jack "nosed" or rubbed his face against the pony's. No expression of mutual gratulation on the completion of a self-imposed duty could have been more significant.

There is an interesting parallelism between the conclusions drawn by Mr. Jones from his observations on the motives of animals and the conclusions concerning human motives contained in chapter 4, "The Sentiment of Justice." The distinction between "rectal-moral" and "conventional-moral" made by him, obviously corresponds with the distinction made in that chapter between the altruistic sentiment and the proaltruistic sentiment. This correspondence is the more noteworthy because it tends to justify the belief in a natural genesis of a developed moral sentiment in the one case as in the other. If in inferior animals the consciousness of duty may be produced by the discipline of life, then, *a fortiori,* it may be so produced in mankind.

Probably many readers will remark that the anecdotes Mr. Jones gives, recall the common saying—"Man is the god of the dog"; and prove that the sentiment of duty developed in the dog arises out of his personal relation to his master, just as the sentiment of duty in man arises out of his relation to his maker. There is good ground for this interpretation in respect of those actions of dogs which Mr. Jones distinguishes as "conventional-moral"; but it does not hold of those which he distinguishes as "rectal-moral." Especially in the case of the dog which would not bite when bitten, but contented himself with preventing his antagonist from biting again (showing a literally Christian feeling not shown by one Christian in a thousand) the act was not prompted by dutifulness to a superior. And this extreme case verifies the inference otherwise drawn, that the sentiment of duty was independent of the sentiment of subordination.

But even were it true that such sentiment of duty as may exist in the relatively undeveloped minds of the higher animals, is exclusively generated by personal relation to a superior, it would not follow that in the much more developed minds of men, there cannot be generated a sentiment of duty which is independent of personal relation to a superior. For experience shows that, in the wider intelligence of the human being, apart from the pleasing of God as a motive, there may arise the benefiting of fellow men as a motive; and that the sentiment of duty may come to be associated with the last as with the first. Beyond question there are many who are constrained by their natures to devote their energies to philanthropic ends, and do this without any regard for personal benefit. Indeed there are here and there men who would consider themselves insulted if told that what they did was done with the view of obtaining divine favor.

APPENDIX E

Replies to Criticisms

[The following replies to criticisms originally appeared in Mind *for January 1881. I have thought it well to give them here a permanent place, because, in making them, I have had occasion further to elucidate certain of the doctrines set forth in the preceding pages.]*

An ethical writer who was required to treat of right and wrong conduct, while saying nothing about any purpose to be effected by conduct, would be greatly perplexed. Were he forbidden to bring in the thoughts of good, better and best in relation to results, moral distinctions among actions would not be easily expressed. I make this remark because Mr. Sidgwick, in his article in *Mind*, XVIII, entitled "Mr. Spencer's Ethical System," quoting from me the phrase, "conduct falling short of its ideal," remarks: "The frankly teleological point of view from which, in this book, Mr. Spencer contemplates the phenomena of life generally, seems worthy of notice, since in his *Principles of Biology* he seems to have taken some pains to avoid 'teleological implications.' "

That a science which has for its subject matter the characters of the ends pursued by men, and the characters of the means used for achieving such ends, can restrict itself to statements in which ends are not implied, is a strange assumption. Teleology of a kind is necessarily involved; and the only question is whether it is of the legitimate or the illegitimate kind. The contrast between the two may readily be shown by a biological illustration. If I speculate concerning the stony shell of a gromwell seed, so hard that it is uninjured by the beak of a bird which swallows the seed, and effectually resists the grinding actions of the bird's gizzard, and if I argue that this hard shell was provided for the purpose of protecting the seed and thus securing its eventual germination, I am arguing teleologically in the vicious way. If, on the other hand, my interpretation is that among the seeds of some remote ancestral plant one with an unusually thick shell passed away uninjured by a bird's beak and stomach, while the rest with thinner shells were broken up and digested; and if I infer that among the seeds of the plant originating from the undigested seed, generally inheriting this greater thickness, those most frequently lived and propagated which had the thickest or hardest shells, until, by survival of the fittest, shells of this extreme density, completely protective, were produced; and if I argue that maintenance of the species was throughout this process the end more effectually subserved; I am also arguing teleologically, but in the legitimate way. There enters the conception of a cause for the genesis of the hard shell, which is, in a sense, a final cause—not that proximate cause constituted by the physiological processes going on in the plant, but a cause remote from these, which, nevertheless, so far determines them that in its absence they would not exist. And it is thus with biological interpretations of structures and functions in general. The welfare of the organism, or of the species, is in every case the end to further which a structure exists; and the difference between a legitimate and an illegitimate teleology is that, while the one explains its existence as having gradually arisen by furthering the end, the other gives no explanation of its existence other than that it was put there to further the end—a final cause of the "barren virgin" sort.

Throughout the *Data of Ethics*, as throughout every ethical treatise, ends are constantly in view, and the interpretations have unceasing reference to them. I have, indeed, in a chapter on "The Physical View" of ethics, treated of conduct as low or high, according as it subserves in a less or greater degree, maintenance of a moving equilibrium; which is, I think, a more unteleological way of regarding it than has been followed by any ethical writer. In this chapter, the evolution of that which we ordinarily conceive as higher conduct, is presented as a process expressible in terms of matter and motion. For the implication of the argument (in harmony with an argument contained in two chapters in the *Principles of Biology* on direct and indirect equilibration) is that, inevitably, those aggregates in which the moving equilibrium is the best, are those which remain outstanding when others disappear; and that so, by inheritance, the tendency is to the establishment of an ever-better moving equilibrium: higher conduct is defined apart even from consciousness—apart from alleged human ends or assumed divine ends. When, in the next chapter, it is shown that what we call, in physical language, a better moving equilibrium, is, in biological language, a better fulfillment of functions, and, consequently, a life which is at once wider and longer; the implication is that a wider and longer life being the end, conduct is to be judged by its conduciveness to this end; and throughout two subsequent chapters this point of view is maintained. But these chapters are nowhere illegitimately teleological. Had I accepted the moral-sense doctrine as ordinarily understood—had I alleged in mankind a supernaturally-given consciousness of obligation—had I asserted that men are endowed with sympathy to enable them the better to cooperate in the social state; I should have been chargeable with teleological interpretation of the vicious kind. But since my interpretation is avowedly opposed to this—since I regard those faculties, which produce a conduct favorable to welfare under the conditions imposed by the social state, as themselves the products of social life, and contend that they have step by step established themselves by furthering social life, the charge seems to me peculiarly inapplicable.

Another criticism made by Mr. Sidgwick is that I have not given that disproof of pessimism which, for the substantiation of my doctrine, I am bound to give. He writes: "Now, after all that has been said of the importance of considering human conduct in connection with the 'universal conduct' of which it is a part, I think that this transition from 'quantity of life' which was stated to be the end of the latter to 'quantity of pleasure' is too rapidly and lightly made. Pessimism, as Mr. Spencer himself says, stands in the way, declaring that life does not bring with it a surplus of agreeable feeling. We expect therefore a scientific confutation of Pessimism; and I am unable to perceive that this expectation is ever adequately realized. Indeed I am unable to find any passage in which Mr. Spencer expressly undertakes such a confutation. And yet he can hardly think that Pessimism is sufficiently confuted by demonstrating that the common moral judgments of mankind imply the assumption that life, on the average, yields a surplus of pleasure over pain. This is not establishing morality on a scientific basis."

I am surprised that one so acute in making distinctions as Mr. Sidgwick, should have so greatly misapprehended my position. It is perfectly true that I nowhere expressly undertake a confutation of Pessimism; but it is also true that it nowhere devolves upon me to do this. If Mr. Sidgwick will re-read the chapter in which is referred to the controversy of Pessimism *versus* Optimism, he will perceive that I have uttered no judgment concerning the issue, and that, for the purpose of my argument, no such judgment is called for. My motive for comparing their views, was to show that "there is one postulate in which pessimists and optimists agree. Both their arguments assume it to be self-evident that life is good or bad, according as it does, or does not, bring a surplus of agreeable feeling." By proving that the two schools have this postulate in common, I am not committed to any judgment concerning the truth of either of their conclusions. I have said that *if* the pessimist is right, "actions furthering its [life's] continuance, either in self or others, must be reprobated"; while, conversely, they must be approved *if* the optimist is right: the implication being that opposite systems of ethics emerge according as one or other of their estimates of life is accepted, but that both systems proceed upon the assumption that happiness is the end of conduct. The sole object of the chapter is to show "that no school can avoid taking for the ultimate moral aim, a desirable state of feeling, called by whatever name—gratification, enjoyment, happiness." Surely it is one thing to contend that optimists and pessimists agree in the belief that life is of value only if it has, on the average, an accompaniment of desirable consciousness, and another thing to contend that it has such an accompaniment. Had Mr. Sidgwick said that by the general argument of the work I have tacitly committed myself to the optimistic view, he would have said rightly. But, as shown, my reference to the controversy was made without any such purpose as that of justifying optimism; and my position was clearly enough implied to be that the arguments of the work are valid only for optimists.

But now, having pointed out that the conclusions contained in the *Data of Ethics,* in common with the conclusions contained in ethical treatises at large, can reasonably be accepted only by those who hold that life in the aggregate brings more pleasure than pain, or, at any rate, is capable of bringing more pleasure than pain, I go on to show that the tacit optimism which pervades the work, has a wider basis than Mr. Sidgwick recognizes. He says that "in Mr. Spencer's view, pessimism is indirectly confuted by the argument—given as an 'inevitable deduction from the hypothesis of evolution'— which shows that 'necessarily throughout the animate world at large, pains are the correlatives of actions injurious to the organism, while pleasures are the correlatives of actions conducive to its welfare.' " This is true as far as it goes; but, ignoring as he does all passages concerning the universal process of adaptation, Mr. Sidgwick omits a large part of the evidence favoring optimism. The chapter on the "Relativity of Pains and Pleasures," sets forth and illustrates the biological truth that everywhere faculties adjust themselves to the conditions of existence, in such wise that the activities those conditions require become pleasurable. The pains accompanying the inactions of faculties for which changed conditions have left no spheres, diminish as the faculties decrease; while the pains accompanying the actions of faculties overtaxed under the new conditions, diminish as the faculties grow, and become pleasures when those faculties have acquired the strengths which fulfillment of the conditions requires. This law is alike inferable *a priori* and proved *a posteriori*, and yields a qualified optimism as its corollary—an optimism qualified by the conclusion that the life of every species of creature is happy or miserable according to the degree of congruity or incongruity between its nature and its environment; but that everywhere, decrease of the misery or increase of the happiness, accompanies the inevitable progress towards congruity. Whence it follows that in the case of mankind, pessimism may be locally true under certain conditions (as those which have fostered the creed which makes annihilation a blessing), while optimism may be locally true under conditions of a more favorable kind; but that with the increasing adaptation of humanity to social life, the excess of pleasures over pains which warrants optimism, must become ever greater. And here let me point out in passing, how, in so far as judgment of an ethical system depends on the tacit acceptance of optimistic or pessimistic views, it can be rightly guided only by a knowledge of biological laws. Mr. Sidgwick is at one with moralists in general in thinking that the truth or falsehood or moral doctrines may be determined without study of the laws of life. He asks, "In what way then does science—that is, biology, psychology, and sociology—provide a basis for this 'truer ethics' "; and in a large measure the purpose of his criticism is to show that such science does this in no appreciable way. Above, however, we see that the acceptability of a system of ethics, depending as it does on the preacceptance of optimism or pessimism, depends on the pre-acceptance or prerejection of certain ultimate biological generalizations. It is, indeed, looked at broadly, a remarkable belief that while ethical science is concerned with certain phenomena of life, it is a matter of indifference in judging about these phenomena, whether the laws of life are known or not.

The way in which Mr. Sidgwick ignores biological generalizations, is curiously shown in a subsequent passage, in which, respecting the ethical method I contend for, he says:

> For instance, its scientific claims are plainly declared in chapter v., on "Ways of Judging Conduct"; from which we learn that Mr. Spencer's way of judging it is to be a high priori road. He will not rely on mere generalization from observation of the actual consequences of different kinds of conduct; it is the defect of current utilitarianism that it does not get beyond these merely empirical generalizations; Mr. Spencer, on the other hand, proposes to "ascertain necessary relations" between actions and their consequences, and so to "deduce from fundamental principles what conduct *must* be detrimental and what *must* be beneficial." Those are brave words, &c.

If, concerning an artillery officer who, instead of ascertaining experimentally the ranges given by certain elevations of his gun, calculated these ranges from the laws of motion and atmospheric resistance, Mr. Sidgwick were to say that he pursued the "high priori road," he would apply this expression with much the same propriety; since the method I contend for is that of deducing from the laws of life under given conditions, results which follow from them in the same necessary way as does the trajectory of a cannon shot from the laws of motion and atmospheric resistance. All developed science may be characterized as "high priori," if the drawing of deductions from premises positively ascertained by induction, is to be so called. Had I given no explanation of my meaning, I should have been less surprised at the passage above quoted. But by a series of examples, beginning with the innutrition of a limb which follows tying of its main artery and ending with the social mischiefs caused by calumny, I have, in section 22, shown what I mean by the derivation of ethical principles from the laws of life; and I have, in subsequent chapters, exhibited this derivation systematically. Nevertheless, because, during our transitional state, in which humanity is changing and social conditions are changing, this method does not suffice for development of a code of conduct in full detail, Mr. Sidgwick, ignoring the derivations of the leading moral restraints in the section I have named, and in the subsequent chapters, thinks the reader will be "disappointed." With equal reason might he represent the biological student as disappointed because, from physiological laws as at present ascertained, the details of pathology and therapeutics cannot be inferred.

All this, however, is introductory to Mr. Sidgwick's criticism on the view I take of the relation between absolute ethics and relative ethics. My position is that, as all ethical theory is concerned with ideas of worse and better in conduct, and that as the conception of better involves the conception of best, there is, in all cases, an ideal conduct tacitly assumed; that before valid conclusions can be drawn, this ideal conduct must be conceived not in a vague and shifting way, but definitely and consistently; and that no definite and consistent conception of ideal conduct can be framed without assuming ideal social conditions. Mr. Sidgwick does not, I think, show that this position is untenable, but contents himself with raising difficulties. Into the details of his criticism I cannot follow him without occupying too much space. I may, however, deal generally with the view he finally implies, that such an ideal is useless, and that the theory of human and social evolution has no practical bearing on the guidance of conduct. He says:

> Even if we could construct scientifically Mr. Spencer's ideal code, I do not think such a code would be of much avail in solving the practical problems of actual humanity. . . . Even supposing that this ideal society is ultimately to be realized, it must at any rate be separated from us by a considerable interval of evolution; hence it is not

unlikely that the best way of progressing towards it is some other than the apparently directest way, and that we shall reach it more easily if we begin by moving away from it.

And Mr. Sidgwick concludes that "the humble and imperfect empirical method" can be our only guide.

Here, then, we have a distinct statement of the opinion that for practical purposes it comes to the same thing whether we do or do not entertain an ideal of conduct and of society. In our estimate of a proximately best, it will make no difference whether we have or have not any conception of an ultimately best. So long as the immediate effects of a measure promise to be good, it is needless to consider whether, while achieving them, we cause changes in men and society, and whether, if we cause changes, these will carry men and society toward, or away from, their highest forms. This position may be dealt with first generally and then more specially.

The empirical method, as upheld by Mr. Sidgwick, estimating, as well as may be, good and evil results, that is, totals of pleasures and pains, postulates as a necessary basis for its conclusions, constancy of relation between pleasures and their causes and between pains and their causes. If, from experience of men as we now know them, it is inferred that a certain policy will be conducive to a surplus of pleasures over pains; and if the establishment of that policy, say by public institutions, is considered as therefore ethically justifiable, or rather, imperative; then the implied assumption is that the surplus of pleasures over pains producible by this course in existing men, will also be producible in their descendants. This, however, cannot be inferred unless it is assumed that men will remain the same. Hence the question whether men are or are not changing, becomes an essential question. If they are not changing, the empirical estimates may be valid. If they are changing, these estimates must be doubtful, and may be entirely false. It needs but to contrast the pleasures of combat, which a Norseman conceived as those of his heaven, with the pleasures pursued by a modern man of letters, or to contrast the repugnance which a savage shows to continued industry, with the eager pursuit of business by a citizen, to see that this change in the relations between actions and the accompanying feelings, is no nominal difficulty in the way of the empirical method. It becomes manifest that if humanity is undergoing modifications, then, guidance of conduct by valuations of pleasures and pains, assuming as it does that what is true now will continue to be true, is a guidance likely to be erroneous. Be it a policy advocated, a law passed, an agency set up, a discipline used, an injunction urged, if its sole warrant is that of furthering the happiness of men as they are, then, if men are becoming other than they are, furtherance of their happiness in future cannot be inferred; and there may result hindrance to their happiness.

Mark, now, another implication. If it is admitted, as it must be, that guidance by estimated surplus of pleasures over pains, as now observable, is vitiated if the relations between actions and feelings change; then it must also be admitted that guidance by such estimated surplus can be made trustworthy, only by knowledge of the ways in which these relations change. If we simply know that these relations between actions and feelings will change, without knowing how they will change, then we simply know that our empirical guidance will go wrong, without knowing the way in which it will go wrong. Hence the question, whether there is at work that adaptation of constitution to conditions which the doctrine of evolution implies, becomes the cardinal question. If, recognizing the relativity of pleasures and pains, we conclude that those activities which social life necessitates in men, tend to become more pleasurable, while the pains caused by the restraints on unfit activities diminish, then the question of first importance becomes—What general form of activities is it to which humanity is being adjusted?—what are the ideal social conditions to which men's natures are being so molded that they will have no desires out of harmony with those conditions? If we can frame a conception of the ideal social state, and of human conduct as carried on in it, then we have a means of correcting whatever empirical guidance may be obtained by valuation of pleasures and pains as now experienced; since, beyond the immediate effects of any course, we are enabled to see whether the ultimate effects are such as further or hinder the required remolding of human nature.

The contrast between Mr. Sidgwick's belief and mine, respecting the relation between ethical doctrine and the theory of human and social evolution, will best be shown by an analogy. In the moral education of a child, proximately good results may be obtained in various ways. Its crying may be stopped by a *bon-bon;* or its mother may alarm it by a threat; it may be led to learn a lesson by fear, or by the promise of a treat, or by the desire to please; and in later childhood there may come, on the part of the father, a control which maintains order by regulating every action, or one which allows a considerable amount of freedom and concomitant experience of good and evil results. Is it, or is it not, desirable to keep in view the fact that presently the child will be a man, and to frame a conception of what the man ought to be? Very frequently the mother, pursuing the empirical method and achieving proximately good results, ignores the question of this ideal and the conduciveness of her discipline to achievement of it; and not uncommonly the father, especially if of the clerical sort, making numerous peremptory rules, considers scarcely at all whether his much-regulated boy is acquiring the qualities which will make him a self-regulating man. Shall we say that such proximately beneficial methods are the best which can be devised; or shall we not rather say that there can be no good education which does not bear the ideal constantly in view, and consider methods partly in reference to their immediate results, but still more in reference to their ultimate results? And if so, must we not say the same with respect to adult humanity, which undergoes an education by social discipline? Of course if Mr. Sidgwick agrees with those who hold that human nature is unchangeable, his position is tenable. But if he admits that man is adaptable, it becomes of some importance to consider of every proposed course, whether, by the

controversy carried on between us respecting the test of truth, I have not read it since. I go on to remark that, as the passage itself shows, and as appears more fully on turning to the volume, the analogy as used by Mr. Mill refers to social science; while the analogy is used by me in elucidation of ethical science. Professor Means says it is "used by Mill for precisely the same purpose." Now though it is true that politics and morals are intimately related, the belief that they are identical is, I think, peculiar to Professor Means, and is likely to remain so.

Let us, however, turn to the main issue—whether the utilitarianism of Mr. Mill and previous writers of the same school, did or did not recognize that dependence of ethical laws upon the laws of life, which I have insisted upon, and did or did not propose to establish them deductively from such laws. To whatever extent it may be true that utilitarians have been conscious of a relation between rules or right conduct and the furtherance, direct or indirect, of vital activities, there could not come the full conception of a resulting method, until biological generalizations of the widest kind had been reached and accepted as data for ethical reasoning. Now up to recent times, biological generalizations of this widest kind had either not been reached at all, or were known only by naturalists, and accepted by very few of these. In Bentham's day, the consequences deducible from the universal law of adaptation, could not take their place in ethical speculation; for the reason that, in the sense involved by the doctrine of evolution, this law had not been heard of by ninety-nine cultivated people out of a hundred, and was pooh-poohed by nearly all those who had heard of it. Again, whatever occasional observations had been made respecting the relations of pleasures and pains to bodily welfare, could not lead to any such ethical conclusions as those involved by acceptance of the doctrine of evolution, which implies that life of the sentient kind has continued and developed only in virtue of these relations. Nor, without the doctrine of the relativity of pains and pleasures, established by a wide biological induction, could there be completed the necessary basis for a scientific ethics. Similarly, into that division of ethics which is concerned with its psychology, the theory of mental evolution enters as an indispensable factor. Though Mr. Mill did not combat the hypothesis of inherited mental modifications, yet he never adopted it in such a way as to qualify his experiential interpretation of ideas and feelings; and, consequently, he was debarred from entertaining that view of the moral sentiments and moral intuitions, which yields an explanation of their varying functions under varying social conditions, and affords a warrant for inferring their ultimate adjustment to an ultimate social state. In brief, then, the laws of life and of mind, referred to by me as those from which a scientific ethics is to be deduced, are laws which were either not known, or not admitted, by utilitarians of the empirical school; and it was therefore not possible for them to entertain that conception of rational ethics which I have put in antithesis to empirical ethics.

Professor Means comments on the contrast I have drawn between justice as an end and happiness as an end. He quotes me as saying that

> Justice "is concerned exclusively with *quantity* under *stated conditions*, whereas happiness is concerned with both *quantity* and *quality* under *conditions not stated.*" It refers to "the relative amounts of actions, or products, or benefits, the natures of which are recognized only as far as is needful for saying whether *as much* has been given, or done, or allowed, by each concerned, as was implied by tacit or overt understanding, to be an equivalent."

To which he objects that

> "Differences of age, of growth, of constitutional need, differences of activity and consequent expenditure, differences of desires and tastes," which Mr. Spencer thinks impossible to be estimated by a utilitarian, must all be estimated before any course of action can be said to be *equivalent* to any other course. And if a comparison of pleasures is impossible, this estimate is impossible.

The reply is that justice as I have defined it, justice as formulated in law, and justice as commonly understood, is satisfied when those concerned have so acted that no one has been trespassed against by another, and, in case of contract, each has done all that was agreed to be done by him. If there has been direct aggression, greater liberty of action has been taken by the aggressor than by the one aggressed upon. If there has been indirect aggression by breach of contract, such greater liberty of action has again been taken: one has broken the understanding while the other has not—one has seized some advantage beyond that given as an equivalent, while the other has not. Justice is not concerned with the relative values of benefits or happinesses, as Professor Means implies, but only with the relative degrees of freedom used in pursuing benefits or happinesses; and if neither by direct or indirect trespass have these degrees been made unequal, there is no injustice. If it be said, as by Professor Means concerning wages given for labor, that very often men are practically coerced by social arrangements into making agreements they would not otherwise have made; then, the injustice exists not in the agreements unwillingly made, but in the social arrangements which have interfered with free volition. If, as appears from his argument, Professor Means holds that justice comprises, not simply a regulation of actions such that each man shall leave others as much freedom to pursue their ends as he himself takes, but that justice involves the establishment of equivalence between advantages gained by cooperation, then the reply is that I am not concerned with justice as so conceived. There are socialists who hold that there should be an equal division of benefits among men, irrespective of the values of their several labors. To many it seems unjust that the hard work of a ploughman should bring in a week, not so much as a physician easily gains in a quarter of an hour. Some persons contend that it is unjust that children born to the poor should not have educational advantages like those of children born to the rich. But such deficiencies in the shares of happiness some men get by cooperation, as arise from the inferior natures they inherit, or from the inferior circumstances into which their inferior ancestors have fallen, are deficiencies with which justice, as I understand it, has nothing to do. The injustice which entails on posterity diseases and deformities—the injustice which inflicts on offspring the painful results of stupidity and misconduct in parents—the injustice which compels those who inherit incapacities to struggle with resulting difficulties—the injustice which leaves in comparative poverty the great majority, whose powers, of low order, bring them small returns, is an injustice of a kind lying outside of my argument. We have to accept, as we may, the established constitution of things, though under it an inferiority for which the individual is not blamable, brings its evils, and a superiority for which he can claim no merit, brings its benefits; and we have to accept, as we may, all those resulting inequalities of advantages which citizens gain by their respective activities. But while it does not devolve upon me to defend the order of Nature, I may say again, as I have said at greater length already (sec. 69), that only in virtue of the law under which every creature takes the good and bad results entailed by its inherited organization, has life advanced to its present height and can continue to advance. A so-called justice which should equalize advantages apart from capacities, would be fatal; while the justice, rightly so-called, which insists that each shall be as free as others to make the best of his powers, and that nothing shall intervene between his efforts and the returns they naturally bring (as decided by agreement) is beneficent immediately and remotely. This is the justice which, as an end, I have contended is more intelligible than happiness as an end; and I decline to be entangled by Professor Means in the difficulties which arise when there is substituted a justice which contemplates equivalence of results.

The remainder of Professor Means' criticisms I must pass over with the remark that, throughout, they similarly display an unusual facility in identifying things which are different.

I turn, now, to the article of Mr. Alfred W. Benn, "Another View of Mr. Spencer's Ethics," contained in the last number of *Mind*. Here, too, I must limit myself to the earlier criticisms.

Mr. Benn blames me for expressing a positive opinion respecting the inevitableness of the hedonistic view of morals. He says: "To declare pleasure a necessary form of moral intuition must in the present state of the controversy be pronounced a piece of unwarrantable dogmatism." As commonly understood, dogmatism implies authoritative assertion without the giving of reasons. Considering that the passage to which Mr. Benn refers, closes a chapter devoted to an examination of all the various standards of goodness in conduct; and considering that the analysis aims to show, and does, I think, show, that happiness as an ultimate end is in every case involved; it seems to me an unusual application of the word to characterize as dogmatic, a proposition which sums up the results of the inquiry. A dogmatism which appeals step by step to the judgment of the reader, is of a species not before known.

I remark this by way of introduction to Mr. Benn's first criticism. Respecting my statement that optimists and pessimists by their arguments both imply acceptance of the hedonistic view, Mr. Benn says:

> Here with all deference I must observe that Mr. Spencer is doubly if not trebly mistaken. In the first place, although Schopenhauer and his school are hedonists, it is perfectly possible to be a pessimist without thinking that pleasure is the end of life and that we do not get enough of it. Some persons if they were convinced that certain knowledge was unattainable, even if they expected it to yield them no pleasure, might regard that as a reason for preferring nonexistence to existence. In the second place, as it is generally better if possible to meet your adversary on his own ground, an optimist who believes that life affords a surplus of pleasurable feeling may very well advance that argument without conceding that such a surplus alone makes life worth having. And, thirdly, as a matter of fact the optimists do not make this concession. M. Caro, an eminent representative of the spiritualistic school in France, has distinctly declared that granting the excess of pain over pleasure to be possible and even probable, he still

remains an optimist, that even an unhappy life is worth living, and
that suffering is preferable to nonentity.

The first of the three proofs that I am mistaken is curiously
hypothetical. "Some persons" "*might* regard" nonexistence as
preferable to existence, *if* they thought "certain knowledge
was unattainable," even *if* they expected no pleasure from
attaining it. Disproof of my statement concerning the beings
we know, by the help of supposable beings, is not, I think,
very satisfactory. But passing over this, let me point out that if
the attainment of "certain knowledge" were an adequate motive for existence, and inability to attain it a motive for preferring nonexistence, it is difficult to conceive otherwise than
that the attainment of it would be a satisfaction; and a satisfaction of whatever nature is a kind of pleasure. To say that the
attainment of the knowledge was not expected to yield them
any pleasure, is to say that they would regard the attainment
of the knowledge with indifference; and if they were indifferent to the attainment of it, how could attainment of it be
regarded as a sufficient reason for *preferring* existence to
nonexistence?

Mr. Benn's second disproof, somewhat hypothetical also,
does not, I think, much strengthen his case. He says: "An
optimist who believes that life affords a surplus of pleasurable
feeling may very well advance that argument without conceding that such a surplus alone makes life worth having." Is this
really another disproof, or only the same restated? Without
naming any end, other than pleasurable feeling, which
"makes life worth having," it alleges that even an optimist
may believe in such an end. I do not see that by leaving this
end unspecified, and supposing an optimist who thinks it a
sufficient end, the argument is made different from the last,
and the same reply serves. The end, of whatever nature, being
one which it is desirable to attain rather than not attain,
implies satisfaction of desire, or pleasure. The third argument
states in the concrete that which is stated in the abstract in the
preceding two, and is the sole argument. This argument is

that M. Caro thinks "even an unhappy life is worth living." Now I suspect that were M. Caro cross-examined, it would turn out that the unhappy life which he thinks worth living, is one which, though it brings misery to the possessor, does not bring misery to others, but conduces to their happiness.* If M. Caro means that life is worth living even on condition that its possessor, suffering misery himself in common with all individuals, shall aid them in living that they may continue to suffer misery, and shall beget and rear children that they, too, may pass lives of misery; and if M. Caro means that misery is to be the fate of all, not only here but during the hereafter he believes in: then, indeed, and only then, does he exclude happiness as an end. But if M. Caro says he believes that even under such conditions life would be worth living, then I venture to class him with those who have not practiced introspection. I once heard a person assert that a cat thrown across a room could drop in the middle if it pleased; and, presumably, this person thought he could himself do the same. The defective consciousness of his mechanical powers which this person displayed, is, I think, paralleled by M. Caro's defective consciousness of his mental powers, if he thinks he can believe that existence would be preferable to nonexistence did it bring pain to all men throughout all time.

Mr. Benn, however, regards this testimony of M. Caro as conclusive. If there is anyone who says he thinks that universal and eternal human misery is better than nonexistence, we must accept his self-interpretation as settling the question; for men never misconceive their own thoughts or fail to understand their own feelings. And then Mr. Benn continues: "*A fortiori* would such persons maintain that a perfectly neutral

---

* Since this was written I have referred to M. Caro's essay, and find he says that if there is really an excess of suffering in the average of human life, "il ne faut pas s'empresser d'en conclure que le pessimisme a raison, que le mal de la vie est absolu, *qu'il est incurable.*" Which makes it clear that M. Caro had in the background of his consciousness the conception of misery to be diminished, that is, happiness to be increased, as a reason for tolerating present misery; and probably this conception was not wholly absent when he wrote—"la souffrance vaut mieux que le néant."

state of consciousness, a life totally devoid both of pleasure and pain, is worth having. Thus the appeal to authority completely breaks down, a single recusant being enough to invalidate it." Passing over the question whether any such recusant exists, it may be as well, before admitting the alleged breakdown, to ask what is the meaning of the word "worth," as used in the above relation. There presents itself the problem to define "worth" in terms which exclude all reference, direct or indirect, to satisfaction, or pleasure, or gratification. It is required to find a case in which men, or things, or acts, are contrasted as having worth and as being worthless, without there entering the conception of preference; or if the conception of preference enters, then it is required to state what kind of preference it is which takes place between things of which one is not liked more than the other; or if difference of liking is admitted, then the question to be answered is what kind of liking is it which does not connote pleasure. Similarly with the words used in a sentence which shortly follows: "For the question is not whether pleasure is a good and pain an evil, but whether pleasure is the only good and pain the only evil." Which question at once raises the inquiry for the kind of evil which, neither proximately nor remotely, to the actor or to any other being, now or hereafter, produces any pain. Until some such kind of evil has been pointed out, I do not see any proposition against which I have to contend. There is merely the alleged possibility of a proposition.

As already hinted, I cannot follow further the course of Mr. Benn's argument, but must leave its validity to be judged by that of this first portion. The only remark I will add, concerns, not a matter of argument but a matter of evidence. Referring to my account of the origin of the religious sanction, Mr. Benn says: "It seems a pity to disturb such an ingenious and symmetrical theory, but I am not aware that it is supported by any external evidence, while there are strong reasons for dissenting from it." Does Mr. Benn mean that no such external evidence is contained in the *Data of Ethics?* If he does, then the reply is that such evidence, occupying more space than that afforded by the entire volume, would have rather too much interrupted the thread of the argument. Does he mean that I have not given such external evidence elsewhere? Then the reply is that in the first division of the *Principles of Sociology,* evidence so great in quantity is set forth, that I have been blamed for overburdening my argument with it; and a further reply is that if Mr. Benn wishes for still more such evidence, he will find abundance of it in Nos. II, III, IV, V and VI of the *Descriptive Sociology,* where the religious ideas of some eighty uncivilized and semicivilized peoples are described in detail. In disproof of my view concerning the genesis of the political and religious controls, Mr. Benn goes on to say: "Modern inquiries into the history of jural conceptions show that among primitive men kings were not legislators but judges," and by way of showing what happens among "primitive men" he instances "the original judgments or Themistes" of the Greeks. On this my comment is that Mr. Benn seems unacquainted with inquiries, more "modern" than those he refers to, which show that theories about primitive ideas and institutions, based on facts furnished by historic peoples, are utterly misleading. The origins of religious and jural conceptions and usages, Mr. Benn thinks may fitly be sought in the traditions of the early Greek world; though, as Curtius remarks (Bk. I. 136–37), this "is not . . . a world of beginnings; it is no world still engaged in an uncertain development, but one thoroughly complete, matured and defined by fixed rules and orders of life." For myself, in seeking for origins, I prefer to look for them among peoples who have not yet arrived at a stage in which there are metal weapons and metal armor, two-horse war chariots, walled towns, temples, palaces, and seagoing ships.

I had originally intended to notice briefly, certain other criticisms—one by Professor Calderwood, which formed the inaugural lecture to his class at Edinburgh in the session of 1879, and was afterward published in the *Contemporary Review;* and the other by Professor Wace of King's College, which was

253. *Cimmarróns* (Osw. 61)—*Wolves* (Rom. 436). **254.** *Beavers* (Dal. in C.N.H. iii, 99)—*Crows and Rooks* (Rom. 323–25). **255.** *Bisons* (Rom. 334–35)—*Elephants* (Rom. 400–1)—*Monkeys* (Gill. 170). **259.** *Abors* (Dalt. in J.A.S.B. xiv, 426). **268.** *Dogribs* (Lub. 509)—*Fuegians* (Wed. 175)—*Greeks* (Pla. Jow. 229). **269.** *Communists* (Lav. in *Contemporary Review,* Feb. 1890; Bel. 101). **271.** *Germany* (Daily Papers, Feb. 1890). **276.** *Lepchas* (Camp. in J.E.S.L. July, 1869)—*Hos* (Dalt. 206)—*Wood-Veddah* (Tenn. ii, 444)—*Kant* (Ka. 54–55). **277.** *Austin* (Aust. 30). **279.** *Benthamism* (Mill, 93; Bel. in *Cont. Rev.,* July, 1890). **285.** *Fijians* (Will. i, 112)—*Wends* (Grimm, 488)—*Herulians* (Grimm, 487)—*Greeks* (Gro. ii, 33)—*Europeans* (Grimm, 289; Green, 13)—*English* (Steph. ii, 204, 209). **286.** *Early Germans, &c.* (Mai. 370)—*Anc. Russia* (Holtz. i, 225–26). **290.** *Abors.* (Dalt. in J.A.S.B. xiv, 426)—*Nagas* (Stew. in J.A.S.B. xxiv, 608)—*Lepchas* (Camp. in J.E.S.L. July, 1869)—*Jakuns* (Fav. in J.I.A. ii). **291.** *Fijians* (Ersk. 492)—*Hebrews* (*Ex.* xxi; *Deut.* xv; *Lev.* xxv. 45, 46)—*Christians* (1 *Cor.* vii. 21)—*Greeks* (Gro. ii, 37, 468–69)—*Spartans* (Gro. ii. 309)—*English* (Green, 56, 91, 90, 247)—*Artizans* (Mart. i, 343). **297.** *Suanctians* (Fresh. in P.R.G.S. June, 1888, p. 335)—*Dahomans* (Burt. i, 260). **299.** *Locke* (Sec. Treat. on Gov. sec. 27)—*Comanches* (Scho. i, 232)—*Chippewayans* (Scho. v. 177)—*Irish* (Green, 431)—*China* (Wil. i, 1–2)—*India* (Lav. 310, etc.). **300.** *Maine* (Mai. 184). **305.** *Romans* (cop. 2)—*English* (Rob. in Ency. Brit., art. "Copyright"). **306.** *Monopolies* (Hayd. 489). **307.** *Roman Law* (Pat. 154–55)—*Buddhists* (Pat. 181, *note*)—*English* (Pat. 53). **308.** *English* (13 Eliz. c. 5; 29 Eliz. c. 5). **309.** *Polynesians* (Ell. P.R. ii, 346; Tho. i, 96)—*Sumatra* (Mars. 244)—*Hottentots* (Kolb. i, 300)—*Damaras* (And. 228)—*Gold Coast* (J.E.S. (1856) IV, 20)—*Congo* (Proy. in Pink, xvi, 571)—*Eghas* (Burt. Abeokuta, i, 208)—*Timbuctoo* (Shab. 18)—*Ashantis* (Bee. 117)—*Arabs* (Burck. i, 131)—*Todas* (Mar. 206)—*Gonds* (His. 12)—*Bodo and Dhimals* (Hodg. in J.A.S.B. xviii, 718)—*Kasias* (Hook, ii, 275)—*Karens* (Mas. in J.A.S.B. xxxvii, pt. ii, 142)—*Mishmis* (Grif. 35)—*Primitive Germans* (Tac. Germ. xx)—*Celts* (Bello. iii, 398)—*Saxons and Frisians* (König. 152–3)—*Merovingians* (König. 158–60)—*France* (Civil Code, sec. 967, etc.). **314.** *Polynesians* (U.S. Ex. Ex. iii, 22; Ang. ii, 50; Ell. Hawaii, 390; St. John, ii, 260)—*Bechuanas* (Burch. ii, 395)—*Inland Negroes* (Land. i, 250)—*Ashantis* (Bee. 148)—*Shoa* (Harr. ii, 26)—*Congo* (Proy. in Pink. xvi, 578)—*Dahomans* (Burt. Miss. i, 52)—*Fulahs* (Wint. i, 170)—*Hebrews* (*Deut.* xxii, 8, etc.)—*Phoenicians* (Möv. ii, 108–110)—*Mexicans* (Zur. 223)—*Cent. Americans* (Xim. 203; Pala. 84; Sqi. ii, 341)—*Patagonians* (Fitz. ii, 150)—*Mundrucus* (Bates, 274)—*Diocletian* (Lév. i, 82–3). **315.** *Hebrews* (*Deut.* xxiii, 19–20)—*Cicero* (Arn. 50)—*England* (Ree. iii, 292; Steph. Com. ii, 90)—*France* (Lec. Rationalism, 293–4). **317.** *England* (Cunn. 200; Thor. i, 118; Craik, i, 108–9; Rog. i, 575; Ree. iii, 262, 590; Pict. Hist. ii, 809, 812, viii, 635)—*France* (Tocque. 427; Lév. iii, 286). **319.** *Guinea* (Bast. iii, 225)—*Fijians* (Lub. 357; Ersk. 450; Will. i, 121)—*Greeks* (Plato: Laws, bk. x; Smith, *Class. Dict.* 714; Ency. Brit. ii, 1). **323.** *Henry* IV. (Green, 258)—*Nonconformists* (Green, 609–13)—*Athenians* (Pat. 76)—*Romans* (Pat. 77)—*English* (Pat. 79, 94)—*Plato* (Pat. 50)—*English* (Pat. 50–1). **335.** *Fijians* (Will. i, 210)—*Fuegians* (Fitz. Voyage, ii, 2)—*Australians* (Trans. Eth. Sec. N.S. iii, 248, 288)—*Egyptians* (Ebers, i, 307–8)—*Aryans* (Tac. Germ. xviii)—*Prim. Germans* (Gri. 450)—*Early Teutons* (Mai. 153)—*Old English* (Lapp. ii, 338–9)—*Romans* (Hunt. 32–3)—*Fulc the Black* (Green, 95). **340.** *Greeks and Romans* (Lec. ii, 26)—*Teutons and Celts* (Gri. 455, etc.). *Fuegians* (Fitz. ii, 171)—*New Guinea* (Kolff, 301)—*New Zealanders* (Cook's Last Voy. 54)—*Dyaks* (Broo. i, 75)—*Malagasy* (Wai. ii, 437)—*Hebrews* (*Ex.* xxi, 7; 2 *Kings* iv, l; *Job* xxiv, 9)—*Romans* (Lec. ii, 31)—*Celts* (König. 86–7)—*Germans* (Gri. 461)—*Romans* (Hunt. 29; König. 87)—*France* (Bern. 189–193; Gonc. 10–12; Bern. 161) **347.** *Esquimaux* (Hear. 161)—*Greeks* (Gro. ii, 468)—*Bodo, Dhimal and Kocch* (Hodg. 157; Hodg. in J.A.S.B. xviii, 741). **356.** *Esquimaux* (Cran. i, 164–5)—*Fuegians* (Wed. 168)—*Veddahs* (Tenn. ii, 440)—*Tasmanians* (Bon. 81)—*Mountain Snakes* (Ross, i, 250)—*Fish-eaters* (Scho. i, 207)—*Shirrydikas* (Lew. & Clarke, 306)—*Comanches* (Scho. ii, 127). **357.** *Snakes* (Lew. & Clark, 306)—*Creeks* (Scho. v, 277)—*Dacotahs* (Scho. ii,

183–5)—*Comanches* (Scho. i, 231)—*Uaupés* (Wal. 499)—*Patagonians* (Falk. 123)—
Araucanians (Thomp. i, 405)—*Bechuanas* (Licht. ii, 329)—*East Africans* (Burt. C.A. ii,
365)—*Coast Negroes* (J.E.S. 1848, i, 215; Wint. i, 127)—*Abyssinia* (Park, ii, 236–8)—*Arabs*
(Palg. 53; Burck. i, 284)—*Bhils* (Mal. i, 576)—*Khonds* (Macph. 44)—*Karens* (Mas. in
J.A.S.B. xxxvii, Pt. II, 142)—*Early Teutons* (Kemb. i, 268, 272; Thor. i, 447)—*English*
(Green, 197)—*French* (Gué. ccviii). **362.** *Paternal Government* (Mai. 133). **363.** *Plato*
(Laws, bks. vi, vii; Rep. bk. v)—*Aristotle* (Rep. bk. vii, 14–16)—*Plato* (Rep. iv, 19)—
Aristotle (Rep. bk. vii, 9–10). **366.** *Feudalism* (Bonne, i, 269)—*Fiji* (Will. i, 30)—
Church-and-King Mob (Hux. 103). **376.** *Thieves* (Daily Papers: date lost).
377. *Shrewsbury* (Jev. 37). **378.** *Penny Post* (Ency. Brit. xix, 565)—*Boy Messengers Co.*
(Daily Papers, March, 1891). **421.** *Ptah-hotep* (*see* Records of the Past, *2nd Series*, iii,
20). **455.** *Mansion House Fund, &c.* (Annual Report of Charity Organization Society,
1885–6, pp. 14, 20; Charity Organization Review, May, 1892). **464.** *Gold Coast* (Bee.
229). **468.** *American on Party-Government* (R.W. Tayler, in Brooklyn Ethical Association Lectures, 1892, p. 503).

TITLES OF WORKS REFERRED TO

And.—Andersson (C.J.) *Lake Ngami.*
Ang.—Angas (G.F.) *Savage Life and Scenes in Australia and New Zealand.*
Arist.—Aristotle's *Politics and Economics.* Trans. by E. Walford. (Bohn's Series). Lon-
    don, 1871.
Arn.—Arnold (W.T.) *Roman Provincial Administration.* London, 1879.
Aust.—Austin (John) *The Province of Jurisprudence Determined.* 2nd Ed. 8vo. London,
    1861.
Bast.—Bastian (A.) *Der Mensch in der Geschichte.* 3 vols.
Bates.—Bates (H.W.) *The Naturalist on the River Amazon.* 2nd Ed. London, 1864.
Bee.—Beecham (J.) *Ashanti and the Gold Coast.*
Bel.—Bellamy (E.) *Looking Backward.*
Bel.—Bellamy in *Contemporary Review.*
Bello.—Belloguet (R. Baron de) *Ethnogénie Gauloise.*
Bern.—Bernard (P.) *Histoire de l'Autorité paternelle en France.* Montdidier, 1863.
Bon.—Bonnemère (E.) *Histoire des Paysans.* 2nd Ed. 2 vols. Paris, 1874.
Bonw.—Bonwick (J.) *Daily Life and Origin of the Tasmanians.* 8vo. London, 1870.
Broo.—Brooke (C.) *Ten Years in Saráwak.*
Burch.—Burchell (W.J.) *Travels into the Interior of Southern Africa.*
Burck.—Burckhardt (J.L.) *Notes on Bedouins and Wahábys.* London, 1831.
Burt.—Burton (R.F.) *Abeokuta and the Cameroon Mountains.* 2 vols. 1863.
Burt.—Burton (R.F.) *The Lake Regions of Central Africa.* 2 vols. 8vo. 1860.
Burt.—Burton (R.F.) *Mission to Gelele, King of Dahomey.* London, 1864.
C.N.H.—*Cassell's Natural History,* ed. by P.M. Duncan. 6 vols. roy. 8vo. London,
    18[77]–1883.
Camp.—Campbell in *Journal of the Ethnological Society, London.*
Cook.—*Journal of Captain Cook's Last Voyage, 1776–79.* London, 1781.
Cop.—Copinger (W.A.) *The Law of Copyright.* 2nd Ed.
Craik.—Craik (G.L.) *History of English Commerce.* 1844.
Cran.—Crantz (D.) *History of Greenland.* London, 1820.
Cunn.—Cunningham (W.) *The Growth of English Industry and Commerce, etc.* 8vo.
    Cambridge, 1890.
Dal.—Dallas in *Cassell's Natural History.*
Dalt.—Dalton (Col. E.J.) *Descriptive Ethnology of Bengal.* Calcutta, 1872.
Dalt.—Dalton in *Journal of the Asiatic Society, Bengal.*

Ebers.—Ebers (G.) *Aegypten und die Bücher Moses.* Leipzig, 1868.
Ell.—Ellis (Rev. W.) *Narrative of a Tour through Hawaii.* 1827.
Ell.—Ellis (Rev. W.) *Polynesian Researches.* 1829.
Ency. Brit.—*Encyclopedia Britannica.* 9th Ed.
Ersk.—Erskine (Capt. J.E.) *Journal of a Cruize Among the Islands of the Western Pacific.* 8vo. 1853.
Falk.—Falkner (T.) *Description of Patagonia.*
Fav.—Favre (Rev. P.) in *Journal of the Indian Archipelago.* Vol. II. Singapore.
Fitz.—Fitzroy (Admiral) *Narrative of the Surveying Voyages of the 'Adventure' and 'Beagle,' etc.* London, 1839–40.
Fresh.—Freshfield (D.) in *Proceedings of the Royal Geographical Society.*
Gill.—Gillmore (P.) *The Hunter's Arcadia.*
Gonc.—Goncourt (E. & J. de) *La Femme au XVIIIe Siècle.* 8vo. 1862.
Green.—Green (J.R.) *A Short History of the English People.* 1880.
Gri.—Grimm (Jacob) *Deutsche Rechtsalterthümer.* Göttingen, 1828.
Grif.—Griffith (W.) *Journal of Travels in Assam, etc.* Calcutta, 1847.
Gro.—Grote (G.) *A History of Greece.* 10 vols. 4th Ed.
Gué.—Guérard (B.) *Cartulaire de l'abbaye de St. Père de Chartres.* 2 vols. Paris, 1840.
Harr.—Harris (W.C.) *Highlands of Æthiopia.* London, 1844.
Hay.—*Haydn's Dictionary of Dates.* 12th Ed., by Vincent. London, 1866.
Hear.—Hearne (S.) *Journey from Prince of Wales's Fort, etc.* Dublin, 1796.
His.—Hislop (Rev. S.) *Aboriginal Tribes of the Central Provinces.* 1860.
Hodg.—Hodgson (B.H.) *Kocch, Bodo and Dhimál Tribes.* Calcutta.
Hodg.—Hodgson (B.H.) in *Journal of the Asiatic Society, Bengal.*
Holtz.—Holtzendorf-Vietmannsdorf (F. von) *Handbuch des deutschen Strafrechts.* 4 vols. 8vo. Berlin, 1871.
Hook.—Hooker (J.D.) *Himalayan Journals.* 2 vols. 8vo. 1854.
Hunt.—Hunter (W.A.) *Introduction to Roman Law.* London, 1880.
Hux.—Huxley (T.H.) *Science and Culture, and Other Essays.* London, 1881.
J.A.S.B.—*Journal of the Asiatic Society, Bengal.*
J.E.S.L.—*Journal of the Ethnological Society, London.*
Jev.—Jevons (W. Stanley) *The State in Relation to Labour.* London, 1882.
Ka.—Kant's (E.) *Theory of Ethics.* Trans. by T.K. Abbott. London, 1873.
Kemb.—Kemble (J.M.) *The Saxons in England.* 2 vols 8vo. 1849.
Kolb.—Kolben (P.) *Present State of the Cape of Good Hope.* Trans. by Medley. 1731.
Kolff.—Kolff (D.H.) *Voyages of the Dutch Brig the 'Dourga' Through the Molucca Archipelago, etc.* Trans. by G.W. Earl 1840.
König.—Königswarter (L.J.) *Histoire de l'organisation de la Famille en France.* Paris, 1851.
Land.—Lander (R.) *Journal of an Expedition to the Course and Termination of the Niger.* London, 1832.
Lapp.—Lappenberg (J.M.) *England under the Saxon Kings.* Trans. by B. Thorpe. 2 vols. 8vo. 1845.
Lav.—Laveleye (E. de) in *The Contemporary Review.*
Lav.—Laveleye (E. de) in *Primitive Property.* London, 1878.
Lec.—Lecky (W.E.H.) *History of European Morals.* 3rd Ed. 2 vols. London, 1877.
Lec.—Lecky (W.E.H.) *On Rationalism in Europe.* 2 vols. 8vo. 1865.
Lév.—Lévasseur (C) *Histoire des classes ouvrières.* 1st and 2nd series. 4 vols. Paris, 1859–67.
Lew.—Lewis (M.) and Capt. Clarke. *Travels to the Source of the Missouri, etc.* London, 1814.
Licht.—Lichtenstein (H.) *Travels in Southern Africa in the Years 1803–1806.* Trans. by A. Plumptre. 2 vols. 4to. 1812–15.
Locke.—Locke (J.) *Two Treatises of Government.* 5th Ed. London, 1728.
Lub.—Lubbock (Sir J.) *Pre-Historic Times.* 2nd Ed. 8vo. London, 1869.

Macph.—Macpherson (Lieut.) *Report upon the Khonds of Ganjam and Cuttack.* Calcutta, 1842
Mai.—Maine (Sir H.S.) *Ancient Law.* 3rd Ed. London, 1866.
Mal.—Malcolm (Sir J.) *Memoir of Central Asia.* London, 1823.
Mar.—Marsden (W.) *History of Sumatra.*
Marsh.—Marshall (Lieut.-Col. W.E.) *A Phrenologist amongst the Todas.* London, 1873.
Mart.—Martineau (H.) *History of England during the Thirty Years' Peace.* 1849–50.
Mas.—Mason in *Journal of the Asiatic Society, Bengal.*
Mill.–Mill *(John Stuart) Utilitarianism.* 2nd Ed. 8vo. London, 1864.
Möv.—Mövers (D.F.C.) *Die Phönizier.* 2 vols. in 4, 8vo. Bonn, 1841–56.
Osw.—Oswald (F.) *Zoological Sketches.*
Pala.—Palacio. *San Salvador and Honduras in 1576* (in Squier, *Collection* No. 1).
Palg.—Palgrave (W.G.) *Journey through Central and Eastern Arabia.* London, 1865.
Park.—Parkyns (M.) *Life in Abyssinia, etc.* 2 vols. 8vo. 1853.
Pat.—Paterson (J.) *The Liberty of the Press, etc.* London, 1880.
Pict. Hist.—*Pictorial History of England.* 6 vols. 1837–41.
Pla. Jow.—Plato's *Republic.* Trans. by B. Jowett. 2nd Ed. 8vo. Oxford, 1881.
Proy.—Proyart (Abbé) *History of Loango.* (In Pinkerton's *Collection,* XVI.)
Ree.—Reeves (J.) *History of the English Law.* Ed Finlason. 3 vols. 8vo 1869.
Rob.—Robertson in *Encyclopedia Britannica.* 9th Ed.
Rog.—Rogers (J.E.T.) *History of Agriculture and Prices in England.* Vol. I. 1866.
Rom.—Romanes (G.J.) *Animal Intelligence.* 8vo. London, 1882.
Ross.—Ross (Alex) *Fur Hunters of Far West.* London, 1855.
St. John.—St. John (S.) *Life in the Forests of the Far East.*
Scho.—Schoolcraft (H.R.) *Information Respecting the Indian Tribes of the United States.* 5 vols. 4to. London, 1853–56.
Shab.—Shabeeny (El Hage abd Salam) *Account of Timbuctoo, etc.* pub. by J.G. Jackson. 1820.
Squi.—Squier (E.G.) *Nicaragua.* New York, 1852.
Steph.—Stephen (H.J.) *New Commentaries on the Laws of England.* 6th Ed.
Steph.—Stephen (J.F.) *A History of the Criminal Law of England.* 3 vols. 8vo. 1883.
Stew.—Stewart in *Journal of the Asiatic Society, Bengal.*
Tac.—Taciti (C.C.) *Germania.* Trans. by Aikin. Warrington, 1777.
Tenn.—Tennant (Sir J.E.) *Ceylon: An Account of the Island, etc.* 3rd Ed. London, 1859.
Thomp.—Thompson (G.A.) *Alcedo's Geographical and Historical Dictionary of America, etc.* London, 1812.
Thoms.—Thomson (Dr. A.S.) *The Story of New Zealand, etc.* 2 vols. 8vo. 1859.
Thor.—Thorpe (B.) *Ancient Laws and Institutions.*
Tocque.—Tocqueville (A. de) *The State of Society in France Before the Revolution.* Trans. by Reeve. 8vo. London, 1856.
U.S. Ex. Ex.—*Narrative of the United States' Exploring Expedition,* by Commander C. Wilkes. 5 vols. Philad., 1845.
Wai.—Waitz (T.) *Anthropologie.*
Wal.—Wallace (A.R.) *Travels on the Amazon and Rio Negro, etc.* 8vo. London, 1853.
Wed.—Weddell (James) *Voyage Towards the South Pole.* 1825.
Wil.—Williams (S.W.) *The Middle Kingdom.* 2 vols. New York.
Will.—Williams (Rev. T.) and J. Calvert. *Fiji and the Fijians.* 2 vols. 8vo. 1858.
Wint.—Winterbottom (T.) *Account of the Native Africans in the Neighbourhood of Sierra Leone.* London, 1803.
Xim.—Ximenez (F.) *Las Historias del Origen de los Indios de Guatemala* [1721] Publ. por C. Sherzer. Viena, 1857.
Zur.—Zurita (Al. de) *Rapport sur les différentes classes de chefs de la Nouvelle-Espagne.* Trad. par H. Ternaux-Compans. Paris, 1840.

INDEX TO VOLUME II

ability
    restraints on displays of, 325–29
Abors, 36, 90
Abyssinia, 225
Act of 8th Elizabeth, 264
adaptation, 41, 168
Agave (Statius), 125
aggression, 36, 43, 62, 67, 81
    counteraggression and, 63
    deterrent from, 45–46
agriculture, 35
    early stages of, 102–4
air
    right to, 97, 99–101
alms, 393
altruism, 314, 390, 446
    acts of, in animals, 20, 288
    divisions of, 288–89, 290
    irrational, 384
    kinds of, 283–95
    root of, 445
    sentiment of justice and, 46–48
America, 129, 138, 142, 264, 268
    politics in, 428, 429
    women in, 182
American Express Company, 267
amity
    ethics of, 67
    religion of, 240
anarchism, 291, 292
anarchists, 156

Anaxagoras, 155
Ancient Law (Maine), 75
anger, 338, 379
    in animals, 470, 474
Ani, 370
animals
    conscience in, 469–80
    duty and, 470, 471, 472, 475–80
    motive in, 472, 475–77
a posteriori reasoning, 70, 71–72, 221, 222
appearance, 417–20
a priori reasoning, 70–75, 221, 222
Arabs, 137, 225, 445
Araucanians, 225
Aristotle, 203, 272
    Politics, 55, 238
army, 251. *See also* soldiers
artisans, 298, 299
Aryans, 181, 225, 235
ascetics, 74
Ashantis, 137, 144
Assyrians, 223
atheism, 161
Athenians, 161, 238
Austin, 70
Australians, 181, 387

Bain (professor), 283
Bankruptcy Court, 252
beauty, 418
Bechuanas, 144, 225

Beecham, 421
beggars, 403
Bellamy, 74
    Looking Backward, 57
Belloguet, 138
beneficence, 298
    altruism and, 288–95
    at-large, 437–47
    effects of, 295
    endangered and, 379–86
    filial, 369–72
    friends and, 387–92
    functions of, 439, 443–44
    ill-used and, 379–86
    injury and, 373–78
    kinds of, 294–95
    marital, 353–60
    negative. *See* beneficence, negative
    objections to, 439–46
    parental, 361–68
    political, 425–35
    poor and, 393–409
    positive. *See* beneficence, positive
    relatives and, 387–92
    sickness and, 373–78
    social, 411–24
beneficence, negative, 34
    ability and, 325–29
    altruism and, 283–95
    blame and, 331–38
    competition and, 297–305
    contract and, 307–16
    praise and, 339–45
    superior, 318
    ultimate sanctions and, 347–49
    undeserved payments and, 317–24
beneficence, positive, 34
    at-large beneficence and, 437–47
    endangered and, 379–86
    filial beneficence and, 369–72
    friends and, 387–92
    ill-used and, 379–86
    injury and, 373–78
    marital beneficence and, 353–60
    political beneficence and, 425–35
    poor and, 393–409
    relatives and, 387–92
    sickness and, 373–78
    social beneficence and, 411–24
Benn, Alfred W.
    vs. Spencer, 499–503
Bentham, 74, 80, 493
    ethical theory of, 56–57

bequest(s)
    gift as implying, 136–37
    limitations on right of, 138–39, 140–41
    right of, 135–42
Bheels, 225
Bible, 476
Black Death, 93, 261
Blackstone, 69
blame
    employment relations and, 333–34
    excessive restraints on, 336–37
    family relations and, 332–33
    friends and, 336
    restraints on, 331–38
    strangers and, 335–36
blameworthiness
    reputation and, 132–33
    See also blame
Bodo, 137, 205
Boy Messengers' Company, 267
Bradfield Union, 265
Buddhism, 133
Bunyan (author-preacher), 161
Burdett, F., 162

cabdrivers, 319–20
Calderwood (professor), 503
cannibalism, 101
    slavery as limitation of, 91
Carlyle, 95, 319
Caro, 499, 501
causation, 65–66
Celts, 189, 455
Chapman, John
    Medical Charity: Its Abuses, and How to Remedy Them, 402 n
character, 271–79
    artificial molding of, 278
    natural molding of, 278
    parental molding of, 363
    society and, 273–74
charity, 440
    difficulties concerning, 408–9
    imperfections of individual, 403–5
    law-enforced, 394–97, 408
    natural form of, 405–7
    privately administered, 398–402, 408
Charity Organization Society, 136
Charlemagne, 189
Charles I (king of England), 425
Charles II (king of England), 125, 146, 267
childbearing, 356

children, 361
    adults' rights distinguished from those of, 185–86
    beneficence of, to parents, 369–72
    claims of, 186–87
    duties of, 187–88
    parental responsibilities to, 361–68, 373–74
    recognition of claims of, 188–90
    rights of, 185–91
    spoiling of, 363–64
China, 114
Chippewayans, 112
Chitty
    Equity Index, 252
Christ, 92, 160, 161, 464, 476
Christianity, 161, 189, 380, 464
    "golden rule" of, 68
    slavery and, 91–92
Christians, 287, 446, 464. *See also* Christianity
church(es), 400, 434. *See also* Christianity
Cicero, 146
class legislation, 212
clergy, 399
    benefit of, 83
    nonconforming, 161
Commanches, 112, 223, 225
common law, 125
communism, 57, 74, 118, 291, 292, 366
    justice violated by, 117
competition, 249–50
    inventions and, 304
    professionals and, 302–4
    restraints on free, 297–305
    unionism and, 298–300
Complete Suffrage Movement, 398 n
compromise, 165, 239, 309
Comte, 464
Congo, 137, 144
conscience
    animals as possessing, 469–81
consciousness
    limitation of, 193–94
consumers, 298
Contemporary Review, 503
contract
    enforcement of, 307, 308
    free, 143–47
    restraints on free, 146–47, 307–16
    system of, 203, 406, 426
conventions
    conformity to, 415–20

conventions (*cont.*)
    resisting, 420–24
cooperation
    advantages of, 36
    compulsory, 250
    nongovernmental, 249
Copinger, 125
copyright, 123–26
    background of, 125
    duration of, 125–26
    monopoly and, 123–24
Copyright Commission, 123–24
Corn Law(s), 145, 147, 398 n
Cossacks, 103
courage, 379–80, 381–83, 416
Coventry, 337
Creeks, 225
crime, 387
criminals, 337
Crown (English), 106
Curtius, 501
Czar, 95

Dacotahs, 225
Dahomans, 106, 144
Dahomey. *See* Dahomans
Damaras, 137
Danes, 105, 455, 456
Data of Ethics, The (Spencer), 466, 467, 485, 487, 502
Davies, J. Llewelyn, 461
    vs. Spencer, 461–68
death
    ownership after, 138–39, 140–42
    penal, 161
    rescuing from, 383–86
deductive school, 73. See also *a priori* reasoning
defense
    ineptitude in national, 251–52
    national, 147, 238
    self- , 232
deity, 46
Descriptive Sociology, 501
despotism, 156
Dhimáls, 137, 205
Digest of the Criminal Law (Stephen), 252
Diocletian, 144, 261
discrimination, 290
    intelligence and, 283–88
    need for, 293–94
disease
    communication of, 86

disease (*cont.*)
  infectious, 374
dissent(ers)
  political, 154
  religious, 155, 243–44, 414
divine right of kings, 156
doctors, 302, 303
Dogribs, 53
dress, 416–17
duty
  animals and, 470, 471, 472, 475–81
  conception of, 466–67, 468
  motive of, 462, 463, 464–65
Dyaks, 189

economists
  neo- , 298
economy
  political, 319
education, 238
Edward I (king of England), 133
Edward III (king of England), 150
egalitarianism, 116–17
Eghas, 137
egoism
  acts of, in animals, 20, 288
  pure, 45
  rational, 384, 390
Egyptians, 181, 223
Elizabeth (queen of England), 136, 162,
    458
Emerson, 343
employee(s), 311–15, 324
  blame in relation of employer to,
    333–34
employer(s), 311–15, 324
  blame in relation of employee to,
    333–34
endangered (the)
  rescuing, 383–85
  succoring, 379–86
enemies, 228–29
Englishmen, 44, 273, 455
English Poor, The (Mackay), 458
enmity
  ethics of, 67
  religion of, 240
environment, 101
equality
  government power and, 211–12, 213–14
  justice and, 56–58, 496–98
  See also inequality

equilibrium
  theory of, 64
equity, 66
Equity Index (Chitty), 252
Esquimaux, 204, 222
ethics
  absolute, 87, 88, 95, 102, 118, 119, 440,
    488–92
  animal. *See* ethics, animal
  background of, 166
  criticism of Spencer's system of, 483–
    504
  endangerment and, 385
  organic evolution's relation to, 41
  political, 39
  quasi- , 23, 39
  relative, 87–88, 95, 118, 119, 440, 489–93
  scope of, 19
  teleology and, 481–84
  utilitarianism in relation to, 499–97
ethics, animal, 19–23, 166
  altruism and, 20
  conscience and, 469–81
  egoism and, 20
Eunuchus (Terence), 125
Europe
  feudal, 36
evolution, 33, 42, 446–47
  mutability of, 201–2
  relation of organic, to ethics, 41
  See also survival of the fittest
exchange
  free, 143–47
  limitations on free, 146–47
"eye for an eye. . . ," 63, 84

family, 58
  blame in relations of, 332–33
  ethics of, 185, 190, 216
  pecuniary aid to, 388–90
  praise among, 340, 341
fear
  four kinds of, 45–46
feudalism, 226
Fijians, 82, 91, 154, 155, 181, 244, 466
First Principles (Spencer), 465
flattery, 339
  praise and, 342–43
Fortnightly Review, The, 466
France, 138, 147
  children in, 190
  equality vs. liberty in, 151
  revolution in. *See* French revolution

franchise, 196
  rights vs. universal, 199
  women and, 215, 218
freedom, 453
  governmental duty and, 241–45
  restriction of, 79
  See also freedom, law of equal; liberty
freedom, law of equal, 80, 81, 82, 97, 98,
    99, 119, 127, 156, 163, 460
  breaches of, 242, 243
  exchange and, 143–44
French, 146
  Republic, 196–97
French revolution, 150–51, 161, 261
Friendly Societies, 376
friends
  pecuniary aid to, 387–92
friendship, 412
Frisians, 138, 455
Fuegians, 53, 181, 189
Fulahs, 137, 144
Fulc the Black, 182
funerals, 421

generosity, 60
George III (king of England), 150
Germans, 189
  primitive, 137–38, 181
Germany, 60
  married women in, 180
  North, 82
Ghonds, 137
gift(s)
  bequest implied by, 136–37
  right of, 135–42
Glaucon, 54
God, 155, 465
Gold Coast, 137, 421
"golden rule," 68
government, 195
  character formation and, 271–79
  control by, 90
  costs of, 219–20
  equality of power and, 211–12, 213–14
  indirect effects of measures of, 263–66
  ineptitude compounded by, 254
  ineptitude of, 251–54
  paternal, 235–37
  primary function of, 226, 229
  primitive administration of, 224–27
  representative, 198–99, 429
  secondary function of, 226–27, 229–31
  security and, 158

government (*cont.*)
  self-interest and, 212–13
  toleration of ineptitude of, 255
  war and, 222–24, 237–39
  See also state
Grant (governor of Colorado), 265
Great Charter, 93, 94
Greece, 38, 202
Greek (language)
  learning of, 194
Greeks, 53–55, 92, 189, 205, 217, 501
  Homeric, 82
gregariousness, 30–31, 32, 35, 290
  tendencies of, 46–47
Grimm, 82
Grote (historian), 82
Guardian, The, 461, 462, 464, 469
Guinea, 154

Habeas Corpus Act, 94
happiness, 427, 446, 497
  principle of greatest, 56, 74–75, 81
  pursuit of, 259–60
Hastie, W., 452
Hebrews, 144, 146, 189
  commandments of, 68, 116
  industry of, 149
  See also Jews
Hecyra (Terence), 125
hedonism, 21, 497
Henry II (king of England), 113
Henry IV (king of England), 161
Henry V (king of England), 367
Henry VIII (king of England), 146
Herald, The, 158
heroism, 385
Herulians, 82
Highlanders, 456
Hindus, 160, 445
Hobart (chief justice), 69
Hobbes (philosopher), 224
  on state, 221–22
honesty, 54
Hos, 66
Hottentots, 137
House of Commons. *See* Parliament
Huish, 268
humanity
  welfare of, 240
Hunt, Leigh, 162
Huss (reformer), 161
Huxley, 465

ill-used (the)
  succoring, 379–86
Inclosure-Acts, 106
India, 114, 160, 202
indignation. *See* anger
individual(s), 453
  consequences belonging to, 76
  preservation of, 87, 95, 142
  worth of, 25
  See also individuality
individuality, 425, 453
  law of, 76, 87
  species vs., 22, 23
  See also individual(s)
inductive school, 73. See also *a posteriori*
  reasoning
industry, 247
  constitution of state and, 210–12
  meaning of free, 146
  right to free, 149–51
inequality
  denial of, 57
  justice and, 53–56
  pecuniary, 366
  sexual, 355, 356
  See also equality
infants
  murder of, 242
inferiority, 329
  sociableness and, 413–15
  unionism and, 299–300
inheritance, 136–38, 276. *See also* be-
  quest(s); gift(s); primogeniture
injury
  beneficence toward those with, 373–78
  bodily, 82, 86
Inquiry Commission (1887), 251
integrity, physical, 81–88
  bodily injury and, 82–86
  disease and, 86
  murder and, 81–84
intelligence
  discrimination and, 283–88
invention(s), 126–30
  competition and, 304
  monopoly and, 127, 128–29
Ireland, 397

Jackson, 154, 466
Jakuns, 90
James I (king of England), 146, 150
Jesus Christ. *See* Christ
Jews, 155, 160. *See also* Hebrews

Johnson, E.C.
  On the Track of the Crescent, 52 n
Jones, T. Mann, 470, 471, 480, 481
  research of, on animals, 472–81
Jowett, 54
Juangs, 217
justice, 298, 427, 453, 496–98
  altruism and, 46–48, 168, 288–95
  crude forms of, 63
  egoistic, 168
  equality and, 56–58
  formula of, 61–77
  happiness vs., 56–57
  human. See justice, human
  idea of, 51–60
  inequality and, 53–56
  negative element of, 122
  objections against formula of, 66–75
  pure, 34
  sentiment of, 41–49, 51
  subhuman. *See* justice, subhuman
  true conception of, 58
justice, human, 33–39, 140, 167, 292
  progress of 34–35
  warfare and, 37–39
  See also justice
justice, subhuman, 25–32, 140, 167
  decidedness of, 27–28
  imperfection of, 26–27
  law of, 26

Kanakas, 445
Kant, 64, 68, 461
  *Philosophy of Law, An Exposition of the
    Fundamental Principles of Jurispru-
    dence as the Science of Right, The,* 452
  theory of rights of, 451–53
Karens, 137, 225
Kasia, 137
Kemble, 226
Khonds, 225
Kocch, 205
Koenigswarter, 138
Krapotkin (prince), 57

labor
  division of, 204
  poor and, 395–97
laborers, 298, 299. *See also* unionism
laissez-faire
  miserable, 60, 462
land, 455–60. *See also* landownership

landownership, 394, 395
  development of private, 102–9, 455–56
  equity in, 456–58
Larkspur, 285
Latin
  learning of, 194
Laveleye, de, 57
law
  biological, 486–87
  causation and, 258–59
  civil, 426
  common. See common law
  criminal, 426
  natural. *See* law, natural
  Roman, 69, 133
  social, 67
law, natural, 255
  theory of, 69
lawyers, 230, 302, 303
legislators, 265–67, 279, 287
Lepchas, 66, 90
Levasseur, 151
lex talionis, 225
libel, 133
liberty, 62
  political rights and, 196–97
  rights and, 79–80, 198
  slavery vs., 93–95
  See also freedom
Liberty and Property Defense League,
    The, 107
life
  sacredness of, 82–83, 85
light
  right to, 97–99
loans
  to family, 388–90
  to relatives, 390–91
Locke (philosopher)
  on property, 111–12
locomotion, free, 89–96
Logic (Mill), 492
Looking Backward (Bellamy), 57
Louis XV (king of France), 146
love, 386
Luther (reformer), 161

machinery
  protest against, 299
  social, 402
Mackay, T.
  English Poor, The, 458
Mackintosh, James, 69

Maine, Henry, 69, 116, 235
  Ancient Law, 75
Maitland, F.W., 451
majority, 299–300
  right of, 244
Maker. *See* God
Malagasy, 189
man, 33
Mansion House Fund, 399
marital relations, 178–80
  beneficence and, 353–60, 373–75
Mark system, 93
Masai, 204
Means (professor)
  vs. Spencer, 492–96
*Medical Charity: Its Abuses, and How to
    Remedy Them* (Chapman), 402 n
men
  duties of, 355–57
  inferior, 175–76
  marriage and, 178–80, 353–60
  women vs., 177, 355
Merovingian period, 138
Mexicans, 144
militancy, 247
  constitution of state and, 209–10, 214
Mill (philosopher), 74, 494, 495, 496
  Logic, 494
  Utilitarianism, 56
Milne-Edwards, 248
Milton (poet), 162
Mind, 481, 492
minority, 244, 299–300
Mishmis, 137
Monkshood, 285
monopoly
  copyright as, 123–24
  inventions and, 127, 128–29
moralists, 74
morals, 65, 74
  hedonistic view of, 499
  motive of, 461–68
  reputation and, 130–31
motion, free, 89–96
motive(s)
  animals and, 472, 474–77
  duty and, 462, 463, 464–65
  moral, 461–68
Mugwump, 429
Mulhall, 458, 459
Mundrucus, 144
murder, 81–84, 242
  law of, 293

murder (*cont.*)
  primitive punishment of, 226–27
  views of, 82–83
Musheras, 404 n
musicians, 318

Nagas, 90
Napoleon III, 197
navy, 251–52
Negro(es), 44, 445
  coast, 225
  Inland, 144
New Guinea, 189
New Zealanders, 189, 424
Nicholls, G., 458, 459
Nineteenth Century, The, 268, 461
Normans, 105, 455, 456
Norsemen, 455, 456, 491
nurses, 377

On the Track of the Crescent (Johnson), 52 n
optimism, 486–89, 499–500
organization, social
  industrial, 59
  militant, 59
Owl, The, 423 n
ownership
  death and, 138–39
  See also landownership

pain, 47, 81, 339, 379, 491–93
Papuan islands, 205
parenthood, 37
  beneficent, 361–68
Parliament, 59, 109, 165, 212, 244, 267, 428, 431, 435
  Long, 162
Parliamentary Blue Books, 397
Patagonians, 144, 225
patriotism
  ethics of, 380
Pattison (naturalist), 471
Paul (apostle), 160
payment(s)
  instances of undeserved, 318–23
  restraints on undeserved, 317–24
peasants, 93–94
Penny Readings, 413
persecution, 243–44
Persia, 38
pessimism, 486–90, 499
philanthropy, 420
  hotheaded, 289–90

philanthropy (*cont.*)
  indiscriminate, 291
Philosophy of Law, An Exposition of the Fundamental Principles of Jurisprudence as the Science of Right, The (Kant), 452
Phoenicians, 144
Plantagenets, 83
Plato, 155, 238, 272
  censors advocated by, 162
  dialogues of, 53–54
pleasure, 47, 340, 412, 413, 491–93
political rights, 193–99
  illusions regarding, 195–96
  means-ends confusion regarding, 195–97
  women's, 182–83
politics, 65, 74, 287
  beneficence and, 425–35
  disregard of duty to, 426–27
  empirical, tested, 260–63
  party loyalty in, 428–30
  party warfare of, 428
  responsibility of citizens to, 426, 430–35
Politics (Aristotle), 55
pollution
  air, 99–101
polygamy, 160
Polynesians, 137, 144
poor (the)
  difficulties in relieving, 408–9
  individual charity for, 403–5
  labor and, 395–97
  natural form of charity for, 405–7
  privately administered charity for, 398–402
  relief of, 393–409, 458–59
  state's relation to, 394
Poor Law(s), 80, 265, 394, 398, 399, 407, 458
Pope (Roman Catholic), 244
Post Office, 267
Power Unknowable, 21
praise
  flattery and, 342–43
  love of, 417
  public honor and, 343–44
  restraints on, 339–45
preservation
  of self. *See* self-preservation
  of species, 22–23, 31, 33, 95, 347–49
primogeniture, 136–37

Principles of Biology (Spencer), 481
Principles of Psychology (Spencer), 47, 283, 344
Principles of Sociology (Spencer), 503
prizefights, 67
propaganda, 158
property, 44
  bequest of, to children, 139–40
  communism and, 117, 118
  death and bequest of, 139–42
  gift based on, 135, 138
  public, vs. incorporeal, 123–24
  right of, 111–19
  right of incorporeal, 121–33
  warfare and, 118
Protestants, 155
Ptah-hotep, 339
publication
  limits to free, 158, 159–60, 162–63
  right to free, 157–63
punishment, 211, 337–38
  fear of, 46
  primitive societies and, 36, 226–27
  religion and, 161

Ravachol, 292
Reform Bill, 158
relatives
  pecuniary aid to, 387–92
religion
  right to freedom of, 153–56
reprobation
  fear of, 45–46
reputation, 130–33
  blameworthiness and, 132–33
retaliation, 81
  family, 84
  fear of, 45
  See also revenge
revenge, 63. *See also* retaliation
Richard II (king of England), 133
Riff pirates, 467
right(s)
  basis of, 79–80
  bequest as, 135–42
  children's, 185–91
  conception of a, 198
  divine. *See* divine right of kings
  free contract as, 143–47
  freedom of religion as, 153–56
  free exchange as, 143–47
  free industry as, 149–51
  free locomotion as, 89–96

right(s) (*cont.*)
  free motion as, 89–96
  free publication as, 157–63
  free speech as, 157–63
  gift as, 135–42
  incorporeal property as, 121–33
  Kantian idea of, 451–53
  natural-media usage as, 97–109
  physical integrity as, 81–88
  political. *See* political rights
  property as, 111–19
  state and, 80
  women's, 175–83
roads, macadamized, 432–33 n
Robertson, 125
Roman Catholics, 155
Roman emperors, 161, 189
Romanes (professor), 471
Romans, 69, 75, 161. *See also* Rome
Rome
  early, 181–82, 189
Russia, 104, 163
  ancient, 84
  See also Russians
Russia (Wallace), 103
Russians, 102–3, 445

Salisbury, Lord, 260, 262, 263
Salvation Army, 154
Samoans, 154
Saxons, 138
school
  ethics of public, 380
Schoolcraft, 112
Schopenhauer, 499
science, 65
self-denial, 317
self-interest
  role of, in government, 212–13
selfishness, 326
self-preservation
  individual vs. social, 87, 142
self-sacrifice, 340, 444
  marriage and, 356, 357, 374–75
self-subordination, 37–39
Semites, 235
serfs, 93–94
Shirry-dikas, 223
Shoa, 144
Shoshones, 223
sick (the)
  beneficence toward, 373–78
  tyranny of, 375

Sidgwick
  vs. Spencer, 481–92
sincerity, 341, 342
Skye-crofters, 308
slavery, 146, 242–43
  cannibalism and, 91
  Christianity and, 91–92
  England and, 93
  Greece and, 92
smoke
  industrial, 100
  tobacco, 100
Snakes, 223, 225
sociableness
  vs. solitude, 411–13
social forces
  beneficent working of, 266–68
socialism, 59, 60, 264, 366. *See also*
  socialists
socialists, 57, 298, 495. *See also* socialism
Social Statics (Spencer), 246, 451, 453, 460
society
  character molding and, 273–74
  distinctions in, 273
Socrates, 54, 155, 238
soldier-king, 238
soldiers, 67, 228
solitude
  sociableness vs., 411–13
Solon, 161
Sparta, 92, 238
species
  association among, 29
  destruction of, 26
  law of, 25–26
  preservation of, 22–23, 31, 33, 95,
    347–49
  self-subordination among, 30–31
Spectator, 265
speech
  limits to free, 158, 159–60, 162–63
  right to free, 157–63
Spencer, Thomas, 398 n
Standard, The, 158, 268
state, 58
  constitution of, 209–20
  duties of, 221–33
  ethics of, 185, 190, 216
  evolution's lesson on, 202
  inhabited territory and, 231–32
  limits on duties of, 235–79
  nature of, 201–7
  poor and, 394–97, 408

state (*cont.*)
  purpose of, 206
  relinquishment of functions by, 248–49
  rights as related to, 80
  varied actions of, 203–6
  varied natures of, 202–3
  See also government
Statius
  Agave, 125
status
  system of, 203, 406, 426
Statute of Labourers, 261
Statute of Merton, 261
steam engine, 193
Stephen, James
  Digest of the Criminal Law, 252
Stewart (businessman), 301
Suanetians, 105
Suez Canal, 267
Sultan (man-of-war), 252
Sumatrans, 102, 137
Sunday Schools, 414
superiority, 325–29
  advantages of, 301
  sociableness and, 413–15
  unionism and, 299–300
supply and demand, 249–50
survival of the fittest, 25, 29, 30, 33, 277,
    408. *See also* evolution
sympathy, 46–47, 305, 317, 379, 445
  relapse of, 60

Tacitus, 137, 181
Tasmanians, 222
taxation, 119, 220
  injustice of, 397
  poor and, 394
Tennant, 222
Terence
  Eunuchus, 125
  Hecyra, 125
Teutons, 189
theft, 242
Thompsons (naturalists), 471
Tibet, 160
Timbuctoo, 137
tipping, 321–23
Todas, 137
Toleration Act (1688), 155
truth, 339–40, 343
  politics and, 428–30

Uaupes, 225
unionism, 314, 315
   competition and, 298–300
utilitarianism, 73, 494–98
   empirical, 260, 494
   ethics as related to, 495–97
   rational, 260
Utilitarianism (Mill), 56
utopia
   communistic, 57

Veddahs, 222
vigilance, eternal, 433–35
voting. *See* franchise

Wace (professor), 501
Wallace
   Russia, 103
War-are-aree-kas, 223
warfare, 37–39, 272–73, 278
   defensive, 87, 96, 210
   government and, 222–24, 237–39
   offensive, 96

warfare (*cont.*)
   property and, 118
Wars of the Roses, 94
Watt (inventor), 128
Weddell, 222
weddings, 421
Welsh, 456
Wends, 82
White, Arnold, 265
Williams, 155
women
   character of, 216–18
   franchise and, 215, 218
   ill-treatment of, 353–54
   impulsiveness of, 215
   intellectual capacity of, 215–16
   marriage and, 178–80, 353–60
   men vs., 177, 355
   political powers and, 215–18
   political rights of, 182–83
   primitive societies and, 180–82
   rights of, 175–83
Wood-Veddah, 66

Tibor R. Machan teaches at Chapman University, California. He is a research fellow at the Hoover Institution on War, Revolution and Peace, Stanford University, California.

The Palatino typeface used in this volume is the work of Hermann Zapf, the noted European type designer and master calligrapher. Palatino is basically an "old style" letterform, yet it is strongly endowed with Zapf's distinctive exquisiteness. With concern not solely for the individual letter but also for the working visual relationship in a page of text, Zapf's edged pen has given this type a brisk, natural motion.

Printed on paper that is acid-free and meets
the requirements of the American National Standard
for Permanence of Paper for
Printed Library Materials, Z39.84, 1984 ♾

Book Design by JMH Corporation, Indianapolis, Indiana
Typography by Weimer Typesetting Co., Inc., Indianapolis, Indiana
Printed and bound by Edwards Brothers, Inc., Ann Arbor, Michigan